Ira Tiwari

OXFORD
SCHOOL
ATLAS

33RD EDITION

OXFORD
UNIVERSITY PRESS

OXFORD
UNIVERSITY PRESS

Oxford University Press is a department of the University of Oxford.
It furthers the University's objective of excellence in research, scholarship,
and education by publishing worldwide. Oxford is a registered trade mark of
Oxford University Press in the UK and in certain other countries.

Published in India by
Oxford University Press
YMCA Library Building, 1 Jai Singh Road, New Delhi 110001, India

© Oxford University Press 1915, 2012

The moral rights of the author/s have been asserted.

First Edition published in 1915
Thirtieth Edition published in 2000
Thirtieth revised Edition published in 2002
Thirty-first Edition published in 2006
Thirty-second Edition published in 2009
Thirty-third Edition published in 2012
Tenth impression 2013

ISBN-13: 978-0-19-807382-6
ISBN-10: 0-19-807382-8

Printed in India by M.P. Printers (A Unit of D B Corp. Ltd), Noida 201305

Cartographed by Oxford University Press, India

Acknowledgements

The following are applicable to all the maps in this atlas wherever India-
International boundaries and coastlines appear:

- © Government of India, Copyright, 2011.
- Based upon Survey of India maps with the permission of the Surveyor General
  of India.
- The responsibility for the correctness of internal details rests with the publisher.
- The territorial waters of India extend into the sea to a distance of twelve nautical
  miles measured from the appropriate base line.
- The administrative headquarters of Chandigarh, Haryana and Punjab are
  at Chandigarh.
- The interstate boundaries amongst Arunachal Pradesh, Assam and Meghalaya
  shown on this map are as interpreted from the "North-Eastern Areas
  (Reorganization) Act' 1971", but have yet to be verified.
- The external boundaries and coastlines of India on the maps agree with the
  Record/Master Copy certified by the Survey of India, Dehra Dun vide their
  letter no. TB-515/62-A-3/29 dated 23.11.2011.
- Topographical sheet nos. 45 D/7 and 45 D/10 reproduced with permission of the
  Survey of India.
- The state boundaries between Uttarakhand & Uttar Pradesh, Bihar & Jharkhand
  and Chhattisgarh & Madhya Pradesh have not been verified by the
  Governments concerned.
- The spellings of names in this map, have been taken from various sources.

CONTENTS

History of Cartography

The history of cartography is not older than 5,000 years. The earliest maps of which we have knowledge were made by the Babylonians on clay tablets, dating around 2300 BC (Fig.1). Early attempts at maps were severely limited by lack of knowledge of anything other than very local features. Of course what constitutes a map is hard to say, especially when one goes back to the very earliest times. In around 6200 BC in **Catal Hyük** in Anatolia a wall painting was made depicting the positions of the streets and houses of the town together with surrounding features such as the volcano close to the town. Whether it is a map or a stylised painting is a matter of debate. Early world maps also reflect the religious beliefs of the form of the world.

Fig. 1: A clay tablet showing land holdings of Babylon

The earliest ancient Greek who is said to have constructed a map of the world is **Anaximander**, who was born in 610 BC in Miletus (now in Turkey) and died in 546 BC. Sadly, no details of his map have survived. Notable Greek philosophers and mathematicians such as Pythagoras, Aristotle, Eratosthenes and Hipparchus made notable contributions to the study of ancient cartography.

The final ancient Greek contribution to cartography, considered the most important, was written by a noted mathematician. In about AD 140 **Ptolemy** wrote his major work, *Guide to Geography*, in eight books, which attempted to map the known world giving coordinates of the major places in terms of what are essentially latitude and longitude (Fig. 2). Given the way that he gathered the data it is not surprising that the maps were inaccurate but they did represent a considerable advance on all previous maps and it would be many centuries before more accurate world maps would be drawn.

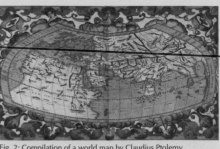

Fig. 2: Compilation of a world map by Claudius Ptolemy

In 1569, **Gerardus Mercator** of Flanders, Belgium, the leading cartographer of the 16th century developed a map projection and drew a world map (Fig.3). Mercator made many new maps and globes, but his greatest contribution to cartography was what is now known as the Mercator projection.

Since then, several leading cartographers from Europe and Asia developed cartographic techniques, giving a boost to map production and the invention

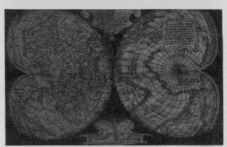

Fig. 3: The first map of the entire world by Gerardus Mercator

of different scientific surveying techniques, instruments and projections. In addition to these developments, the broadening of knowledge with the introduction of new fields of studies such as astronomy, geology, meteorology, biology, and the social sciences gave rise to thematic cartography.

As the world advances, as the unknown is revealed and surveyed, as humans alter the face of the earth with their new settlements, new states, railways, canals, land reclamation and cultivation, these changes are reflected in the maps of the times.

The Age of Modern Cartography: Remote Sensing and GIS

In the 20th century, the invention of the airplane followed by satellite remote sensing technology added a new dimension to mapping and widened its scope through the method of remote sensing. This provided a bird´s-eye view of the earth and saved time and money required for conventional surveying of ground realities.

In the broadest sense, remote sensing is the measurement or acquisition of information of an object or phenomenon, by a recording device that is not in physical or intimate contact with the object. It is the utilization at a distance (as from aircraft, spacecraft, satellite, or ship) of any device for gathering information about the environment. The technique can make use of devices such as a camera, laser, radar, sonar, seismograph or a gravimeter. Modern remote sensing normally includes digital processes but can be done as well with non-digital methods.

Fig. 4: An aerial photograph of North Male Atoll, Maldives

Aerial photography is the original form of remote sensing. An aerial photograph can be defined as a photograph taken from an aircraft with a camera specially designed for aircraft use (Fig.4). The occurrence of the two world wars led to a demand for aerial photography for military purposes. In India, aerial photographs have been in use since 1920 for aerial surveys and for interpretation of specific fields such as topographical mapping, geology, engineering, environmental studies, and exploration of oil and minerals.

With the development of satellite technology between 1970 and 1980, remote sensing through satellites received more attention from researchers, cartographers and general users. An image taken from space using a spacecraft as the platform and scanners or specially designed cameras as sensors to detect the given area of the earth´s surface is termed **satellite imagery** (Fig. 5). The remote sensor system makes use of the emitted or reflected electromagnetic radiation of the examined object and measures a larger area of the earth. Satellite imagery can be widely applied and is extensively used by scientists, researchers, and planners in map-making, urban and regional planning, agriculture, forestry, ecology and environment, soil survey, natural resource mapping, oil and mineral exploration, and so on.

Fig. 5: A satellite image showing lake Rakas (left) and lake Manasarovar (right)

In traditional cartography, the map represented both the database and the display of geographic information whereas in **GIS** (Geographical Information Systems), the database, analysis, and display are physically and conceptually separate aspects. Geographic information systems include several elements such as computer hardware, software, digital data, people, and institutions for collecting, storing, retrieving, analysing, and displaying georeferenced data or information about the Earth. Modern map-making relies much more on GIS, which provides flexible computer-aided database and maps.

Scale

A scale is essential for reading a map accurately. It is defined as the ratio between two points on the ground and their corresponding distance on a piece of paper (the map). A scale can be expressed as:

1. Representative Fraction (R.F.)

The units of measurement of distances are the same both on the ground and on paper. It is always expressed as a ratio, e.g. 1:100,000, where 1 cm on the map represents 100,000 cm or 1 inch =100,000 inches.

2. Written statement

The system of measurement is clearly stated, e.g.
1 cm = 1 km
or 1 inch = 1 mile.

3. Graphical method

A diagram of a ruler is drawn to show the given scale, e.g. 1 cm = 1 km or 1:100,000. A segment of a ruler measuring 15 cm will represent 15 km.

km 1   0   1   2 km

Maps and Globes

A map is a graphic representation of the round earth or the real world on a flat piece of paper. Maps show us what the earth would look like if we could see it from above. The main purpose of preparing a map is to show the things as they appear in their true location, in terms of latitudes and longitudes, either in isolation or in relation to some other feature. On the other hand, a globe represents the whole surface in the form of a sphere on which all its continents and features are shown at the same scale and with their correct shapes and areas.

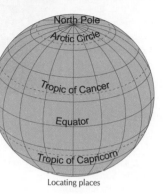

Locating places

Map Projections

A map projection is a systematic and orderly drawing of a grid of parallels of latitude and meridians of longitude used to represent the spherical surface of the earth, or a part of it, on a reduced scale on a flat piece of paper. It is not possible to make a map (of the world or of any part of it) that is accurate in area, shape, distance and direction. Every map is distorted in at least one of these aspects.

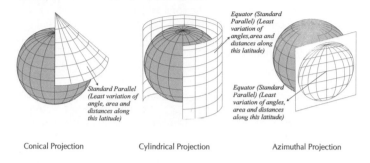

Conical Projection   Cylindrical Projection   Azimuthal Projection

---

Types of Maps

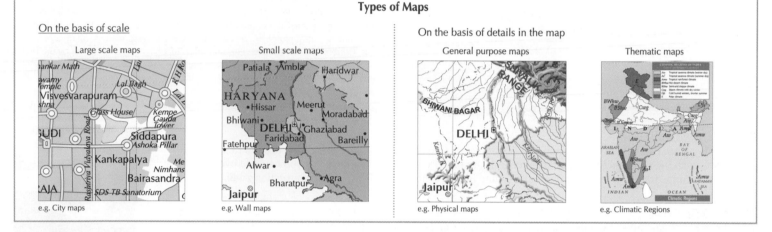

On the basis of scale

Large scale maps   Small scale maps

e.g. City maps   e.g. Wall maps

On the basis of details in the map

General purpose maps   Thematic maps

e.g. Physical maps   e.g. Climatic Regions

Physical Relief: Representation of the Earth's Surface

One of the challenges of map-making is to adequately represent the physical relief of any region i.e., the delineation of hills and plains, the distinguishing of high ground and low ground. The two methods generally used to represent physical relief are *hill-shading and contour lines,* each of which may be treated in a variety of ways and are sometimes combined.

Figure A shows a mountainous island with the hill slopes indicated by a method of hill–shading called `hachures' (lines indicating the direction of the slope). Figure B shows the same island with the hills indicated by contour lines. The principle of showing elevation by contour lines can be seen by comparing Figure C with the profile section in Figure B.

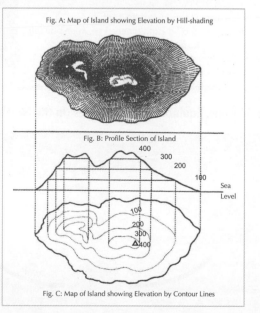

Fig. A: Map of Island showing Elevation by Hill-shading

Fig. B: Profile Section of Island

Fig. C: Map of Island showing Elevation by Contour Lines

Symbols and Shades

Maps cannot show everything nor can the features of the landscape be contained in a limited area. Therefore, symbols, often termed as conventional symbols, have been developed to represent the features on a map. Some symbols are like pictures while others are initial letters such as `PO' for post office. Colours are also used as symbols such as green for forests or woodlands and blue for water. Shades ranging from deepest to lightest can represent the range of occurrences of any phenomenon, such as altitude.

Conventional symbols can be found on a topographical sheet, a weather chart, or on physical or thematic maps. It is always important to refer to the key or legend of a map to find out what the symbols mean. Symbols are designed to be easy to remember.

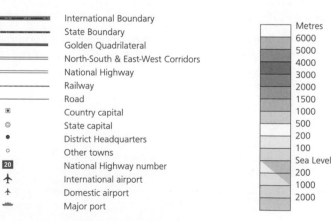

The Solar System

The solar system was formed about 4,600 million years ago. It is located in the Orion arm of the Milky Way galaxy, around two-thirds away from the central bulge, about 27,000 light-years from the centre of the galaxy. It takes the solar system about 220 million years to orbit the galaxy once.

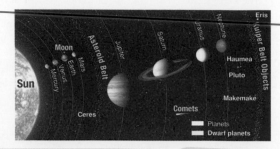

The solar planets can be divided into an inner system of four small, solid planets made up of materials similar to that of the Earth. The outer system of four larger planets, known as the `gas giants´, has rings and lots of moons. The gas giants are made up mostly of hydrogen, helium, frozen water, ammonia, methane, and carbon monoxide. Pluto does not belong to any group but is a tiny rocky body at the edge of the solar system. Some people think it is a giant comet rather than a planet. Its composition is similar to a comet (ice and rock) but its orbit is different from the other comets and planets. Between these two planetary systems is a belt of asteroids containing pieces of rock of varying size.

Planet Profile

Planet	Mean distance from Sun (million km)	Orbital period	Diameter (km)	No. of known satellites
Mercury	57.9	88.0 days	4,879	0
Venus	108.2	224.7 days	12,104	0
Earth	149.6	365.3 days	12,756	1
Mars	227.9	687.0 days	6,787	2
Jupiter	778.4	11.86 years	142,800	64
Saturn	1426.7	29.46 years	120,660	62
Uranus	2871.0	84.01 years	51,118	27
Neptune	4498.73	164.8 years	49,528	13

Dwarf Planets and Plutoids

Pluto, which was considered to be a planet since its discovery in 1930, was reclassified as a 'dwarf planet' on 24 August 2006 by the International Astronomical Union.

According to the IAU, a dwarf planet fulfils the following criteria:
• It is in orbit around the Sun.
• It has sufficient mass for its self-gravity to overcome rigid body forces so that it assumes a hydrostatic equilibrium (nearly round) shape.
• It has not `cleared the neighbourhood´ around its orbit.
• It is not a satellite of a planet, or other non-stellar body.

Two years after coining the term `dwarf planets´, the IAU has decided to call trans-neptunian dwarf planets similar to Pluto, `plutoids´. While all plutoids are dwarf planets, all dwarf planets are not plutoids. Currently, there are five celestial bodies that have been redefined by the IAU as dwarf planets, of which four belong to the subset plutoids. Eris, Pluto, and most recently, MakeMake and Haumea have been classified as plutoids and dwarf planets, while Ceres remains in the category dwarf planet.

Sun

The Sun is a giant ball of hot gas, 150 million kilometers from the Earth. The surface of this burning ball of gas is 5500°C, with the core reaching an unimaginable 15.6 million°C. The Sun is so large that you could fit over one million Earths inside it. The Sun's internal structure includes the core, radiation zone, convection zone, and photosphere.

The turbulence in the photosphere is visible from the earth in the form of sunspots, solar flares, prominences and small patches of gas called granules. The Sun consumes four million tonnes of hydrogen every second. Even so, it is so vast that our star has enough fuel to keep it shining for another five billion years.

The corona is the outermost part of the Sun's atmosphere, visible during a solar eclipse only.

Phases of the Moon

The moon seems to have different shapes at different times of the month because of its changing position in relation to the Earth. These different shapes are known as the phases of the Moon. The interval between one full Moon and the next is 29.5 days.

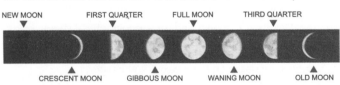

NEW MOON   FIRST QUARTER   FULL MOON   THIRD QUARTER

CRESCENT MOON   GIBBOUS MOON   WANING MOON   OLD MOON

Facts about the Moon

The lunar surface

• The only natural satellite of the planet Earth
• Distance from Earth– 384,400 km
• Diameter– 3,476 km
• Mass– 0.0123 of the Earth's
• Surface gravity– 0.165 of the Earth's
• Time taken to orbit Earth (interval between one full moon and the next) – 29.53 days or 709 hours
• Surface temperature– 120 °C maximum to –163 °C at night

Tides

At new Moon and full Moon, when the Moon and the Sun are in line with the Earth, tides are at their highest and are called **spring tides.**

At quarter and three-quarter Moon, the Sun and Moon are at right angles, so that the gravitational pull of the Moon is partly cancelled out by the gravitational pull of the Sun, the tides are at their lowest and are called **neap tides**.

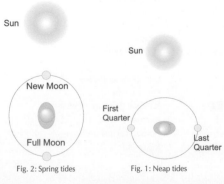

Sun

Sun

New Moon

First Quarter

Full Moon

Last Quarter

Fig. 2: Spring tides   Fig. 1: Neap tides

The Seasons, Equinoxes and Solstices (in the Northern Hemisphere)

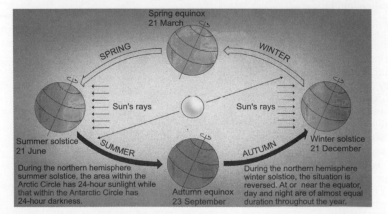

Spring equinox 21 March

SPRING   WINTER

Sun's rays   Sun's rays

Summer solstice 21 June   Winter solstice 21 December

SUMMER   AUTUMN

During the northern hemisphere summer solstice, the area within the Arctic Circle has 24-hour sunlight while that within the Antarctic Circle has 24-hour darkness.

Autumn equinox 23 September

During the northern hemisphere winter solstice, the situation is reversed. At or near the equator, day and night are of almost equal duration throughout the year.

Continental Drift

The Earth's crust is not a single continuous layer. It is made up of a number of gigantic pieces like a huge jigsaw puzzle. Each piece is called a crustal plate. Currents of molten rock rise up through the mantle like boiling water in a saucepan. These form convection cells that drive the movement of the plates so that they are continuously moving away or towards each other. Geologically, the most important things happen at the plate boundaries, including most of the earthquakes, volcanoes, igneous rocks, major metamorphism, and mountain building processes. There are 10 crustal plates:

1. Pacific
2. Antarctic
3. Indian
4. African
5. South American
6. Nazca
7. North American
8. Eurasian
9. Cocos
10. Australian

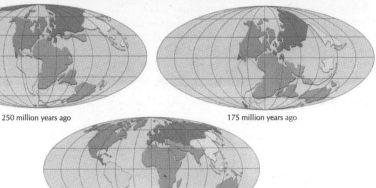
250 million years ago

175 million years ago

Present day

The Giant Jigsaw Puzzle

Alfred Wegener (1880-1930), a German meteorologist and geologist, was the first person to propose the theory of continental drift. In his book, **Origin of Continents and Oceans**, he calculated that 200 million years ago the continents were originally joined together, forming a large supercontinent. He named this supercontinent Pangaea, meaning `All-earth´. Pangaea split into plates to form Eurasia in the north and Gondwanaland in the south. Further splitting over millions of years formed the continents as we know them today. Wegener's concept was originally based on the apparent `jigsaw´ fit. The continents look as if they were pieces of a giant jigsaw puzzle that could fit together to make one giant super-continent. The bulge of Africa fits the shape of the coast of North America while Brazil fits along the coast of Africa beneath the bulge. There are three kinds of plate boundaries:

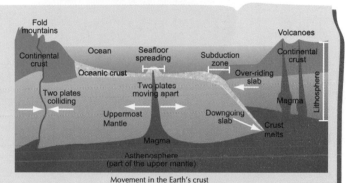
Movement in the Earth's crust

Divergent boundaries are where plates separate from each other, and magma oozes up from the mantle into the crack (a fissure volcano) making the ocean basin wider. This is known as sea floor spreading.

Convergent boundaries are where plates come together, but to do so one of the plates must dive below the surface into the mantle along a subduction zone. These often result in deep-sea trenches. Convergent boundaries also produce mountain chains and very large, explosive volcanoes.

Plates slide past each other where transform boundaries occur, ideally with little or no vertical movement. Most transform boundaries are below sea level and therefore not easy to see. The San Andreas fault in California is a transform boundary. It has been estimated that these plates are moving at a speed of 1 to 10 cm per year.

Inside the Earth

The Earth is made up of four main layers—the **inner core**, **outer core**, the **mantle**, and the **crust** (Fig.23). We live on the outer part of the Earth, which is called the crust. This layer consists of the upper 30-100 km. The crust mostly consists of igneous rocks; the rest consists of sedimentary and metamorphic rocks. The layer from 0-20 km is called the **sial** as the two main constituents are **silicon** and **aluminium**. It is 2.7 times denser than water. The next layer is known as **sima** as a large quantity of **silicon** and **magnesium** is found in this layer. The average density of this layer is 3.4 times that of water.

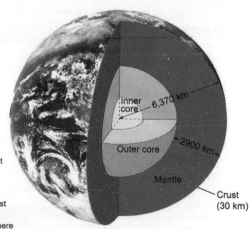

The next layer called the **mantle** is 100-2,900 km thick. The upper part of the mantle is a plastic layer over which the crust floats. The mantle is composed of silicate material, but it is chemically distinct from the crust.

The Earth's **outer core** (2,900-5,100 km) is composed of liquid metallic material (primarily iron and nickel). The solid **inner core** (5,100-6,370 km) of the Earth is made up of iron. It has been discovered that the inner core is rotating and is the cause of Earth's magnetic field.

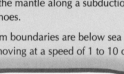

Rocks and Minerals

Rocks are the substances that make up the Earth. They include loose and unconsolidated deposits, as well as the hard, solid parts that make up the Earth's lithosphere. Rocks can be classified into three main groups on the basis of their origin—igneous, sedimentary and metamorphic. Minerals are the building materials of rocks. Rocks may be composed of only one mineral, while others contain many of them.

Granite

Igneous (or primary) rocks are the first rocks to be formed from magma or molten rock beneath the earth's crust, e.g. granite and basalt.

Limestone

Sedimentary (stratified or layered) rocks are formed by the collection of sediments over a long span of time, e.g. sandstone and shale.

Marble

Metamorphic rocks are formed when the nature of any rock is altered by subjecting it to intense heat and/or pressure, e.g. graphite (from coal) and quartzite (from sandstone).

The lithosphere (geosphere), atmosphere and hydrosphere comprise the three realms of the Earth. We can define the biosphere (the fourth realm of the Earth) as the parts of the Earth's lithosphere (land), hydrosphere (water) and atmosphere (air) occupied by living organisms.

Lithosphere or Geosphere

The lithosphere or geosphere is the solid, rocky crust covering the entire planet. This crust is inorganic and is composed of rocks, minerals and elements. It covers the entire surface of the Earth from the top of Mount Everest to the bottom of the Mariana Trench. On the surface of the Earth, the lithosphere is composed of three main types of rocks—igneous, sedimentary and metamorphic. The land area constitutes about 29 per cent of the total surface area of the Earth.

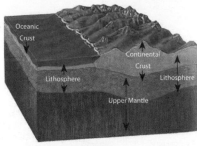

Structure of the lithosphere

Hydrosphere

The hydrosphere is the combined mass of water found on, under and over the surface of the Earth. About 71 per cent of the Earth's surface is covered by water in the form of oceans, seas, bays, gulfs, lakes, rivers, etc. The oceans contain most of the Earth's surface water. Most fresh water is frozen into glaciers. Most available fresh water is stored underground as groundwater.

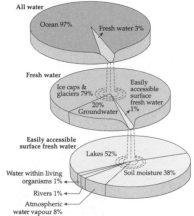

Atmosphere

The atmosphere is made up of gases such as nitrogen (78 per cent), oxygen (21 per cent) and small amounts of carbon dioxide, argon, ammonia and a few others. Water vapour (1 per cent approximately) is also present in the atmosphere. The atmosphere has several different layers. Higher up, the air gets thinner and colder, and there is less oxygen to breathe. In the very highest layers there is hardly any air at all.

Structure of the Atmosphere

The layers of the atmosphere are not of uniform thickness or density. They also vary in other aspects.

Troposphere
It is the lowest layer of the atmosphere. It contains 75 per cent of the gases in the atmosphere. All weather phenomena that we experience on the Earth occur in this sphere.

Stratosphere
The stratosphere has a layer of ozone which protects life on Earth from the harmful ultraviolet light of the Sun.

Mesosphere
The temperature in the mesosphere decreases with height, reaching about –100°C in the upper mesosphere. This is the coldest region of the atmosphere.

Thermosphere
The temperature in the thermosphere increases with height. The thermosphere is also known as the heat sphere of the atmosphere.

Exosphere
It is the outermost layer of the atmosphere. This layer has the lightest gases like hydrogen and helium in extremely low densities. Most of the Earth's satellites orbit here.

Biosphere

The biosphere is made up of all living organisms of the Earth, as well as the physical environment in which they live and with which they interact. Most living organisms actually live within a small area in the biosphere, from about 500 m below the ocean's surface to about 6 km above sea level.

Structure of the atmosphere

Atmospheric Clouds

High-level clouds such as cirrus, cirrostratus and cirrocumulus are usually thin and white in appearance.

Mid-level clouds are the altocumulus and altostratus clouds.

While altocumulus may appear as parallel bands or rounded masses of clouds, altostratus clouds are generally uniform grey sheet or layered clouds.

Low clouds are the cumulus, stratus, nimbostratus and stratocumulus clouds. Cumulus clouds are 'puffy' clouds; stratus clouds are flat, featureless clouds; and nimbostratus and stratocumulus clouds are large, dark clouds.

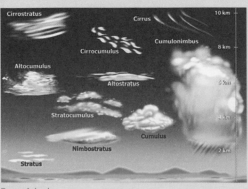

Types of cloud

Heat Budget of the Earth

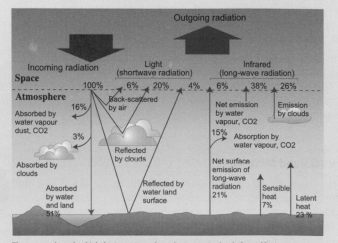

The process through which the incoming solar radiation on Earth is balanced by its outgoing terrestrial radiation is called heat balance. It is essential for the maintenance of the correct temperature of the planet to prevent it from getting hotter or cooler.

Contours and Landforms—One of the challenges of map-making is to adequately represent the physical relief of any region, i.e., the delineation of hills and plains, the distinguishing of high ground and low ground. The main method of showing relief features on a flat sheet of paper is by using contours. A contour is a line on a map joining all points which are of the same height above sea level. Contour lines are used to show the height and shapes of landforms in lowland and highland areas. Some of the relief features or landforms are shown below using certain contour patterns.

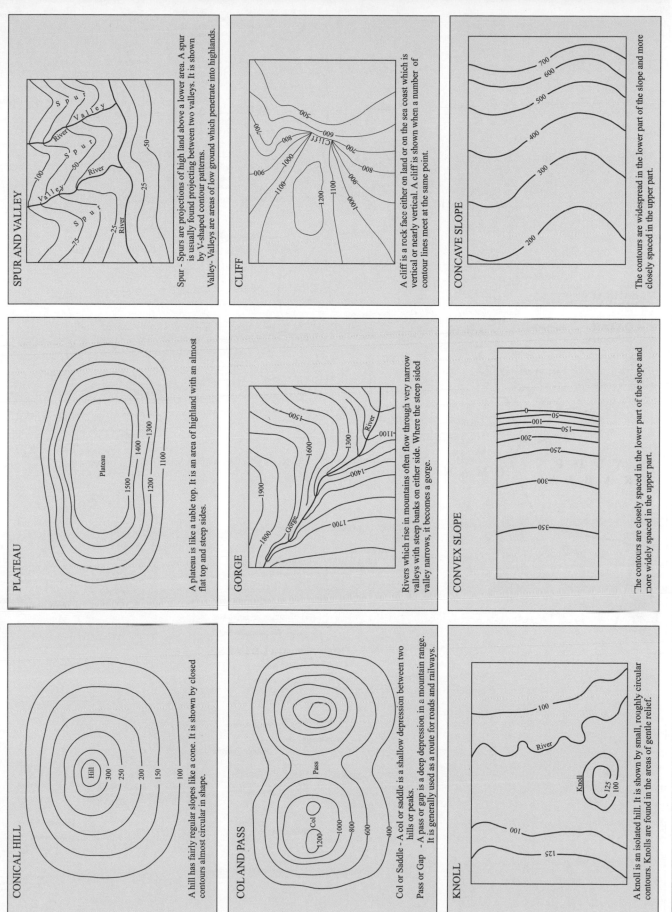

SPUR AND VALLEY

Spur - Spurs are projections of high land above a lower area. A spur is usually found projecting between two valleys. It is shown by V-shaped contour patterns.
Valley- Valleys are areas of low ground which penetrate into highlands.

CLIFF

A cliff is a rock face either on land or on the sea coast which is vertical or nearly vertical. A cliff is shown when a number of contour lines meet at the same point.

CONCAVE SLOPE

The contours are widespread in the lower part of the slope and more closely spaced in the upper part.

PLATEAU

A plateau is like a table top. It is an area of highland with an almost flat top and steep sides.

GORGE

Rivers which rise in mountains often flow through very narrow valleys with steep banks on either side. Where the steep sided valley narrows, it becomes a gorge.

CONVEX SLOPE

The contours are closely spaced in the lower part of the slope and more widely spaced in the upper part.

CONICAL HILL

A hill has fairly regular slopes like a cone. It is shown by closed contours almost circular in shape.

COL AND PASS

Col or Saddle - A col or saddle is a shallow depression between two hills or peaks.
Pass or Gap - A pass or gap is a deep depression in a mountain range. It is generally used as a route for roads and railways.

KNOLL

A knoll is an isolated hill. It is shown by small, roughly circular contours. Knolls are found in the areas of gentle relief.

Heights given are in metres

9

SCALE 1: 12 500 000

0 100 200 300 400 km

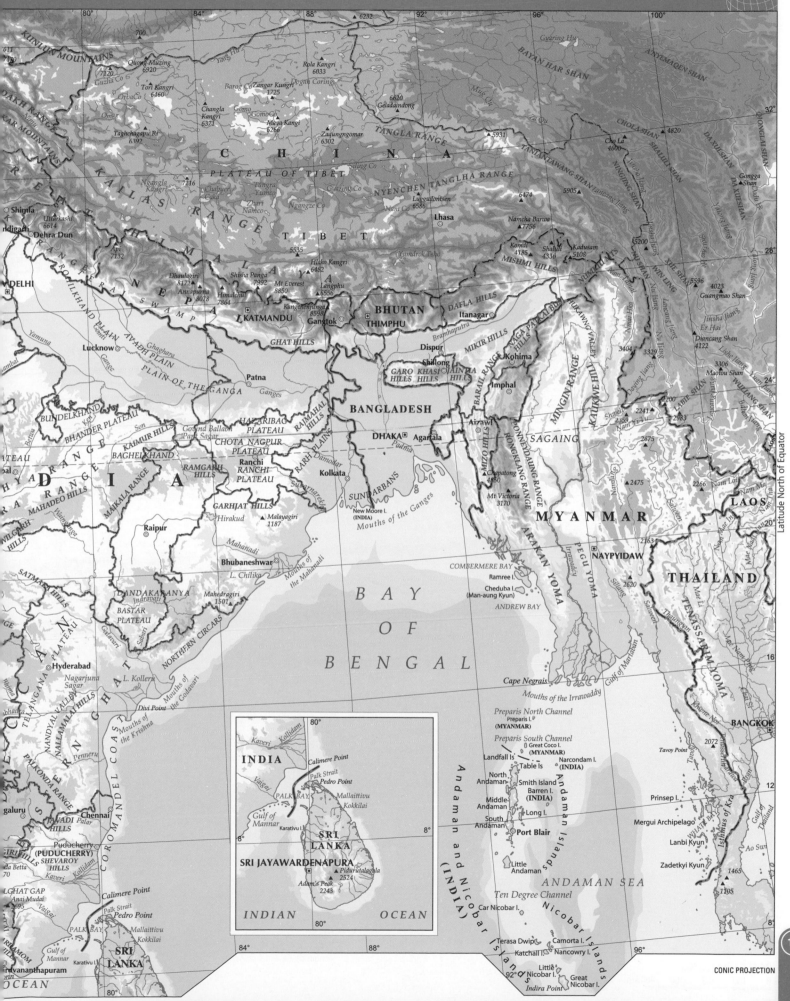

KUNLUN MOUNTAINS
611
470
700
LADAKH RANGE
KARAKORAM MOUNTAINS
Quong Muzing 6920
Guzha Co
7120
Tori Kangri 6460
OrbaCo
Omar
Taghchagapu Ri 6392
Changla Kangri 6371
Como
GomoCo
Maya Kangi 6266
Rola Kangri 6033
Barog Co
Zangar Kangri 1725
Pogan Coring
Zaqungngomar 6302
6232
6620
Geladaindong
BAYAN HAR SHAN
Gyaring Hu
A'NYEMAQEN SHAN
Mub Qu
Za Qu
32°
CHINA
CHOLA SHAN 4820
Cho La 4600
SHALULI SHAN
DAXUESHAN
QIONGLAI SHAN
PLATEAU OF TIBET
Siling Co
Zangal Yumco
Zhari Namco
Giaring Co
Ngangze Co
Nam Co 6586
Luggudontsen
NYENCHEN TANGLHA RANGE
6474
5905
NINGING SHAN
YUN LING
5596
4023
Guangmao Shan
Gongga Shan
TANGLA RANGE
5931
TANTANTAWANG SHAN
XIE SHAN
Lancang Jiang
Nu Jiang
Jinsha Jiang
Yalong Jiang
Dadu He
28°
Shinla
Uttarkashi 6614
Dehra Dun
ndigarh
Api 7132
Ngangla Kangri 7216
Chulyyer Caka
5535
Yamdrok Tsho
Lhasa
Namcha Barwa 7756
Kondai 4185
Shaluli 4336
Kadusam 5108
5200
Er Hai
Jinsha Jiang
Diancang Shan 4122
DELHI
Dhaulagiri 8172
Annapurna 8078
Himalchuli 7864
NEPAL
Shisha Panga 7992
Mt Everest 8850
6482
Langphu 6556
Kangchenjunga 6598
MISHMI HILLS
NU SHAN
3404
3329
3306
Maotou Shan
WULIANG SHAN
24°
ROHILKHAND
Ganges
TERAI
SWAMP
AVADH PLAIN
KATMANDU
Gangtok
BHUTAN
THIMPHU
GHAT HILLS
DAFLA HILLS
Itanagar
Bramhaputra
MIKIR HILLS
Kohima
NAGA PAKAI RAJ
PATKAI BUM
FUKANG VALLEY
MINGIN RANGE
LABEI SHAN
3306
Maotou Shan
Lucknow
Yamuna
PLAIN OF THE GANGA
Ghaghara
Patna
Ganges
BANGLADESH
Dispur
Shillong
GARO HILLS
KHASI HILLS
JAINTIA HILLS
BARAIL RANGE
Imphal
MIZO HILLS
CHIN HILLS
PONNEDAUNG RANGE
SAGAING
2241
2359
2983
2675
2675
Nam Yit Mt
Nam Lot
2266
LAOS
BUNDELKHAND
BHANDER PLATEAU
Betwa
Son
Govind Ballabh 'Park Sagar
HAZARIBAG PLATEAU
CHOTA NAGPUR PLATEAU
RAJMAHAL HILLS
Ranchi
RANCHI PLATEAU
Kolkata
RARH PLAINS
Damodar
DHAKA
Padma
Agartala
SUNDARBANS
2475
2266
Nam Mai
NAM LOI
2620
VINDHYA RANGE
KAIMUR HILLS
BAGHELKHAND
RAMGARH HILLS
GARHJAT HILLS
Subarnarekha
Mt Victoria 3170
Chapatong 4850
RONGKLANG RANGE
ARAKAN YOMA
PEGU YOMA
THAILAND
MAHADEO HILLS
MAIKALA RANGE
INDIA
Hirakud
Malayagiri 1187
Mahanadi
New Moore I. (INDIA)
Mouths of the Ganges
Raipur
Bhubaneshwar
L. Chilika
Mouths of the Mahanadi
2163
NAYPYIDAW
SATMAI HILLS
DANDAKARANYA
Indravati
BASTAR PLATEAU
Godavari
Mahedragiri 1501
NORTHERN CIRCARS
BAY OF BENGAL
COMBERMERE BAY
Ramree I.
Cheduba I. (Man-aung Kyun)
ANDREW BAY
2620
Sittang
DECCAN
Hyderabad
Nagarjuna Sagar
TELANGANA PLATEAU
Wainganga
L. Kolleru
Krishna
Mouths of the Godavari
Cape Negrais
Mouths of the Irrawaddy
TENASSERIM YOMA
Tavoy Point
2072
BANGKOK
WESTERN GHATS
Bhima
NANDYAL VALLEY
NALLAMALAI HILLS
Penneru
Divi Point
Mouths of the Krishna
INDIA
Kaveri
Kollidam
Calimere Point
80°
Preparis North Channel
Preparis I. (MYANMAR)
Preparis South Channel
Great Coco I. (MYANMAR)
Landfall Is
Narcondam I. (INDIA)
North Andaman
Table Is
Smith Island
Barren I. (INDIA)
Middle Andaman
Long I.
South Andaman
Port Blair
Andaman Islands
Mergui Archipelago
Lanbi Kyun
Zadetkyi Kyun
1465
1105
EASTERN GHATS
PALKONDA RANGE
galuru
JAWADI HILLS
Palar
Chennai
COROMANDEL COAST
Vaigai
PALK BAY
Gulf of Mannar
Karativu I.
SRI LANKA
SRI JAYAWARDENAPURA
Pidurutalagala 2524
Adam's Peak 2243
Palk Strait
Pedro Point
Mallaittivu
Kokkilai
8°
8°
INDIAN OCEAN
80°
Andaman and Nicobar Islands (INDIA)
Prinsep I.
ANDAMAN SEA
Ten Degree Channel
Car Nicobar I.
Nicobar Islands
SHEVAROY HILLS
Anai Mudai 2695
Kollidam
Calimere Point
Palk Strait
Pedro Point
PALK BAY
Mallaittivu
Kokkilai
Gulf of Mannar
Karativu I.
SRI LANKA
rvananthapuram
Terasa Dwip
Camorta I.
Katchall I.
Nancowry I.
Little Nicobar I.
Great Nicobar I.
Indira Point
96°
84°
88°
92°
8°
12
16
20°
24°
28°
32°

Latitude North of Equator

CONIC PROJECTION

Map labels

IRAN

Qom · Dasht-e Kavir · Daryacheh-ye Namak · Kashmar · Mashhad · TURKMENISTAN · Shibirghan · Sar-e Pul · Mazar-e Sharif · Aibak · Taloqan · Kunduz · Gilgit · Indus

Kah-e Garbosh · Chah-e Malek · Esfahan · Birjand · Bala Murghab · Qal'ah-ye Now · Herat · Bamiyan · Charikar · KABUL · Mehtar Lam · Paruti · Baramula · Srinagar

Ahvaz · Yazd · Kerman · Shindand · AFGHANISTAN · Ghazni · Gardez · Jalalabad · ISLAMABAD · Gulmarg · Jammu

Kharki · Zaindeh · Namakzar-e Shadad · Harut · Farah Rud · Farah · Delaram · Tarin Kot · Sharan · Rawalpindi · Jhelum · Chenab

Kerman · Shur Ab · Gereshk · Helmand · Arghandab · Qalat · Kandahar · Lashkar Gah · Multan · Lahore · Amritsar · Jaland · Ludhiana · PUNJA

Daryacheh-ye Bakhtegan · Shiraz · Nosratabad · Zaranj · Zahedan · Quetta · Loralai · Ravi · Sutlej · Bhatinda

Ridge Mand · Rud-e Mand · Kharan · Bam · Qila Safed · Hamun Pu · Khash Rud · Nushki · Sibi · Sukkur · Bahawalpur · Ganganagar · HARYA

Persian Gulf · Ad Dammam · BAHRAIN · MANAMA · Sheykh Sho'eyb · Hendorabi · Bandar-e Abbas · Iranshahr · Hamun-e Jaz Murian · Saravan · Kuhak · Diz · Shikarpur · Larkana · Rahimyar Khan · Sardarshahr · Bikaner · Fatehpur · Bhi

QATAR · DOHA · Jazireh-ye Sirri · Qeshm I. · Strait of Hormuz · Al Khasab · OMAN · Gwadar · Turbat · Bela · Dadu · Nawabshah · Jaisalmer · Jodhpur · Luni · Nagaur · L. Sambhar · Jaipur · RAJASTHAN

Dubai · Gulf of Oman · Jiwani · Pasni · Karachi · Hyderabad · Mirpur Khas · Barmer · Ajmer

ABU DHABI · UNITED ARAB EMIRATES · Suhar · SONMIANI BAY · Uthal · Abu · Bhilwara · Udaipur

Tropic of Cancer · MUSCAT · Ar Rustaq · Mouths of the Indus · Radhanpur · Mahesana

SAUDI ARABIA · Sur · Bhuj · Gandhinagar · Ahmadabad · Godhra · Ratlam · Indore

Umm as Samim · Wadi Andam · Gulf of Kachchh · Kandla · GUJARAT · Rajkot · Vadodara · Narmada · Mh

OMAN · Dwarka · Bhavnagar · Surat · Tapi · Dhule

YEMEN · Wadi Muqshin · Jazirat Masirah · Porbandar · Somnath · Diu (D&D) · Gulf of Khambhat · Daman (D&D) · Silvassa · Dhule

DADRA & NAGAR HAVELI · Nasik · Godavari · MAHARASHTI

ARABIAN SEA · Mumbai · Ahmadnagar

Pune

Maldives inset

8° · 72° · Eight Degree Channel

Thiladummathi Atoll
Miladhunmadulu Atoll
North Maalhosmadulu Atoll · Faadhippolhu Atoll
Maalhosmadulu Atoll · **MALDIVES**
Gatani Atoll
Ari Atoll · Male
Vaadhu Channel
Felidhu Channel
Nilandhoo Atoll · Mulakatholhu
Kolhumadulu Atoll · Hadhdhunmathi Atoll
One and a Half Degree Channel
4°
Huvadhu Atoll
Equator
INDIAN OCEAN
Addu Atoll
Hitaddu · Midu
On same scale · Longitude East of Greenwich

Lower right

Satara · Solapur

Ratnagiri

Bijap · Krishna

Kudal · Belgaum

Panaji · Hubli

GOA · KARNATA

Davangere · Chitra

Linganamakki Reservoir

Udupi · Hal · Belur

Mangalore · Hass

Cherbaniani Reef · Byramgore Reef · Chettlatt I. · Bitra I. · Kiltann I. · Mahe · PUDUCHERRY

Kadamatt I. · Amindivi Islands · Kozhikode

Laccadive Islands · Andrott I. · Thris

Kavaratti · Cheriyam I. · LAKSHADWEEP SEA

Suheli I. · Kalpeni I. · (INDIA)

Nine Degree Channel · Alap

Minicoy I.

Eight Degree Channel · INDIA

SCALE 1: 12 500 000

0 · 100 · 200 · 300 · 400 km

Longitude East of Greenwich

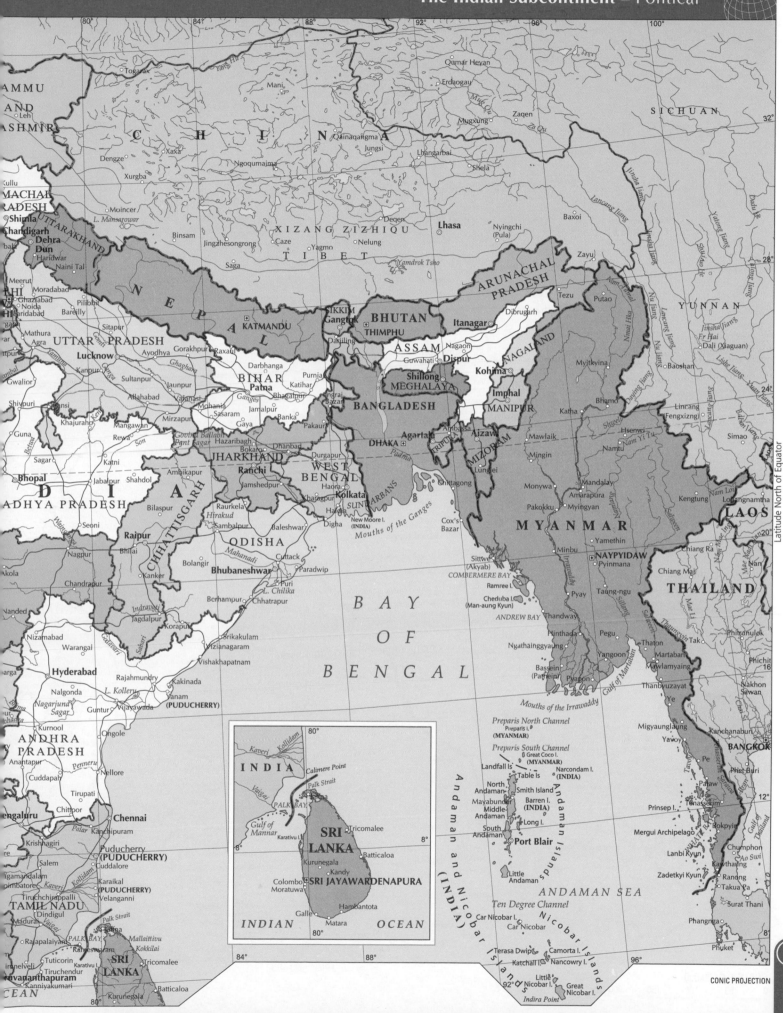

CONIC PROJECTION

Latitude North of Equator

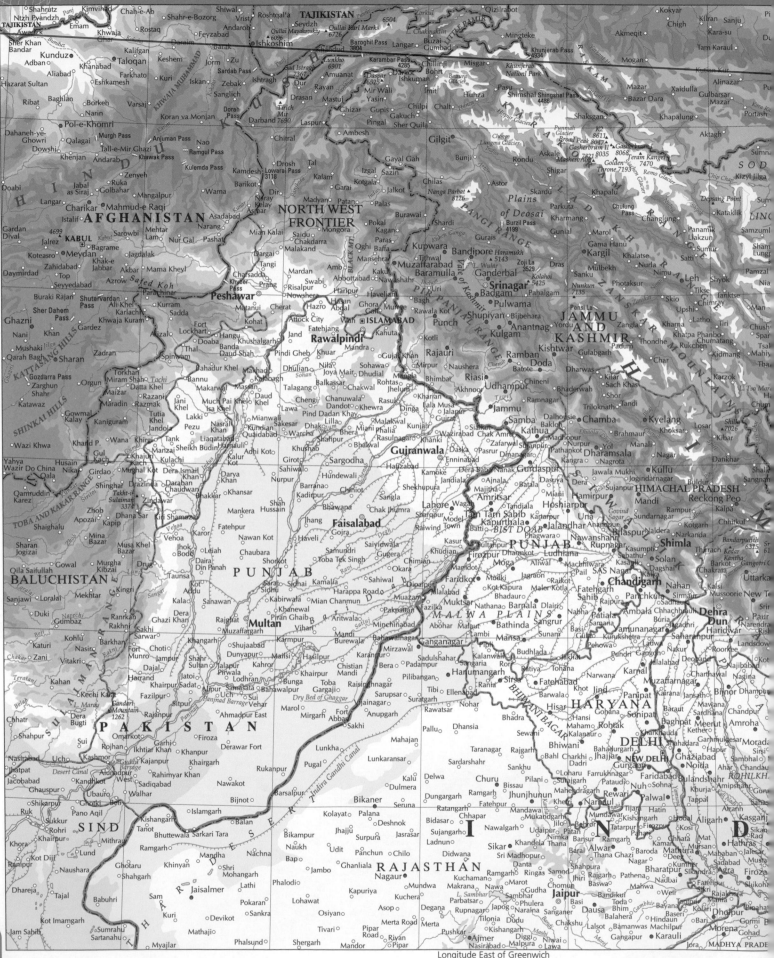

SCALE 1:5 000 000

0   50   100   150   200 km

Longitude East of Greenwich

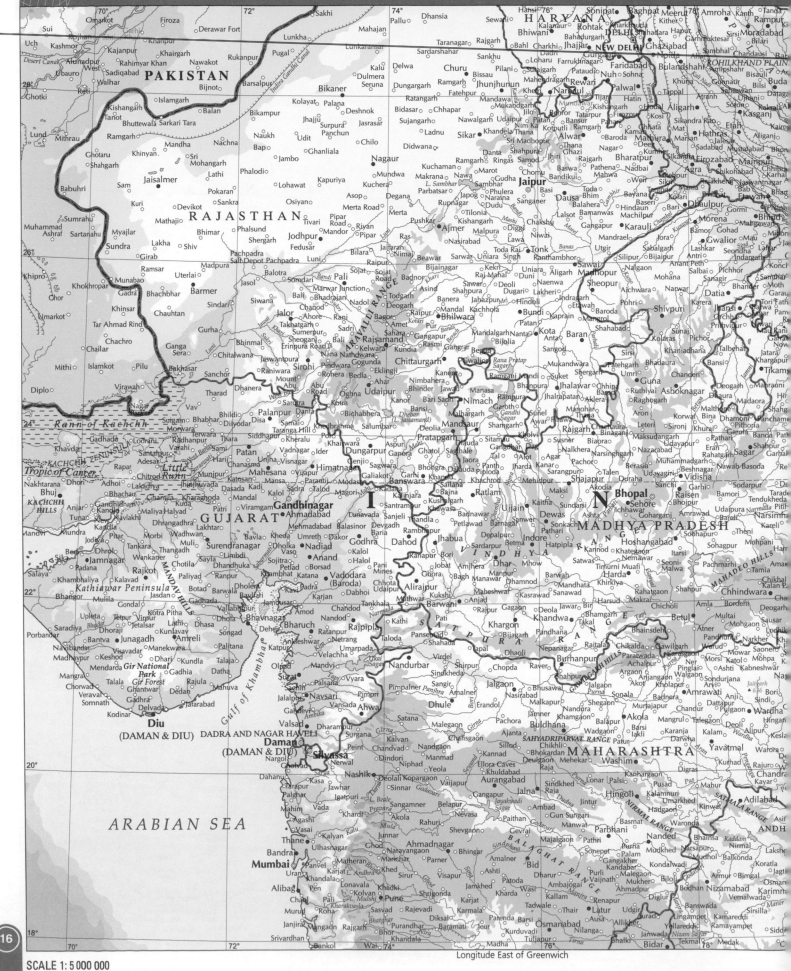

SCALE 1:5 000 000

0   50   100   150   200 km

Longitude East of Greenwich

SCALE 1: 5 000 000

0   50   100   150   200 km

Latitude North of Equator

CONIC PROJECTION

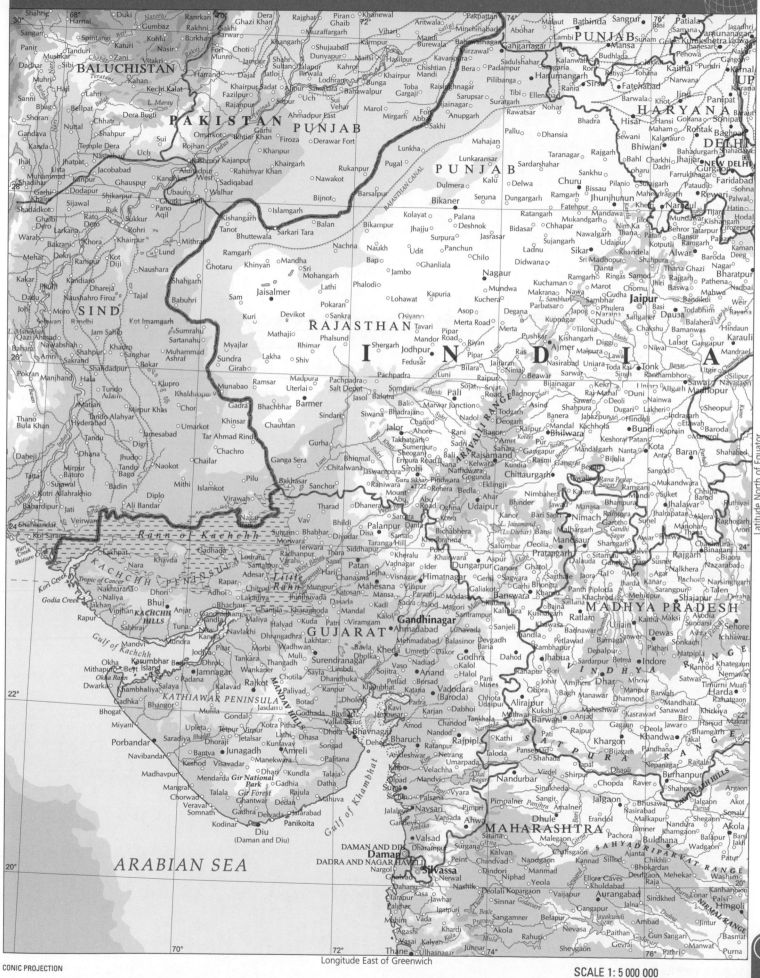

CONIC PROJECTION

Longitude East of Greenwich

SCALE 1 : 5 000 000

0   50   100   150   200 km

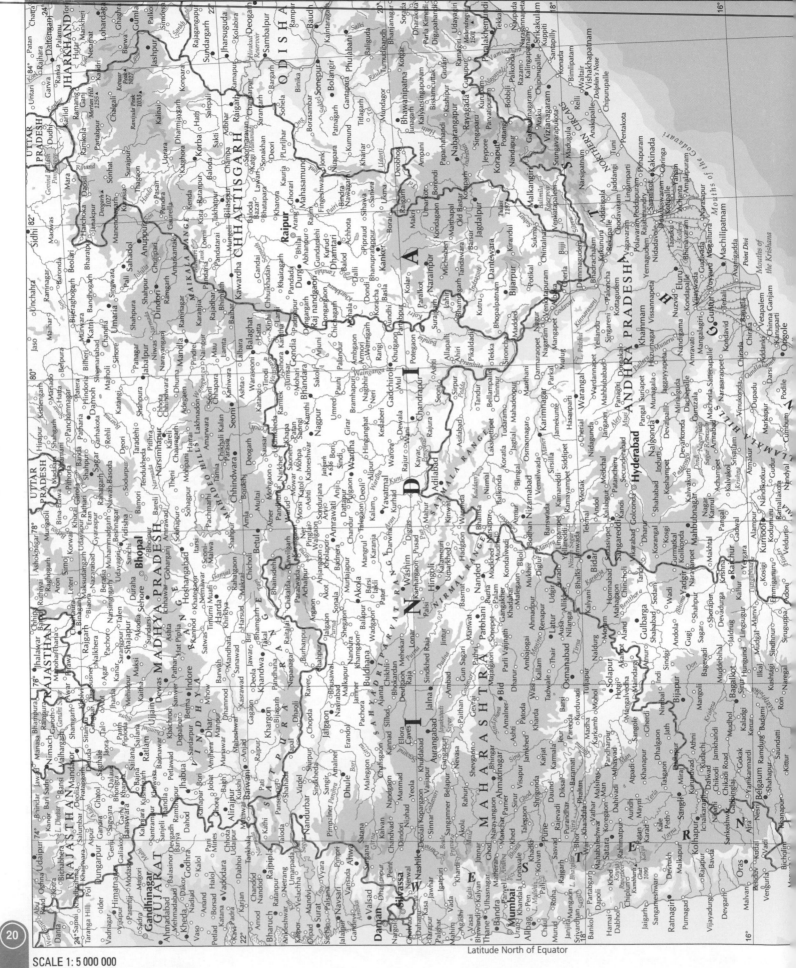

Latitude North of Equator

SCALE 1 : 5 000 000

0   50   100   150   200 km

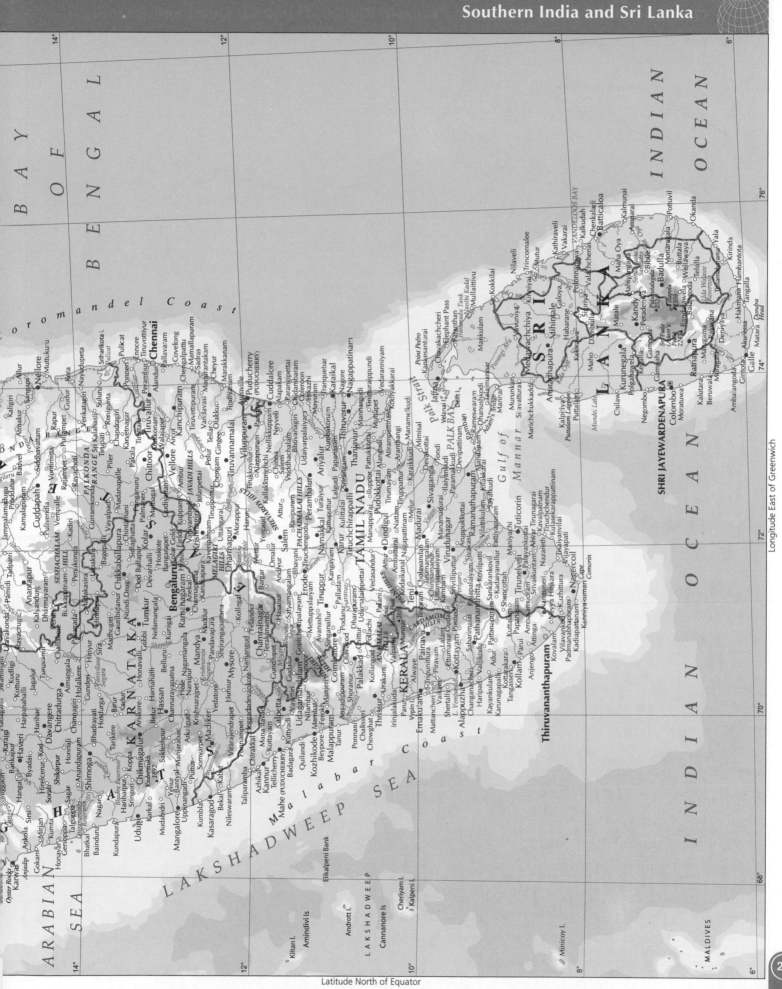

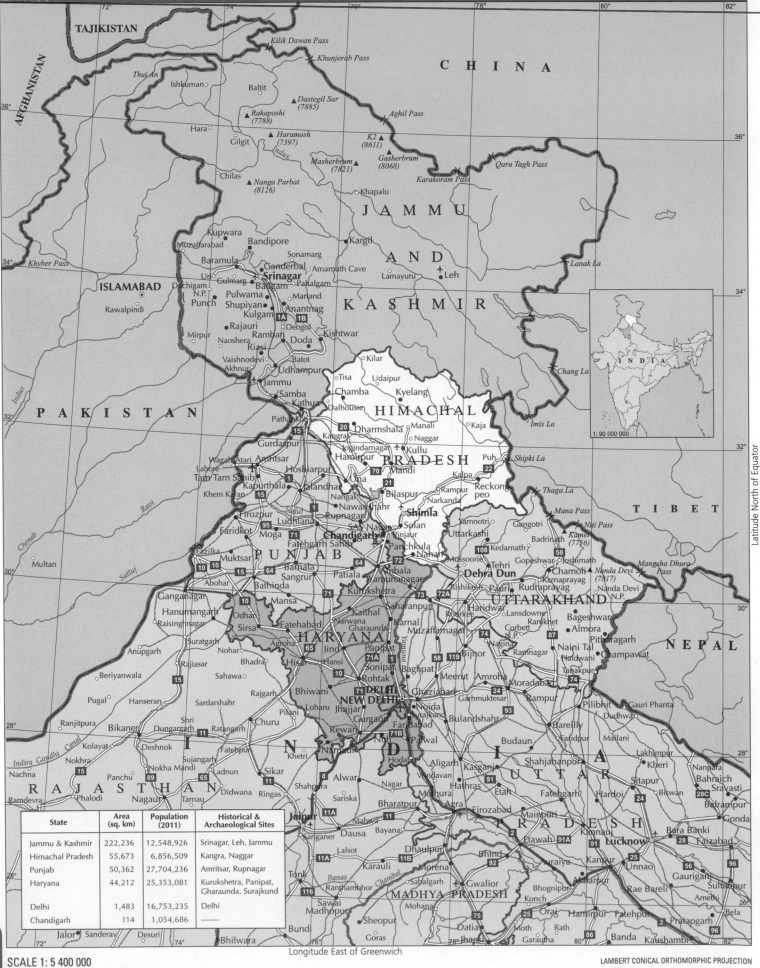

State	Area (sq. km)	Population (2011)	Historical & Archaeological Sites
Jammu & Kashmir	222,236	12,548,926	Srinagar, Leh, Jammu
Himachal Pradesh	55,673	6,856,509	Kangra, Naggar
Punjab	50,362	27,704,236	Amritsar, Rupnagar
Haryana	44,212	25,353,081	Kurukshetra, Panipat, Gharaunda, Surajkund
Delhi	1,483	16,753,235	Delhi
Chandigarh	114	1,054,686	-------

SCALE 1: 5 400 000

0   50   100   150   200 km

Longitude East of Greenwich

Latitude North of Equator

LAMBERT CONICAL ORTHOMORPHIC PROJECTION

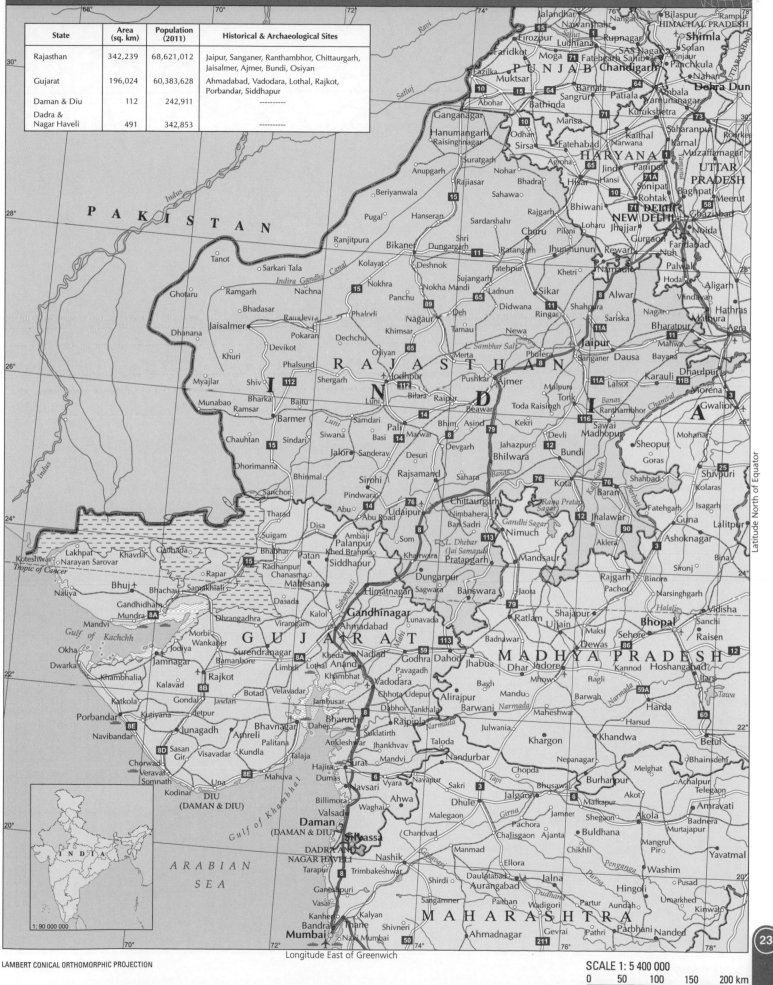

State	Area (sq. km)	Population (2011)	Historical & Archaeological Sites
Rajasthan	342,239	68,621,012	Jaipur, Sanganer, Ranthambhor, Chittaurgarh, Jaisalmer, Ajmer, Bundi, Osiyan
Gujarat	196,024	60,383,628	Ahmadabad, Vadodara, Lothal, Rajkot, Porbandar, Siddhapur
Daman & Diu	112	242,911	----------
Dadra & Nagar Haveli	491	342,853	----------

LAMBERT CONICAL ORTHOMORPHIC PROJECTION

Longitude East of Greenwich

SCALE 1: 5 400 000

0   50   100   150   200 km

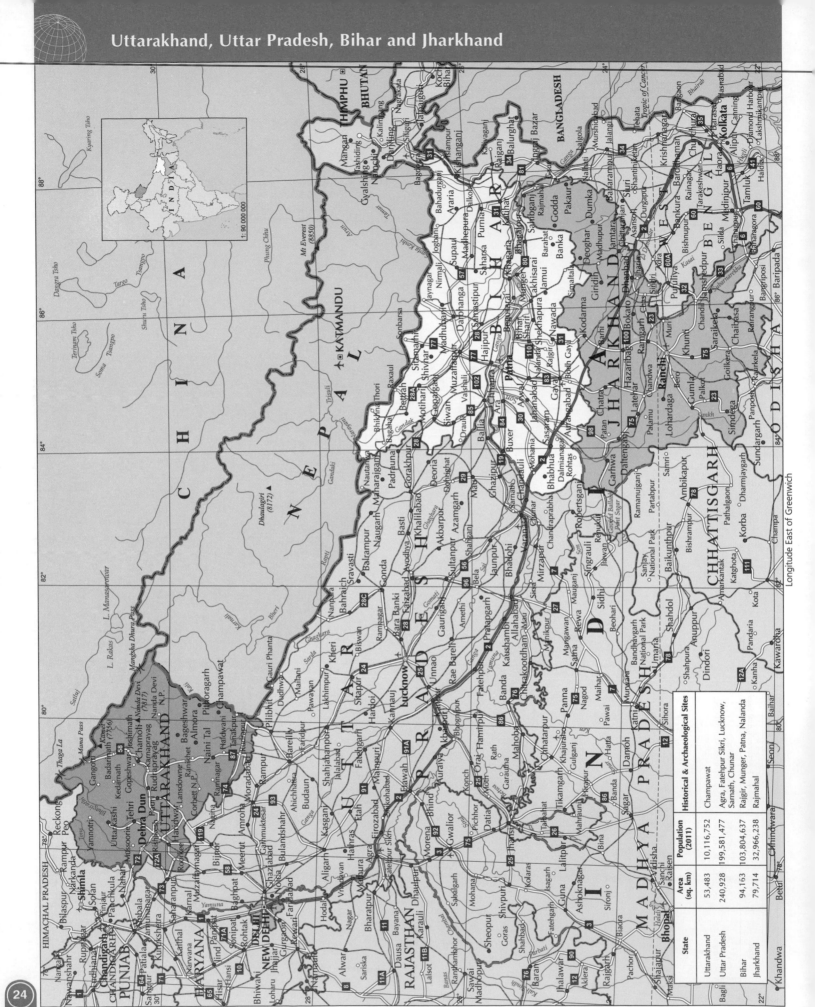

State	Area (sq. km)	Population (2011)	Historical & Archaeological Sites
Uttarakhand	53,483	10,116,752	Champawat
Uttar Pradesh	240,928	199,581,477	Agra, Fatehpur Sikri, Lucknow, Sarnath, Chunar
Bihar	94,163	103,804,637	Rajgir, Munger, Patna, Nalanda
Jharkhand	79,714	32,966,238	Rajmahal

Latitude North of Equator

Longitude East of Greenwich

SCALE 1: 5 400 000

0   50   100   150   200 km

LAMBERT CONICAL ORTHOMORPHIC PROJECTION

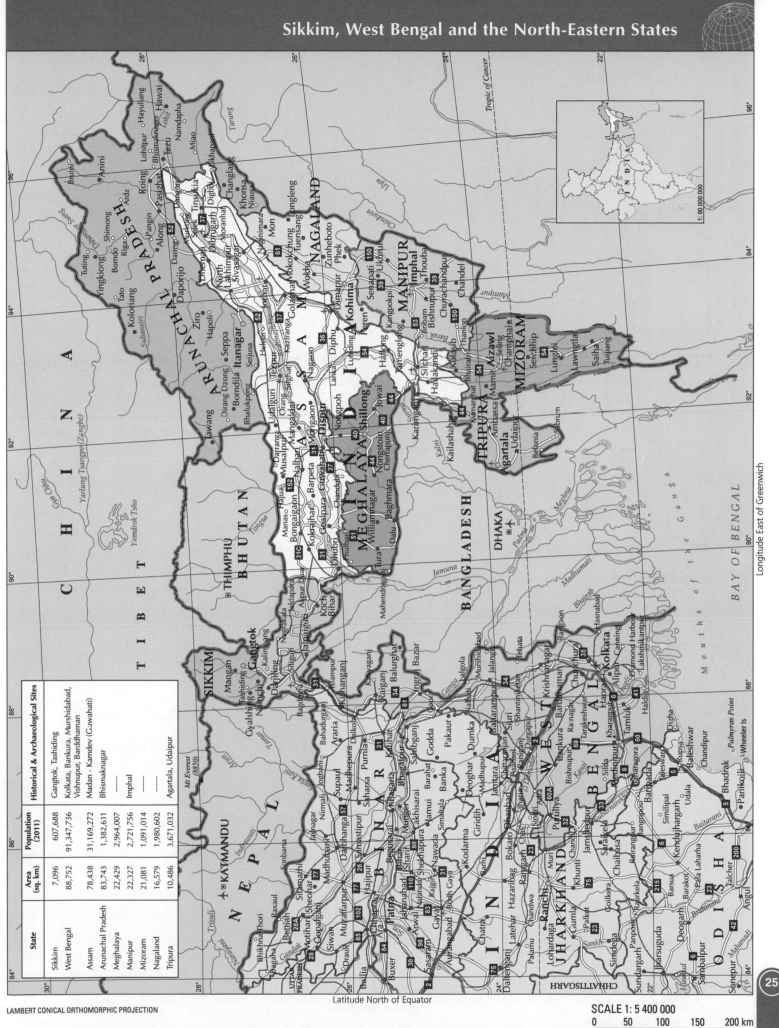

State	Area (sq. km)	Population (2011)	Historical & Archaeological Sites
Sikkim	7,096	607,688	Gangtok, Tashiding
West Bengal	88,752	91,347,736	Kolkata, Bankura, Murshidabad, Vishnupur, Barddhaman
Assam	78,438	31,169,272	Madan – Kamdev (Guwahati)
Arunachal Pradesh	83,743	1,382,611	Bhismaknagar
Meghalaya	22,429	2,964,007	-----
Manipur	22,327	2,721,756	Imphal
Mizoram	21,081	1,091,014	-----
Nagaland	16,579	1,980,602	-----
Tripura	10,486	3,671,032	Agartala, Udaipur

LAMBERT CONICAL ORTHOMORPHIC PROJECTION

Latitude North of Equator

Longitude East of Greenwich

SCALE 1: 5 400 000

0   50   100   150   200 km

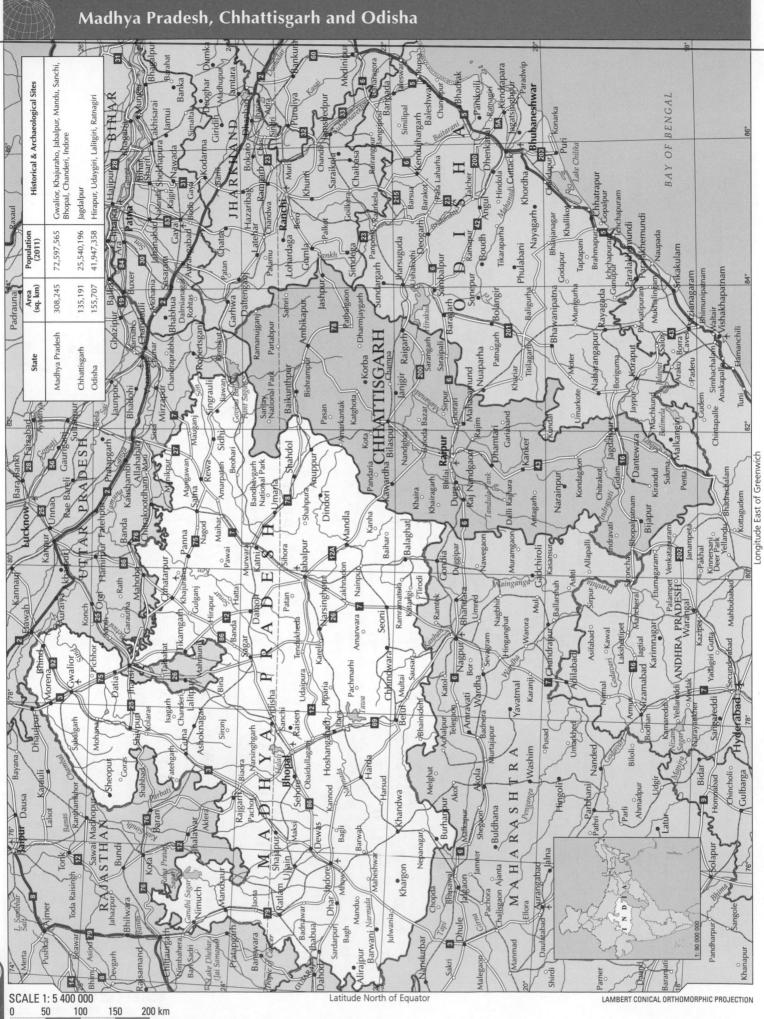

State	Area (sq. km)	Population (2011)	Historical & Archaeological Sites
Madhya Pradesh	308,245	72,597,565	Gwalior, Khajuraho, Jabalpur, Mandu, Sanchi, Bhopal, Chanderi, Indore
Chhattisgarh	135,191	25,540,196	Jagdalpur
Odisha	155,707	41,947,358	Hirapur, Udaygiri, Lalitgiri, Ratnagiri

SCALE 1: 5 400 000

0   50   100   150   200 km

Latitude North of Equator

LAMBERT CONICAL ORTHOMORPHIC PROJECTION

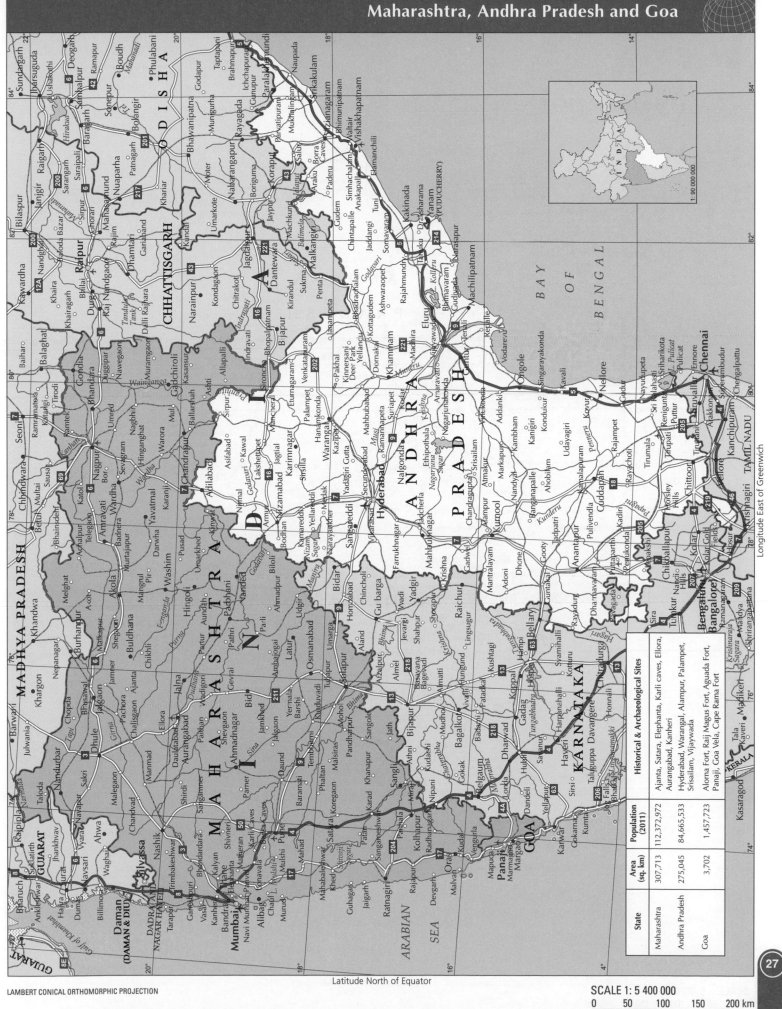

State	Area (sq. km)	Population (2011)	Historical & Archaeological Sites
Maharashtra	307,713	112,372,972	Ajanta, Satara, Elephanta, Karli caves, Ellora, Aurangabad, Kanheri
Andhra Pradesh	275,045	84,665,533	Hyderabad, Warangal, Alampur, Palampet, Srisailam, Vijaywada
Goa	3,702	1,457,723	Aloma Fort, Raij Magus Fort, Aguada Fort, Panaji, Goa Vela, Cape Rama Fort

Latitude North of Equator

LAMBERT CONICAL ORTHOMORPHIC PROJECTION

SCALE 1 : 5 400 000

0   50   100   150   200 km

27

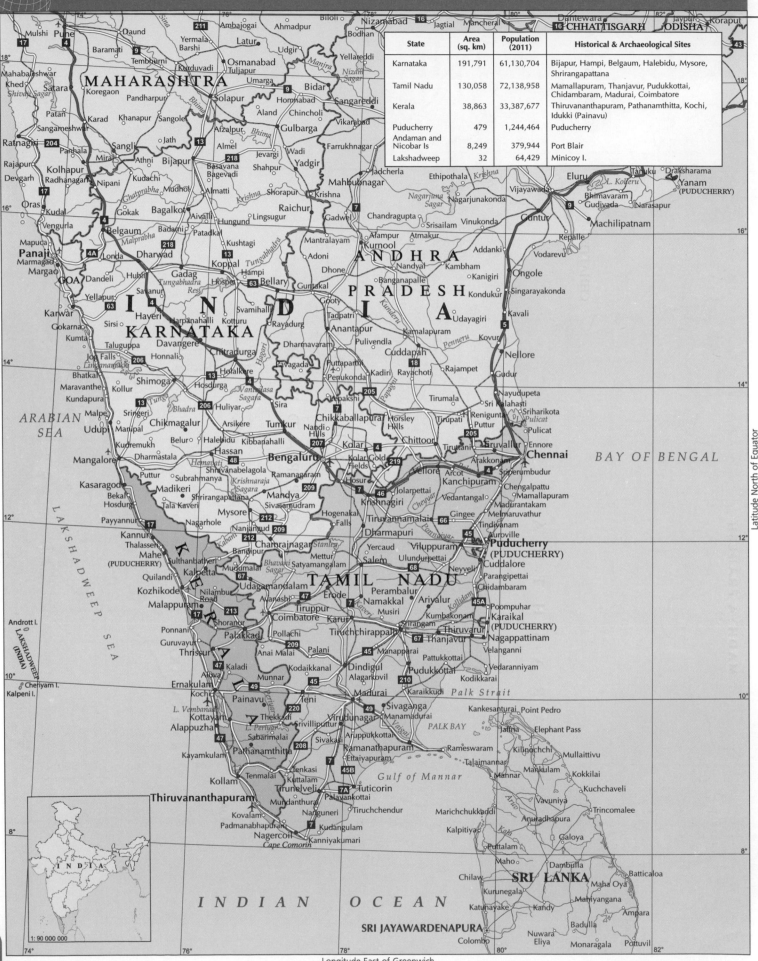

State	Area (sq. km)	Population (2011)	Historical & Archaeological Sites
Karnataka	191,791	61,130,704	Bijapur, Hampi, Belgaum, Halebidu, Mysore, Shrirangapattana
Tamil Nadu	130,058	72,138,958	Mamallapuram, Thanjavur, Pudukkottai, Chidambaram, Madurai, Coimbatore
Kerala	38,863	33,387,677	Thiruvananthapuram, Pathanamthitta, Kochi, Idukki (Painavu)
Puducherry	479	1,244,464	Puducherry
Andaman and Nicobar Is	8,249	379,944	Port Blair
Lakshadweep	32	64,429	Minicoy I.

Longitude East of Greenwich

Latitude North of Equator

LAMBERT CONICAL ORTHOMORPHIC PROJECTION

SCALE 1: 5 400 000

0   50   100   150   200 km

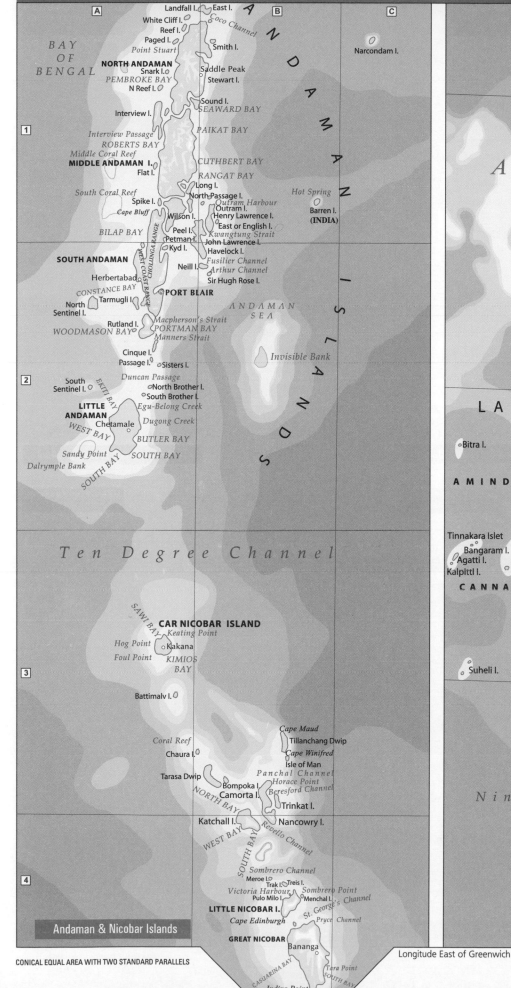

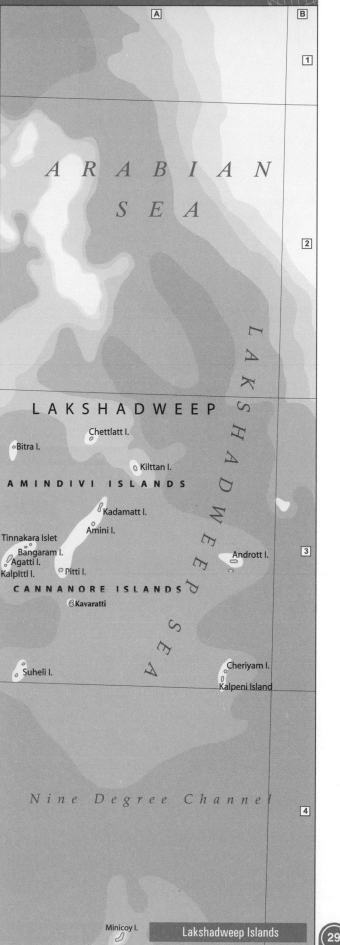

Andaman & Nicobar Islands

Lakshadweep Islands

CONICAL EQUAL AREA WITH TWO STANDARD PARALLELS

Longitude East of Greenwich

SCALE 1 : 2 850 000

0   25   50   75   100 km

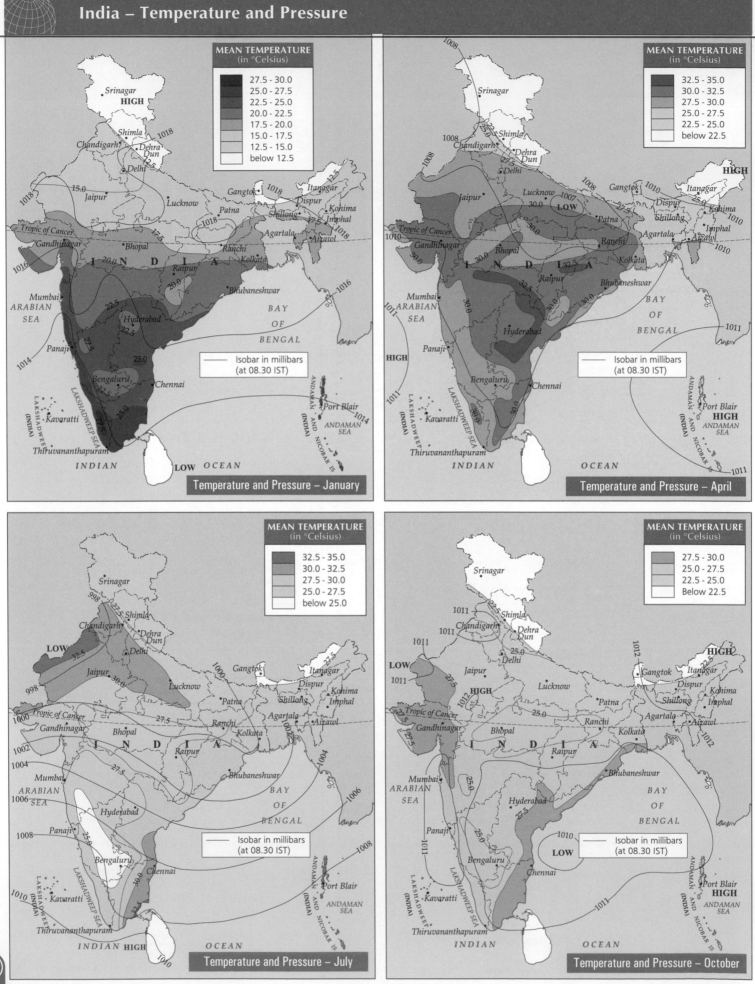

Temperature and Pressure – January

Temperature and Pressure – April

Temperature and Pressure – July

Temperature and Pressure – October

MEAN TEMPERATURE
(in °Celsius)

27.5 - 30.0
25.0 - 27.5
22.5 - 25.0
20.0 - 22.5
17.5 - 20.0
15.0 - 17.5
12.5 - 15.0
below 12.5

MEAN TEMPERATURE
(in °Celsius)

32.5 - 35.0
30.0 - 32.5
27.5 - 30.0
25.0 - 27.5
22.5 - 25.0
below 22.5

MEAN TEMPERATURE
(in °Celsius)

32.5 - 35.0
30.0 - 32.5
27.5 - 30.0
25.0 - 27.5
below 25.0

MEAN TEMPERATURE
(in °Celsius)

27.5 - 30.0
25.0 - 27.5
22.5 - 25.0
Below 22.5

Isobar in millibars
(at 08.30 IST)

SCALE 1: 30 500 000

0   300   600   900   1200 km

LAMBERT CONICAL ORTHOMORPHIC PROJECTION

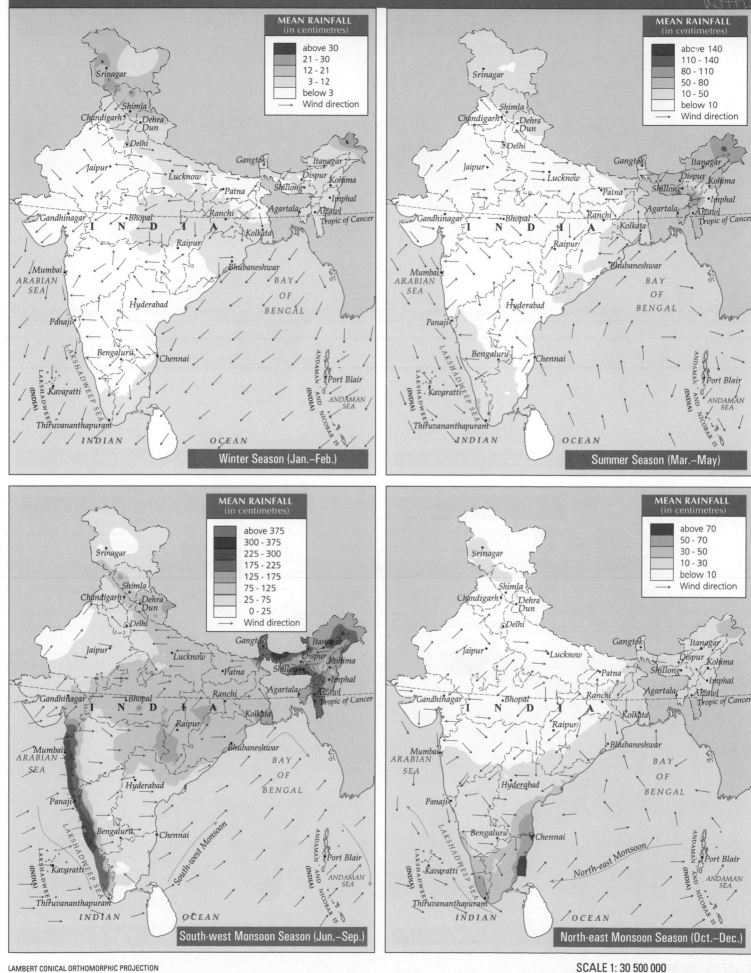

MEAN RAINFALL
(in centimetres)

- above 30
- 21 - 30
- 12 - 21
- 3 - 12
- below 3
- → Wind direction

Winter Season (Jan.–Feb.)

MEAN RAINFALL
(in centimetres)

- above 140
- 110 - 140
- 80 - 110
- 50 - 80
- 10 - 50
- below 10
- → Wind direction

Summer Season (Mar.–May)

MEAN RAINFALL
(in centimetres)

- above 375
- 300 - 375
- 225 - 300
- 175 - 225
- 125 - 175
- 75 - 125
- 25 - 75
- 0 - 25
- → Wind direction

South-west Monsoon Season (Jun.–Sep.)

MEAN RAINFALL
(in centimetres)

- above 70
- 50 - 70
- 30 - 50
- 10 - 30
- below 10
- → Wind direction

North-east Monsoon Season (Oct.–Dec.)

LAMBERT CONICAL ORTHOMORPHIC PROJECTION

SCALE 1: 30 500 000

0   300   600   900   1200 km

India – Relative Humidity, Annual Rainfall & Monsoon and Climatic Regions

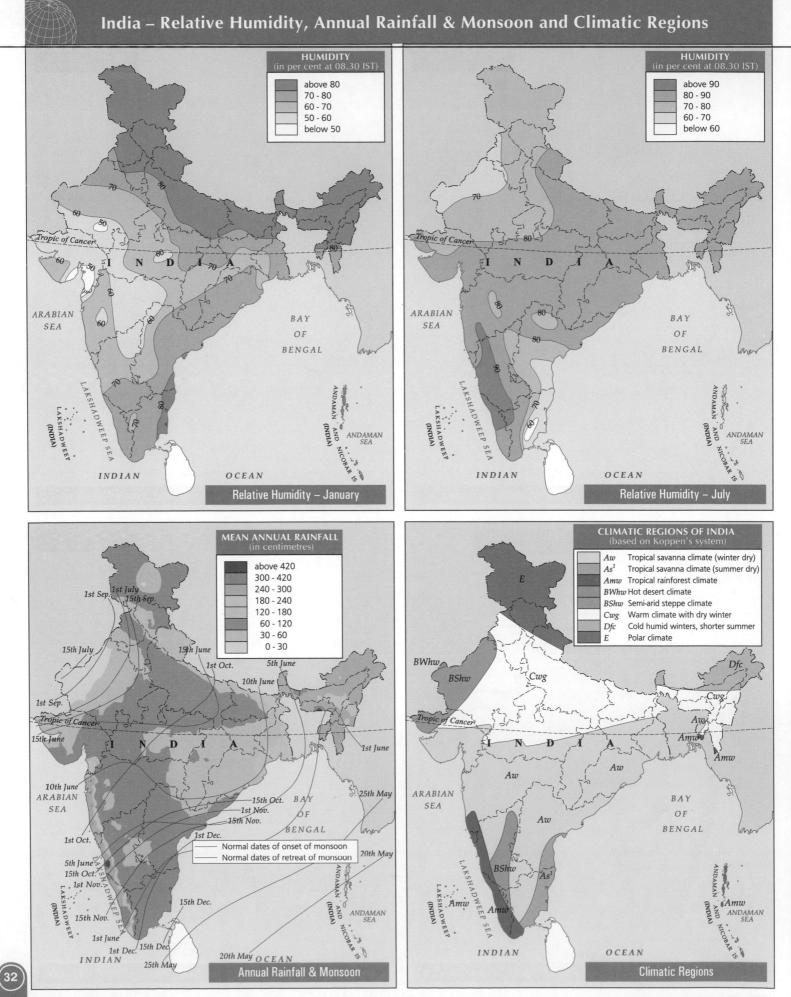

HUMIDITY
(in per cent at 08.30 IST)

- above 80
- 70 - 80
- 60 - 70
- 50 - 60
- below 50

Relative Humidity – January

HUMIDITY
(in per cent at 08.30 IST)

- above 90
- 80 - 90
- 70 - 80
- 60 - 70
- below 60

Relative Humidity – July

MEAN ANNUAL RAINFALL
(in centimetres)

- above 420
- 300 - 420
- 240 - 300
- 180 - 240
- 120 - 180
- 60 - 120
- 30 - 60
- 0 - 30

— Normal dates of onset of monsoon
— Normal dates of retreat of monsoon

Annual Rainfall & Monsoon

CLIMATIC REGIONS OF INDIA
(based on Koppen's system)

Aw	Tropical savanna climate (winter dry)
As¹	Tropical savanna climate (summer dry)
Amw	Tropical rainforest climate
BWhw	Hot desert climate
BShw	Semi-arid steppe climate
Cwg	Warm climate with dry winter
Dfc	Cold humid winters, shorter summer
E	Polar climate

Climatic Regions

SCALE 1: 30 500 000

0   300   600   900   1200 km

LAMBERT CONICAL ORTHOMORPHIC PROJECTION

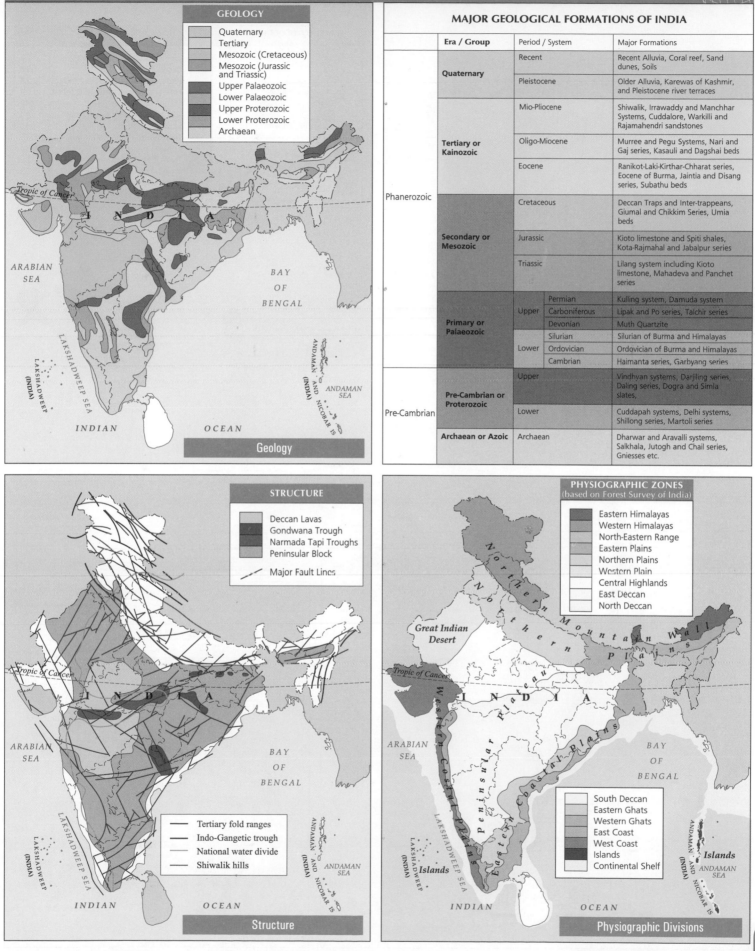

GEOLOGY

- Quaternary
- Tertiary
- Mesozoic (Cretaceous)
- Mesozoic (Jurassic and Triassic)
- Upper Palaeozoic
- Lower Palaeozoic
- Upper Proterozoic
- Lower Proterozoic
- Archaean

Geology

MAJOR GEOLOGICAL FORMATIONS OF INDIA

Era / Group		Period / System		Major Formations
Phanerozoic	Quaternary	Recent		Recent Alluvia, Coral reef, Sand dunes, Soils
		Pleistocene		Older Alluvia, Karewas of Kashmir, and Pleistocene river terraces
	Tertiary or Kainozoic	Mio-Pliocene		Shiwalik, Irrawaddy and Manchhar Systems, Cuddalore, Warkilli and Rajamahendri sandstones
		Oligo-Miocene		Murree and Pegu Systems, Nari and Gaj series, Kasauli and Dagshai beds
		Eocene		Ranikot-Laki-Kirthar-Chharat series, Eocene of Burma, Jaintia and Disang series, Subathu beds
	Secondary or Mesozoic	Cretaceous		Deccan Traps and Inter-trappeans, Giumal and Chikkim Series, Umia beds
		Jurassic		Kioto limestone and Spiti shales, Kota-Rajmahal and Jabalpur series
		Triassic		Lilang system including Kioto limestone, Mahadeva and Panchet series
	Primary or Palaeozoic	Upper	Permian	Kulling system, Damuda system
			Carboniferous	Lipak and Po series, Talchir series
			Devonian	Muth Quartzite
		Lower	Silurian	Silurian of Burma and Himalayas
			Ordovician	Ordovician of Burma and Himalayas
			Cambrian	Haimanta series, Garbyang series
Pre-Cambrian	Pre-Cambrian or Proterozoic	Upper		Vindhyan systems, Darjiling series, Daling series, Dogra and Simla slates,
		Lower		Cuddapah systems, Delhi systems, Shillong series, Martoli series
	Archaean or Azoic	Archaean		Dharwar and Aravalli systems, Salkhala, Jutogh and Chail series, Gniesses etc.

STRUCTURE

- Deccan Lavas
- Gondwana Trough
- Narmada Tapi Troughs
- Peninsular Block
- Major Fault Lines

—— Tertiary fold ranges
—— Indo-Gangetic trough
—— National water divide
—— Shiwalik hills

Structure

PHYSIOGRAPHIC ZONES
(based on Forest Survey of India)

- Eastern Himalayas
- Western Himalayas
- North-Eastern Range
- Eastern Plains
- Northern Plains
- Western Plain
- Central Highlands
- East Deccan
- North Deccan
- South Deccan
- Eastern Ghats
- Western Ghats
- East Coast
- West Coast
- Islands
- Continental Shelf

Great Indian Desert

Physiographic Divisions

LAMBERT CONICAL ORTHOMORPHIC PROJECTION

SCALE 1: 30 500 000

0   300   600   900   1200 km

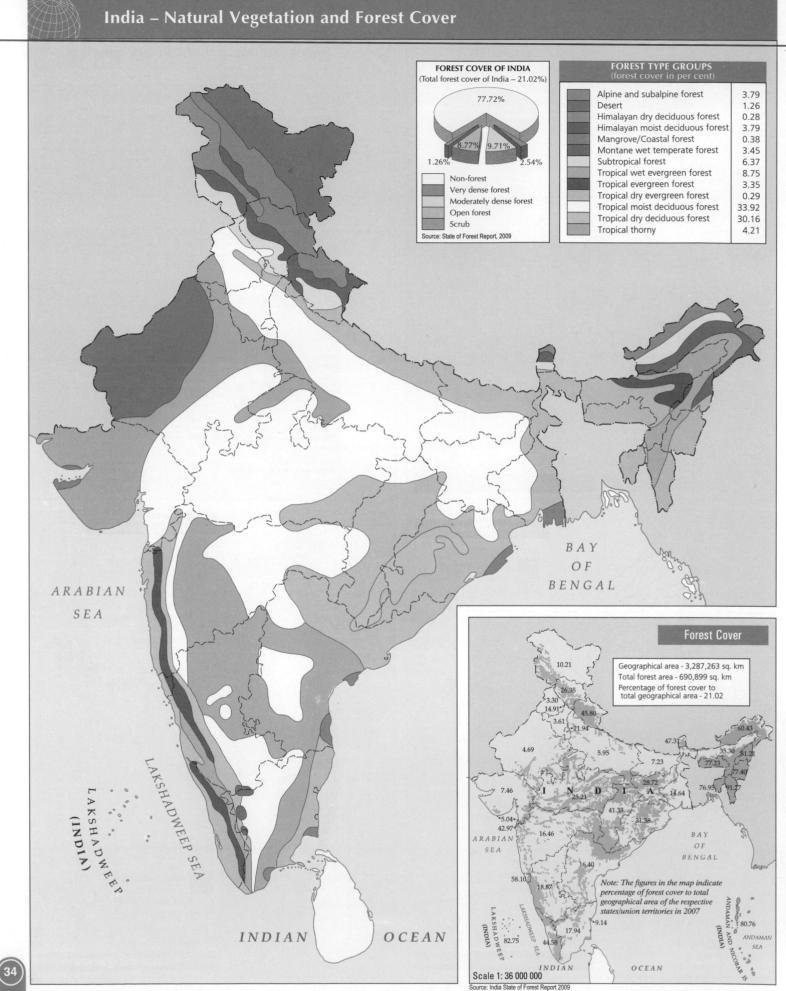

FOREST COVER OF INDIA
(Total forest cover of India – 21.02%)

77.72%

8.77% 9.71%

1.26% 2.54%

- Non-forest
- Very dense forest
- Moderately dense forest
- Open forest
- Scrub

Source: State of Forest Report, 2009

FOREST TYPE GROUPS
(forest cover in per cent)

Forest Type	Per cent
Alpine and subalpine forest	3.79
Desert	1.26
Himalayan dry deciduous forest	0.28
Himalayan moist deciduous forest	3.79
Mangrove/Coastal forest	0.38
Montane wet temperate forest	3.45
Subtropical forest	6.37
Tropical wet evergreen forest	8.75
Tropical evergreen forest	3.35
Tropical dry evergreen forest	0.29
Tropical moist deciduous forest	33.92
Tropical dry deciduous forest	30.16
Tropical thorny	4.21

ARABIAN SEA

BAY OF BENGAL

LAKSHADWEEP SEA

LAKSHADWEEP (INDIA)

INDIAN OCEAN

Forest Cover

Geographical area - 3,287,263 sq. km

Total forest area - 690,899 sq. km

Percentage of forest cover to total geographical area - 21.02

Note: The figures in the map indicate percentage of forest cover to total geographical area of the respective states/union territories in 2007

Scale 1: 36 000 000

Source: India State of Forest Report 2009

SCALE 1: 15 000 000

0   150   300   450   600 km

LAMBERT CONICAL ORTHOMORPHIC PROJECTION

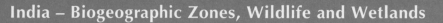
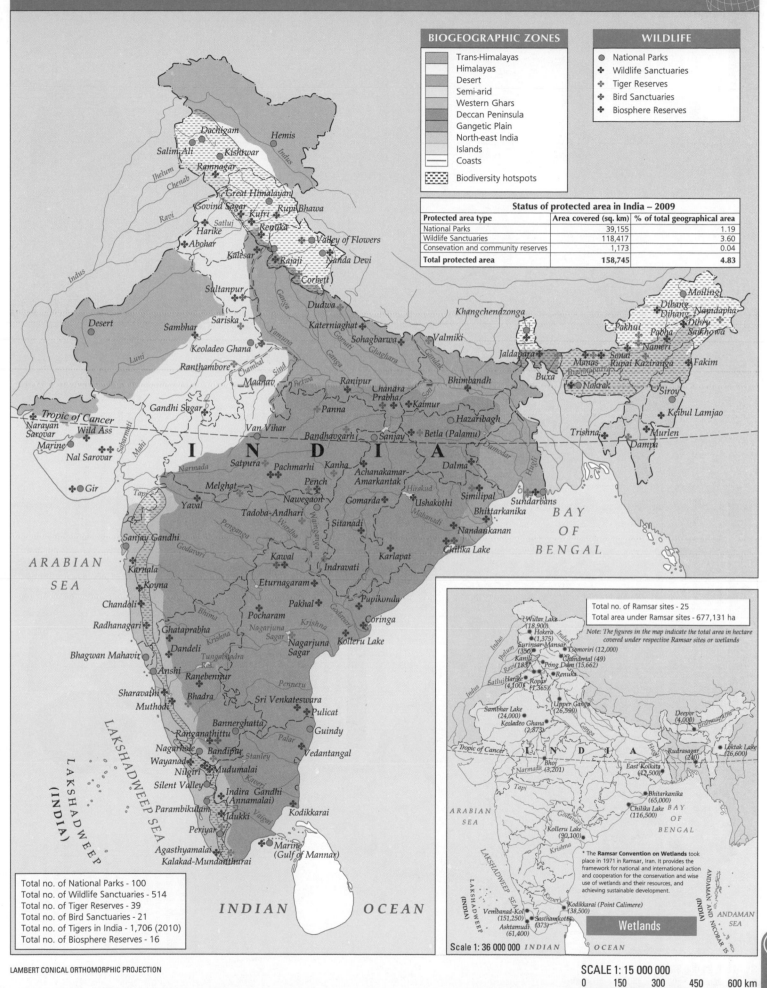

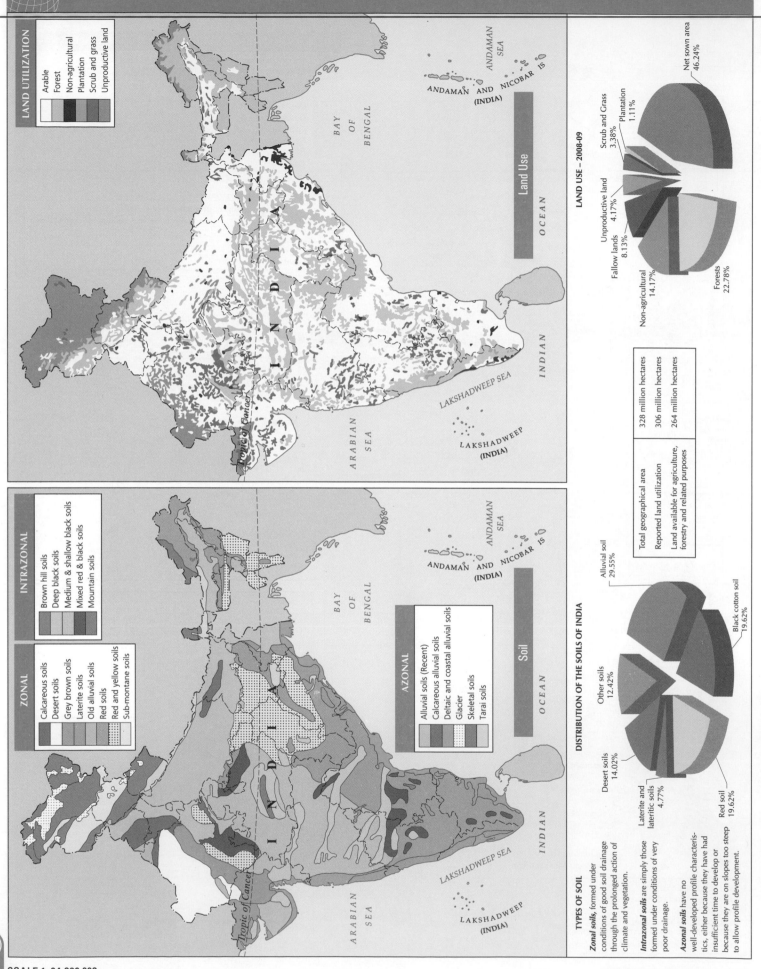

LAND UTILIZATION

- Arable
- Forest
- Non-agricultural
- Plantation
- Scrub and grass
- Unproductive land

Land Use

ZONAL

- Calcareous soils
- Desert soils
- Grey brown soils
- Laterite soils
- Old alluvial soils
- Red soils
- Red and yellow soils
- Sub-montane soils

INTRAZONAL

- Brown hill soils
- Deep black soils
- Medium & shallow black soils
- Mixed red & black soils
- Mountain soils

AZONAL

- Alluvial soils (Recent)
- Calcareous alluvial soils
- Deltaic and coastal alluvial soils
- Glacier
- Skeletal soils
- Tarai soils

Soil

TYPES OF SOIL

Zonal soils, formed under conditions of good soil drainage through the prolonged action of climate and vegetation.

Intrazonal soils are simply those formed under conditions of very poor drainage.

Azonal soils have no well-developed profile characteristics, either because they have had insufficient time to develop or because they are on slopes too steep to allow profile development.

DISTRIBUTION OF THE SOILS OF INDIA

- Alluvial soil 29.55%
- Black cotton soil 19.62%
- Red soil 19.62%
- Laterite and lateritic soils 4.77%
- Desert soils 14.02%
- Other soils 12.42%

LAND USE – 2008-09

- Net sown area 46.24%
- Scrub and Grass 3.38%
- Plantation 1.11%
- Forests 22.78%
- Non-agricultural 14.17%
- Fallow lands 8.13%
- Unproductive land 4.17%

Total geographical area	328 million hectares
Reported land utilization	306 million hectares
Land available for agriculture, forestry and related purposes	264 million hectares

SCALE 1: 24 000 000

0   250   500   750   1000 km

LAMBERT CONICAL ORTHOMORPHIC PROJECTION

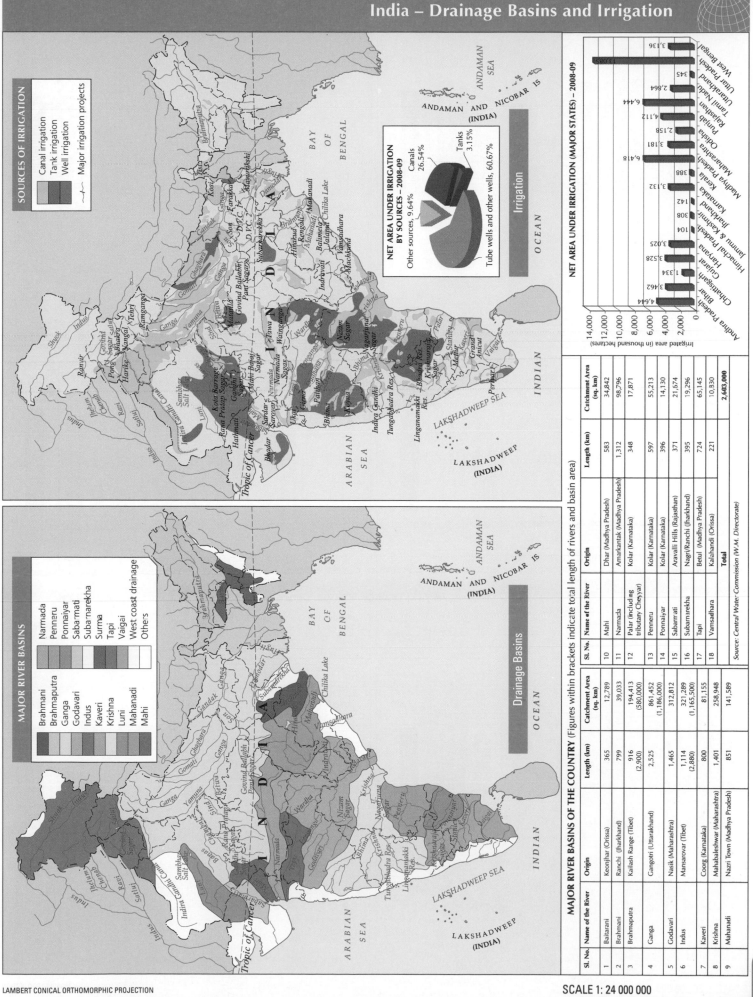

SOURCES OF IRRIGATION
- Canal irrigation
- Tank irrigation
- Well irrigation
- Major irrigation projects

MAJOR RIVER BASINS
- Brahmani
- Brahmaputra
- Ganga
- Godavari
- Indus
- Kaveri
- Krishna
- Luni
- Mahanadi
- Mahi
- Narmada
- Penneru
- Ponnaiyar
- Sabarmati
- Subarnarekha
- Surma
- Tapi
- Vaigai
- West coast drainage
- Others

NET AREA UNDER IRRIGATION BY SOURCES – 2008-09
- Canals 26.54%
- Tanks 3.15%
- Tube wells and other wells, 60.67%
- Other sources, 9.64%

NET AREA UNDER IRRIGATION (MAJOR STATES) – 2008-09

(Irrigated area in thousand hectares)

Andhra Pradesh	4,644
Bihar	3,462
Chhattisgarh	1,334
Gujarat	3,528
Haryana	3,025
Himachal Pradesh	104
Jammu & Kashmir	308
Jharkhand	142
Karnataka	3,132
Kerala	388
Madhya Pradesh	6,418
Maharashtra	3,181
Odisha	2,158
Punjab	4,112
Rajasthan	6,444
Tamil Nadu	2,664
Uttarakhand	345
Uttar Pradesh	13,085
West Bengal	3,136

MAJOR RIVER BASINS OF THE COUNTRY (Figures within brackets indicate total length of rivers and basin area)

Sl. No.	Name of the River	Origin	Length (km)	Catchment Area (sq. km)
1	Baitarani	Keonjhar (Orissa)	365	12,789
2	Brahmani	Ranchi (Jharkhand)	799	39,033
3	Brahmaputra	Kailash Range (Tibet)	916 (2,900)	194,413 (580,000)
4	Ganga	Gangotri (Uttarakhand)	2,525	861,452 (1,186,000)
5	Godavari	Nasik (Maharashtra)	1,465	312,812
6	Indus	Mansarovar (Tibet)	1,114 (2,880)	321,289 (1,165,500)
7	Kaveri	Coorg (Karnataka)	800	81,155
8	Krishna	Mahabaleshwar (Maharashtra)	1,401	258,948
9	Mahanadi	Nazri Town (Madhya Pradesh)	851	141,589
10	Mahi	Dhar (Madhya Pradesh)	583	34,842
11	Narmada	Amarkantak (Madhya Pradesh)	1,312	98,796
12	Palar (including tributary Cheyyar)	Kolar (Karnataka)	348	17,871
13	Penneru	Kolar (Karnataka)	597	55,213
14	Ponnaiyar	Kolar (Karnataka)	396	14,130
15	Sabarmati	Aravalli Hills (Rajasthan)	371	21,674
16	Subarnarekha	Nagri/Ranchi (Jharkhand)	395	19,296
17	Tapi	Betul (Madhya Pradesh)	724	65,145
18	Vamsadhara	Kalahandi (Orissa)	221	10,830
	Total			2,683,000

Source: Central Water Commission (W.M. Directorate)

LAMBERT CONICAL ORTHOMORPHIC PROJECTION

SCALE 1: 24 000 000

0   250   500   750   1000 km

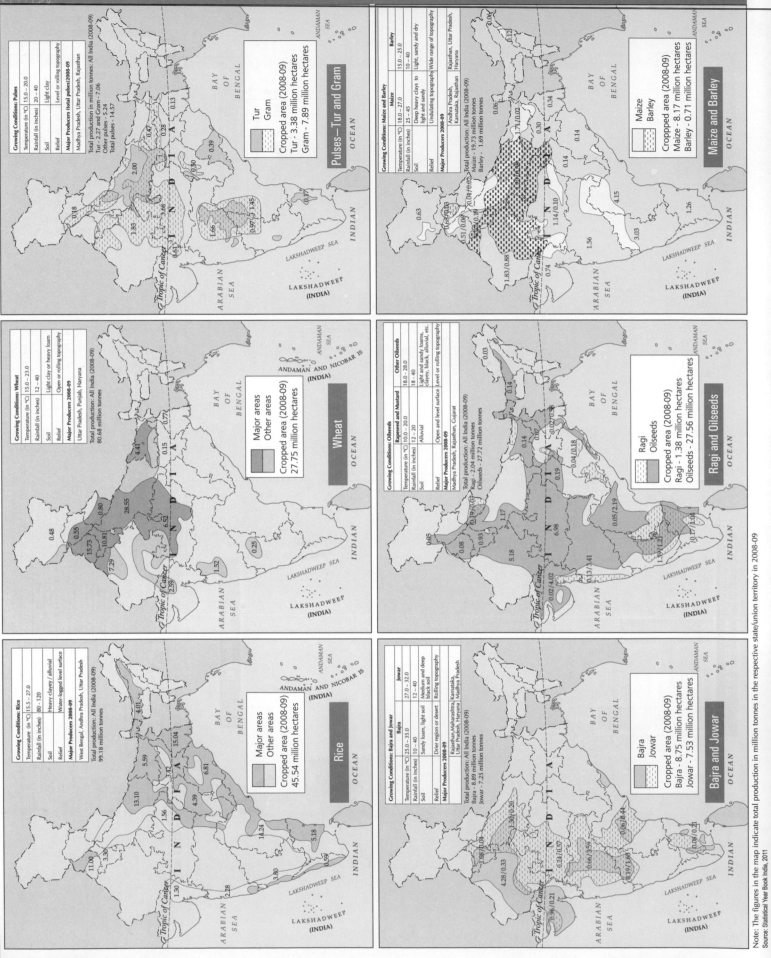

Pulses—Tur and Gram

Growing Conditions: Pulses	
Temperature (in °C)	15.0 – 20.0
Rainfall (in inches)	20 – 40
Soil	Light clay
Relief	Level or rolling topography

Major Producers (total pulses)2008-09
Madhya Pradesh, Uttar Pradesh, Rajasthan

Total production in million tonnes: All India (2008-09)
Tur – 2.27 and Gram – 7.06
Other pulses – 5.24
Total pulses – 14.57

Tur
Gram

Cropped area (2008-09)
Tur – 3.38 million hectares
Gram – 7.89 million hectares

Maize and Barley

Growing Conditions: Maize and Barley	Maize	Barley
Temperature (in °C)	18.0 – 27.0	15.0 – 25.0
Rainfall (in inches)	25 – 45	10 – 40
Soil	Deep heavy clays, to light and sandy	Light, sandy and dry
Relief	Undulating topography	Wide range of topography

Major Producers 2008-09
Andhra Pradesh, Karnataka, Rajasthan
Rajasthan, Uttar Pradesh, Haryana

Total production: All India (2008-09)
Maize – 19.73 million tonnes
Barley – 1.69 million tonnes

Maize
Barley

Croppped area (2008-09)
Maize – 8.17 million hectares
Barley – 0.71 million hectares

Wheat

Growing Conditions: Wheat	
Temperature (in °C)	15.0 – 23.0
Rainfall (in inches)	12 – 40
Soil	Light clay or heavy loam
Relief	Open or rolling topography

Major Producers 2008-09
Uttar Pradesh, Punjab, Haryana

Total production: All India (2008-09)
80.68 million tonnes

Major areas
Other areas

Cropped area (2008-09)
27.75 million hectares

Ragi and Oilseeds

Growing Conditions: Oilseeds	Rapeseed and Mustard	Other Oilseeds
Temperature (in °C)	10.0 – 20.0	18.0 – 28.0
Rainfall (in inches)	12 – 20	12 – 40
Soil	Alluvial	Light and sandy loams, clayey, black, alluvial, etc.
Relief	Open and level surface	Level or rolling topography

Major Producers 2008-09
Madhya Pradesh, Rajasthan, Gujarat

Ragi – 2.04 million tonnes
Oilseeds – 27.72 million tonnes

Ragi
Oilseeds

Cropped area (2008-09)
Ragi – 1.38 million hectares
Oilseeds – 27.56 million hectares

Rice

Growing Conditions: Rice	
Temperature (in °C)	15.5 – 27.0
Rainfall (in inches)	80 – 120
Soil	Heavy clayey / alluvial
Relief	Water-logged level surface

Major Producers 2008-09
West Bengal, Andhra Pradesh, Uttar Pradesh

Total production: All India (2008-09)
99.18 million tonnes

Major areas
Other areas

Cropped area (2008-09)
45.54 million hectares

Bajra and Jowar

Growing Conditions: Bajra and Jowar	Bajra	Jowar
Temperature (in °C)	25.0 – 35.0	27.0 – 32.0
Rainfall (in inches)	10 – 40	12 – 40
Soil	Sandy loam, light soil	Medium and deep black soil
Relief	Drier region or desert	Rolling topography

Major Producers 2008-09
Rajasthan, Maharashtra, Karnataka, Uttar Pradesh, Haryana, Madhya Pradesh

Total production: All India (2008-09)
Bajra – 8.89 million tonnes
Jowar – 7.25 million tonnes

Bajra
Jowar

Cropped area (2008-09)
Bajra – 8.75 million hectares
Jowar – 7.53 million hectares

SCALE 1 : 36 000 000

0   350   700   1050   1400 km

Note: The figures in the map indicate total production in million tonnes in the respective state/union territory in 2008-09
Source: Statistical Year Book India, 2011

LAMBERT CONICAL ORTHOMORPHIC PROJECTION

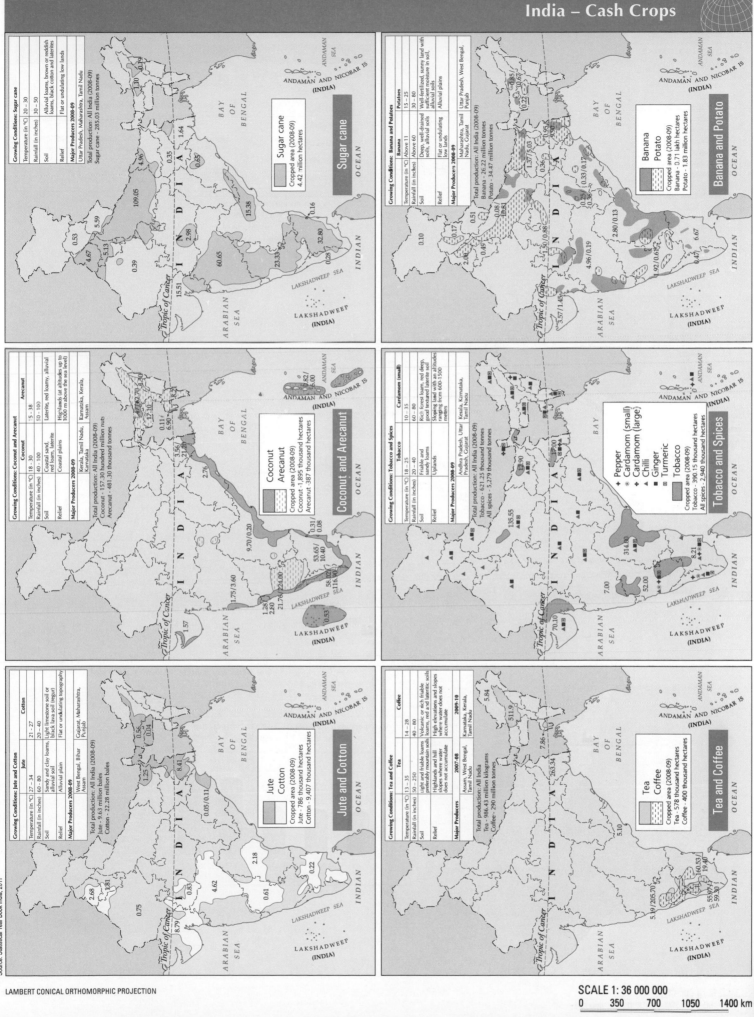

Note: The figures in the map indicate total production in million tonnes in the respective state/union territory in 2008-09
Source: Statistical Year Book India, 2011

Sugar cane

Growing Conditions: Sugar cane		
Temperature (in °C)	20 – 30	30 – 50
Rainfall (in inches)	30 – 50	
Soil	Alluvial loams, brown or reddish loams, black cotton and laterites	
Relief	Flat or undulating low lands	
Major Producers 2008-09	Uttar Pradesh, Maharashtra, Tamil Nadu	

Total production - All India (2008-09)
Sugar cane - 285.03 million tonnes

Sugar cane
Cropped area (2008-09)
4.42 million hectares

Banana and Potato

Growing Conditions: Banana and Potatoes		
	Banana	Potatoes
Temperature (in °C)	Above 11	15 – 25
Rainfall (in inches)	Above 60	30 – 80
Soil	Deep, well-drained soils, alluvial soils	Well-fertilized, sunny land with sufficient moisture in soil, alluvial plains
Relief	Flat or undulating low lands	Alluvial plains
Major Producers 2008-09	Maharashtra, Tamil Nadu, Gujarat	Uttar Pradesh, West Bengal, Punjab

Total production - All India (2008-09)
Banana - 26.22 million tonnes
Potato - 34.47 million tonnes

Banana
Potato
Cropped area (2008-09)
Banana - 0.71 lakh hectares
Potato - 1.83 million hectares

Coconut and Arecanut

Growing Conditions: Coconut and Arecanut		
	Coconut	Arecanut
Temperature (in °C)	18 – 30	15 – 38
Rainfall (in inches)	40 – 100	50 – 100
Soil	Coastal sand, red loam, laterite	Laterite, red loamy, alluvial
Relief	Coastal plains	Highlands (at altitudes up to 1000 m above the sea level)
Major Producers 2008-09	Kerala, Tamil Nadu, Karnataka	Karnataka, Kerala, Assam

Total production - All India (2008-09)
Coconut - 157.30 hundred million nuts
Arecanut - 481.30 thousand tonnes

Coconut
Arecanut
Cropped area (2008-09)
Coconut -1,895 thousand hectares
Arecanut - 387 thousand hectares

Tobacco and Spices

Growing Conditions: Tobacco and Spices		
	Tobacco	Cardamom (small)
Temperature (in °C)	18 – 25	10 – 35
Rainfall (in inches)	20 – 40	60 – 80
Soil	Friable and sandy loams	Rich forest loam, red deep, good textured laterite soil
Relief	Uplands	Sloping land with an altitudes ranging from 600-1500 meters
Major Producers 2008-09	Andhra Pradesh, Uttar Pradesh, Gujarat	Kerala, Karnataka, Tamil Nadu

Total production - All India (2008-09)
Tobacco - 621.25 thousand tonnes
All spices - 5,279 thousand tonnes

Pepper
Cardamom (small)
Cardamom (large)
Chilli
Ginger
Turmeric
Tobacco
Cropped area (2008-09)
Tobacco - 390.15 thousand hectares
All spices - 2,940 thousand hectares

Jute and Cotton

Growing Conditions: Jute and Cotton		
	Jute	Cotton
Temperature (in °C)	27 – 34	21 – 27
Rainfall (in inches)	60 – 80	20 – 40
Soil	Sandy and clay loams, alluvial soil	Light limestone soil or black lava soil (regur)
Relief	Alluvial plain	Flat or undulating topography
Major Producers 2008-09	West Bengal, Bihar, Assam	Gujarat, Maharashtra, Punjab

Total production - All India (2008-09)
Jute - 9.63 million bales
Cotton - 22.28 million bales

Jute
Cotton
Cropped area (2008-09)
Jute - 786 thousand hectares
Cotton - 9,407 thousand hectares

Tea and Coffee

Growing Conditions: Tea and Coffee		
	Tea	Coffee
Temperature (in °C)	13 – 35	14 – 28
Rainfall (in inches)	50 – 250	40 – 80
Soil	Light and friable loams preferably mountain soils	Volcanic or rich friable loams, red and lateritic soils
Relief	Highlands and hill slopes where water does not accumulate	High elevations and slopes where water does not accumulate
Major Producers	Assam, West Bengal, Tamil Nadu	Karnataka, Kerala, Tamil Nadu

Total production - All India
Tea - 986.43 million kilograms
Coffee - 290 million tonnes

Tea
Coffee
Cropped area (2008-09)
Tea - 578 thousand hectares
Coffee - 400 thousand hectares

LAMBERT CONICAL ORTHOMORPHIC PROJECTION

SCALE 1: 36 000 000
0   350   700   1050   1400 km

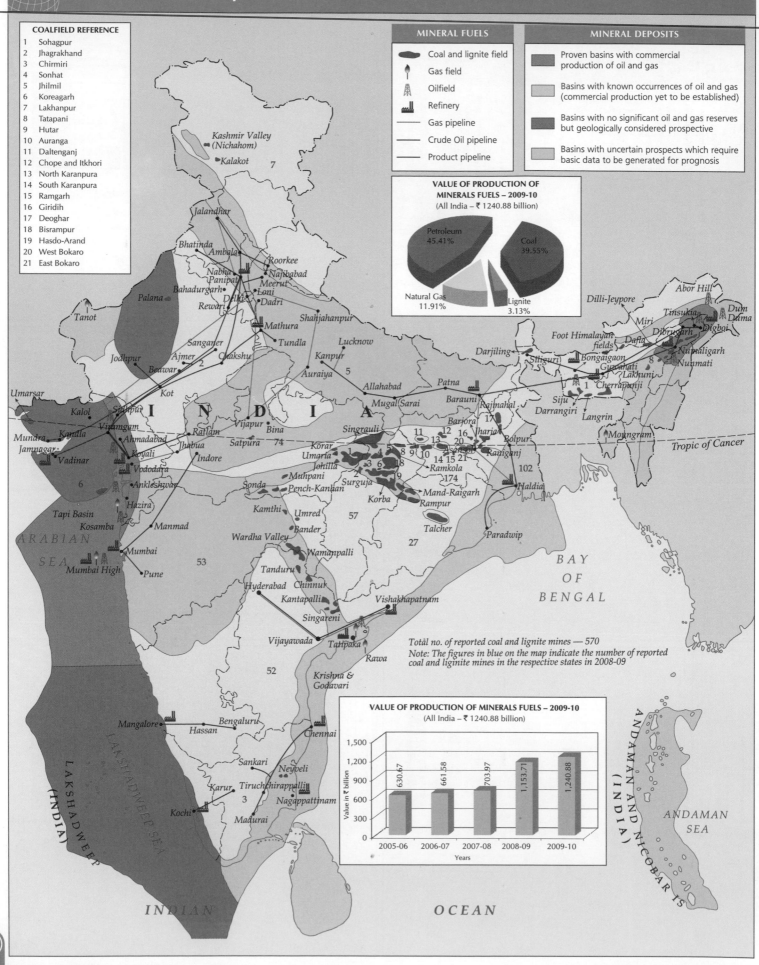

COALFIELD REFERENCE
1 Sohagpur
2 Jhagrakhand
3 Chirmiri
4 Sonhat
5 Jhilmil
6 Koreagarh
7 Lakhanpur
8 Tatapani
9 Hutar
10 Auranga
11 Daltenganj
12 Chope and Itkhori
13 North Karanpura
14 South Karanpura
15 Ramgarh
16 Giridih
17 Deoghar
18 Bisrampur
19 Hasdo-Arand
20 West Bokaro
21 East Bokaro

MINERAL FUELS
Coal and lignite field
Gas field
Oilfield
Refinery
Gas pipeline
Crude Oil pipeline
Product pipeline

MINERAL DEPOSITS
Proven basins with commercial production of oil and gas
Basins with known occurrences of oil and gas (commercial production yet to be established)
Basins with no significant oil and gas reserves but geologically considered prospective
Basins with uncertain prospects which require basic data to be generated for prognosis

VALUE OF PRODUCTION OF MINERALS FUELS – 2009-10
(All India – ₹ 1240.88 billion)

Petroleum 45.41%
Coal 39.55%
Natural Gas 11.91%
Lignite 3.13%

Total no. of reported coal and lignite mines — 570
Note: The figures in blue on the map indicate the number of reported coal and lignite mines in the respective states in 2008-09

VALUE OF PRODUCTION OF MINERALS FUELS – 2009-10
(All India – ₹ 1240.88 billion)

Years	Value in ₹ billion
2005-06	630.67
2006-07	661.58
2007-08	703.97
2008-09	1,153.71
2009-10	1,240.88

SCALE 1: 15 000 000
0   150   300   450   600 km

LAMBERT CONICAL ORTHOMORPHIC PROJECTION

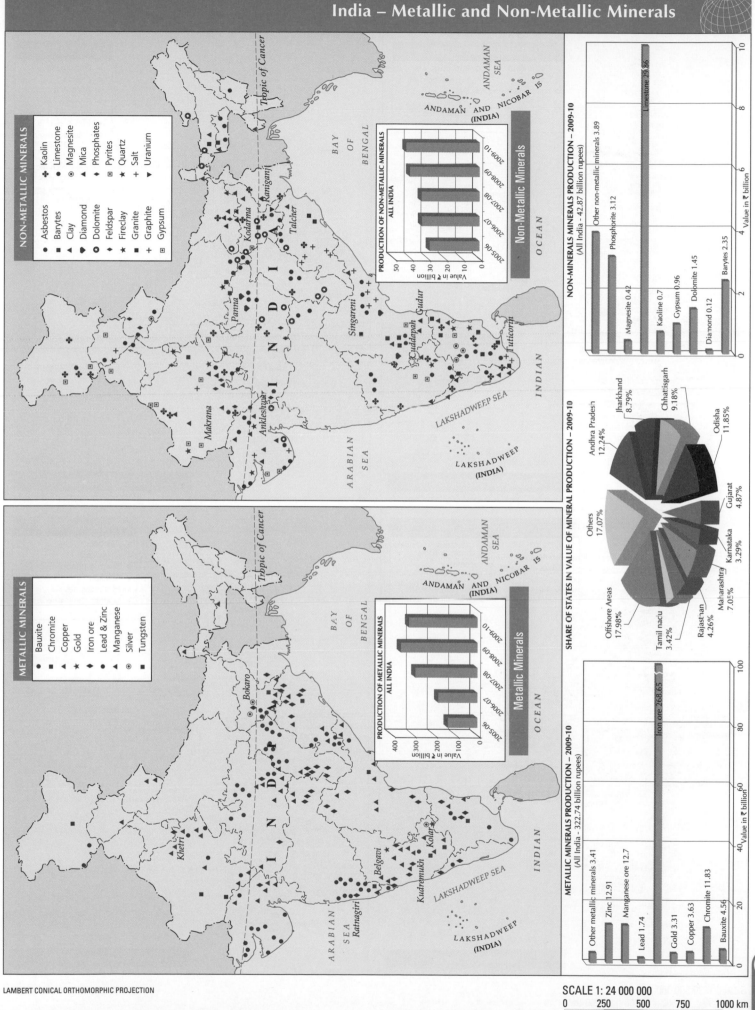

NON-METALLIC MINERALS

Asbestos	Kaolin		
Barytes	Limestone		
Clay	Magnesite		
Diamond	Mica		
Dolomite	Phosphates		
Feldspar	Pyrites		
Fireclay	Quartz		
Granite	Salt		
Graphite	Uranium		
Gypsum			

PRODUCTION OF NON-METALLIC MINERALS
ALL INDIA

Non-Metallic Minerals

NON-MINERALS MINERALS PRODUCTION – 2009-10
(All India - 42.87 billion rupees)

- Other non-metallic minerals 3.89
- Phosphorite 3.12
- Magnesite 0.42
- Limestone 29.86
- Kaoline 0.7
- Gypsum 0.96
- Dolomite 1.45
- Diamond 0.12
- Barytes 2.35

SHARE OF STATES IN VALUE OF MINERAL PRODUCTION – 2009-10

- Andhra Pradesh 12.24%
- Jharkhand 8.79%
- Chhatisgarh 9.18%
- Odisha 11.85%
- Gujarat 4.87%
- Karnataka 3.29%
- Maharashtra 7.0%
- Rajasthan 4.26%
- Tamil nadu 3.42%
- Offshore Areas 17.98%
- Others 17.07%

METALLIC MINERALS

Bauxite	
Chromite	
Copper	
Gold	
Iron ore	
Lead & Zinc	
Manganese	
Silver	
Tungsten	

PRODUCTION OF METALLIC MINERALS
ALL INDIA

Metallic Minerals

METALLIC MINERALS PRODUCTION – 2009-10
(All India - 322.74 billion rupees)

- Other metallic minerals 3.41
- Zinc 12.91
- Manganese ore 12.7
- Lead 1.74
- Iron ore 268.65
- Gold 3.31
- Copper 3.63
- Chromite 11.83
- Bauxite 4.56

LAMBERT CONICAL ORTHOMORPHIC PROJECTION

SCALE 1: 24 000 000

0   250   500   750   1000 km

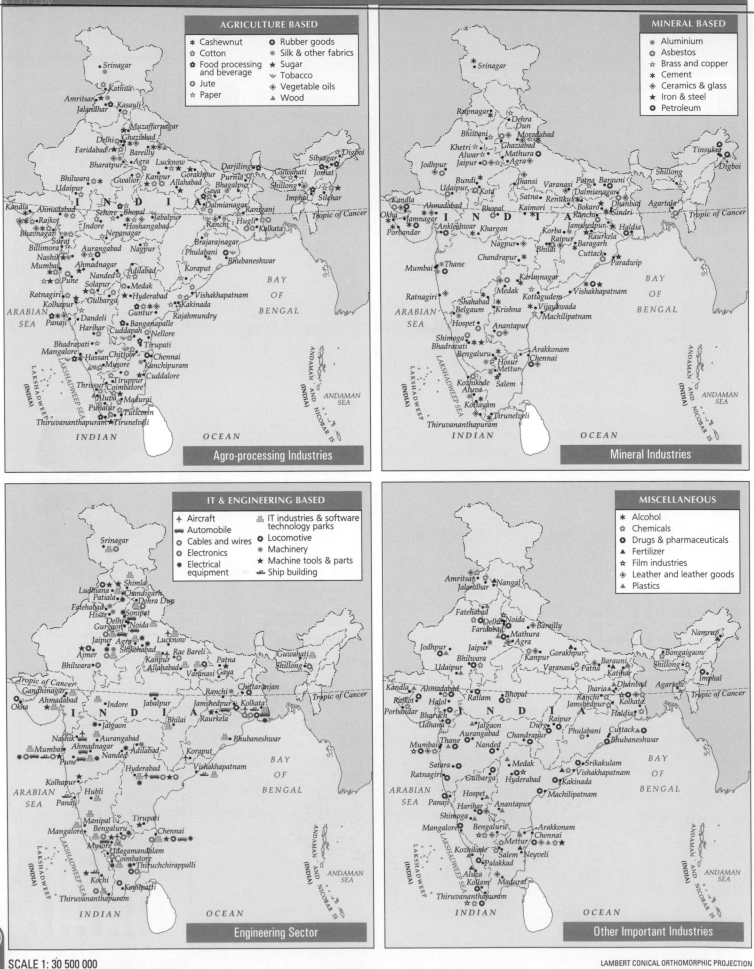

Agro-processing Industries

AGRICULTURE BASED

- ✳ Cashewnut
- ⬠ Cotton
- ⬟ Food processing and beverage
- ◉ Jute
- ✶ Paper
- ◈ Rubber goods
- ✦ Silk & other fabrics
- ★ Sugar
- ⌄ Tobacco
- ▽ Vegetable oils
- ▲ Wood

Mineral Industries

MINERAL BASED

- ● Aluminium
- ◉ Asbestos
- ☆ Brass and copper
- ◆ Cement
- ◇ Ceramics & glass
- ★ Iron & steel
- ◉ Petroleum

Engineering Sector

IT & ENGINEERING BASED

- ✈ Aircraft
- ▭ Automobile
- ◎ Cables and wires
- ◉ Electronics
- ■ Electrical equipment
- ⊞ IT industries & software technology parks
- ◆ Locomotive
- ▣ Machinery
- ★ Machine tools & parts
- ⚓ Ship building

Other Important Industries

MISCELLANEOUS

- ✳ Alcohol
- ⬠ Chemicals
- ◉ Drugs & pharmaceuticals
- ▲ Fertilizer
- ☆ Film industries
- ◈ Leather and leather goods
- ▲ Plastics

SCALE 1 : 30 500 000

0   300   600   900   1200 km

LAMBERT CONICAL ORTHOMORPHIC PROJECTION

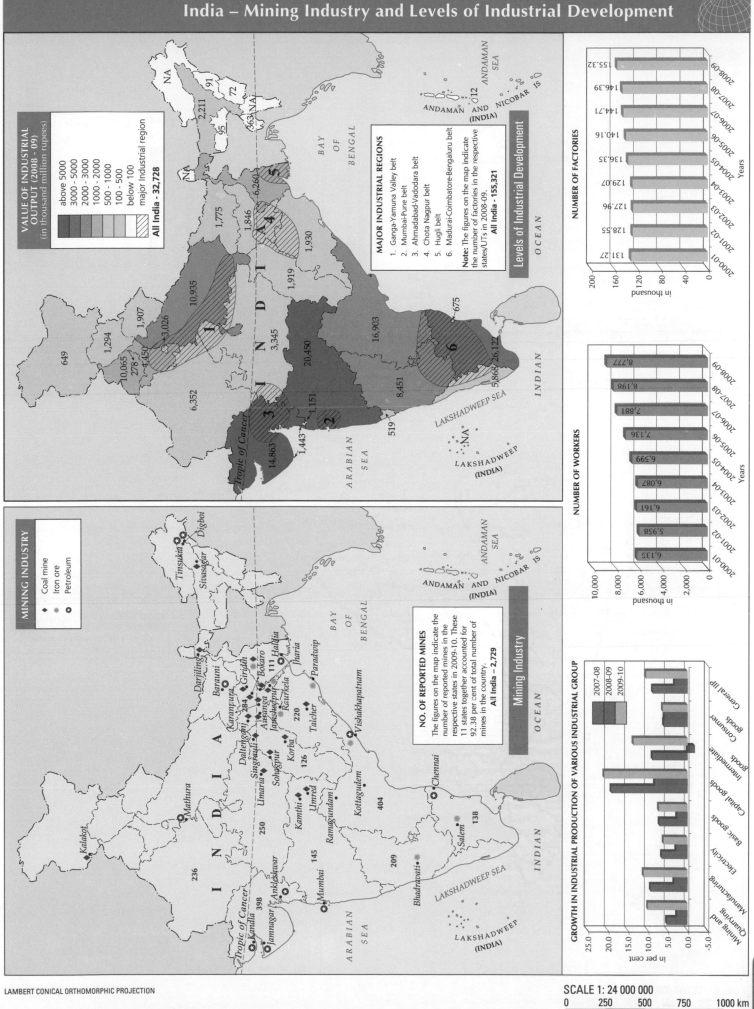

VALUE OF INDUSTRIAL OUTPUT (2008 - 09)
(in thousand million rupees)

- above 5000
- 3000 - 5000
- 2000 - 3000
- 1000 - 2000
- 500 - 1000
- 100 - 500
- below 100
- major Industrial region

All India - 32,728

MAJOR INDUSTRIAL REGIONS

1. Ganga-Yamuna Valley belt
2. Mumbai-Pune belt
3. Ahmadabad-Vadodara belt
4. Chota Nagpur belt
5. Hugli belt
6. Madurai-Coimbatore-Bengaluru belt

Note: The figures on the map indicate the number of factories in the respective states/UTs in 2008-09.

All India - 155,321

Levels of Industrial Development

NUMBER OF FACTORIES

in thousand

131.27 — 2000-01
128.55 — 2001-02
127.96 — 2002-03
129.07 — 2003-04
136.35 — 2004-05
140.16 — 2005-06
144.71 — 2006-07
146.39 — 2007-08
155.32 — 2008-09

NUMBER OF WORKERS

in thousand

6,135 — 2000-01
5,958 — 2001-02
6,161 — 2002-03
6,087 — 2003-04
6,599 — 2004-05
7,136 — 2005-06
7,881 — 2006-07
8,198 — 2007-08
8,777 — 2008-09

MINING INDUSTRY

- ◆ Coal mine
- ✳ Iron ore
- ✸ Petroleum

NO. OF REPORTED MINES

The figures on the map indicate the number of reported mines in the respective states in 2009-10. These 11 states together accounted for 92.38 per cent of total number of mines in the country.

All India - 2,729

Mining Industry

GROWTH IN INDUSTRIAL PRODUCTION OF VARIOUS INDUSTRIAL GROUP

in per cent

- 2007-08
- 2008-09
- 2009-10

Industrial groups: Mining and Quarrying, Manufacturing, Electricity, Basic Goods, Capital Goods, Intermediate Goods, Consumer Goods, General (IIP)

LAMBERT CONICAL ORTHOMORPHIC PROJECTION

SCALE 1: 24 000 000

0   250   500   750   1000 km

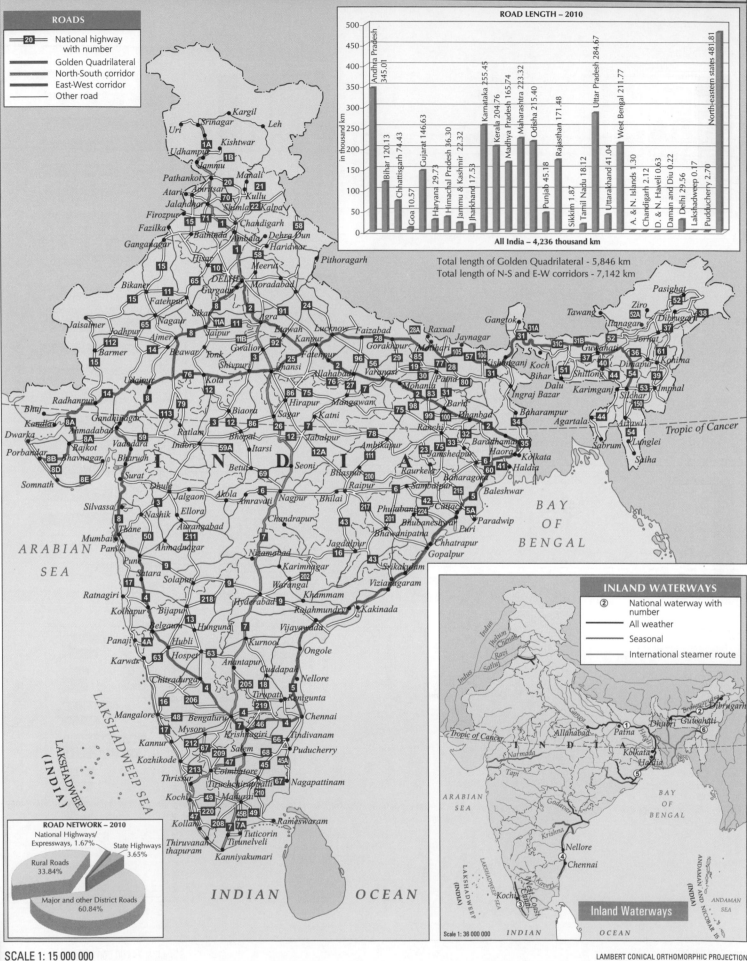

SCALE 1 : 15 000 000

0   150   300   450   600 km

LAMBERT CONICAL ORTHOMORPHIC PROJECTION

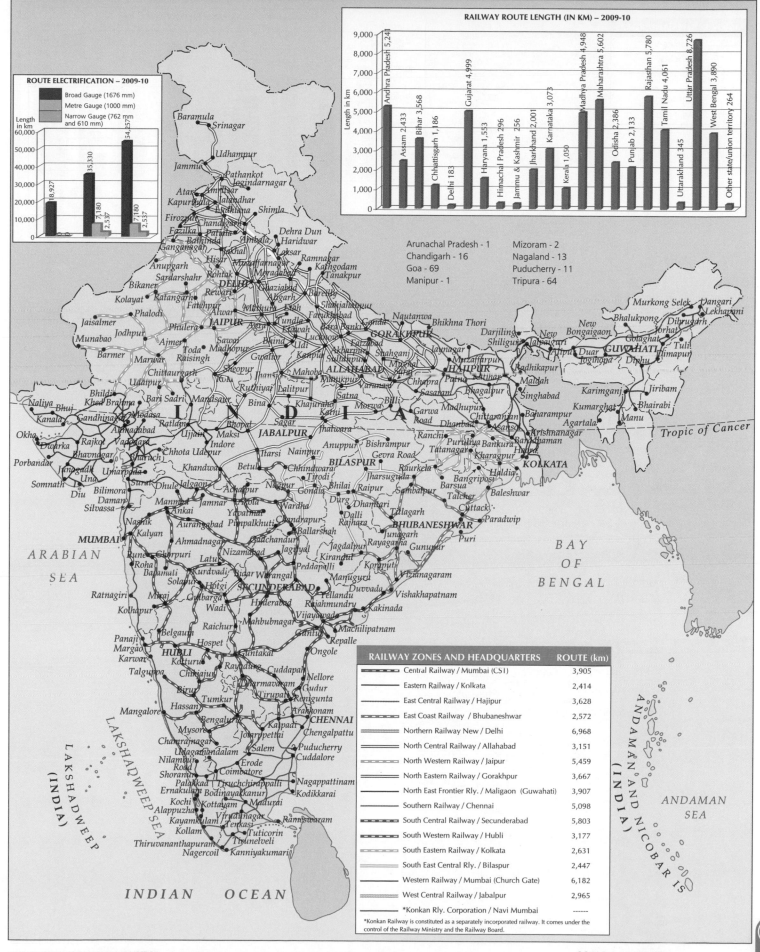

LAMBERT CONICAL ORTHOMORPHIC PROJECTION

SCALE 1: 15 000 000

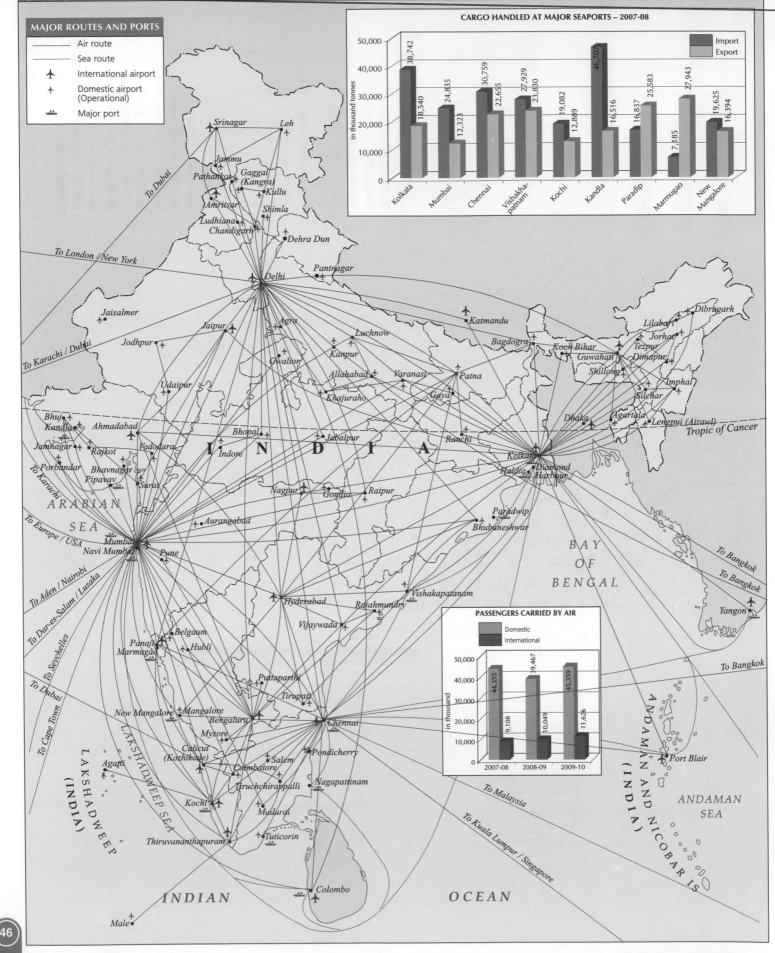

MAJOR ROUTES AND PORTS

— Air route
— Sea route
✈ International airport
✈ Domestic airport (Operational)
🚢 Major port

CARGO HANDLED AT MAJOR SEAPORTS – 2007-08

in thousand tonnes

- Import
- Export

	Import	Export
Kolkata	38,742	18,540
Mumbai	24,835	12,323
Chennai	30,759	22,655
Vishakhapatnam	27,929	23,830
Kochi	19,082	12,889
Kandla	46,707	16,516
Paradip	16,837	25,583
Marmugao	7,185	27,943
New Mangalore	19,625	16,394

PASSENGERS CARRIED BY AIR

in thousand

- Domestic
- International

	Domestic	International
2007-08	44,355	9,108
2008-09	39,467	10,049
2009-10	45,359	11,626

To Dubai
To London / New York
To Karachi / Dubai
To Europe / USA
To Karachi
To Aden / Nairobi
To Dar-es-Salam / Lusaka
To Seychelles
To Dubai
To Cape Town
To Malaysia
To Kuala Lumpur / Singapore
To Bangkok
To Bangkok
To Bangkok

Srinagar, Leh, Jammu, Pathankot, Gaggal (Kangra), Kullu, Amritsar, Shimla, Ludhiana, Chandigarh, Dehra Dun, Pantnagar, Delhi, Jaisalmer, Jaipur, Agra, Luchnow, Katmandu, Jodhpur, Kanpur, Bagdogra, Koch Bihar, Lilabari, Dibrugarh, Jorhat, Tezpur, Dimapur, Guwahati, Shillong, Gwalion, Allahabad, Varanasi, Patna, Gaya, Imphal, Silchar, Udaipur, Khajuraho, Dhaka, Agartala, Lengpui (Aizawl), Bhuj, Kandla, Ahmadabad, Bhopal, Jabalpur, Ranchi, Kolkata, Jamnagar, Rajkot, Vadodara, Indore, INDIA, Porbandar, Bhavnagar, Pipavav, Surat, Nagpur, Gondia, Raipur, Haldia, Diamond Harbour, Aurangabad, Paradwip, Bhubaneshwar, Mumbai, Navi Mumbai, Pune, Hyderabad, Rajahmundry, Vishakapatanam, Vijaywada, Belgaum, Hubli, Panaji, Marmugao, Puttaparthi, Tirupati, New Mangalore, Mangalore, Bengaluru, Mysore, Chennai, Calicut (Kozhikode), Salem, Pondicherry, Coimbatore, Nagapattinam, Tiruchchirappalli, Kochi, Madurai, Tuticorin, Thiruvananthapuram, Agatti, Port Blair, Yangon, Colombo, Male

ARABIAN SEA
BAY OF BENGAL
LAKSHADWEEP SEA
LAKSHADWEEP (INDIA)
ANDAMAN AND NICOBAR IS (INDIA)
ANDAMAN SEA
INDIAN OCEAN
Tropic of Cancer

SCALE 1: 15 000 000

0   150   300   450   600 km

LAMBERT CONICAL ORTHOMORPHIC PROJECTION

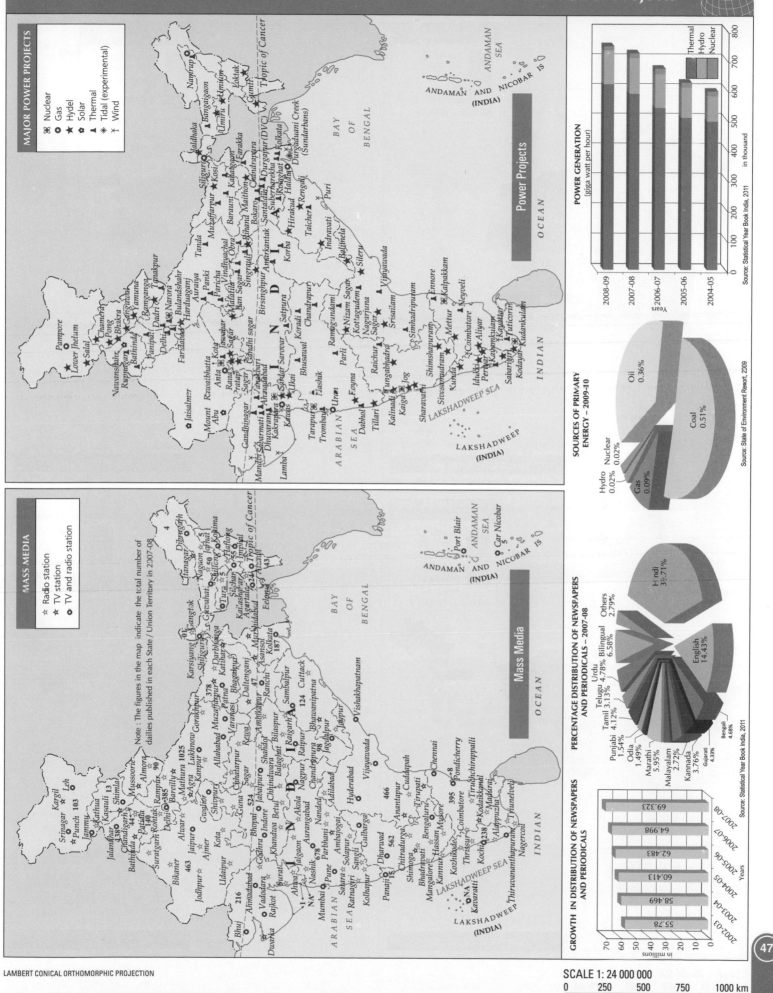

LAMBERT CONICAL ORTHOMORPHIC PROJECTION

SCALE 1: 24 000 000

0   250   500   750   1000 km

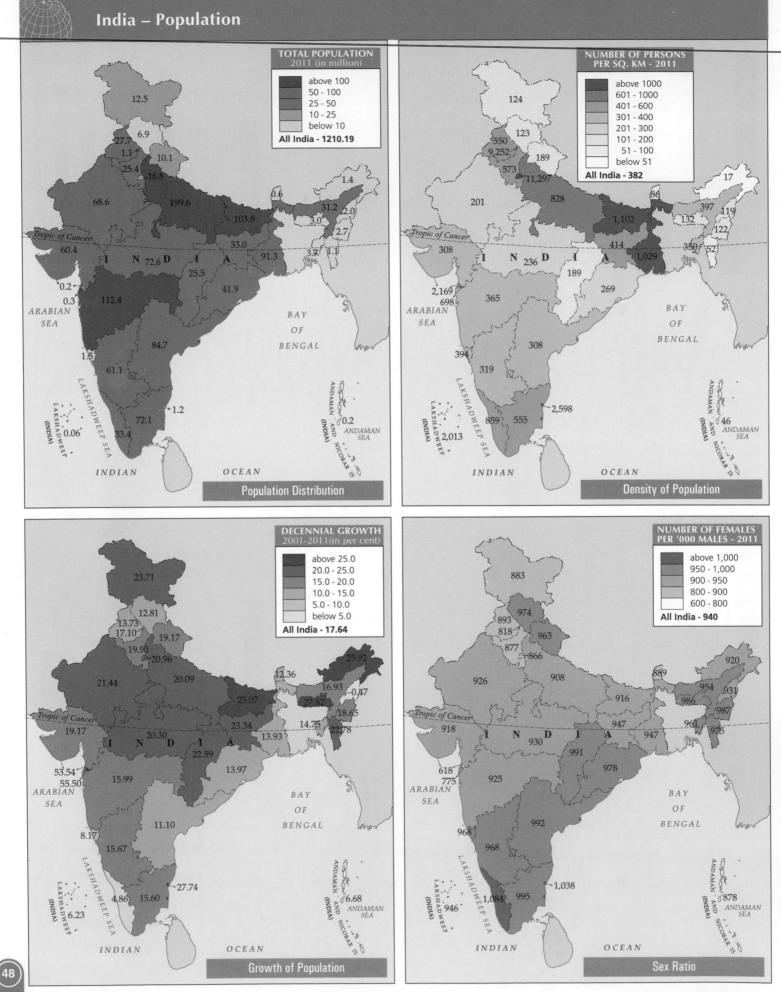

TOTAL POPULATION
2011 (in million)

above 100
50 - 100
25 - 50
10 - 25
below 10

All India - 1210.19

Population Distribution

NUMBER OF PERSONS PER SQ. KM - 2011

above 1000
601 - 1000
401 - 600
301 - 400
201 - 300
101 - 200
51 - 100
below 51

All India - 382

Density of Population

DECENNIAL GROWTH
2001-2011(in per cent)

above 25.0
20.0 - 25.0
15.0 - 20.0
10.0 - 15.0
5.0 - 10.0
below 5.0

All India - 17.64

Growth of Population

NUMBER OF FEMALES PER '000 MALES - 2011

above 1,000
950 - 1,000
900 - 950
800 - 900
600 - 800

All India - 940

Sex Ratio

SCALE 1: 30 500 000

0   300   600   900   1200 km

LAMBERT CONICAL ORTHOMORPHIC PROJECTION

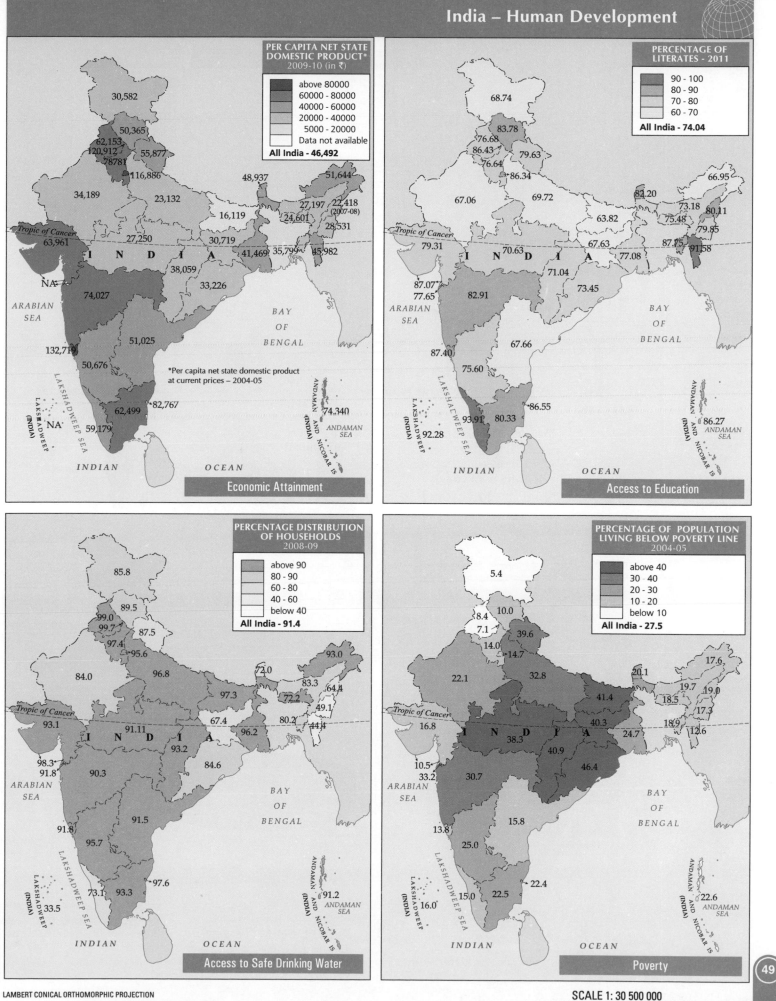

PER CAPITA NET STATE DOMESTIC PRODUCT*
2009-10 (in ₹)

- above 80000
- 60000 - 80000
- 40000 - 60000
- 20000 - 40000
- 5000 - 20000
- Data not available

All India - 46,492

30,582
50,365
62,153
120,912
78781
55,877
116,886
48,937
51,644
34,189
23,132
27,197
22,418 (2007-08)
16,119
24,601
28,531
Tropic of Cancer
63,961
27,250
30,719
35,799
45,982
I N D I A
41,469
38,059
NA
33,226
74,027
ARABIAN SEA
BAY OF BENGAL
132,719
51,025
50,676
*Per capita net state domestic product at current prices – 2004-05
ANDAMAN SEA
82,767
74,340
LAKSHADWEEP SEA
LAKSHADWEEP (INDIA)
NA
62,499
59,179
ANDAMAN AND NICOBAR IS (INDIA)
INDIAN OCEAN

Economic Attainment

PERCENTAGE OF LITERATES - 2011

- 90 - 100
- 80 - 90
- 70 - 80
- 60 - 70

All India - 74.04

68.74
83.78
76.68
86.43
79.63
76.64
86.34
67.06
69.72
82.20
66.95
73.18
80.11
63.82
75.48
79.85
Tropic of Cancer
79.31
70.63
67.63
87.75
91.58
I N D I A
77.08
71.04
87.07*
77.65
82.91
73.45
ARABIAN SEA
BAY OF BENGAL
87.40
67.66
75.60
86.55
LAKSHADWEEP SEA
LAKSHADWEEP (INDIA)
93.91
80.33
92.28
ANDAMAN AND NICOBAR IS (INDIA)
86.27
ANDAMAN SEA
INDIAN OCEAN

Access to Education

PERCENTAGE DISTRIBUTION OF HOUSEHOLDS
2008-09

- above 90
- 80 - 90
- 60 - 80
- 40 - 60
- below 40

All India - 91.4

85.8
89.5
99.0
99.7
87.5
97.4
95.6
93.0
84.0
96.8
72.0
83.3
64.4
97.3
72.2
49.1
Tropic of Cancer
93.1
91.11
67.4
80.2
44.4
I N D I A
96.2
93.2
98.3
90.3
84.6
91.8
91.5
ARABIAN SEA
BAY OF BENGAL
91.8
95.7
LAKSHADWEEP SEA
73.1
93.3
97.6
LAKSHADWEEP (INDIA)
33.5
ANDAMAN AND NICOBAR IS (INDIA)
91.2
ANDAMAN SEA
INDIAN OCEAN

Access to Safe Drinking Water

PERCENTAGE OF POPULATION LIVING BELOW POVERTY LINE
2004-05

- above 40
- 30 - 40
- 20 - 30
- 10 - 20
- below 10

All India - 27.5

5.4
10.0
8.4
7.1
39.6
14.0
14.7
22.1
32.8
20.1
17.6
19.7
19.0
41.4
18.5
17.3
Tropic of Cancer
16.8
38.3
40.3
24.7
18.9
12.6
I N D I A
40.9
10.5
33.2
30.7
46.4
13.8
15.8
ARABIAN SEA
BAY OF BENGAL
25.0
22.4
LAKSHADWEEP SEA
15.0
22.5
LAKSHADWEEP (INDIA)
16.0
ANDAMAN AND NICOBAR IS (INDIA)
22.6
ANDAMAN SEA
INDIAN OCEAN

Poverty

LAMBERT CONICAL ORTHOMORPHIC PROJECTION

SCALE 1: 30 500 000
0   300   600   900   1200 km

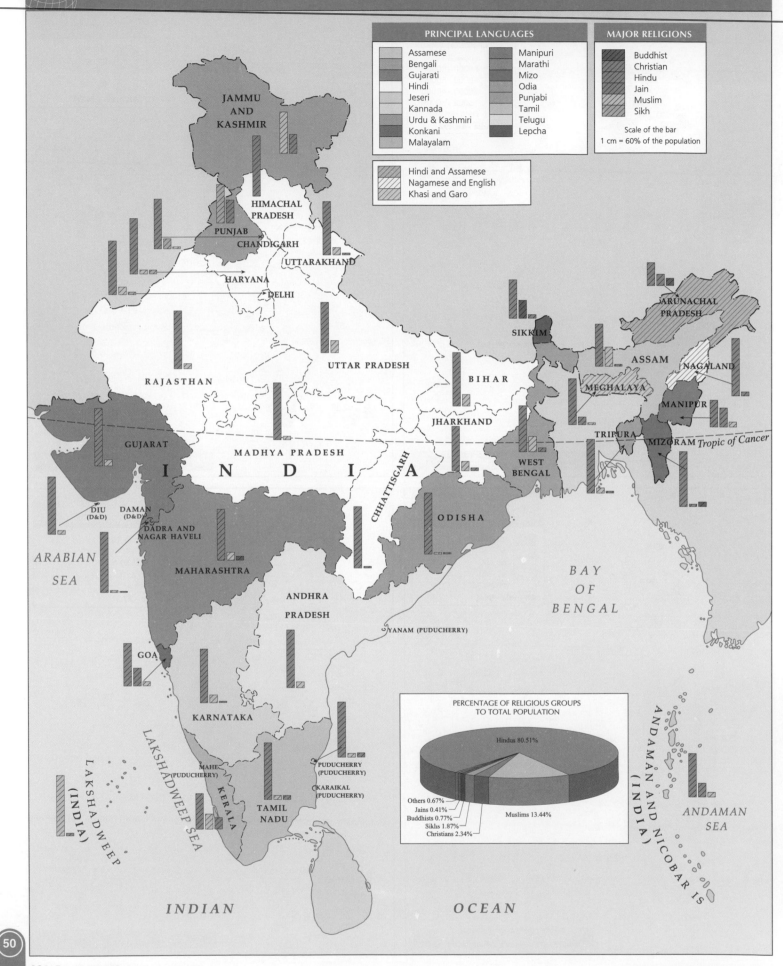

PRINCIPAL LANGUAGES

- Assamese
- Bengali
- Gujarati
- Hindi
- Jeseri
- Kannada
- Urdu & Kashmiri
- Konkani
- Malayalam
- Manipuri
- Marathi
- Mizo
- Odia
- Punjabi
- Tamil
- Telugu
- Lepcha

- Hindi and Assamese
- Nagamese and English
- Khasi and Garo

MAJOR RELIGIONS

- Buddhist
- Christian
- Hindu
- Jain
- Muslim
- Sikh

Scale of the bar
1 cm = 60% of the population

JAMMU AND KASHMIR

HIMACHAL PRADESH

PUNJAB

CHANDIGARH

UTTARAKHAND

HARYANA

DELHI

RAJASTHAN

UTTAR PRADESH

BIHAR

SIKKIM

ARUNACHAL PRADESH

ASSAM

NAGALAND

MEGHALAYA

MANIPUR

JHARKHAND

TRIPURA

MIZORAM *Tropic of Cancer*

GUJARAT

I N D I A

MADHYA PRADESH

CHHATTISGARH

WEST BENGAL

DIU (D&D)

DAMAN (D&D)

DADRA AND NAGAR HAVELI

ODISHA

ARABIAN SEA

MAHARASHTRA

ANDHRA PRADESH

YANAM (PUDUCHERRY)

BAY OF BENGAL

GOA

ANDAMAN AND NICOBAR IS (INDIA)

KARNATAKA

MAHE (PUDUCHERRY)

PUDUCHERRY (PUDUCHERRY)

KARAIKAL (PUDUCHERRY)

LAKSHADWEEP SEA

LAKSHADWEEP (INDIA)

KERALA

TAMIL NADU

ANDAMAN SEA

PERCENTAGE OF RELIGIOUS GROUPS TO TOTAL POPULATION

Hindus 80.51%

Others 0.67%
Jains 0.41%
Buddhists 0.77%
Sikhs 1.87%
Christians 2.34%

Muslims 13.44%

INDIAN

OCEAN

SCALE 1: 15 000 000

0   150   300   450   600 km

LAMBERT CONICAL ORTHOMORPHIC PROJECTION

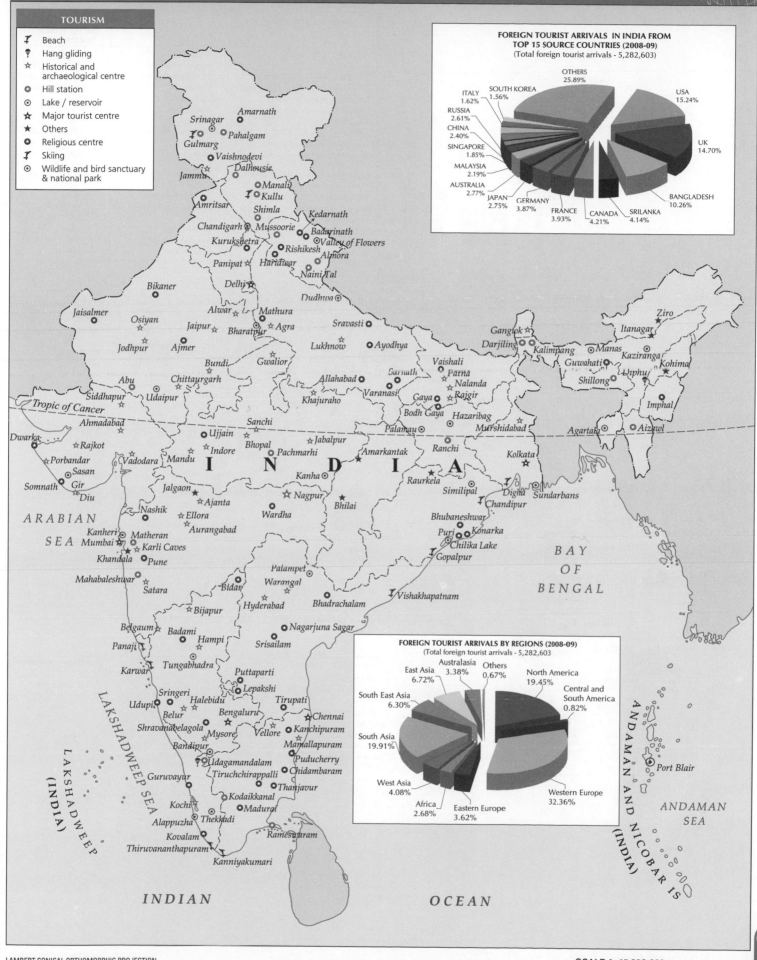

TOURISM

- ⌃ Beach
- ⌄ Hang gliding
- ✶ Historical and archaeological centre
- ⊙ Hill station
- ⊙ Lake / reservoir
- ☆ Major tourist centre
- ★ Others
- ⊕ Religious centre
- ⌃ Skiing
- ⊙ Wildlife and bird sanctuary & national park

FOREIGN TOURIST ARRIVALS IN INDIA FROM TOP 15 SOURCE COUNTRIES (2008-09)
(Total foreign tourist arrivals - 5,282,603)

- OTHERS 25.89%
- USA 15.24%
- UK 14.70%
- BANGLADESH 10.26%
- SRILANKA 4.14%
- CANADA 4.21%
- FRANCE 3.93%
- GERMANY 3.87%
- JAPAN 2.75%
- AUSTRALIA 2.77%
- MALAYSIA 2.19%
- SINGAPORE 1.85%
- CHINA 2.40%
- RUSSIA 2.61%
- ITALY 1.62%
- SOUTH KOREA 1.56%

FOREIGN TOURIST ARRIVALS BY REGIONS (2008-09)
(Total foreign tourist arrivals - 5,282,603)

- North America 19.45%
- Central and South America 0.82%
- Western Europe 32.36%
- Eastern Europe 3.62%
- Africa 2.68%
- West Asia 4.08%
- South Asia 19.91%
- South East Asia 6.30%
- East Asia 6.72%
- Australasia 3.38%
- Others 0.67%

ARABIAN SEA

LAKSHADWEEP SEA

LAKSHADWEEP (INDIA)

I N D I A

BAY OF BENGAL

ANDAMAN AND NICOBAR IS (INDIA)

ANDAMAN SEA

Port Blair

INDIAN OCEAN

Tropic of Cancer

Srinagar, Amarnath, Pahalgam, Gulmarg, Vaishnodevi, Dalhousie, Jammu, Manali, Kullu, Amritsar, Shimla, Kedarnath, Chandigarh, Mussoorie, Badarinath, Kurukshetra, Rishikesh, Valley of Flowers, Almora, Panipat, Haridwar, Naini Tal, Bikaner, Delhi, Dudhwa, Jaisalmer, Alwar, Mathura, Sravasti, Gangtok, Ziro, Itanagar, Darjiling, Kalimpang, Manas, Osiyan, Jaipur, Bharatpur, Agra, Lukhnow, Ayodhya, Kaziranga, Jodhpur, Ajmer, Guwahati, Diphu, Kohima, Bundi, Gwalior, Vaishali, Patna, Shillong, Abu, Chittaurgarh, Allahabad, Sarnath, Nalanda, Siddhapur, Udaipur, Khajuraho, Varanasi, Gaya, Rajgir, Imphal, Bodh Gaya, Ahmadabad, Sanchi, Ujjain, Hazaribag, Murshidabad, Agartala, Aizawl, Palamau, Dwarka, Rajkot, Bhopal, Jabalpur, Amarkantak, Ranchi, Kolkata, Porbandar, Vadodara, Mandu, Indore, Pachmarhi, Sasan, Somnath, Gir, Diu, Jalgaon, Ajanta, Kanha, Raurkela, Similipal, Digha, Sundarbans, Nashik, Ellora, Nagpur, Bhilai, Chandipur, Kanheri, Aurangabad, Wardha, Bhubaneshwar, Mumbai, Matheran, Karli Caves, Puri, Konarka, Khandala, Pune, Chilika Lake, Mahabaleshwar, Palampet, Gopalpur, Satara, Bidar, Warangal, Bijapur, Hyderabad, Bhadrachalam, Vishakhapatnam, Belgaum, Badami, Hampi, Nagarjuna Sagar, Panaji, Srisailam, Karwar, Tungabhadra, Puttaparti, Lepakshi, Sringeri, Halebidu, Tirupati, Udupi, Belur, Bengaluru, Shravanabelagola, Mysore, Vellore, Kanchipuram, Chennai, Bandipur, Mamallapuram, Udagamandalam, Puducherry, Guruvayur, Tiruchirappalli, Chidambaram, Thanjavur, Kochi, Kodaikkanal, Madurai, Alappuzha, Thekkadi, Kovalam, Rameswaram, Thiruvananthapuram, Kanniyakumari

LAMBERT CONICAL ORTHOMORPHIC PROJECTION

SCALE 1: 15 000 000
0 150 300 450 600 km

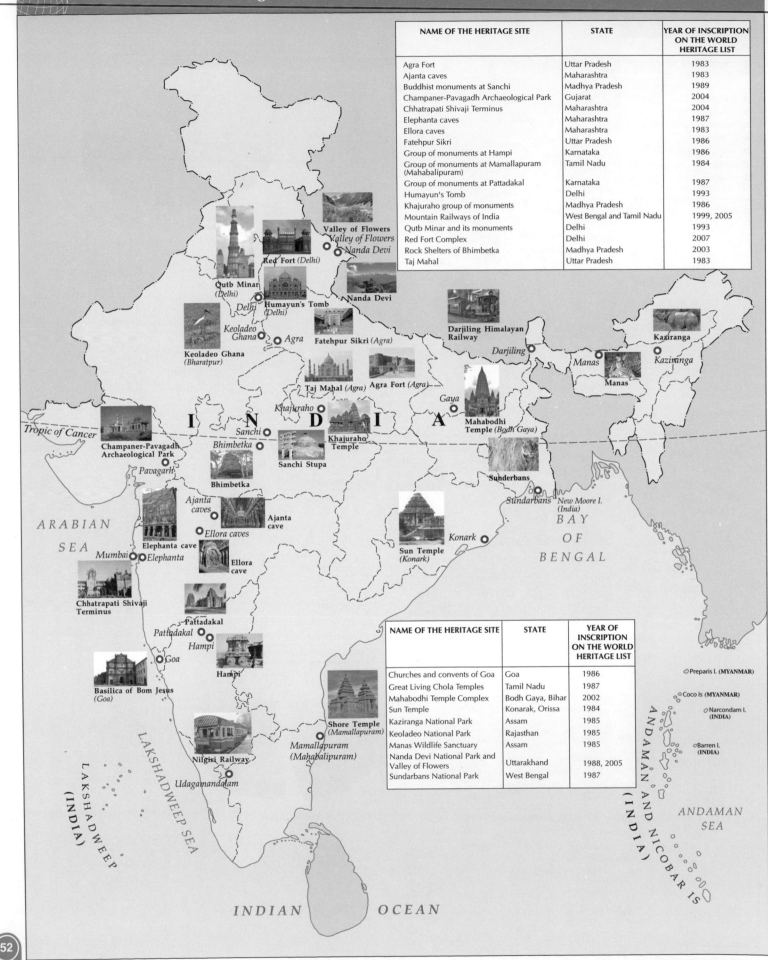

NAME OF THE HERITAGE SITE	STATE	YEAR OF INSCRIPTION ON THE WORLD HERITAGE LIST
Agra Fort	Uttar Pradesh	1983
Ajanta caves	Maharashtra	1983
Buddhist monuments at Sanchi	Madhya Pradesh	1989
Champaner-Pavagadh Archaeological Park	Gujarat	2004
Chhatrapati Shivaji Terminus	Maharashtra	2004
Elephanta caves	Maharashtra	1987
Ellora caves	Maharashtra	1983
Fatehpur Sikri	Uttar Pradesh	1986
Group of monuments at Hampi	Karnataka	1986
Group of monuments at Mamallapuram (Mahabalipuram)	Tamil Nadu	1984
Group of monuments at Pattadakal	Karnataka	1987
Humayun's Tomb	Delhi	1993
Khajuraho group of monuments	Madhya Pradesh	1986
Mountain Railways of India	West Bengal and Tamil Nadu	1999, 2005
Qutb Minar and its monuments	Delhi	1993
Red Fort Complex	Delhi	2007
Rock Shelters of Bhimbetka	Madhya Pradesh	2003
Taj Mahal	Uttar Pradesh	1983

NAME OF THE HERITAGE SITE	STATE	YEAR OF INSCRIPTION ON THE WORLD HERITAGE LIST
Churches and convents of Goa	Goa	1986
Great Living Chola Temples	Tamil Nadu	1987
Mahabodhi Temple Complex	Bodh Gaya, Bihar	2002
Sun Temple	Konarak, Orissa	1984
Kaziranga National Park	Assam	1985
Keoladeo National Park	Rajasthan	1985
Manas Wildlife Sanctuary	Assam	1985
Nanda Devi National Park and Valley of Flowers	Uttarakhand	1988, 2005
Sundarbans National Park	West Bengal	1987

Valley of Flowers

Red Fort (Delhi)

Nanda Devi

Qutb Minar (Delhi)

Humayun's Tomb (Delhi)

Delhi

Nanda Devi

Keoladeo Ghana

Agra

Fatehpur Sikri (Agra)

Darjiling Himalayan Railway

Kaziranga

Keoladeo Ghana (Bharatpur)

Darjiling

Manas

Kaziranga

Manas

Taj Mahal (Agra)   Agra Fort (Agra)

Gaya

Khajuraho

Sanchi

Mahabodhi Temple (Bodh Gaya)

Tropic of Cancer

I N D I A

Champaner-Pavagadh Archaeological Park

Bhimbetka

Khajuraho Temple

Sanchi Stupa

Pavagarh

Bhimbetka

Sunderbans

Sunderbans

New Moore I. (India)

ARABIAN SEA

Ajanta caves

Ajanta cave

Ellora caves

BAY OF BENGAL

Elephanta cave

Mumbai

Elephanta

Ellora cave

Konark

Chhatrapati Shivaji Terminus

Sun Temple (Konark)

Pattadakal

Pattadakal

Hampi

Goa

Hampi

Basilica of Bom Jesus (Goa)

Shore Temple (Mamallapuram)

Nilgiri Railway

Mamallapuram (Mahabalipuram)

LAKSHADWEEP SEA

Udagamandalam

Preparis I. (MYANMAR)

Coco Is (MYANMAR)

Narcondam I. (INDIA)

ANDAMAN AND NICOBAR IS (INDIA)

Barren I. (INDIA)

LAKSHADWEEP (INDIA)

ANDAMAN SEA

INDIAN OCEAN

SCALE 1: 15 000 000

0   150   300   450   600 km

LAMBERT CONICAL ORTHOMORPHIC PROJECTION

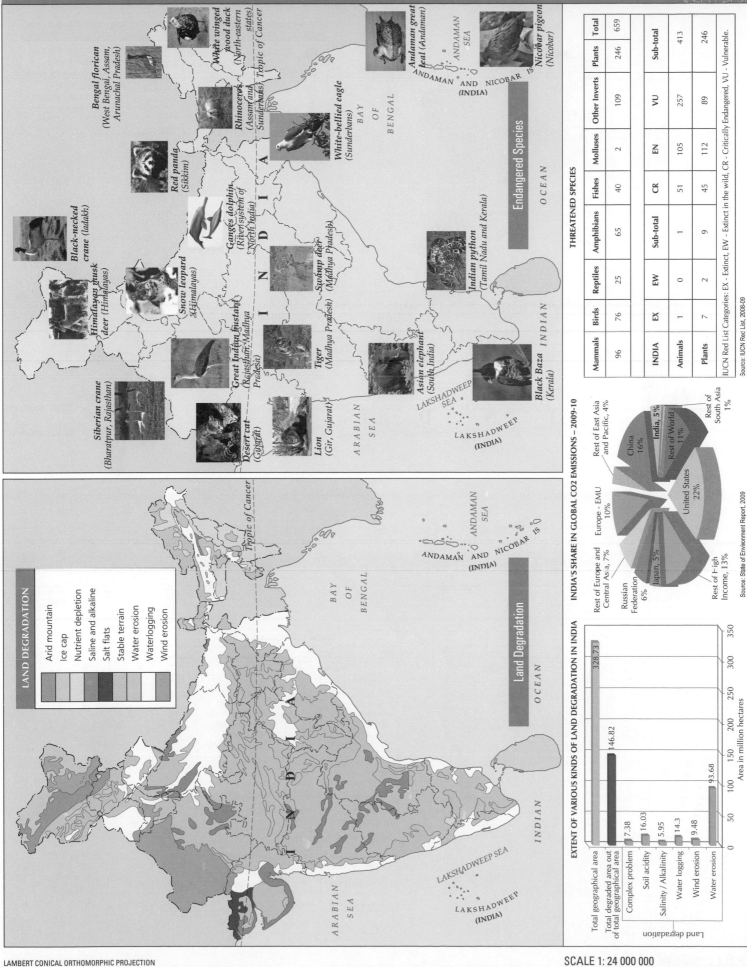

Endangered Species

Bengal florican
(West Bengal, Assam, Arunachal Pradesh)

White winged wood duck
(North-eastern states)

Tropic of Cancer

Rhinoceros
(Assam and Sunderbans)

Andaman great teal (Andaman)

Nicobar pigeon
(Nicobar)

ANDAMAN AND NICOBAR IS
(INDIA)

Red panda
(Sikkim)

White-bellied eagle
(Sunderbans)

Black-necked crane (ladakh)

Ganges dolphin
(River system of North India)

Himalayas musk deer (Himalayas)

Snow leopard
(Himalayas)

Swamp deer
(Madhya Pradesh)

Indian python
(Tamil Nadu and Kerala)

Great Indian bustard
(Rajasthan, Madhya Pradesh)

Tiger
(Madhya Pradesh)

Asian elephant
(South India)

Siberian crane
(Bharatpur, Rajasthan)

Desert cat
(Gujrat)

Lion
(Gir, Gujarat)

Black Baza
(Kerala)

THREATENED SPECIES

	Mammals	Birds	Reptiles	Amphibians	Fishes	Molluses	Other Inverts	Plants	Total
INDIA	96	76	25	65	40	2	109	246	659
	EX	EW	Sub-total	CR	EN	VU	Sub-total		
Animals	1	0	1	51	105	257	413		
Plants	7	2	9	45	112	89	246		

IUCN Red List Categories: EX - Extinct, EW - Extinct in the wild, CR - Critically Endangered, VU - Vulnerable.

Source: IUCN Rec List, 2008-09

INDIA'S SHARE IN GLOBAL CO2 EMISSIONS – 2009-10

Rest of East Asia and Pacific, 4%

India, 5%

Rest of South Asia 1%

China 16%

Rest of World 11%

Europe - EMU 10%

United States 22%

Rest of Europe and Central Asia, 7%

Russian Federation 6%

Japan, 5%

Rest of High Income, 13%

Source: State of Environment Report, 2009

LAND DEGRADATION

- Arid mountain
- Ice cap
- Nutrient depletion
- Saline and alkaline
- Salt flats
- Stable terrain
- Water erosion
- Waterlogging
- Wind erosion

Land Degradation

EXTENT OF VARIOUS KINDS OF LAND DEGRADATION IN INDIA

Land degradation	
Total geographical area	328.73
Total degraded area out of total geographical area	146.82
Complex problem	7.38
Soil acidity	16.03
Salinity / Alkalinity	5.95
Water logging	14.3
Wind erosion	9.48
Water erosion	93.68

Area in million hectares

LAMBERT CONICAL ORTHOMORPHIC PROJECTION

SCALE 1: 24 000 000

0   250   500   750   1000 km

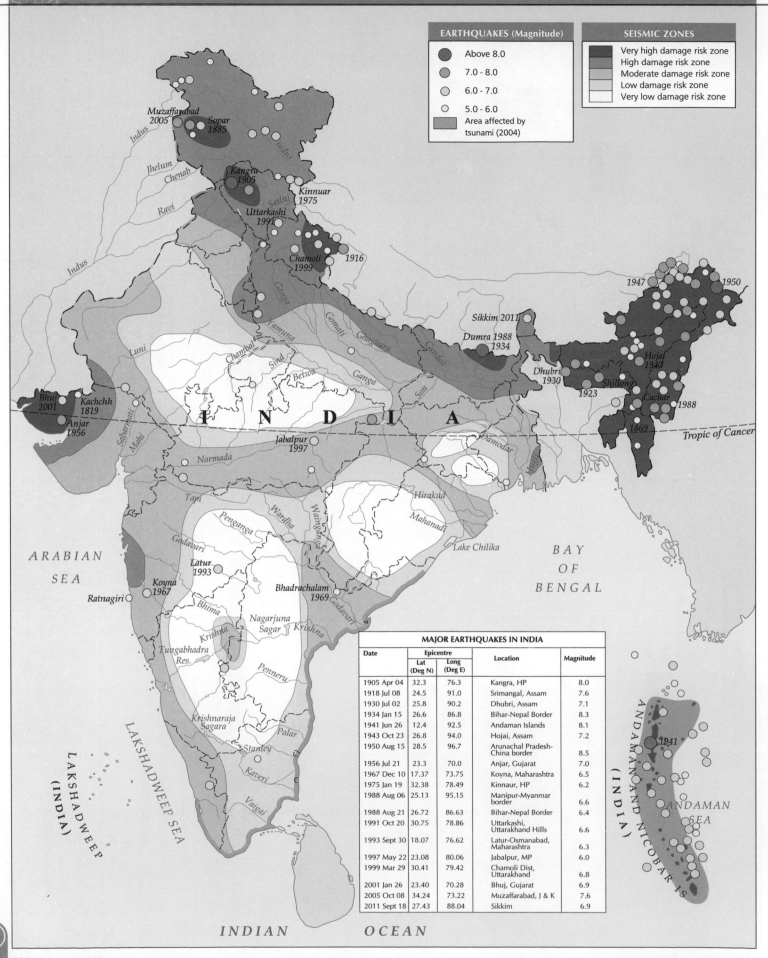

EARTHQUAKES (Magnitude)
- Above 8.0
- 7.0 - 8.0
- 6.0 - 7.0
- 5.0 - 6.0
- Area affected by tsunami (2004)

SEISMIC ZONES
- Very high damage risk zone
- High damage risk zone
- Moderate damage risk zone
- Low damage risk zone
- Very low damage risk zone

MAJOR EARTHQUAKES IN INDIA				
Date	Epicentre		Location	Magnitude
	Lat (Deg N)	Long (Deg E)		
1905 Apr 04	32.3	76.3	Kangra, HP	8.0
1918 Jul 08	24.5	91.0	Srimangal, Assam	7.6
1930 Jul 02	25.8	90.2	Dhubri, Assam	7.1
1934 Jan 15	26.6	86.8	Bihar-Nepal Border	8.3
1941 Jun 26	12.4	92.5	Andaman Islands	8.1
1943 Oct 23	26.8	94.0	Hojai, Assam	7.2
1950 Aug 15	28.5	96.7	Arunachal Pradesh-China border	8.5
1956 Jul 21	23.3	70.0	Anjar, Gujarat	7.0
1967 Dec 10	17.37	73.75	Koyna, Maharashtra	6.5
1975 Jan 19	32.38	78.49	Kinnaur, HP	6.2
1988 Aug 06	25.13	95.15	Manipur-Myanmar border	6.6
1988 Aug 21	26.72	86.63	Bihar-Nepal Border	6.4
1991 Oct 20	30.75	78.86	Uttarkashi, Uttarakhand Hills	6.6
1993 Sept 30	18.07	76.62	Latur-Osmanabad, Maharashtra	6.3
1997 May 22	23.08	80.06	Jabalpur, MP	6.0
1999 Mar 29	30.41	79.42	Chamoli Dist, Uttarakhand	6.8
2001 Jan 26	23.40	70.28	Bhuj, Gujarat	6.9
2005 Oct 08	34.24	73.22	Muzaffarabad, J & K	7.6
2011 Sept 18	27.43	88.04	Sikkim	6.9

SCALE 1: 15 000 000

0   150   300   450   600 km

LAMBERT CONICAL ORTHOMORPHIC PROJECTION

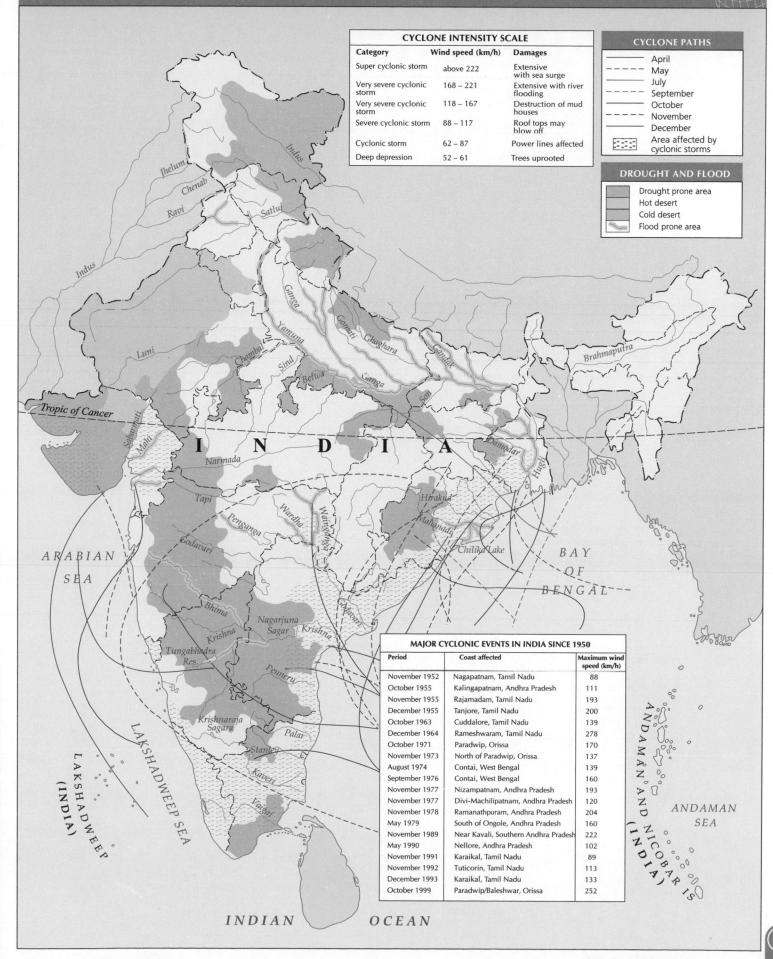

CYCLONE INTENSITY SCALE

Category	Wind speed (km/h)	Damages
Super cyclonic storm	above 222	Extensive with sea surge
Very severe cyclonic storm	168 – 221	Extensive with river flooding
Very severe cyclonic storm	118 – 167	Destruction of mud houses
Severe cyclonic storm	88 – 117	Roof tops may blow off
Cyclonic storm	62 – 87	Power lines affected
Deep depression	52 – 61	Trees uprooted

CYCLONE PATHS

- April
- May
- July
- September
- October
- November
- December
- Area affected by cyclonic storms

DROUGHT AND FLOOD

- Drought prone area
- Hot desert
- Cold desert
- Flood prone area

MAJOR CYCLONIC EVENTS IN INDIA SINCE 1950

Period	Coast affected	Maximum wind speed (km/h)
November 1952	Nagapatnam, Tamil Nadu	88
October 1955	Kalingapatnam, Andhra Pradesh	111
November 1955	Rajamadam, Tamil Nadu	193
December 1955	Tanjore, Tamil Nadu	200
October 1963	Cuddalore, Tamil Nadu	139
December 1964	Rameshwaram, Tamil Nadu	278
October 1971	Paradwip, Orissa	170
November 1973	North of Paradwip, Orissa	137
August 1974	Contai, West Bengal	139
September 1976	Contai, West Bengal	160
November 1977	Nizampatnam, Andhra Pradesh	193
November 1977	Divi-Machilipatnam, Andhra Pradesh	120
November 1978	Ramanathpuram, Andhra Pradesh	204
May 1979	South of Ongole, Andhra Pradesh	160
November 1989	Near Kavali, Southern Andhra Pradesh	222
May 1990	Nellore, Andhra Pradesh	102
November 1991	Karaikal, Tamil Nadu	89
November 1992	Tuticorin, Tamil Nadu	113
December 1993	Karaikal, Tamil Nadu	133
October 1999	Paradwip/Baleshwar, Orissa	252

LAMBERT CONICAL ORTHOMORPHIC PROJECTION

SCALE 1: 15 000 000

0   150   300   450   600 km

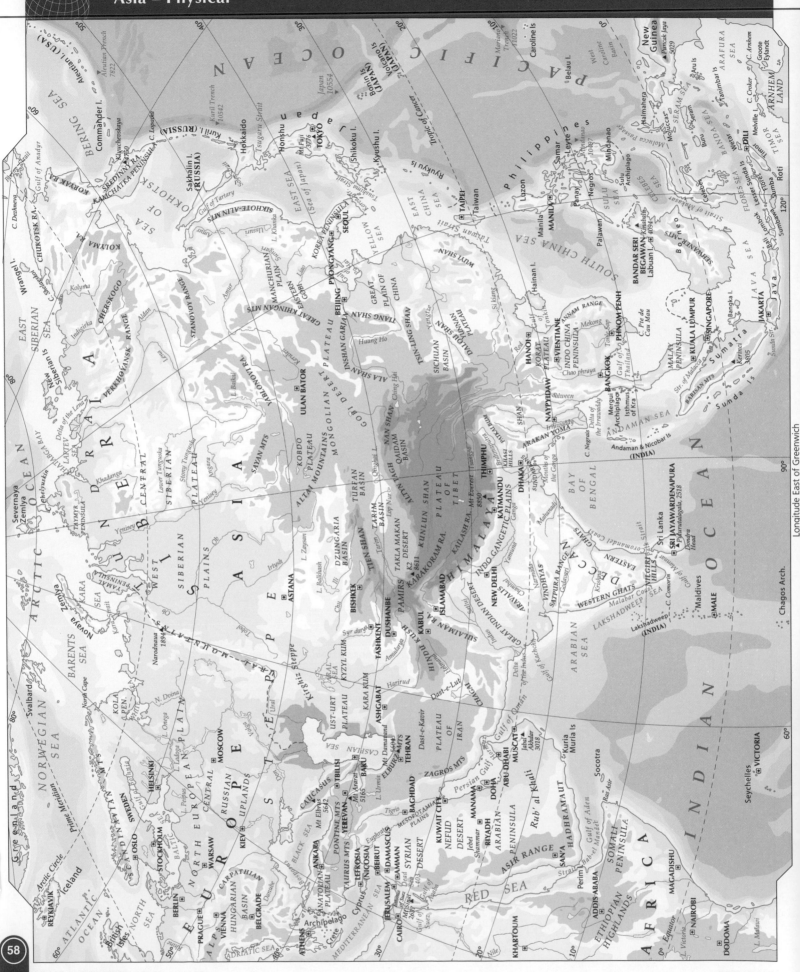

SCALE 1: 47 500 000

0   500   1000   1500   2000 km

BONNE PROJECTION

Longitude East of Greenwich

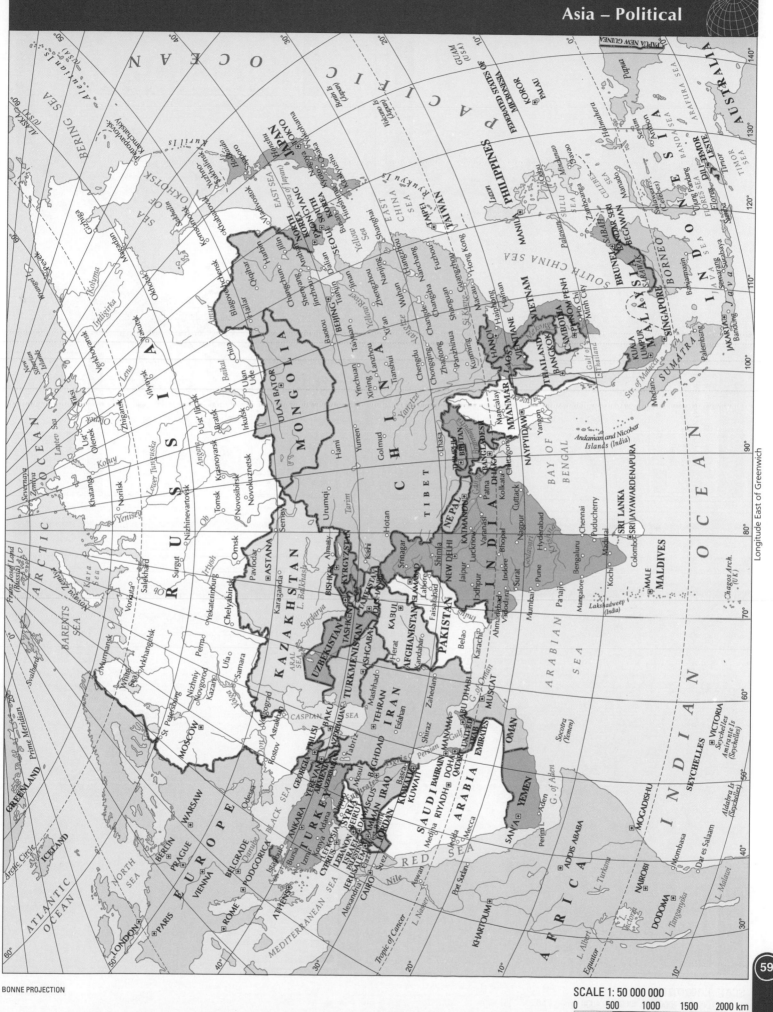

BONNE PROJECTION

Longitude East of Greenwich

SCALE 1: 50 000 000

0   500   1000   1500   2000 km

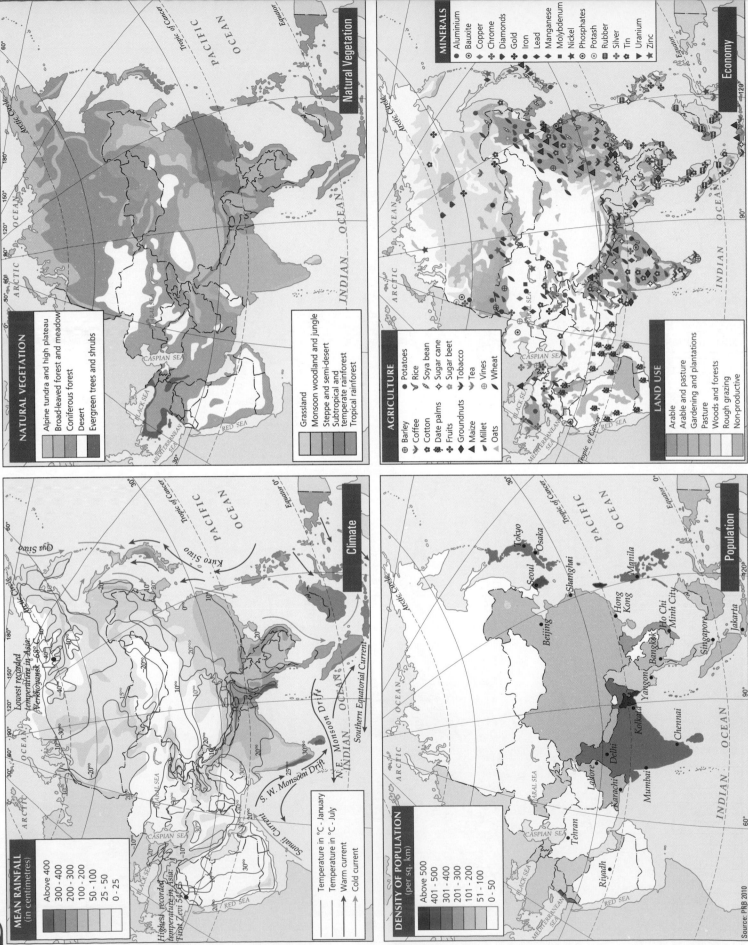

Natural Vegetation

NATURAL VEGETATION

- Alpine tundra and high plateau
- Broad-leaved forest and meadow
- Coniferous forest
- Desert
- Evergreen trees and shrubs
- Grassland
- Monsoon woodland and jungle
- Steppe and semi-desert
- Subtropical and temperate rainforest
- Tropical rainforest

Economy

MINERALS
- Aluminium
- Bauxite
- Copper
- Chrome
- Diamonds
- Gold
- Iron
- Lead
- Manganese
- Molybdenum
- Nickel
- Phosphates
- Potash
- Rubber
- Silver
- Tin
- Uranium
- Zinc

AGRICULTURE
- Barley
- Coffee
- Cotton
- Date palms
- Fruits
- Groundnuts
- Maize
- Millet
- Oats
- Potatoes
- Rice
- Soya bean
- Sugar cane
- Sugar beet
- Tobacco
- Tea
- Vines
- Wheat

LAND USE
- Arable
- Arable and pasture
- Gardening and plantations
- Pasture
- Woods and forests
- Rough grazing
- Non-productive

Climate

MEAN RAINFALL (in centimetres)
- Above 400
- 300 - 400
- 200 - 300
- 100 - 200
- 50 - 100
- 25 - 50
- 0 - 25

- Temperature in °C - January
- Temperature in °C - July
- Warm current
- Cold current

Lowest recorded temperature in Asia: Verkhoyansk – 68°

Highest recorded temperature in Asia: Tirat Zevi 54°

Oya Siwo
Kuro Siwo
S. W. Monsoon Drift
N. E. Monsoon Drift
Southern Equatorial Current
Somali Current

Population

DENSITY OF POPULATION (per sq. km)
- Above 500
- 401 - 500
- 301 - 400
- 201 - 300
- 101 - 200
- 51 - 100
- 0 - 50

Tokyo, Osaka, Seoul, Shanghai, Beijing, Hong Kong, Manila, Ho Chi Minh City, Bangkok, Singapore, Jakarta, Yangon, Chennai, Mumbai, Kolkata, Delhi, Lahore, Karachi, Tehran, Riyadh

Source: PRB 2010

SCALE 1: 100 000 000
0   1000   2000   3000   4000 km

BONNE PROJECTION

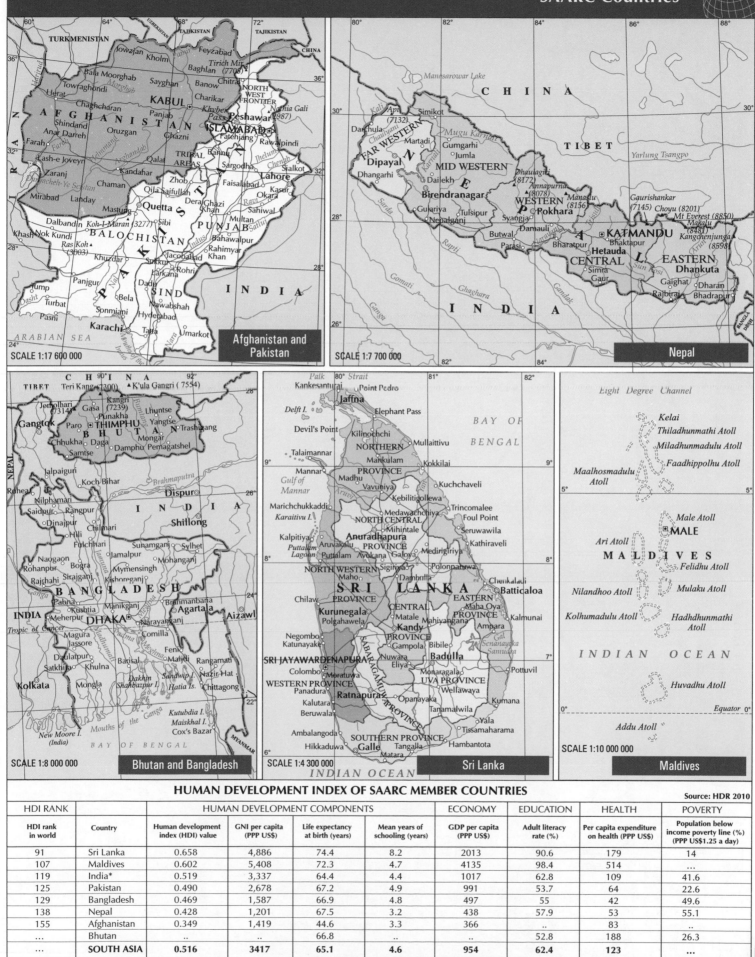

Afghanistan and Pakistan
SCALE 1:17 600 000

Nepal
SCALE 1:7 700 000

Bhutan and Bangladesh
SCALE 1:8 000 000

Sri Lanka
SCALE 1:4 300 000

Maldives
SCALE 1:10 000 000

HUMAN DEVELOPMENT INDEX OF SAARC MEMBER COUNTRIES

Source: HDR 2010

HDI RANK		HUMAN DEVELOPMENT COMPONENTS				ECONOMY	EDUCATION	HEALTH	POVERTY
HDI rank in world	Country	Human development index (HDI) value	GNI per capita (PPP US$)	Life expectancy at birth (years)	Mean years of schooling (years)	GDP per capita (PPP US$)	Adult literacy rate (%)	Per capita expenditure on health (PPP US$)	Population below income poverty line (%) (PPP US$1.25 a day)
91	Sri Lanka	0.658	4,886	74.4	8.2	2013	90.6	179	14
107	Maldives	0.602	5,408	72.3	4.7	4135	98.4	514	...
119	India*	0.519	3,337	64.4	4.4	1017	62.8	109	41.6
125	Pakistan	0.490	2,678	67.2	4.9	991	53.7	64	22.6
129	Bangladesh	0.469	1,587	66.9	4.8	497	55	42	49.6
138	Nepal	0.428	1,201	67.5	3.2	438	57.9	53	55.1
155	Afghanistan	0.349	1,419	44.6	3.3	366	..	83	...
...	Bhutan	..	..	66.8	..	..	52.8	188	26.3
...	SOUTH ASIA	0.516	3417	65.1	4.6	954	62.4	123	...

*Map details of India are given in the preceding pages

Longitude East of Greenwich

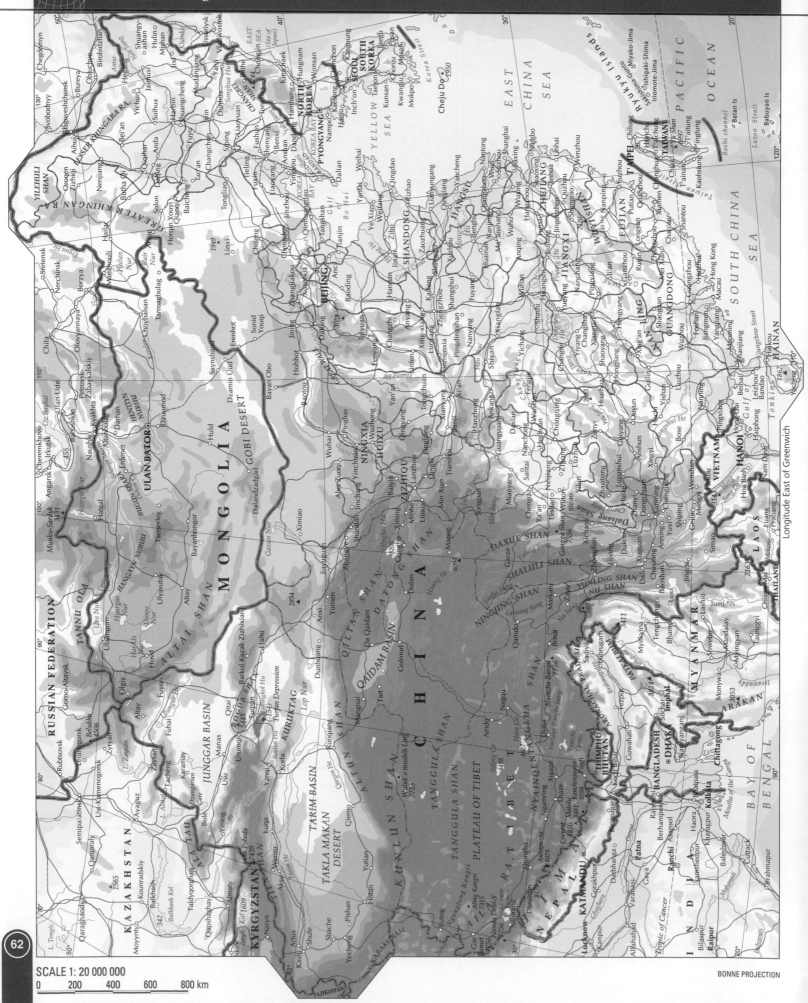

SCALE 1 : 20 000 000

0   200   400   600   800 km

BONNE PROJECTION

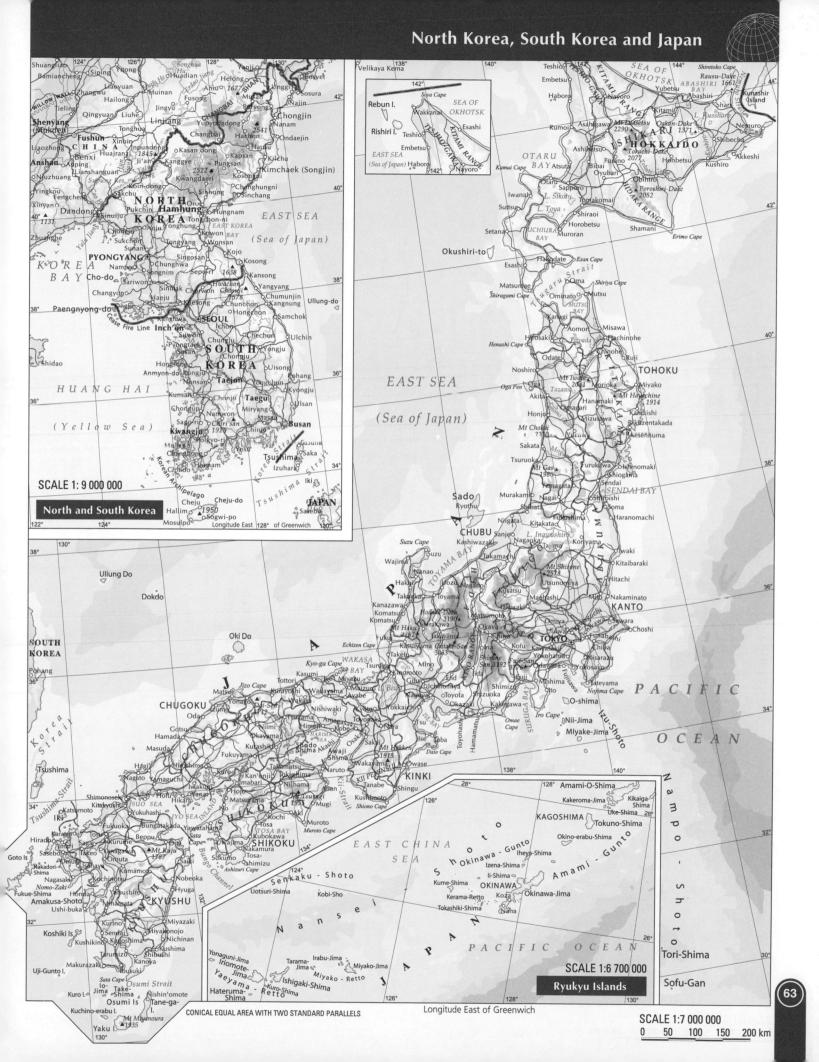

SCALE 1: 9 000 000

North and South Korea

CONICAL EQUAL AREA WITH TWO STANDARD PARALLELS

SCALE 1:6 700 000

Ryukyu Islands

Longitude East of Greenwich

SCALE 1:7 000 000

0   50   100   150   200 km

63

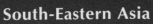

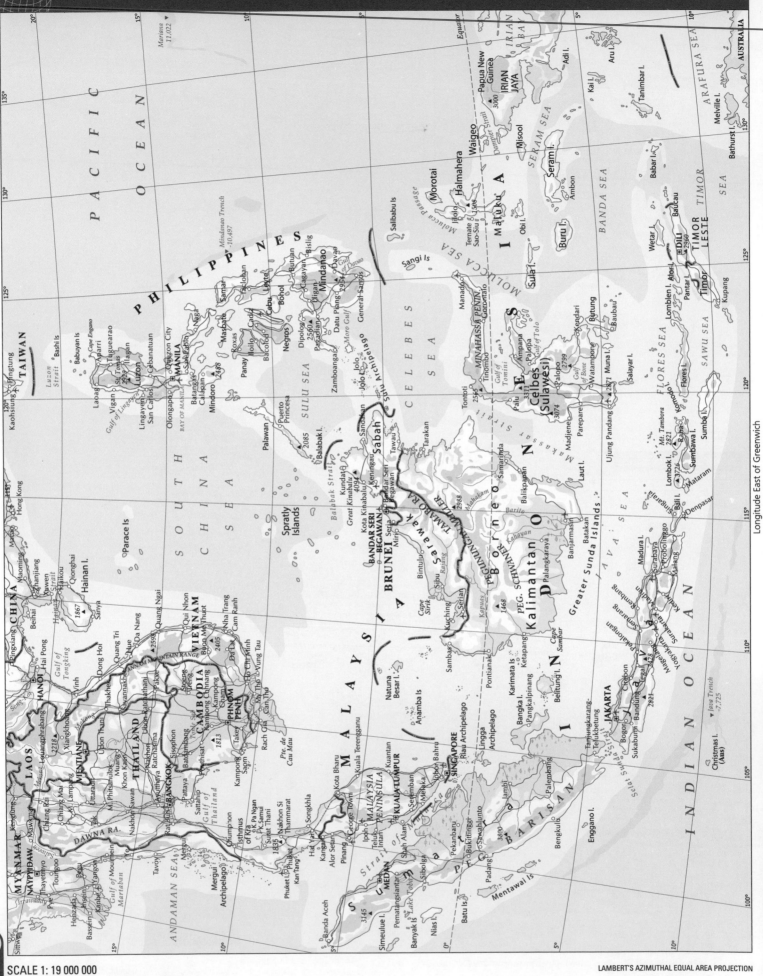

PACIFIC OCEAN

Mariana 11,022 ▼

IRIAN BAY

IRIAN JAYA

Papua New Guinea

AUSTRALIA

ARAFURA SEA

Aru I.

Kai I.

Tanimbar I.

SERAM SEA

Seram I.

Misool

Waigeo

Dampier Strait

3000

Morotai

Halmahera

Ternate

Sao-Siu

Obi I.

BANDA SEA

Babar I.

Buru I.

Ambon

M a l u k u

Wetar I.

TIMOR SEA

Bathurst I.

Melville I.

130°

Baucau

DILI

TIMOR LESTE

Timor

Kupang

TAIWAN

Kaohsiung

Jingtung

Luzon Strait

Bashi Is

Babuyan Is

Cape Engano

PHILIPPINES

Mindanao Trench -10,497

Salibabu Is

Sangi Is

Moluccan Passage

Ilolo

Sao-Siu

MINAHASSA PENIN.

Manado

Gorontalo

MOLUCCA SEA

C E L E B E S   S E A

CELEBES SEA

Tontoli

2556

Palu

3371

Celebes (Sulawesi)

3074

Tinombo

Gulf of Tomini

Ampana

Palopo

Gulf of Tolo

Kendari

Butung

Baubau

Pareparé

2787

Muna I.

Madjene

Gulf of Bone

Watampone

Salayar I.

FLORES SEA

SAWU SEA

Ujung Pandang

Mt. Tambora 2821

Raba

2960

Sumba I.

Flores I.

Komodo I.

Lomblen I.

Alor I.

Pantar I.

Adonara

Bima

Sumbawa I.

Mataram

Lombok I.

3726

Bali I.

Denpasar

Longitude East of Greenwich

SOUTH CHINA SEA

Paracel Is

Hainan I.

1867

Sanya

Qionghai

Haikou

Hoihow

Zhanjiang

Beihai

CHINA

Maoming

Hong Kong

Macao

Pingxiang

Nanning

Qinzhou

Fangcheng

Gulf of Tongking

Spratly Islands

Great Kinabalu 4094

Kota Kinabalu

Sabah

Balabak Strait

Balabak I.

2085

Palawan

Puerto Princesa

SULU SEA

Jolo

Jolo

Sulu Archipelago

Sandakan

Zamboanga

General Santos 2954

Moro Gulf

Datu Piang

Pagadian

Dipolog

Cagayan

Butuan

Surigao

Davao

Gulf of Davao

Mindanao

Bislig

Dinagat

Cebu

Bohol

Leyte

Negros

Bacolod

Tacloban

Samar

Masbate

Roxas

Iloilo

Panay

Calapan

Mindoro

2498

Batangas

Calamian

San Carlos

Lingayen

Gulf of Lingayen

MANILA

BAY OF MANILA

Olongapo

Quezon City

Cabanatuan

2929

San Fernando

Ilagan

Tuguegarao

Aparri

Laoag

Vigan

Luzon

BRUNEI

BANDAR SERI BEGAWAN

Bandar Seri Begawan

Seria

Miri

Kuching

Sibu

Bintulu

Sarawak

Kundat

Kudat

Keningau

Tawau

Tarakan

Nunukan

Samarinda

Balikpapan

Laut I.

Banjarmasin

B o r n e o

Kalimantan

PEG. SCHWANER

PEG. MULLER

Mahakam

2988

Barito

Batakan

Palangkaraya

Lahayan

Kapuas

1468

Cape Sirik

Cape Sambar

Karimata Is

Ketapang

Pontianak

Sambas

Natuna Besar I.

Anambas Is

Greater Sunda Islands

JAVA SEA

Madura I.

Surabaya

Malang

Probolinggo

Pasuruan

Cirebon

Tegal

2821

Bandung

Bogor

JAKARTA

Kembang

Semarang

Pekalongan

Yogyakarta

Sukabumi

Sawahlunto

J a v a

Lingga Archipelago

Lingga

Riau Archipelago

Tanjungkarang-Telukbetung

Jambi

Palembang

Bengkulu

Pangkalpinang

Bangka I.

Belitung I.

Billiton I.

Batam

SINGAPORE

Johor Bahru

Melaka

Seremban

Shah Alam

KUALA LUMPUR

MALAYSIA

Ipoh

George Town

Pinang

Kota Bharu

Kuala Terengganu

Kuantan

MALAY PENINSULA

Alor Setar

Kangar

Hat Yai

Songkhla

Nakhon Si Thammarat

Surat Thani

K. Samui

K. Pha Ngan

Chumphon

Isthmus of Kra

1835

Gulf of Thailand

THAILAND

BANGKOK

Ayutthaya

Pattaya

Nakhon Ratchasima

Ubon Ratchathani

Sisophon

Battambang

Pouthisat

1813

Tonle Sap

Kampong Thom

Kampong Cham

PHNOM PENH

Takeo

Kampong Saom

CAMBODIA

Can Tho

Rach Gia

Pte. de Cau Mau

My Tho

Ho Chi Minh

Vung Tau

Da Lat

2405

Bao Loc

Buon Me Thuot

Qui Nhon

Quang Ngai

Da Nang

2598

Hue

Quang Tri

Dong Hoi

VIETNAM

ANNAM MOUNTAIN RANGE

Vinh

Thanh Hoa

HANOI

Hai Phong

Song Hong

LAOS

VIENTIANE

2218

Louangphrabang

Xiangkhoang

Udon Thani

Khon Kaen

Nakhon Sawan

Phitsanulok

Uttaradit

Lampang

Chiang Mai

Chiang Rai

Kengtung

Mawlamyine

DAWNA RA.

Tak

MYANMAR

NAYPYIDAW

Toungoo

Thayetmyo

Pyay

YANGON

Bassein

Henzada

Pathein

Gulf of Martaban

Mergui

Tavoy

Mergui Archipelago

Phuket

Kan Tang

Trang

ANDAMAN SEA

Mt. Mountain 3145

Banda Aceh

Sibolga

Medan

Pematangsiantar

SUMATRA

Pekanbaru

Padang

PEG. BARISAN

3800

Bukittinggi

Nias I.

Batu Is

Siberut I.

Mentawai Is

Enggano I.

Simeulue I.

Banyak Is

Strait of Malacca

Strait of Sunda

INDIAN OCEAN

Java Trench -7,725 ▼

Christmas I. (Aus)

Selat Sunda

SCALE 1: 19 000 000

0   200   400   600   800 km

LAMBERT'S AZIMUTHAL EQUAL AREA PROJECTION

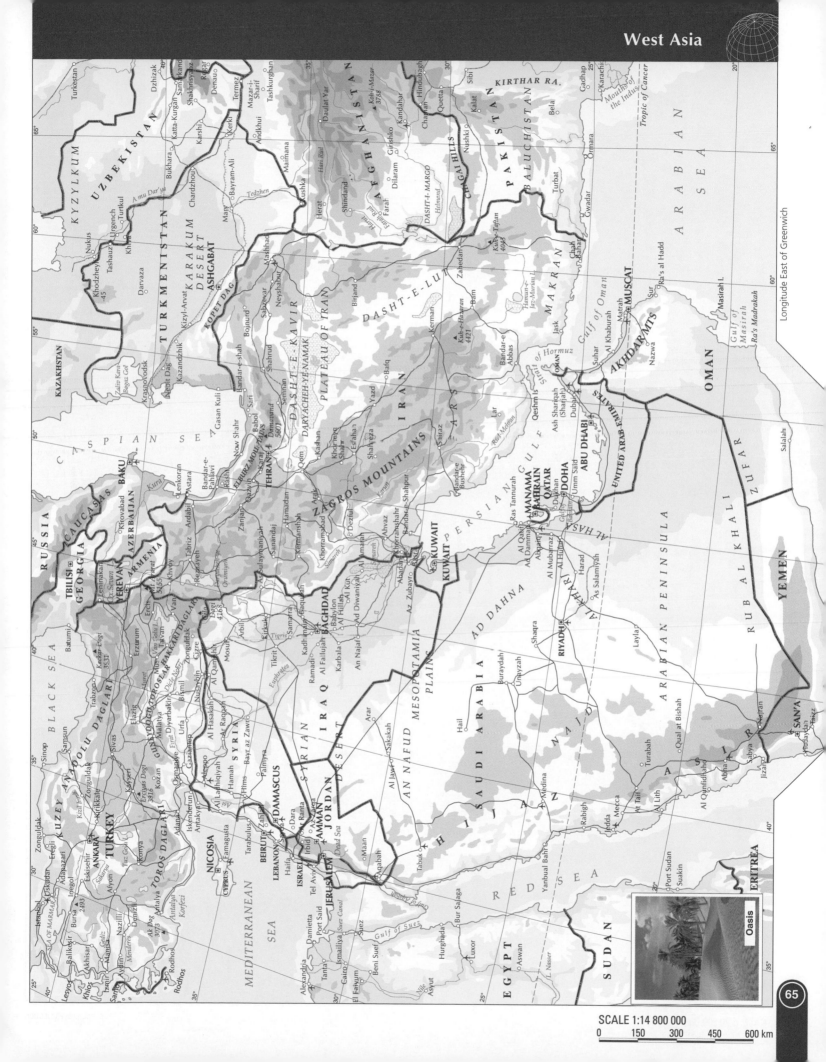

Tropic of Cancer

Longitude East of Greenwich

Oasis

SCALE 1:14 800 000

0   150   300   450   600 km

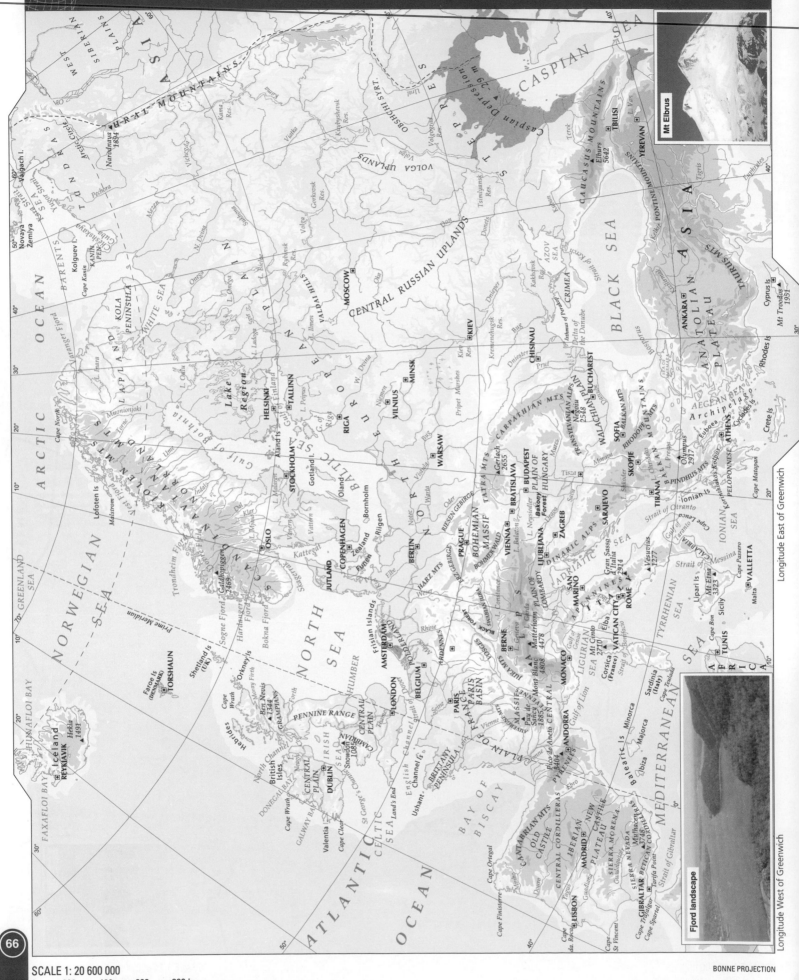

Mt Elbrus

Fjord landscape

SCALE 1: 20 600 000

0   200   400   600   800 km

BONNE PROJECTION

Longitude East of Greenwich

Longitude West of Greenwich

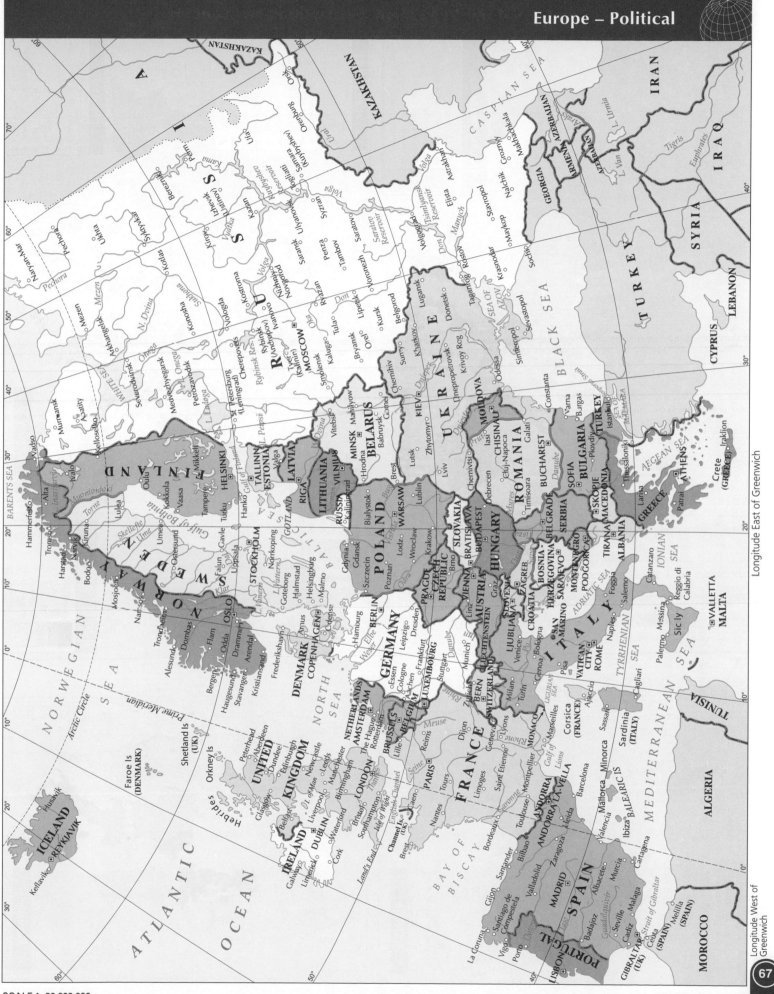

Longitude West of Greenwich

Longitude East of Greenwich

SCALE 1: 20 600 000

0   200   400   600   800 km

BONNE PROJECTION

Europe – Climate, Natural Vegetation, Population and Economy

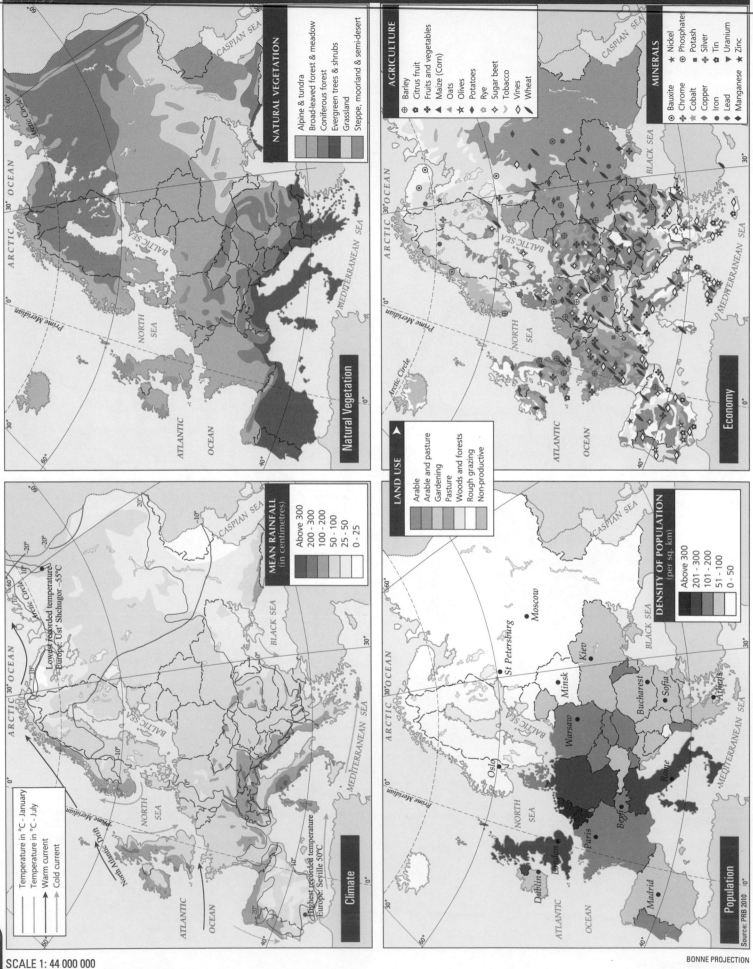

NATURAL VEGETATION
- Alpine & tundra
- Broad-leaved forest & meadow
- Coniferous forest
- Evergreen trees & shrubs
- Grassland
- Steppe, moorland & semi-desert

Natural Vegetation

AGRICULTURE
- ⊕ Barley
- ✿ Citrus fruit
- ✿ Fruits and vegetables
- ▲ Maize (Corn)
- ✦ Oats
- ✧ Olives
- ◆ Potatoes
- ✦ Rye
- ✿ Sugar beet
- ◇ Tobacco
- ✧ Vines
- ◇ Wheat

MINERALS
- ⊙ Bauxite
- ✿ Chrome
- ✶ Cobalt
- ◆ Copper
- ● Iron
- ▼ Lead
- ◆ Manganese
- ★ Nickel
- ⊙ Phosphates
- ■ Potash
- ✿ Silver
- ✿ Tin
- ▼ Uranium
- ★ Zinc

Economy

LAND USE
- Arable
- Arable and pasture
- Gardening
- Pasture
- Woods and forests
- Rough grazing
- Non-productive

MEAN RAINFALL
(in centimetres)
- Above 300
- 200 - 300
- 100 - 200
- 50 - 100
- 25 - 50
- 0 - 25

Lowest recorded temperature
Europe: Ust' Shchugor –55°C

Highest recorded temperature
Europe: Seville 50°C

Temperature in °C - January
Temperature in °C - July
Warm current
Cold current

North Atlantic Drift

Climate

DENSITY OF POPULATION
(per sq. km)
- Above 300
- 201 - 300
- 101 - 200
- 51 - 100
- 0 - 50

Moscow
St Petersburg
Minsk
Kiev
Warsaw
Bucharest
Sofia
Athens
Oslo
Rome
Berlin
Paris
London
Dublin
Madrid

Source: PRB 2010

Population

SCALE 1: 44 000 000

0   400   800   1200   1600 km

BONNE PROJECTION

CONICAL WITH TWO STANDARD PARALLELS

Longitude West of Greenwich

Longitude East of Greenwich

SCALE 1: 5 000 000

0   50   100   150   200 km

69

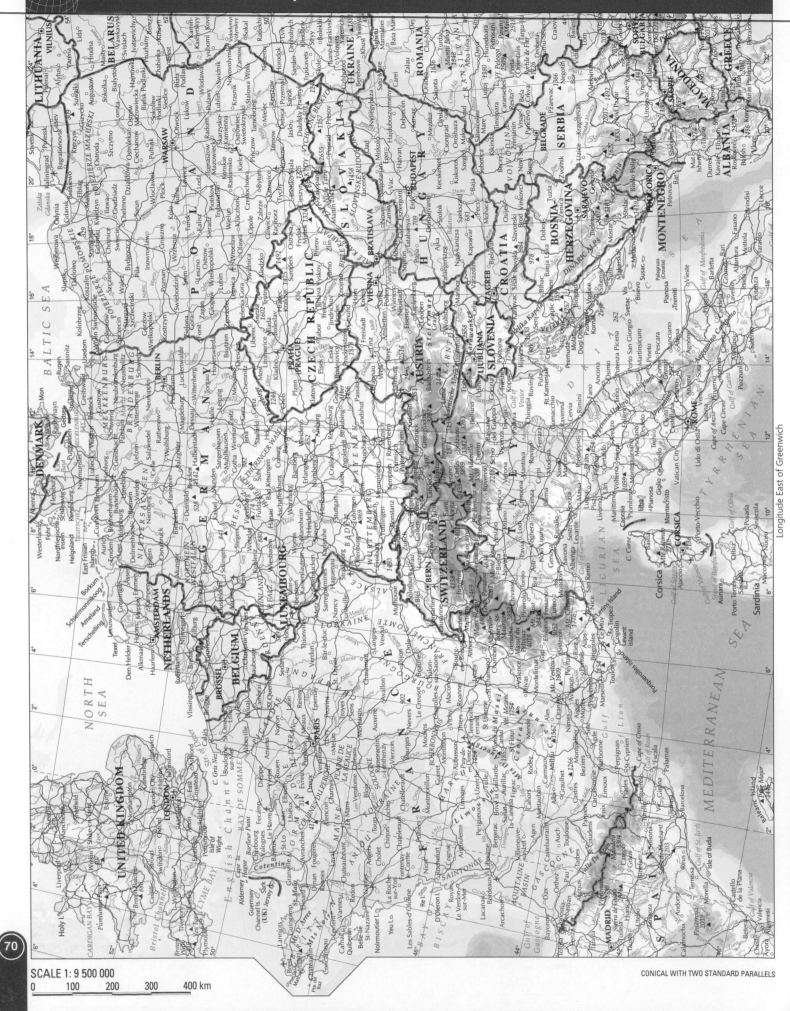

SCALE 1: 9 500 000

0   100   200   300   400 km

CONICAL WITH TWO STANDARD PARALLELS

Longitude East of Greenwich

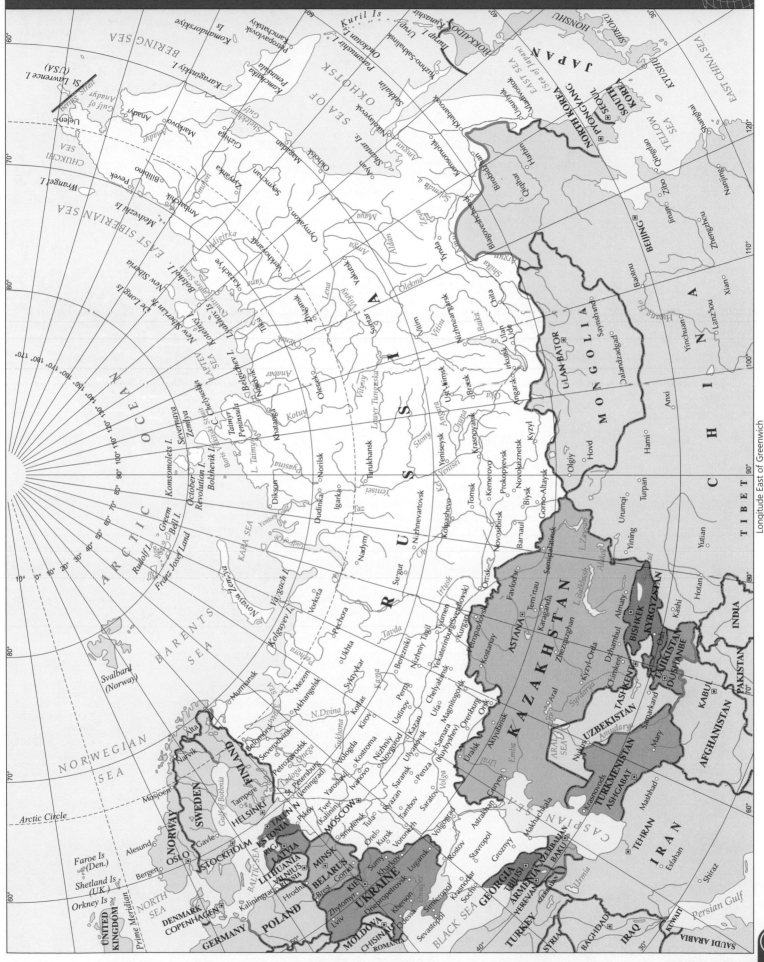

CONIC PROJECTION

SCALE 1 : 34 000 000

| 0 | 300 | 600 | 900 | 1200 km |

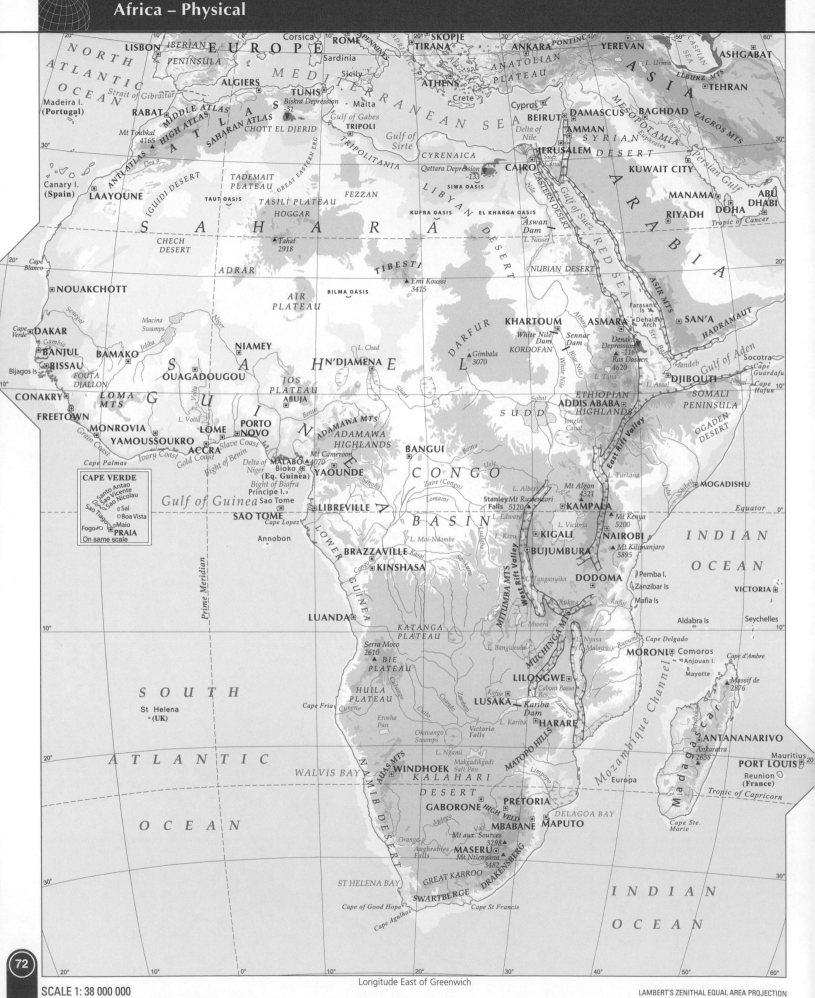

SCALE 1: 38 000 000

0   400   800   1200   1600 km

Longitude East of Greenwich

LAMBERT'S ZENITHAL EQUAL AREA PROJECTION

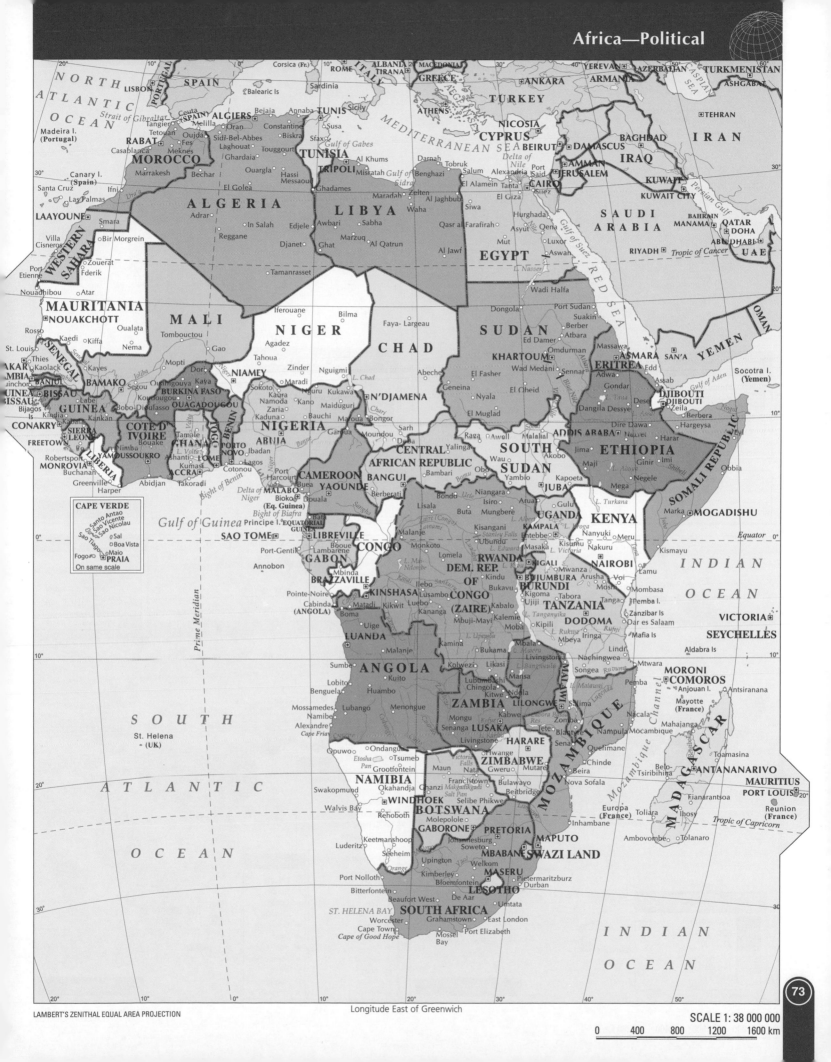

NORTH
ATLANTIC
OCEAN

Corsica (Fr.)
ROME
ITALY
ALBANIA
TIRANA
MACEDONIA
GREECE
ATHENS
ANKARA
ARMENIA
YEREVAN
AZERBAIJAN
TURKMENISTAN
ASHGABAT

LISBON
PORTUGAL
SPAIN
Sardinia
Balearic Is.
Sicily
TURKEY
NICOSIA
CYPRUS
BEIRUT
DAMASCUS
BAGHDAD
TEHRAN

Ceuta (SPAIN)
ALGIERS
Bejaia
Annaba
TUNIS
Susa
IRAN

Tangier
Melilla
Oran
Constantine

RABAT
Tetouan
Oujda
Sidi-Bel-Abbes
Biskra
Sfax
Gulf of Gabes
Al Khums
TRIPOLI
Misratah
Darnah
Tobruk
Salum
Alexandria
Port Said
AMMAN
JERUSALEM
IRAQ
KUWAIT

MOROCCO
Casablanca
Meknes
Fes
Laghouat
Ghardaia
Benghazi
Gulf of Sidra
El Alamein
Tanta
CAIRO
El Giza
Suez
SAUDI
ARABIA
BAHRAIN
MANAMA
QATAR
DOHA
ABU DHABI
KUWAIT CITY

Marrakesh
Bechar
Ouargla
Hassi
Messaoud
Ghadames
Maradah
Zelten
Al Jaghbub
Siwa
Hurghada
Asyut
Qena
Luxor
RIYADH
Tropic of Cancer
UAE

Canary I.
(Spain)
Ifni
El Golea
ALGERIA
LIBYA
Awbari
Sabha
Qasr al Farafirah
Mut
Aswan

Santa Cruz
Las Palmas
Adrar
In Salah
Edjele
Djanet
Ghat
Al Qatrun
Marzuq
Al Jawf
EGYPT
L. Nasser
RED

LAAYOUNE
Smara
Reggane
Tamanrasset

Villa
Cisneros
Bir Morgrein
Zouerat
Fderik
WESTERN
SAHARA
Wadi Halfa

Port
Etienne
Atar
Nouadhibou
MAURITANIA
MALI
Iferouane
Bilma
Faya- Largeau
Dongola
Port Sudan
Suakin
YEMEN
OMAN

Nouakchott
NOUAKCHOTT
Oualata
Nema
NIGER
Agadez
CHAD
SUDAN
Berber
Atbara
Massawa
ASMARA
SAN'A
SEA

Rosso
Kaedi
Kiffa
Tombouctou
Gao
Tahoua
Zinder
Nguigmi
L. Chad
El Fasher
KHARTOUM
Wad Medani
Sennar
ERITREA
Adwa
Edd
Socotra I.
(Yemen)

St. Louis
Thies
Kayes
Mopti
Segou
N'DJAMENA
Abeche
Geneina
Nyala
El Oheid
Gondar
Dangila
Dessye
DJIBOUTI
DJIBOUTI
Zeila
Berbera
Gulf of Aden

SENEGAL
DAKAR
Kaolack
BAMAKO
Koutiala
Dori
Kaya
Sokoto
Maradi
Kano
Maiduguri
Mafoua
El Muglad
Raga
Awoll
Malalal
ADDIS ABABA
Dire Dawa
Harar
Hargeysa

GAMBIA
BANJUL
GUINEA
BISSAU
BISSAU
CONAKRY
Labe
Kankan
BURKINA FASO
OUAGADOUGOU
Bobo-Dioulasso
Kaduna
Bongor
Sarh
Yalinga
SOUTH
Wau
Akobo
Jima
Maji
ETHIOPIA
Ginir
Imi
SOMALI REPUBLIC

Kindia
Kabala
SIERRA
LEONE
FREETOWN
COTE D'IVOIRE
GHANA
TOGO
BENIN
NIGERIA
ABUJA
CENTRAL
AFRICAN REPUBLIC
BANGUI
Bambari
Obo
Yambio
SUDAN
JUBA
Kapoeta
Mega
Negele
Obbia

Robertsport
Harper
LIBERIA
MONROVIA
YAMOUSSOUKRO
Bouake
Tamale
Ibadan
Lagos
Port
Harcourt
CAMEROON
YAOUNDE
Berberati
Bondo
Niangara
Isiro
UGANDA
KENYA
Marka
MOGADISHU

Buchanan
Greenville
Kumasi
ACCRA
Ashanti
L. Volta
LOME
PORTO
NOVO
Cotonou
Delta of
Niger
MALABO
Douala
Bioko
Buea
Uele
Buta
Mungbere
KAMPALA
L. Kyoga
Kisumu
Nanyuki
Meru
Lamu

Abidjan
Takoradi
Bight of Benin
Bight of Biafra
EQUATORIAL
GUINEA
(Eq. Guinea)
Principe I.
Bata
Lisala
Kisangani
Stanley Falls
Ubundu
L. Albert
L. Edward
Masaka
NAIROBI
Kismayu

CAPE VERDE
Santo Antao
Sao Vicente
Sao Nicolau
Sal
Boa Vista
Maio
Santiago
Fogo
PRAIA
On same scale
Gulf of Guinea
SAO TOME
LIBREVILLE
GABON
CONGO
Boue
Lambarene
Monkoto
Lomela
RWANDA
KIGALI
BURUNDI
BUJUMBURA
Bukavu
Ujiji
Mwanza
L. Victoria
Nakuru
Kisumu
Arusha
Moshi
Mombasa
INDIAN
OCEAN

Annobon
Port-Gentil
Mbinda
BRAZZAVILLE
Pointe-Noire
KINSHASA
Matadi
DEM. REP.
OF
CONGO
(ZAIRE)
Kindu
Kalemie
TANZANIA
DODOMA
Tabora
Pemba I.
Zanzibar Is.
Dar es Salaam
VICTORIA
SEYCHELLES

Cabinda
(ANGOLA)
Boma
Kikwit
Luebo
Kananga
Kabalo
Moba
Kipili
L. Tanganyika
Mbeya
Iringa
Mafia I.

Uige
LUANDA
Mbuji-Mayi
Kamina
Bukama
Mbala
L. Rukwa
Ruvi
Lindi
Aldabra Is.

Sumbe
Malanje
Kolwezi
Likasi
Livingstone
Nachingwea
Mtwara
MORONI
COMOROS

ANGOLA
Kuito
Lubumbashi
Chingola
Kitwe
Ndola
L. Malawi
Pemba
Anjouan I.
Antsiranana

Lobito
Benguela
Huambo
Menongue
ZAMBIA
Kabwe
LILONGWE
MALAWI
Nacala
Mayotte
(France)

Mossamedes
Namibe
Lubango
Mongu
Senanga
LUSAKA
Tete
Zomba
Nampula
Mocambique
Mahajanga

Alexandre
Cape Friar
Ondangwa
Opuwo
Etosha
Pan
Tsumeb
Grootfontein
Maun
Victoria
Falls
Kasane
HARARE
Mutare
Beira
Nova Sofala
Quelimane
Tsiribihina
MAURITIUS
PORT LOUIS

SOUTH
ATLANTIC
OCEAN
St. Helena
- (UK)
NAMIBIA
Swakopmund
Walvis Bay
Okahandja
WINDHOEK
Ghanzi
Makgadikgadi
Salt Pan
Francistown
Bulawayo
Beitbridge
ZIMBABWE
Gweru
ANTANANARIVO
Fianarantsoa
Europa
(France)
Reunion
(France)
Tropic of Capricorn

Luderitz
Keetmanshoop
BOTSWANA
Molepolole
GABORONE
Selibe Phikwe
PRETORIA
Johannesburg
Soweto
MAPUTO
Inhambane
Ambovombe
Toliara
Ihosy
Tolanaro
MADAGASCAR

Rehoboth
Seeheim
Upington
Welkom
MBABANE
SWAZI LAND
MASERU
LESOTHO

Port Nolloth
Kimberley
Bloemfontein
Pietermaritzburg
Durban

Bitterfontein
Beaufort West
De Aar
Umtata

St. HELENA BAY
Worcester
Cape Town
Cape of Good Hope
SOUTH AFRICA
Grahamstown
East London
Mossel
Bay
Port Elizabeth
INDIAN
OCEAN

MEDITERRANEAN SEA
Prime Meridian

LAMBERT'S ZENITHAL EQUAL AREA PROJECTION
Longitude East of Greenwich

SCALE 1: 38 000 000
0   400   800   1200   1600 km

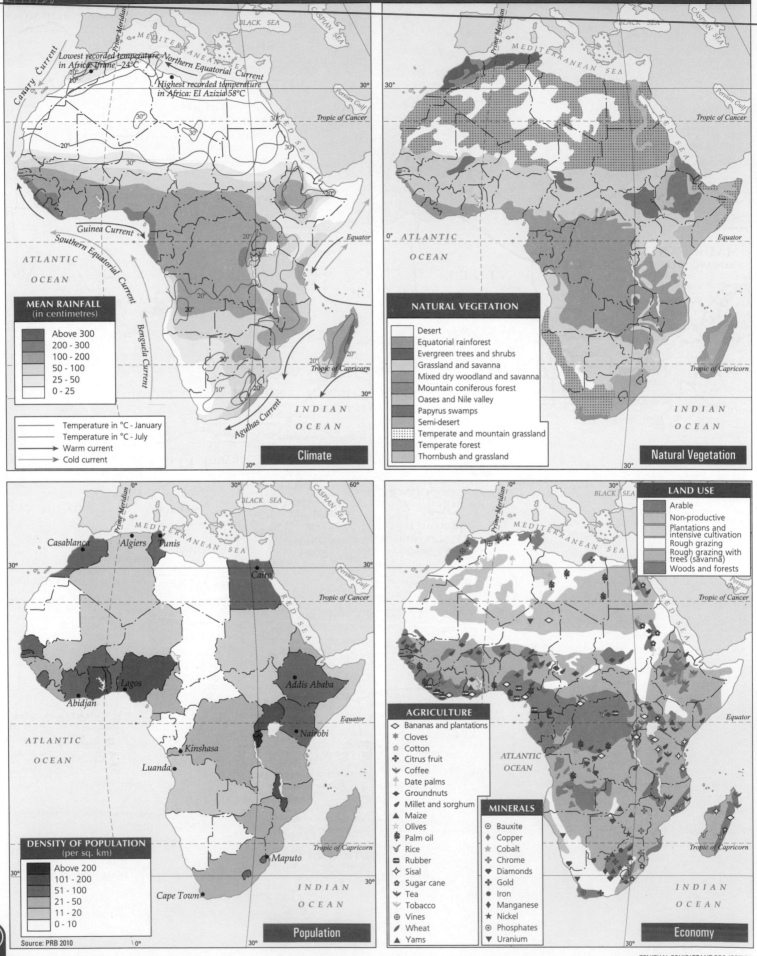

Africa – Climate, Natural Vegetation, Population and Economy

Climate

MEAN RAINFALL
(in centimetres)

- Above 300
- 200 - 300
- 100 - 200
- 50 - 100
- 25 - 50
- 0 - 25

— Temperature in °C - January
— Temperature in °C - July
→ Warm current
→ Cold current

Lowest recorded temperature in Africa: Ifrane −24°C
Highest recorded temperature in Africa: El Azizia 58°C

Canary Current
Northern Equatorial Current
Guinea Current
Southern Equatorial Current
Benguela Current
Agulhas Current

MEDITERRANEAN SEA
BLACK SEA
CASPIAN SEA
Persian Gulf
RED SEA
ATLANTIC OCEAN
INDIAN OCEAN

Tropic of Cancer
Equator
Tropic of Capricorn

Natural Vegetation

NATURAL VEGETATION

- Desert
- Equatorial rainforest
- Evergreen trees and shrubs
- Grassland and savanna
- Mixed dry woodland and savanna
- Mountain coniferous forest
- Oases and Nile valley
- Papyrus swamps
- Semi-desert
- Temperate and mountain grassland
- Temperate forest
- Thornbush and grassland

Population

DENSITY OF POPULATION
(per sq. km)

- Above 200
- 101 - 200
- 51 - 100
- 21 - 50
- 11 - 20
- 0 - 10

Source: PRB 2010

Casablanca
Algiers
Tunis
Cairo
Lagos
Abidjan
Addis Ababa
Nairobi
Kinshasa
Luanda
Maputo
Cape Town

Economy

LAND USE

- Arable
- Non-productive
- Plantations and intensive cultivation
- Rough grazing
- Rough grazing with trees (savanna)
- Woods and forests

AGRICULTURE

- ◇ Bananas and plantations
- ✸ Cloves
- ✿ Cotton
- ✤ Citrus fruit
- ✿ Coffee
- ⚕ Date palms
- ◆ Groundnuts
- ✦ Millet and sorghum
- ▲ Maize
- ☆ Olives
- ✿ Palm oil
- ✓ Rice
- ▣ Rubber
- ✧ Sisal
- ✿ Sugar cane
- ✿ Tea
- ✿ Tobacco
- ✿ Vines
- ✎ Wheat
- ▲ Yams

MINERALS

- ⊙ Bauxite
- ◆ Copper
- ★ Cobalt
- ✤ Chrome
- ▼ Diamonds
- ✦ Gold
- ● Iron
- ◆ Manganese
- ★ Nickel
- ⊙ Phosphates
- ▽ Uranium

SCALE 1: 81 000 000

0   800   1600   2400   3200 km

ZENITHAL EQUIDISTANT PROJECTION

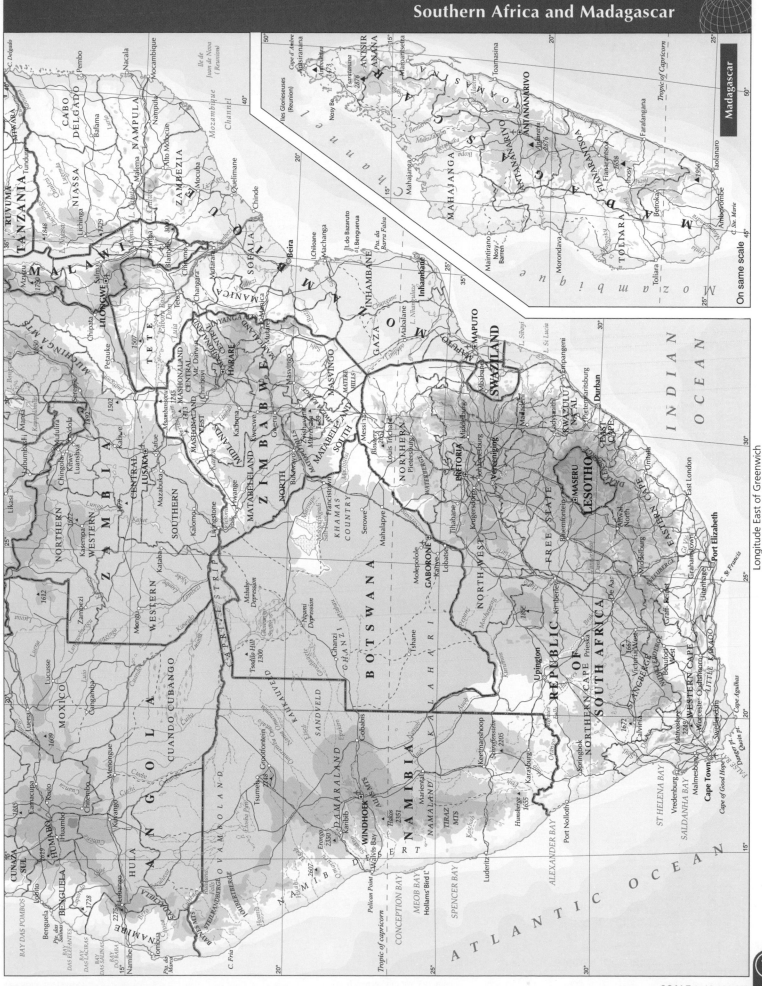

Madagascar

On same scale

Longitude East of Greenwich

75

SCALE 1: 13 100 000

0   100   200   300   400 km

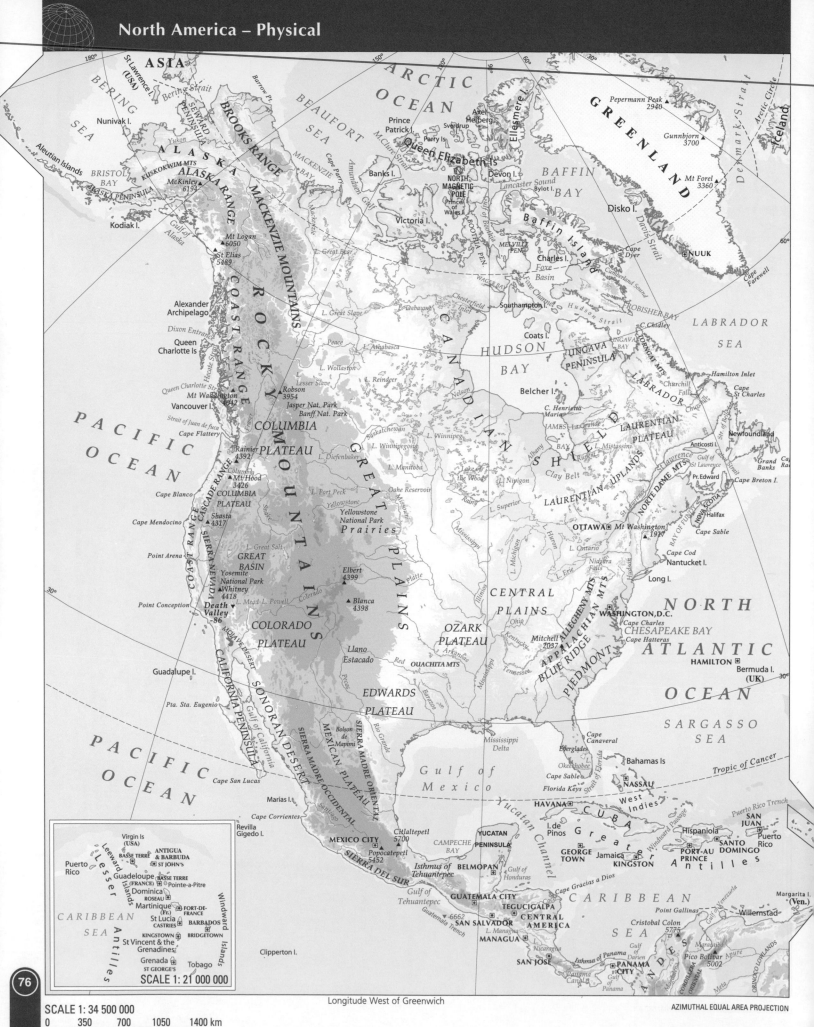

ASIA

BERING
SEA

Nunivak I.

Aleutian Islands

Kodiak I.

BRISTOL
BAY

ALASKA PENINSULA

KUSKOKWIM MTS

McKinley
6194

ALASKA

Yukon

SEWARD
PENINSULA

St Lawrence I.
(USA)

Bering Strait

Barrow Pt.

BEAUFORT
SEA

ARCTIC
OCEAN

Prince
Patrick I.

Banks I.

Victoria I.

Axel
Heiberg I.

Sverdrup

Cape Perry

Amundsen Gulf

McClure Strait

Queen Elizabeth Is

NORTH
MAGNETIC
POLE

Prince
of
Wales I.

BOOTHIA
PEN.

Devon I.

Lancaster Sound

Bylot I.

BAFFIN
BAY

MELVILLE
PEN.

Charles
I.

Foxe
Basin

Cape
Dyer

Baffin Island

Southampton I.

Cumberland Sound

FROBISHER BAY

Hudson Strait

C. Chidley

GREENLAND

Pepermann Peak
2940

Gunnbjorn
3700

Mt Forel
3360

Denmark Strait

Arctic Circle

Iceland

Disko I.

NUUK

Cape
Farewell

60°

LABRADOR
SEA

BROOKS RANGE

MACKENZIE MOUNTAINS

ALASKA RANGE

Mt Logan
6050

St Elias
5489

Gulf of
Alaska

COAST RANGE

Alexander
Archipelago

Dixon Entrance

Queen
Charlotte Is

Hecate Str.

Queen Charlotte Str.

Mt Waddington
4042

Vancouver I.

Strait of Juan de Fuca

Cape Flattery

L. Great Bear

Mackenzie

MACKENZIE

BAY

L. Great Slave

Peace

L. Athabasca

Dabawnt

Chesterfield
Inlet

WAGER BAY

Coats I.

HUDSON
BAY

Belcher I.

C. Henrietta
Maria

JAMES
BAY

Rupert

UNGAVA
PENINSULA

UNGAVA
BAY

TORNGAT MTS

LABRADOR

Churchill
Falls

Hamilton Inlet

Cape
St Charles

PACIFIC
OCEAN

ROCKY

Robson
3954

Jasper Nat. Park
Banff Nat. Park

COLUMBIA
PLATEAU

Rainier
4392

Columbia

Mt Hood
3426

COLUMBIA
PLATEAU

CASCADE RANGE

Shasta
4317

Cape Blanco

Cape Mendocino

Lesser Slave

L. Wollaston

Lesser Slave

Saskatchewan

L. Reindeer

L. Winnipeg

L. Winnipegosis

L. Manitoba

Nelson

Lake of
the Woods

L. Diefenbaker

L. Fort Peck

Yellowstone

Oahe Reservoir

Missouri

Yellowstone
National Park

Prairies

GREAT

Albany

Nelson

La Grande

CANADIAN

SHIELD

Clay Belt

L. Mistassini

Raimy

L. Nipigon

L. Superior

LAURENTIAN
PLATEAU

Anticosti I.

Newfoundland

Gulf of
St Lawrence

Pr. Edward

Grand
Banks

Cape
Ra

MOUNTAINS

SIERRA NEVADA

COAST RANGE

Point Arena

Point Conception

Yosemite
National Park

Whitney
4418

Death
Valley
-86

L. Great Salt

GREAT
BASIN

MOJAVE DESERT

L. Mead

L. Powell

Colorado

COLORADO
PLATEAU

Elbert
4399

Blanca
4398

Platte

PLAINS

Llano
Estacado

Red

Arkansas

CENTRAL
PLAINS

Ohio

Mississippi

L. Michigan

L. Huron

Mitchell
2037

Kentucky

Tennessee

OZARK
PLATEAU

OUACHITA MTS

LAURENTIAN
UPLANDS

OTTAWA

L. Ontario

L. Erie

Niagara
Falls

Mt Washington
1917

NORE DAME MTS

ST Lawrence

NOVA SCOTIA

Halifax

BAY OF FUNDY

Cape Breton I.

Cape Sable

Cape Cod

Nantucket I.

Long I.

WASHINGTON, D.C.

Cape Charles

CHESAPEAKE BAY

Cape Hatteras

APPALACHIAN MTS

ALLEGHENY MTS

BLUE RIDGE

PIEDMONT

NORTH

ATLANTIC

HAMILTON

Bermuda I.
(UK)

OCEAN

SARGASSO
SEA

Guadalupe I.

CALIFORNIA PENINSULA

SONORAN DESERT

SIERRA MADRE OCCIDENTAL

Pta. Sta. Eugenio

Gulf of
California

EDWARDS
PLATEAU

Rio Grande

Bolson
de
Mapimi

SIERRA MADRE ORIENTAL

MEXICAN PLATEAU

Pecos

Barros

Mississippi
Delta

Gulf of
Mexico

Everglades

Okeechobee

Cape Sable

Florida Keys

Cape
Canaveral

Strait of Florida

Bahamas Is

NASSAU

Tropic of Cancer

30°

PACIFIC

OCEAN

Cape San Lucas

Marias I.

Cape Corrientes

Revilla
Gigedo I.

Santiago

Citlaltepetl
5700

MEXICO CITY

Popocatepetl
5452

SIERRA DEL SUR

YUCATAN

CAMPECHE
BAY

YUCATAN
PENINSULA

Isthmus of
Tehuantepec

BELMOPAN

Gulf of
Honduras

Yucatan Channel

West
Indies

HAVANA

I. de
Pinos

CUBA

Greater

Windward Passage

Jamaica

KINGSTON

Antilles

Hispaniola

PORT-AU
PRINCE

SANTO
DOMINGO

Puerto
Rico

SAN
JUAN

Puerto Rico Trench

Gulf of
Tehuantepec

GUATEMALA CITY

Isthmus of Panama

TEGUCIGALPA

SAN SALVADOR

-6662

Guatemala Trench

CENTRAL
AMERICA

MANAGUA

L.
Nicaragua

Cape Gracias a Dios

Coco

CARIBBEAN

SEA

Point Gallinas

Cristobal Colon
5775

ANDES

Margarita I.
(Ven.)

Willemstad

Lago de
Maracaibo

Pico Bolivar
5002

CORDILLERA ORIENTAL

ORINOCO LOWLANDS

Meta

Apure

SAN JOSE

PANAMA
CITY

Panama
Canal

Gulf
of
Panama

Gulf
of
Darien

Clipperton I.

Inset map

Puerto
Rico

Virgin Is
(USA)

BASSE TERRE

ANTIGUA
& BARBUDA

ST JOHN'S

Guadeloupe
(FRANCE)

BASSE TERRE

Pointe-a-Pitre

Leeward Islands

Dominica

ROSEAU

Martinique
(Fr.)

FORT-DE-
FRANCE

St Lucia

CASTRIES

BARBADOS

BRIDGETOWN

KINGSTOWN

St Vincent & the
Grenadines

Grenada

ST GEORGE'S

Tobago

Windward Islands

Lesser Antilles

CARIBBEAN
SEA

Clipperton I.

SCALE 1: 21 000 000

SCALE 1: 34 500 000

0   350   700   1050   1400 km

Longitude West of Greenwich

AZIMUTHAL EQUAL AREA PROJECTION

LAMBERT'S EQUIVALENT AZIMUTHAL PROJECTION

Longitude West of Greenwich

SCALE 1 : 34 500 000

0   350   700   1050   1400 km

North America – Climate, Natural Vegetation, Population and Economy

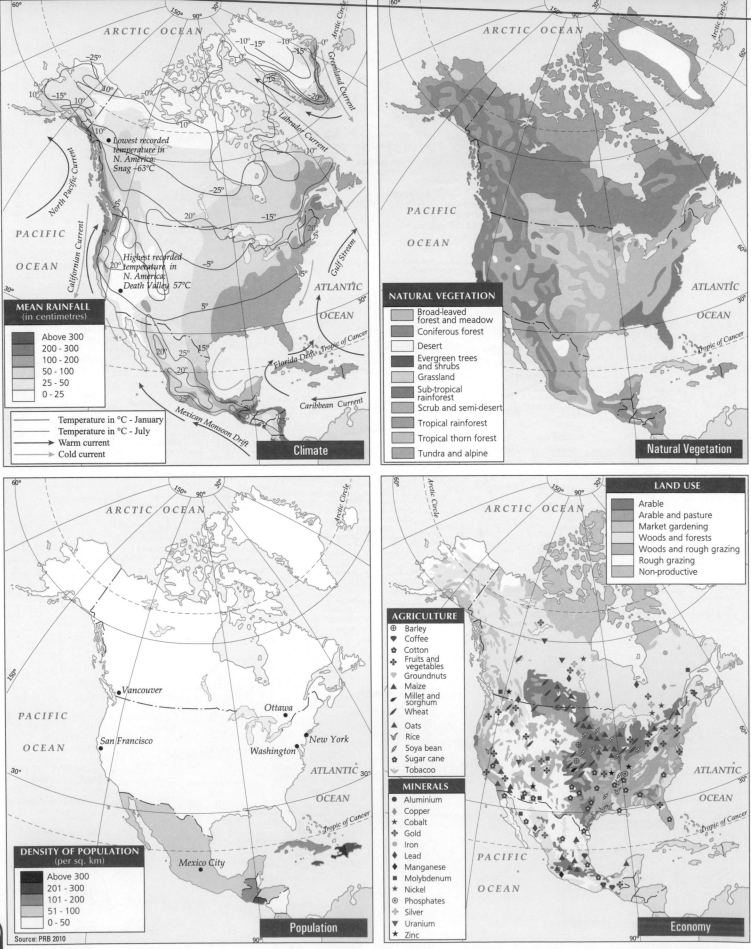

Climate

MEAN RAINFALL
(in centimetres)

- Above 300
- 200 – 300
- 100 – 200
- 50 – 100
- 25 – 50
- 0 – 25

— Temperature in °C – January
— Temperature in °C – July
→ Warm current
→ Cold current

ARCTIC OCEAN
PACIFIC OCEAN
ATLANTIC OCEAN

North Pacific Current
Californian Current
Greenland Current
Labrador Current
Gulf Stream
Florida Drift
Caribbean Current
Mexican Monsoon Drift

Lowest recorded temperature in N. America: Snag –63°C
Highest recorded temperature in N. America: Death Valley 57°C

Tropic of Cancer

Natural Vegetation

NATURAL VEGETATION

- Broad-leaved forest and meadow
- Coniferous forest
- Desert
- Evergreen trees and shrubs
- Grassland
- Sub-tropical rainforest
- Scrub and semi-desert
- Tropical rainforest
- Tropical thorn forest
- Tundra and alpine

ARCTIC OCEAN
PACIFIC OCEAN
ATLANTIC OCEAN
Tropic of Cancer

Population

DENSITY OF POPULATION
(per sq. km)

- Above 300
- 201 – 300
- 101 – 200
- 51 – 100
- 0 – 50

Source: PRB 2010

ARCTIC OCEAN
PACIFIC OCEAN
ATLANTIC OCEAN

Vancouver
Ottawa
San Francisco
New York
Washington
Mexico City

Tropic of Cancer

Economy

LAND USE

- Arable
- Arable and pasture
- Market gardening
- Woods and forests
- Woods and rough grazing
- Rough grazing
- Non-productive

AGRICULTURE

- ⊕ Barley
- ♥ Coffee
- ✿ Cotton
- ✠ Fruits and vegetables
- ♥ Groundnuts
- ▲ Maize
- ⁄ Millet and sorghum
- ⁄ Wheat
- ▲ Oats
- ⴼ Rice
- ⁄ Soya bean
- ✿ Sugar cane
- ✲ Tobacoo

MINERALS

- ● Aluminium
- ◆ Copper
- ★ Cobalt
- ✚ Gold
- ● Iron
- ◆ Lead
- ◆ Manganese
- ■ Molybdenum
- ★ Nickel
- ◉ Phosphates
- ✚ Silver
- ▼ Uranium
- ★ Zinc

ARCTIC OCEAN
PACIFIC OCEAN
ATLANTIC OCEAN
Tropic of Cancer

SCALE 1 : 75 000 000

0   700   1400   2100   2800 km

BONNE PROJECTION

Hawaiian Islands

SCALE 1: 3 800 000

Longitude West of Greenwich

Alaska

SCALE 1: 30 500 000

Longitude West of Greenwich

79

CONICAL ORTHOMORPHIC PROJECTION

SCALE 1: 18 800 000

0   200   400   600   800 km

SCALE 1: 34 500 000

0   350   700   1050   1400 km

Longitude West of Greenwich

LAMBERT EQUAL AREA PROJECTION

LAMBERT EQUAL AREA PROJECTION

Longitude West of Greenwich

81

SCALE 1: 34 500 000

0   350   700   1050   1400 km

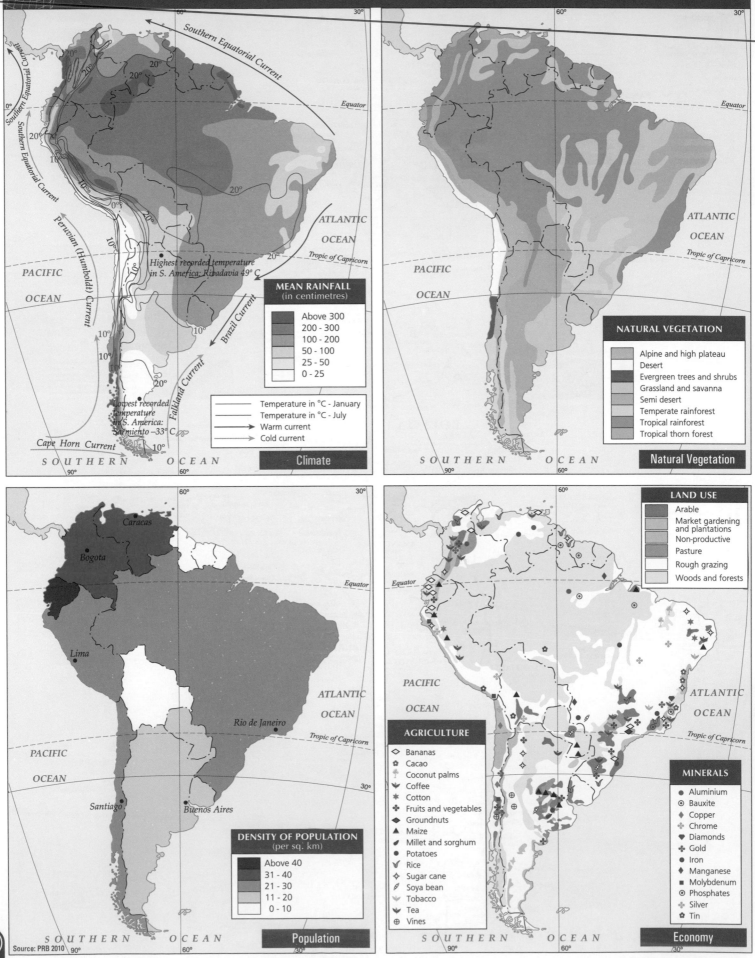

Climate

Southern Equatorial Current

Southern Equatorial Current

Southern Equatorial Current

Peruvian (Humboldt) Current

Brazil Current

Falkland Current

Cape Horn Current

PACIFIC OCEAN

ATLANTIC OCEAN

Equator

Tropic of Capricorn

Highest recorded temperature in S. America: Rivadavia 49° C

Lowest recorded temperature in S. America: Sarmiento –33° C

SOUTHERN OCEAN

MEAN RAINFALL
(in centimetres)

- Above 300
- 200 - 300
- 100 - 200
- 50 - 100
- 25 - 50
- 0 - 25

Temperature in °C - January
Temperature in °C - July
→ Warm current
→ Cold current

Natural Vegetation

PACIFIC OCEAN

ATLANTIC OCEAN

Equator

Tropic of Capricorn

SOUTHERN OCEAN

NATURAL VEGETATION

- Alpine and high plateau
- Desert
- Evergreen trees and shrubs
- Grassland and savanna
- Semi desert
- Temperate rainforest
- Tropical rainforest
- Tropical thorn forest

Population

Caracas
Bogota
Lima
Santiago
Buenos Aires
Rio de Janeiro

PACIFIC OCEAN

ATLANTIC OCEAN

PACIFIC OCEAN

Equator

Tropic of Capricorn

SOUTHERN OCEAN

DENSITY OF POPULATION
(per sq. km)

- Above 40
- 31 - 40
- 21 - 30
- 11 - 20
- 0 - 10

Source: PRB 2010

Economy

PACIFIC OCEAN

ATLANTIC OCEAN

Equator

Tropic of Capricorn

SOUTHERN OCEAN

LAND USE

- Arable
- Market gardening and plantations
- Non-productive
- Pasture
- Rough grazing
- Woods and forests

AGRICULTURE

- ◇ Bananas
- ✿ Cacao
- ⍦ Coconut palms
- ↯ Coffee
- ✳ Cotton
- ♣ Fruits and vegetables
- ◆ Groundnuts
- ▲ Maize
- ◢ Millet and sorghum
- ● Potatoes
- ↯ Rice
- ◇ Sugar cane
- ◎ Soya bean
- ↯ Tobacco
- ↯ Tea
- ⊕ Vines

MINERALS

- ● Aluminium
- ◎ Bauxite
- ◆ Copper
- ✤ Chrome
- ▼ Diamonds
- ✢ Gold
- ● Iron
- ◆ Manganese
- ■ Molybdenum
- ◉ Phosphates
- ✤ Silver
- ✿ Tin

SCALE 1: 66 000 000

0   600   1200   1800   2400 km

LAMBERT AZIMUTHAL EQUAL AREA PROJECTION

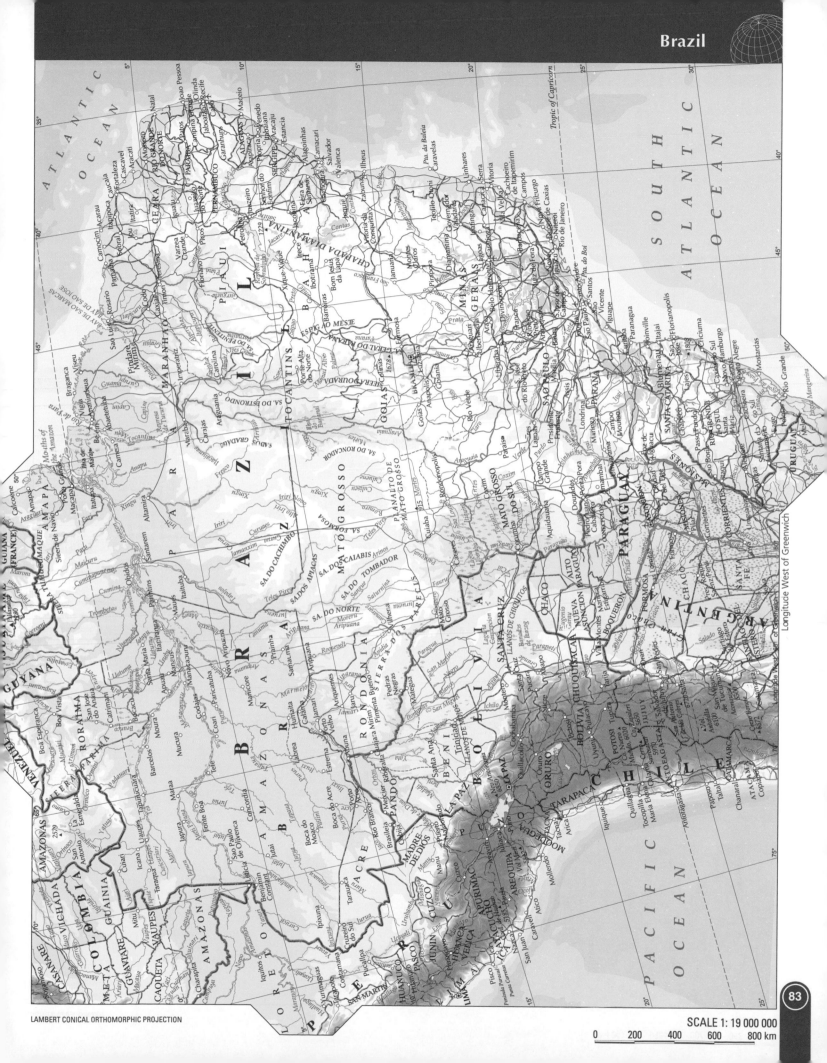

LAMBERT CONICAL ORTHOMORPHIC PROJECTION

SCALE 1: 19 000 000

0   200   400   600   800 km

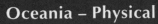
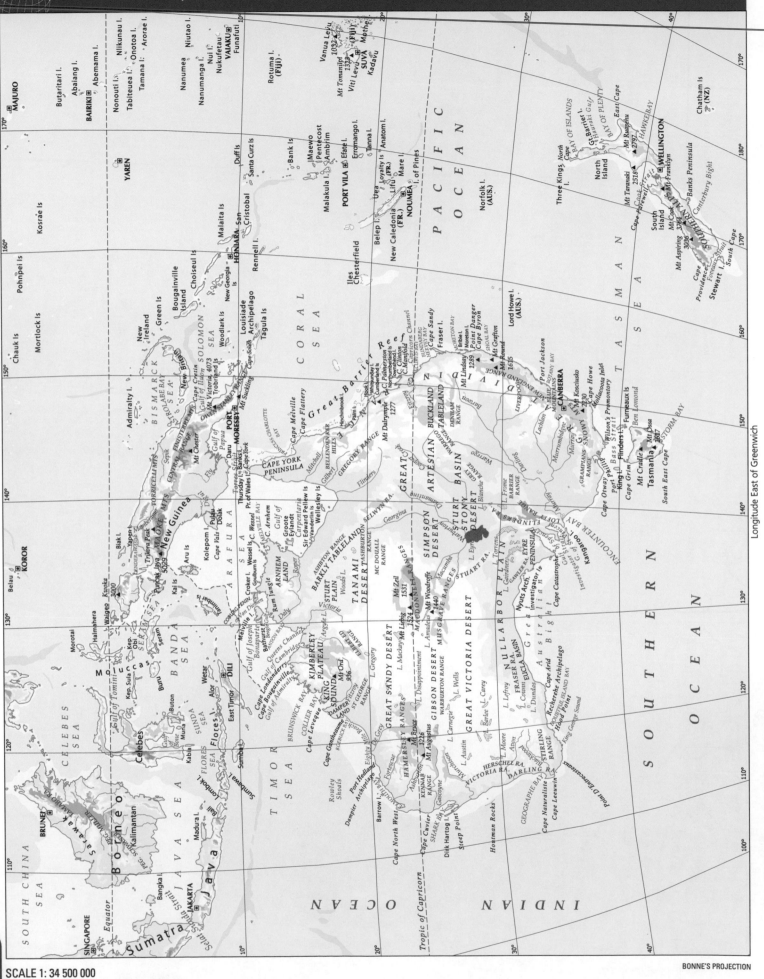

SCALE 1: 34 500 000

0   350   700   1050   1400 km

Longitude East of Greenwich

BONNE'S PROJECTION

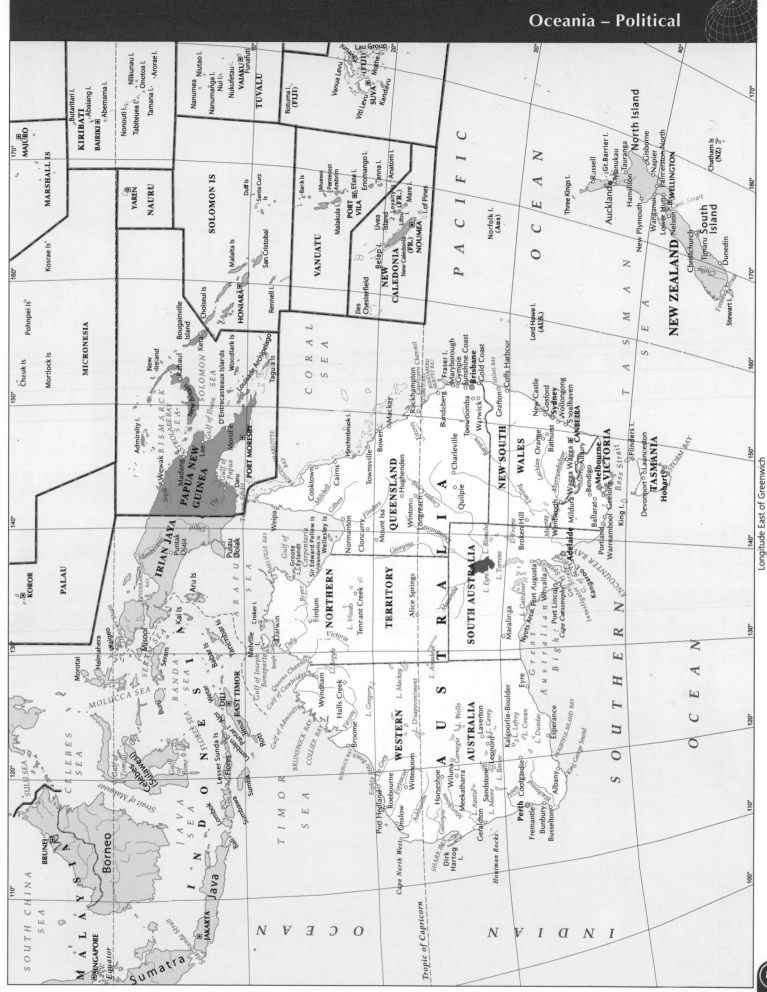

SCALE 1: 34 500 000

0	350	700	1050	1400 km

BONNE'S PROJECTION

Longitude East of Greenwich

85

Oceania – Climate, Natural Vegetation, Population and Economy

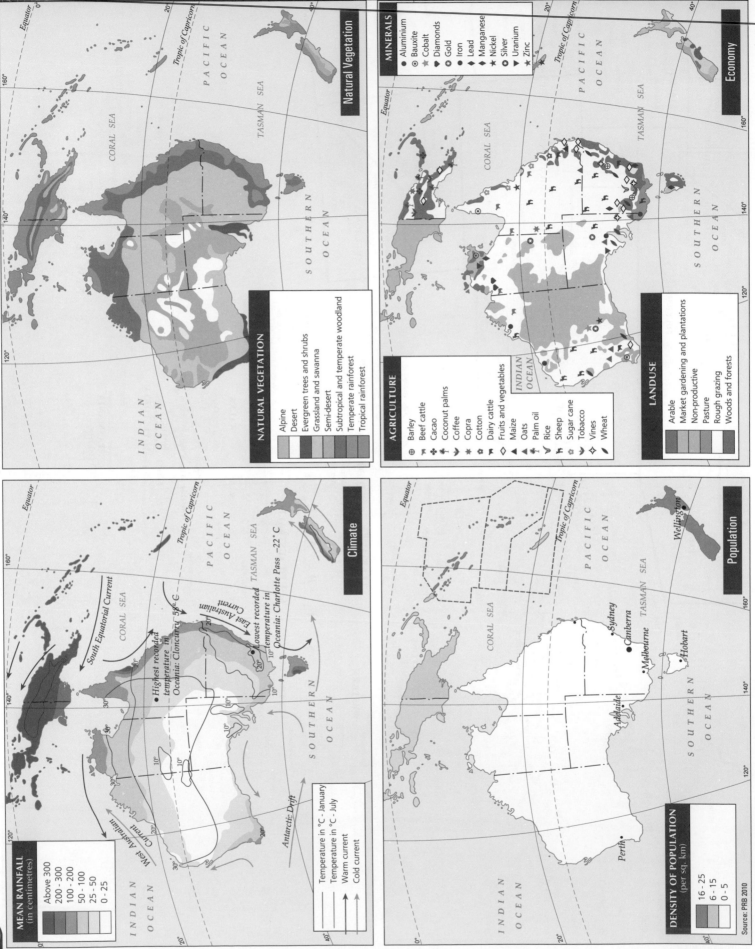

Natural Vegetation

NATURAL VEGETATION

- Alpine
- Desert
- Evergreen trees and shrubs
- Grassland and savanna
- Semi-desert
- Subtropical and temperate woodland
- Temperate rainforest
- Tropical rainforest

Economy

MINERALS

- ⊕ Aluminium
- ⊙ Bauxite
- ★ Cobalt
- ◆ Diamonds
- ▶ Gold
- ✳ Iron
- ✿ Lead
- ◆ Manganese
- ★ Nickel
- ◇ Silver
- ▼ Uranium
- ◆ Zinc

AGRICULTURE

- ⊕ Barley
- ⚒ Beef cattle
- ❀ Cacao
- ✲ Coconut palms
- ➤ Coffee
- ✳ Copra
- ✿ Cotton
- ✦ Dairy cattle
- ◇ Fruits and vegetables
- ◀ Maize
- ◀ Oats
- ✿ Palm oil
- ✈ Rice
- ✿ Sheep
- ➤ Sugar cane
- ➢ Tobacco
- ◇ Vines
- ◣ Wheat

LANDUSE

- Arable
- Market gardening and plantations
- Non-productive
- Pasture
- Rough grazing
- Woods and forests

Climate

Highest recorded temperature in Oceania: Cloncurry 53° C

Lowest recorded temperature in Oceania: Charlotte Pass –22° C

South Equatorial Current

East Australian Current

West Australian Current

Antarctic Drift

MEAN RAINFALL
(in centimetres)

- Above 300
- 200 - 300
- 100 - 200
- 50 - 100
- 25 - 50
- 0 - 25

— Temperature in °C - January
— Temperature in °C - July
→ Warm current
→ Cold current

Population

- Wellington
- Sydney
- Canberra
- Melbourne
- Hobart
- Adelaide
- Perth

DENSITY OF POPULATION
(per sq. km)

- 16 - 25
- 6 - 15
- 0 - 5

Source: PRB 2010

SCALE 1: 62 000 000

0   600   1200   1800   2400 km

BONNE PROJECTION

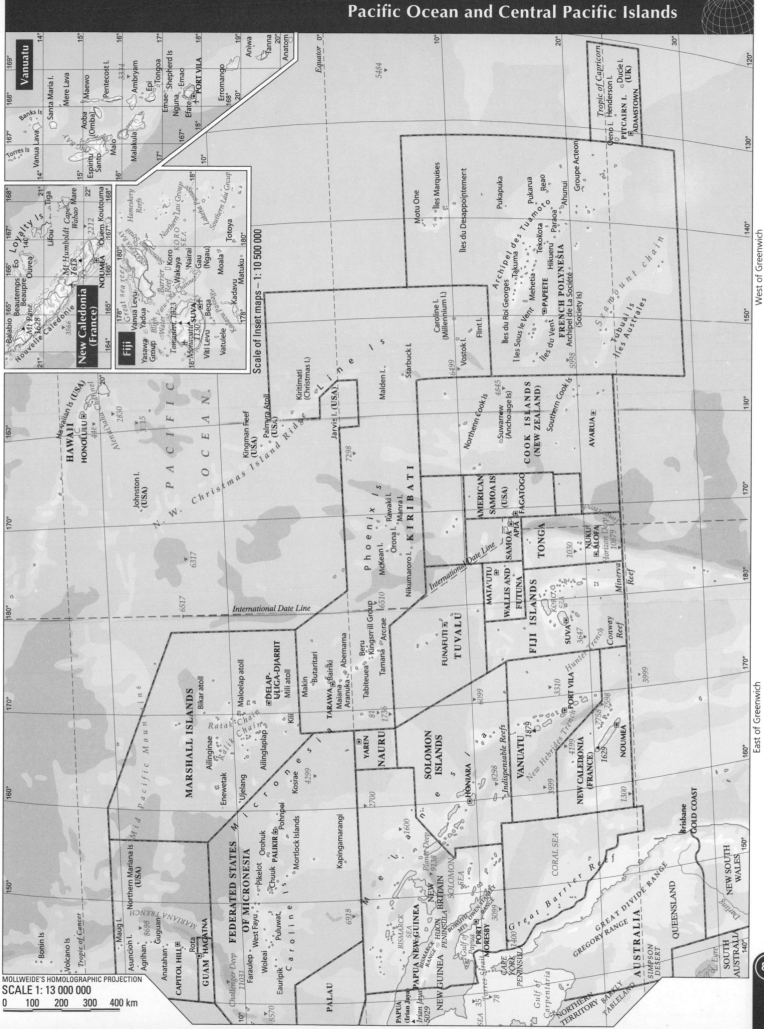

Vanuatu

Santa Maria I.
Mere Lava
Vanua Lava
Banks Is
Torres Is
Espiritu Santo
Malo
Malakula
Aoba (Omba)
Maewo
Pentecost I.
Ambrym
Epi
Emae Shepherd Is
Nguna Emao
Efate
PORT VILA
Erromango
Aniwa
Tanna
Tongoa
Anatom

New Caledonia (France)
Nouvelle Calédonie

Balabio
Beautemps
Beaupré
Mt. Panié
1628
Mt. Humboldt Cape
1618
3566
2212
Ouvéa
Lifou
Tiga
Maré
Wabao
Loyalty Is
Eo
Ouem Koutouma
NOUMÉA

Fiji

Hameskery Reefs
Yasawa Group
Yadua
Vanua Levu
Viti Levu
SUVA
Beqa
Vatulele
Kadavu
Great sea reef
Northern Lau Group
Southern Lau Group
KORO SEA
Koro
Wakaya
Nairai
Gau (Ngau)
Moala
Matuku
Totoya
Wailevu
Ovalau
Nanuya

Scale of Inset maps – 1 : 10 500 000

Equator

5484

Tropic of Capricorn
Oeno I.
Henderson I.
Ducie I.
PITCAIRN I. (UK)
ADAMSTOWN

Motu One
Îles Marquises
Îles du Désappointement
Pukapuka
Pukarua
Takume
Reao
Tekokota
Hikueru
Paraoa
Ahunui
Groupe Acteon
Archipel des Tuamotu
Caroline I. (Millennium I.)
Flint I.
Vostok I.
Îles du Roi Georges
Mehetia
Îles Sous le Vent
PAPEETE
Îles du Vent
French Polynesia
Archipel de la Société (Society Is)
Tubuai Is
Îles Australes
6499
5998
Seamount chain

Líne Is
Kiritimati (Christmas I.)
Malden I.
Starbuck I.
6499

Palmyra Atoll (USA)
Kingman Reef (USA)
Jarvis I. (USA)
7298

HAWAII
HONOLULU
Hawaiian Is (USA)
Kauai Channel
2830
3515
Alenuihaha Channel

Johnston I. (USA)

N. W. PACIFIC OCEAN
Christmas Island Ridge

Suwarrow (Anchorage Is)
4845
Northern Cook Is
COOK ISLANDS (NEW ZEALAND)
AVARUA
Southern Cook Is

AMERICAN SAMOA IS (USA)
FAGATOGO
SAMOA
APIA
Phoenix Is
McKean I.
Rawaki I.
Orona I.
Manra I.
Nikumaroro I.
KIRIBATI
TONGA
NUKU' ALOFA
1030
Horizon Deep 10879
International Date Line
MATA'UTU
WALLIS AND FUTUNA
Minerva Reef
TUVALU
FUNAFUTI
FIJI ISLANDS
SUVA
Koro Sea
3647
Conway Reef
Hunter Trench
3999

6317
6517
16510
International Date Line
Tabiteuea Kingsmill Group
Beru
Tamaná Arorae
Onotoa
81
1736

MARSHALL ISLANDS
Bikar atoll
Maloelap atoll
DELAP-ULIGA-DJARRIT
Mili atoll
Kili
Ratak Chain
Raluk Chain
Ailinginae
Enewetak
Ujelang
Ailinglaplap
TARAWA
Bairiki
Maiana
Aranuka
Abemama
Butaritari
Makin

NAURU
YAREN
2700
4299
Kosrae
Pohnpei
Mid Pacific Mountains

SOLOMON ISLANDS
HONIARA
8298
Indispensable Reefs
6099
VANUATU
1879
PORT VILA
3310
4199
NEW CALEDONIA (FRANCE)
1629
2758
NOUMÉA
7598
3999
1300

FEDERATED STATES OF MICRONESIA
PALIKIR
Chuuk
Orohuk
Pikelot
Mortlock Islands
Kapingamarangi
Micronesia

Northern Mariana Is (USA)
Maug I.
Asunción I.
Agrihan
Guguan
Anatahan
Rota
CAPITOL HILL
GUAM
HAGÅTÑA
Tropic of Cancer
MARIANA TRENCH
8698
11031
Challenger Deep

Bonin Is
Volcano Is
Faraulep
West Fayu
Puluwat
Eauripik
Woleai
Caroline Is
6918
PALAU
8570
5029
PAPUA (Irian Jaya)
Irian Jaya

BISMARCK SEA
NEW GUINEA
NEW BRITAIN
PAPUA NEW GUINEA
HUON PENINSULA
BISMARCK RANGE
PORT MORESBY
Gulf of Papua
CORAL SEA
SOLOMON SEA
9138
Planet Deep
1600
Melanesia
New Hebrides Trench

Brisbane
GOLD COAST
Great Barrier Reef
CORAL SEA
AUSTRALIA
QUEENSLAND
GREAT DIVIDE RANGE
GREGORY RANGE
NEW SOUTH WALES
CAPE YORK PENINSULA
Gulf of Carpentaria
NORTHERN TERRITORY
BARKLY TABLELAND
SIMPSON DESERT
SOUTH AUSTRALIA
Darling

West of Greenwich

East of Greenwich

MOLLWEIDE'S HOMOLOGRAPHIC PROJECTION
SCALE 1: 13 000 000
0   100   200   300   400 km

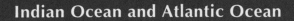

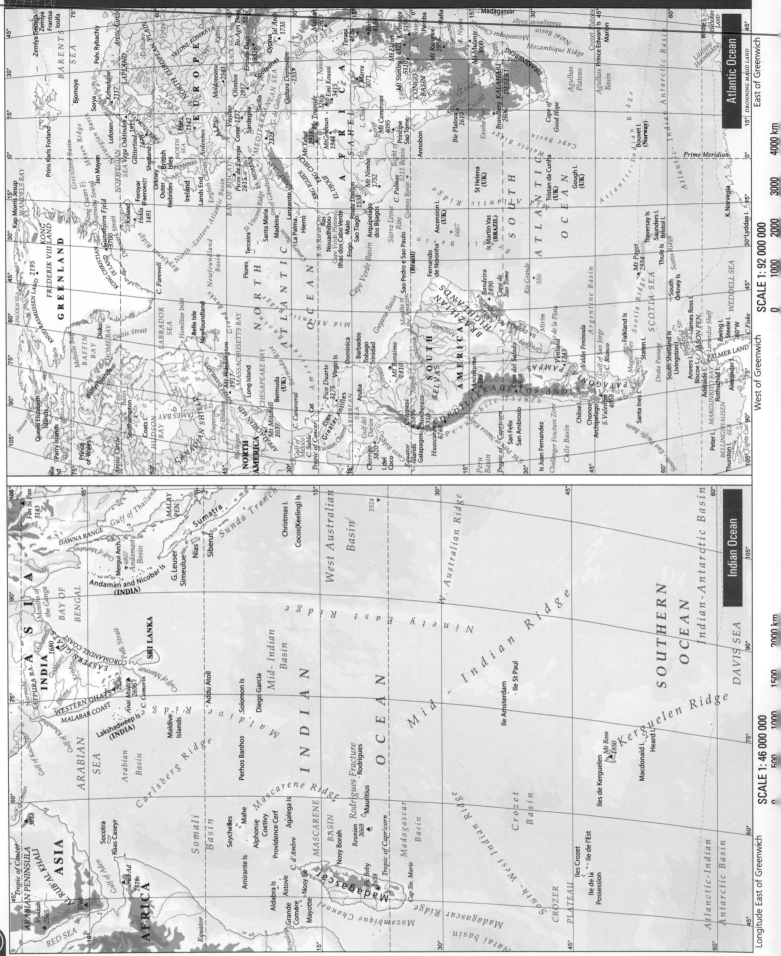

Atlantic Ocean

SCALE 1:92 000 000

West of Greenwich   East of Greenwich

0   1000   2000   3000   4000 km

Prime Meridian

Indian Ocean

SCALE 1:46 000 000

0   500   1000   1500   2000 km

Longitude East of Greenwich

88

GALL'S STEREOGRAPHIC PROJECTION

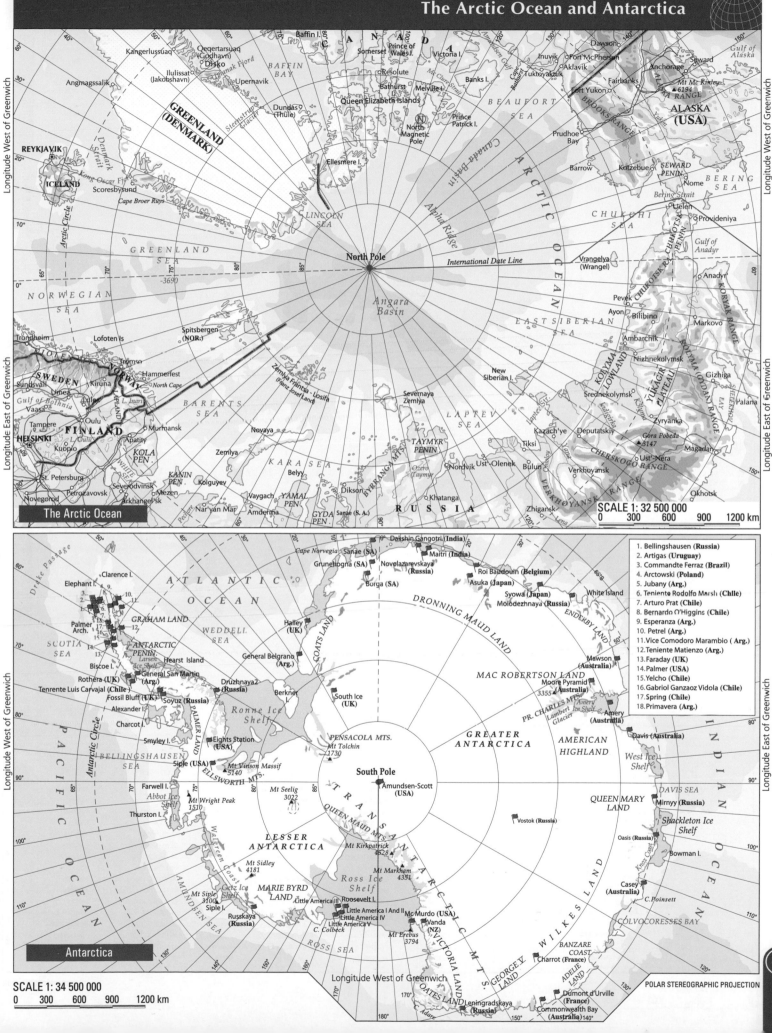

The Arctic Ocean

SCALE 1: 32 500 000

0   300   600   900   1200 km

Antarctica

1. Bellingshausen (**Russia**)
2. Artigas (**Uruguay**)
3. Commandte Ferraz (**Brazil**)
4. Arctowski (**Poland**)
5. Jubany (**Arg.**)
6. Teniente Rodolfo Marsh (**Chile**)
7. Arturo Prat (**Chile**)
8. Bernardo O'Higgins (**Chile**)
9. Esperanza (**Arg.**)
10. Petrel (**Arg.**)
11. Vice Comodoro Marambio (**Arg.**)
12. Teniente Matienzo (**Arg.**)
13. Faraday (**UK**)
14. Palmer (**USA**)
15. Yelcho (**Chile**)
16. Gabriol Ganzaoz Vidola (**Chile**)
17. Spring (**Chile**)
18. Primavera (**Arg.**)

SCALE 1: 34 500 000

0   300   600   900   1200 km

POLAR STEREOGRAPHIC PROJECTION

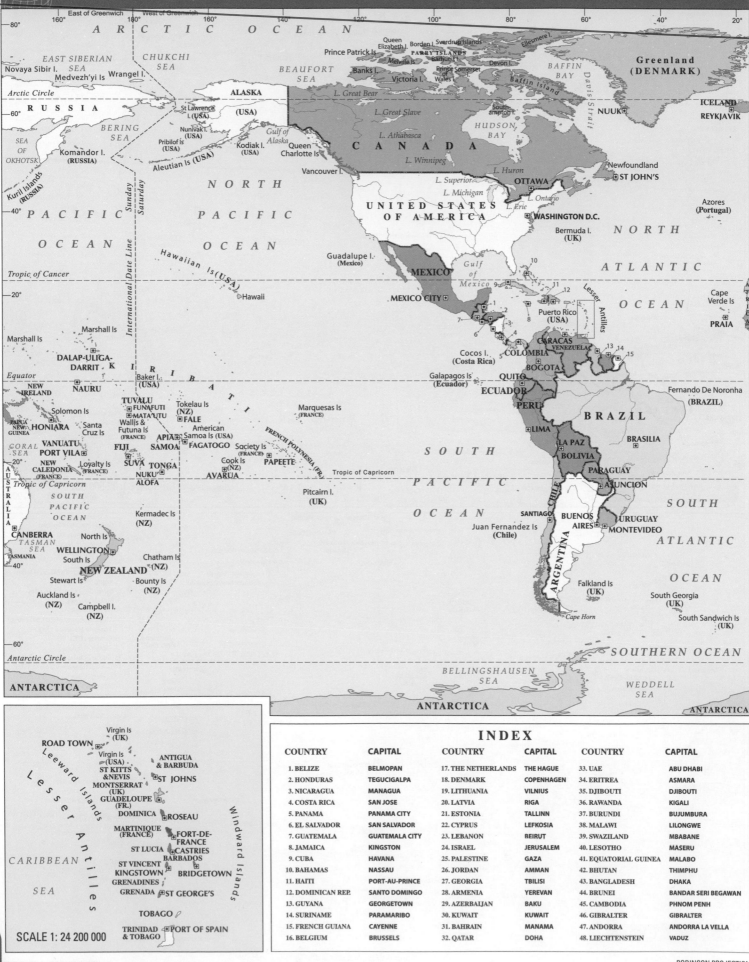

SCALE 1: 24 200 000

SCALE 1: 121 000 000

0   1500   3000   4500   6000 km

ROBINSON PROJECTION

INDEX

COUNTRY	CAPITAL	COUNTRY	CAPITAL	COUNTRY	CAPITAL
1. BELIZE	BELMOPAN	17. THE NETHERLANDS	THE HAGUE	33. UAE	ABU DHABI
2. HONDURAS	TEGUCIGALPA	18. DENMARK	COPENHAGEN	34. ERITREA	ASMARA
3. NICARAGUA	MANAGUA	19. LITHUANIA	VILNIUS	35. DJIBOUTI	DJIBOUTI
4. COSTA RICA	SAN JOSE	20. LATVIA	RIGA	36. RAWANDA	KIGALI
5. PANAMA	PANAMA CITY	21. ESTONIA	TALLINN	37. BURUNDI	BUJUMBURA
6. EL SALVADOR	SAN SALVADOR	22. CYPRUS	LEFKOSIA	38. MALAWI	LILONGWE
7. GUATEMALA	GUATEMALA CITY	23. LEBANON	BEIRUT	39. SWAZILAND	MBABANE
8. JAMAICA	KINGSTON	24. ISRAEL	JERUSALEM	40. LESOTHO	MASERU
9. CUBA	HAVANA	25. PALESTINE	GAZA	41. EQUATORIAL GUINEA	MALABO
10. BAHAMAS	NASSAU	26. JORDAN	AMMAN	42. BHUTAN	THIMPHU
11. HAITI	PORT-AU-PRINCE	27. GEORGIA	TBILISI	43. BANGLADESH	DHAKA
12. DOMINICAN REP.	SANTO DOMINGO	28. ARMENIA	YEREVAN	44. BRUNEI	BANDAR SERI BEGAWAN
13. GUYANA	GEORGETOWN	29. AZERBAIJAN	BAKU	45. CAMBODIA	PHNOM PENH
14. SURINAME	PARAMARIBO	30. KUWAIT	KUWAIT	46. GIBRALTER	GIBRALTER
15. FRENCH GUIANA	CAYENNE	31. BAHRAIN	MANAMA	47. ANDORRA	ANDORRA LA VELLA
16. BELGIUM	BRUSSELS	32. QATAR	DOHA	48. LIECHTENSTEIN	VADUZ

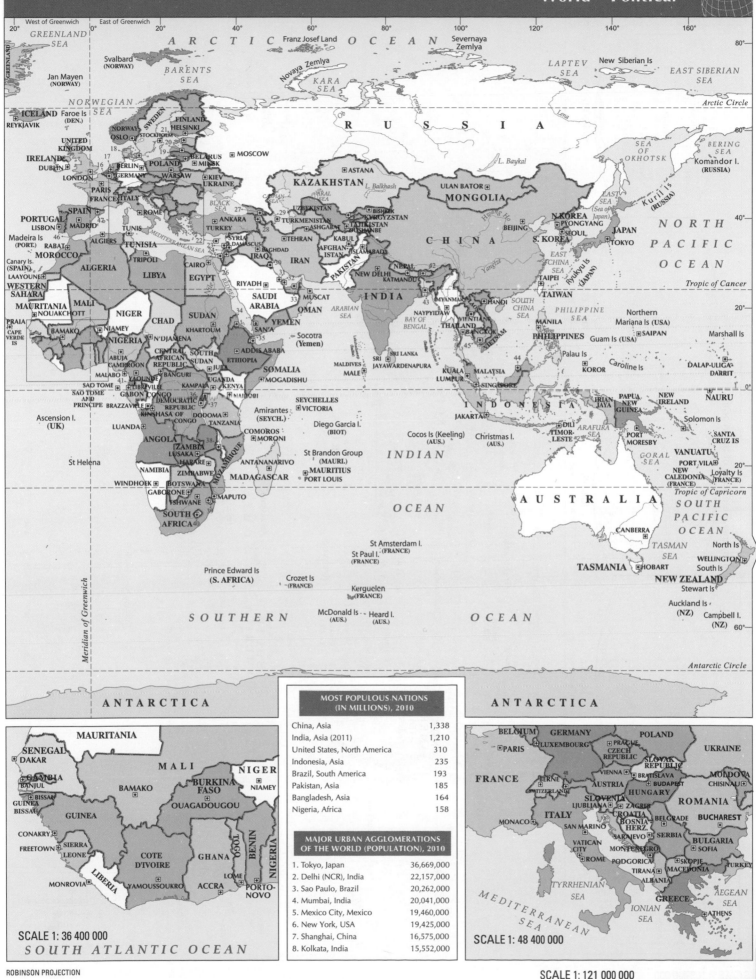

ROBINSON PROJECTION

MOST POPULOUS NATIONS (IN MILLIONS), 2010

China, Asia	1,338
India, Asia (2011)	1,210
United States, North America	310
Indonesia, Asia	235
Brazil, South America	193
Pakistan, Asia	185
Bangladesh, Asia	164
Nigeria, Africa	158

MAJOR URBAN AGGLOMERATIONS OF THE WORLD (POPULATION), 2010

1.	Tokyo, Japan	36,669,000
2.	Delhi (NCR), India	22,157,000
3.	Sao Paulo, Brazil	20,262,000
4.	Mumbai, India	20,041,000
5.	Mexico City, Mexico	19,460,000
6.	New York, USA	19,425,000
7.	Shanghai, China	16,575,000
8.	Kolkata, India	15,552,000

SCALE 1: 36 400 000

SCALE 1: 48 400 000

SCALE 1: 121 000 000

0   1500   3000   4500   6000 km

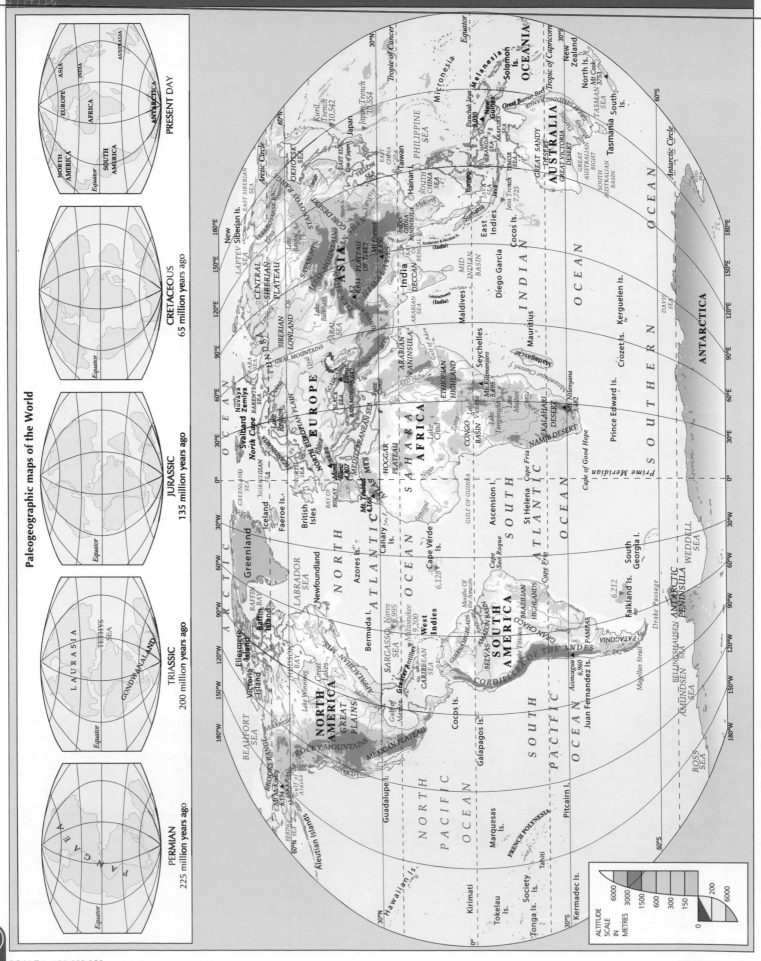

Paleogeographic maps of the World

PRESENT DAY

CRETACEOUS
65 million years ago

JURASSIC
135 million years ago

TRIASSIC
200 million years ago

PERMIAN
225 million years ago

ROBINSON PROJECTION

SCALE 1: 163 000 000

0   1500   3000   4500   6000 km

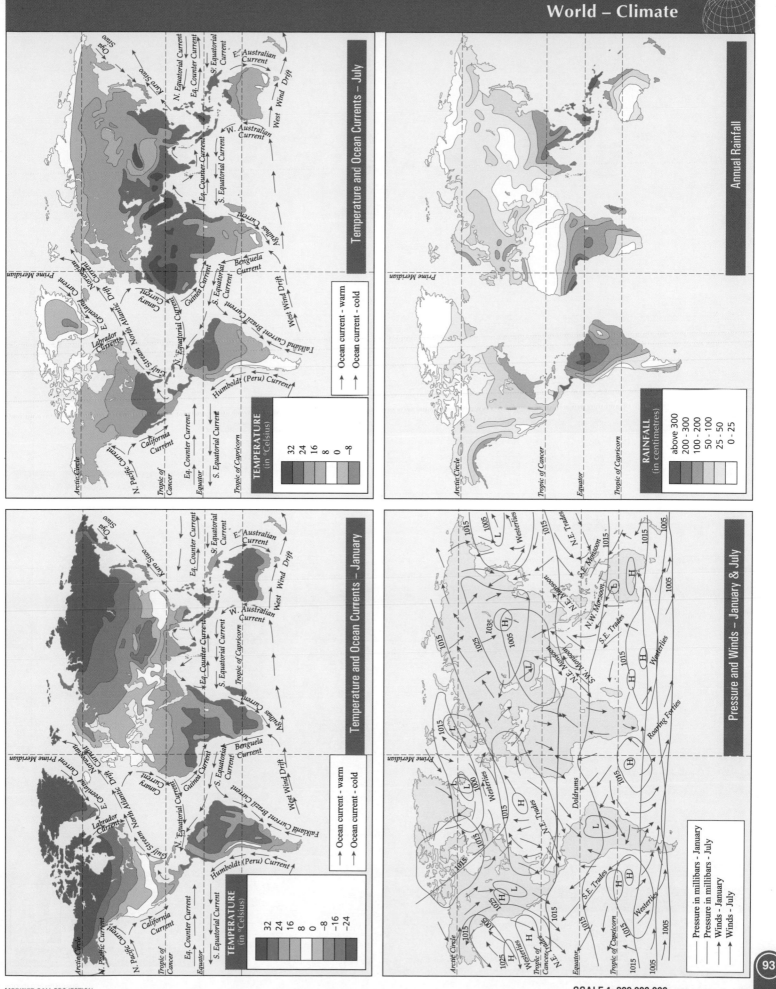

Temperature and Ocean Currents – July

Qya Siwo
Kuro Siwo
N. Equatorial Current
Eq. Counter Current
S. Equatorial Current
E. Australian Current
West Wind Drift
W. Australian Current
Agulhas Current
Benguela Current
S. Equatorial Current
Guinea Current
N. Equatorial Current
West Wind Drift
Norwegian Current
Greenland Current
E. Greenland Drift
Canary Current
Gulf Stream
N. North Atlantic Current
Brazil Current
Falkland Current
Labrador Current
Humboldt (Peru) Current
S. Equatorial Current
Eq. Counter Current
California Current
N. Pacific Current
Prime Meridian
Arctic Circle
Tropic of Cancer
Equator
Tropic of Capricorn

→ Ocean current - warm
→ Ocean current - cold

TEMPERATURE (in °Celsius)
32 24 16 8 0 −8

Annual Rainfall

Prime Meridian
Arctic Circle
Tropic of Cancer
Equator
Tropic of Capricorn

RAINFALL (in centimetres)
above 300
200 - 300
100 - 200
50 - 100
25 - 50
0 - 25

Temperature and Ocean Currents – January

Qya Siwo
Kuro Siwo
N. Pacific Current
Eq. Counter Current
S. Equatorial Current
E. Australian Current
West Wind Drift
W. Australian Current
Agulhas Current
Benguela Current
S. Equatorial Current
Guinea Current
N. Equatorial Current
West Wind Drift
Eq. Counter Current
Norwegian Current
Greenland Current
E. Greenland Drift
Canary Current
Gulf Stream
N. North Atlantic Current
Brazil Current
Falkland Current
Labrador Current
Humboldt (Peru) Current
S. Equatorial Current
Eq. Counter Current
California Current
N. Pacific Current
Prime Meridian
Arctic Circle
Tropic of Cancer
Equator
Tropic of Capricorn

→ Ocean current - warm
→ Ocean current - cold

TEMPERATURE (in °Celsius)
32 24 16 8 0 −8 −16 −24

Pressure and Winds – January & July

1015 1005 1015 1015 1005
1015 1025 1035 1005
L H H H
E
N.E. Trades
N.E. Monsoon
N.W. Monsoon
N.E. Monsoon
S.W. Monsoon
S.E. Trades
Westerlies
Roaring Forties
Doldrums
N.E. Trades
S.E. Trades
Westerlies
Westerlies
Westerlies
N.E.
H H H L
1000 1015 1015 1025 1015 1005
Prime Meridian
Arctic Circle
Tropic of Cancer
Equator
Tropic of Capricorn
1005 1015 1015 1005

— Pressure in millibars - January
— Pressure in millibars - July
→ Winds - January
→ Winds - July

93

SCALE 1: 308 000 000
0   3000   6000   9000   12000 km

World – Climatic Regions and Water Resources

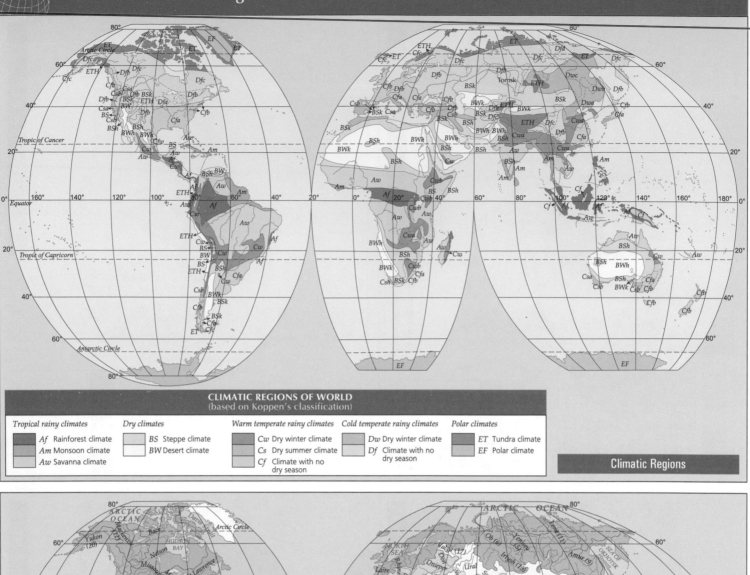

CLIMATIC REGIONS OF WORLD
(based on Koppen's classification)

Tropical rainy climates
- **Af** Rainforest climate
- **Am** Monsoon climate
- **Aw** Savanna climate

Dry climates
- **BS** Steppe climate
- **BW** Desert climate

Warm temperate rainy climates
- **Cw** Dry winter climate
- **Cs** Dry summer climate
- **Cf** Climate with no dry season

Cold temperate rainy climates
- **Dw** Dry winter climate
- **Df** Climate with no dry season

Polar climates
- **ET** Tundra climate
- **EF** Polar climate

Climatic Regions

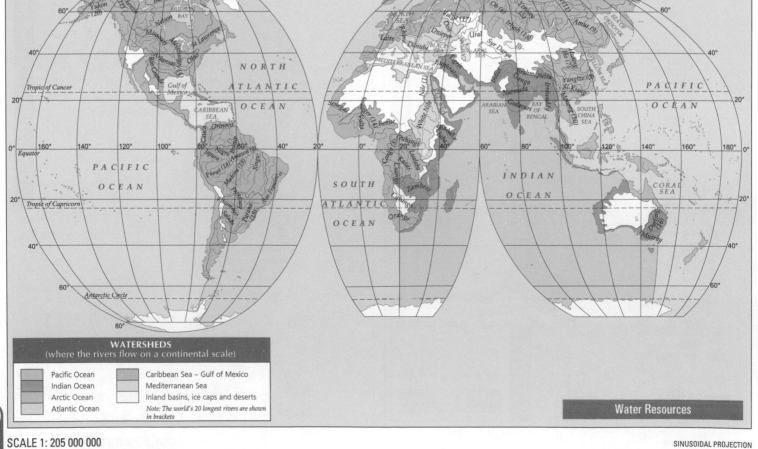

WATERSHEDS
(where the rivers flow on a continental scale)

- Pacific Ocean
- Indian Ocean
- Arctic Ocean
- Atlantic Ocean
- Caribbean Sea – Gulf of Mexico
- Mediterranean Sea
- Inland basins, ice caps and deserts

Note: The world's 20 longest rivers are shown in brackets

Water Resources

SCALE 1: 205 000 000

0   2000   4000   6000   8000 km

SINUSOIDAL PROJECTION

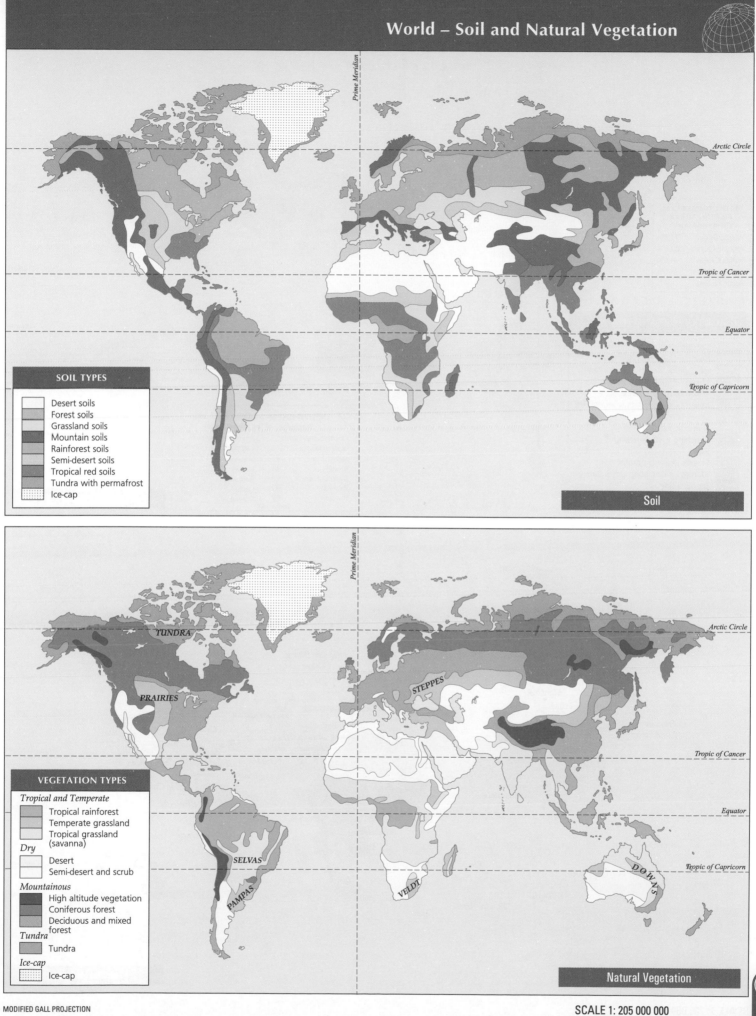

SOIL TYPES

Desert soils
Forest soils
Grassland soils
Mountain soils
Rainforest soils
Semi-desert soils
Tropical red soils
Tundra with permafrost
Ice-cap

Soil

Prime Meridian

Arctic Circle

Tropic of Cancer

Equator

Tropic of Capricorn

TUNDRA

PRAIRIES

STEPPES

SELVAS

PAMPAS

VELDT

DOWNS

VEGETATION TYPES

Tropical and Temperate
Tropical rainforest
Temperate grassland
Tropical grassland (savanna)
Dry
Desert
Semi-desert and scrub
Mountainous
High altitude vegetation
Coniferous forest
Deciduous and mixed forest
Tundra
Tundra
Ice-cap
Ice-cap

Natural Vegetation

MODIFIED GALL PROJECTION

SCALE 1: 205 000 000

0   2000   4000   6000   8000 km

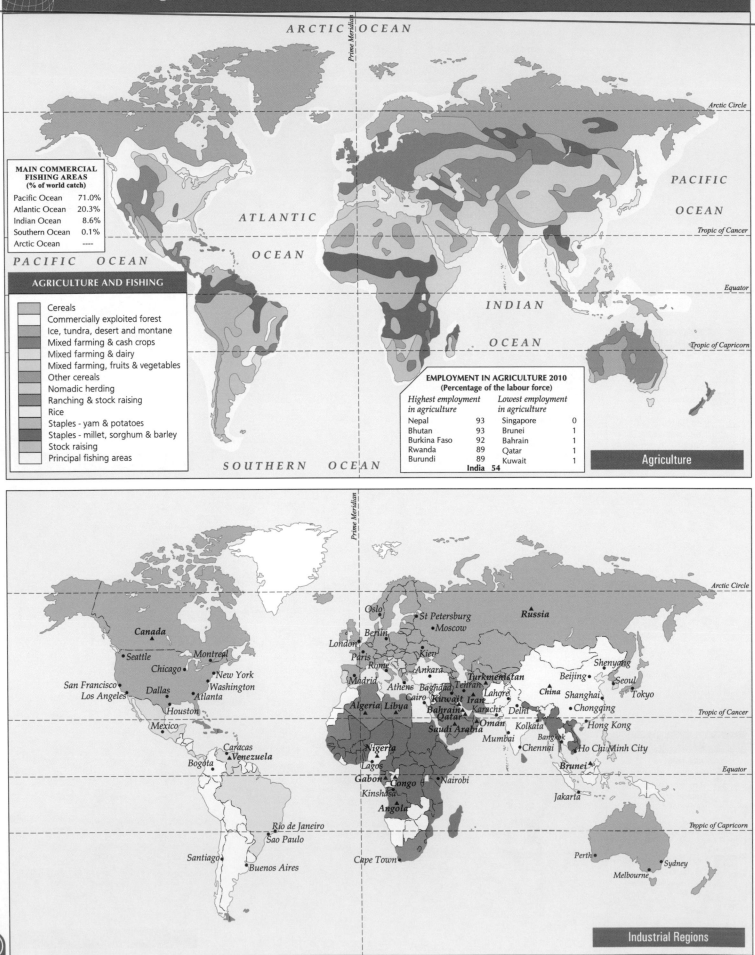

ARCTIC OCEAN

PACIFIC OCEAN

ATLANTIC OCEAN

PACIFIC OCEAN

INDIAN OCEAN

SOUTHERN OCEAN

Arctic Circle

Tropic of Cancer

Equator

Tropic of Capricorn

MAIN COMMERCIAL FISHING AREAS
(% of world catch)

Pacific Ocean	71.0%
Atlantic Ocean	20.3%
Indian Ocean	8.6%
Southern Ocean	0.1%
Arctic Ocean	----

AGRICULTURE AND FISHING

- Cereals
- Commercially exploited forest
- Ice, tundra, desert and montane
- Mixed farming & cash crops
- Mixed farming & dairy
- Mixed farming, fruits & vegetables
- Other cereals
- Nomadic herding
- Ranching & stock raising
- Rice
- Staples - yam & potatoes
- Staples - millet, sorghum & barley
- Stock raising
- Principal fishing areas

EMPLOYMENT IN AGRICULTURE 2010
(Percentage of the labour force)

Highest employment in agriculture		Lowest employment in agriculture	
Nepal	93	Singapore	0
Bhutan	93	Brunei	1
Burkina Faso	92	Bahrain	1
Rwanda	89	Qatar	1
Burundi	89	Kuwait	1
India	54		

Agriculture

Prime Meridian

Arctic Circle

Tropic of Cancer

Equator

Tropic of Capricorn

Canada
Seattle
Chicago
Montreal
San Francisco
Dallas
Los Angeles
Atlanta
New York
Washington
Houston
Mexico
Caracas
Bogotá
Venezuela
Rio de Janeiro
São Paulo
Santiago
Buenos Aires

Oslo
St Petersburg
Moscow
Russia
Berlin
London
Paris
Kiev
Rome
Ankara
Madrid
Athens
Baghdad Tehran
Cairo
Algeria
Libya
Kuwait Iran
Bahrain
Qatar
Saudi Arabia
Nigeria
Lagos
Gabon
Congo
Kinshasa
Angola
Cape Town

Turkmenistan
Lahore
Karachi
Oman
Nairobi

Shenyang
Beijing
Seoul
China
Shanghai
Tokyo
Delhi
Chongqing
Kolkata
Hong Kong
Mumbai
Bangkok
Chennai
Ho Chi Minh City
Brunei
Jakarta
Perth
Sydney
Melbourne

Industrial Regions

SCALE 1: 205 000 000

0   2000   4000   6000   8000 km

MODIFIED GALL PROJECTION

World – Minerals, Mineral Fuels, Trade and Economic Development

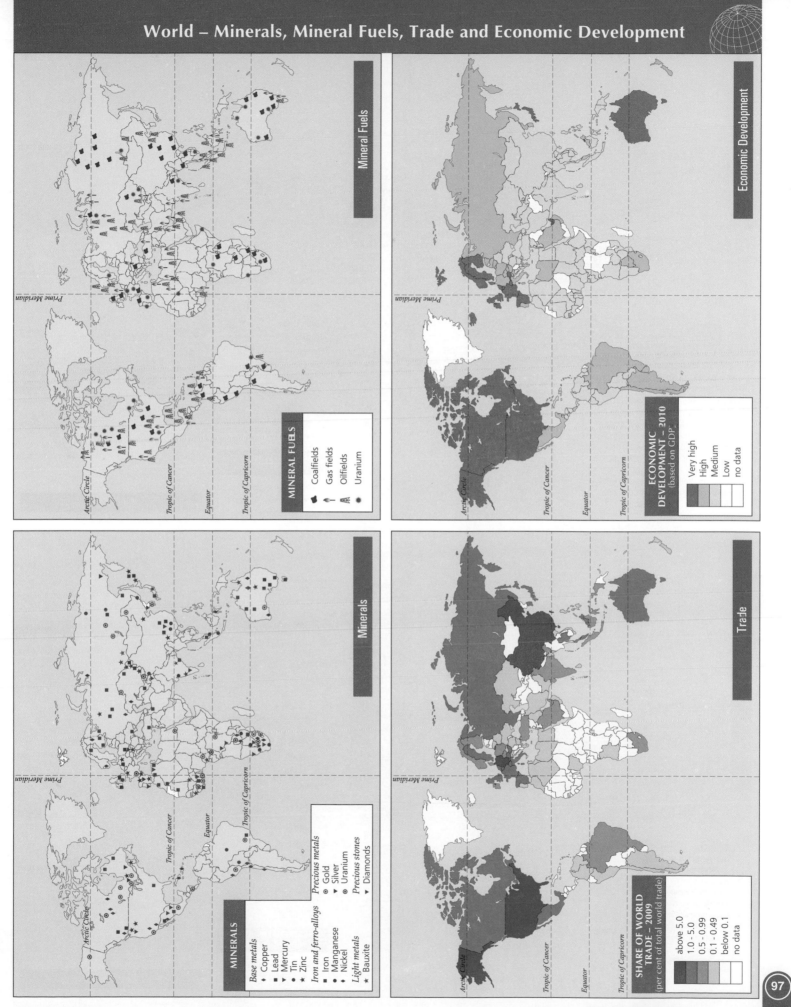

Mineral Fuels

MINERAL FUELS
- Coalfields
- Gas fields
- Oilfields
- Uranium

Economic Development

ECONOMIC DEVELOPMENT – 2010
(based on GDP)
- Very high
- High
- Medium
- Low
- no data

Arctic Circle
Tropic of Cancer
Equator
Tropic of Capricorn
Prime Meridian

Minerals

MINERALS

Base metals
- Copper
- Lead
- Mercury
- Tin
- Zinc

Iron and ferro-alloys
- Iron
- Manganese
- Nickel

Light metals
- Bauxite

Precious metals
- Gold
- Silver
- Uranium

Precious stones
- Diamonds

Trade

SHARE OF WORLD TRADE – 2009
(per cent of total world trade)
- above 5.0
- 1.0 – 5.0
- 0.5 – 0.99
- 0.1 – 0.49
- below 0.1
- no data

MODIFIED GALL PROJECTION

SCALE 1: 308 000 000

0   3000   6000   9000   1200 km

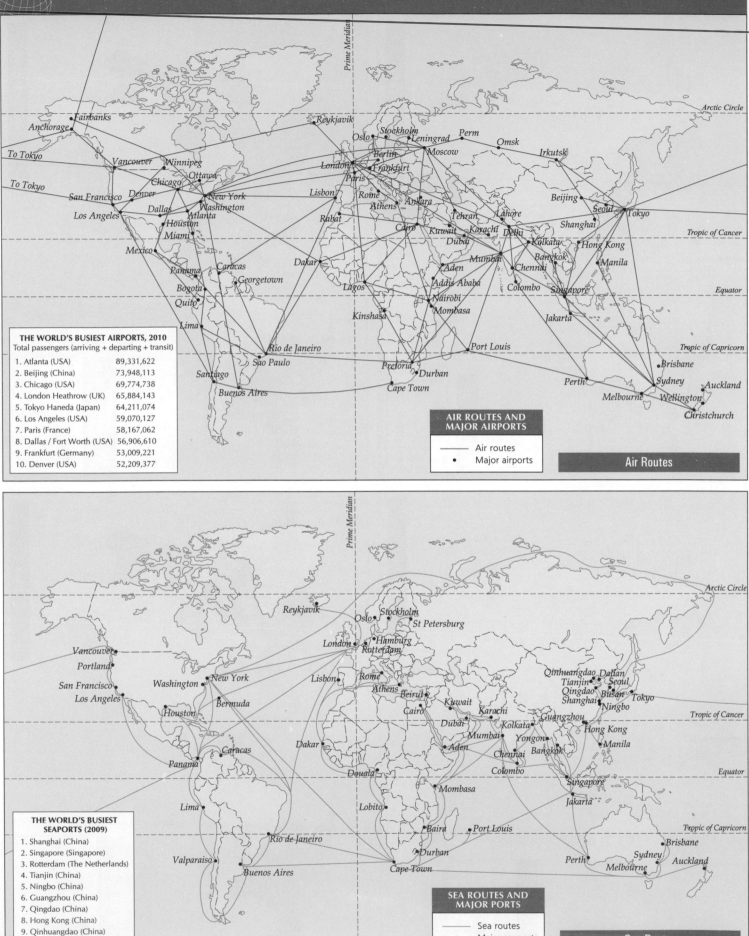

THE WORLD'S BUSIEST AIRPORTS, 2010
Total passengers (arriving + departing + transit)

1. Atlanta (USA)	89,331,622
2. Beijing (China)	73,948,113
3. Chicago (USA)	69,774,738
4. London Heathrow (UK)	65,884,143
5. Tokyo Haneda (Japan)	64,211,074
6. Los Angeles (USA)	59,070,127
7. Paris (France)	58,167,062
8. Dallas / Fort Worth (USA)	56,906,610
9. Frankfurt (Germany)	53,009,221
10. Denver (USA)	52,209,377

AIR ROUTES AND MAJOR AIRPORTS

—— Air routes

• Major airports

Air Routes

THE WORLD'S BUSIEST SEAPORTS (2009)

1. Shanghai (China)
2. Singapore (Singapore)
3. Rotterdam (The Netherlands)
4. Tianjin (China)
5. Ningbo (China)
6. Guangzhou (China)
7. Qingdao (China)
8. Hong Kong (China)
9. Qinhuangdao (China)
10. Busan (South Korea)

SEA ROUTES AND MAJOR PORTS

—— Sea routes

• Major seaports

Sea Routes

SCALE 1: 205 000 000

0   2000   4000   6000   8000 km

MODIFIED GALL PROJECTION

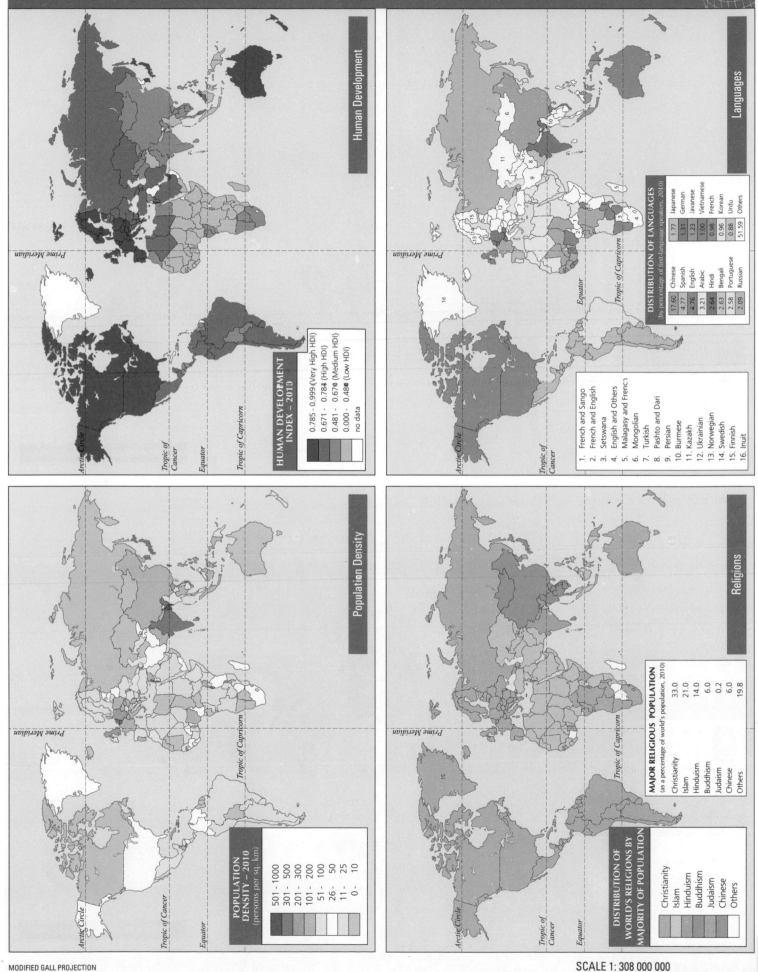

Human Development

HUMAN DEVELOPMENT
INDEX – 2011

- 0.785 - 0.999 (Very High HDI)
- 0.671 - 0.784 (High HDI)
- 0.481 - 0.670 (Medium HDI)
- 0.000 - 0.480 (Low HDI)
- no data

Languages

DISTRIBUTION OF LANGUAGES
(by percentage of first-language speakers, 2010)

Language	%	Language	%
Chinese	17.60	Japanese	1.77
Spanish	4.77	German	1.31
English	4.76	Javanese	1.23
Arabic	3.21	Vietnamese	1.00
Hindi	2.64	French	0.98
Bengali	2.63	Korean	0.96
Portuguese	2.58	Urdu	0.88
Russian	2.09	Others	51.59

1. French and Sango
2. French and English
3. Setswana
4. English and Others
5. Malagasy and French
6. Mongolian
7. Turkish
8. Pashto and Dari
9. Persian
10. Burmese
11. Kazakh
12. Ukrainian
13. Norwegian
14. Swedish
15. Finnish
16. Inuit

Population Density

POPULATION
DENSITY – 2010
(persons per sq. km)

- 501 - 1000
- 301 - 500
- 201 - 300
- 101 - 200
- 51 - 100
- 26 - 50
- 11 - 25
- 0 - 10

Religions

MAJOR RELIGIOUS POPULATION
(as a percentage of world's population, 2010)

Religion	%
Christianity	33.0
Islam	21.0
Hinduism	14.0
Buddhism	6.0
Judaism	0.2
Chinese	6.0
Others	19.8

DISTRIBUTION OF
WORLD'S RELIGIONS BY
MAJORITY OF POPULATION

- Christianity
- Islam
- Hinduism
- Buddhism
- Judaism
- Chinese
- Others

MODIFIED GALL PROJECTION

SCALE 1: 308 000 000

0   3000   6000   9000   12000 km

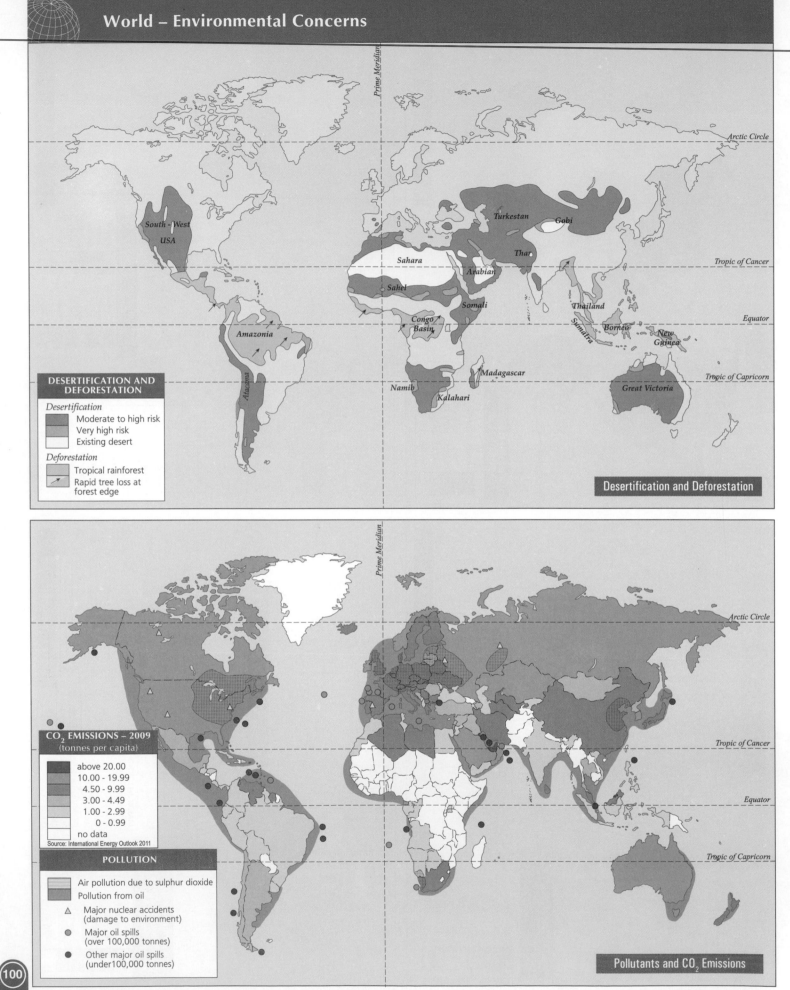

DESERTIFICATION AND DEFORESTATION

Desertification
- Moderate to high risk
- Very high risk
- Existing desert

Deforestation
- Tropical rainforest
- Rapid tree loss at forest edge

Desertification and Deforestation

South – West USA
Amazonia
Atacama
Sahara
Sahel
Arabian
Somali
Congo Basin
Namib
Kalahari
Madagascar
Turkestan
Gobi
Thar
Thailand
Sumatra
Borneo
New Guinea
Great Victoria

Arctic Circle
Tropic of Cancer
Equator
Tropic of Capricorn
Prime Meridian

CO$_2$ EMISSIONS – 2009
(tonnes per capita)

- above 20.00
- 10.00 - 19.99
- 4.50 - 9.99
- 3.00 - 4.49
- 1.00 - 2.99
- 0 - 0.99
- no data

Source: International Energy Outlook 2011

POLLUTION

- Air pollution due to sulphur dioxide
- Pollution from oil
- △ Major nuclear accidents (damage to environment)
- ● Major oil spills (over 100,000 tonnes)
- ● Other major oil spills (under 100,000 tonnes)

Pollutants and CO$_2$ Emissions

100

SCALE 1: 205 000 000

0   2000   4000   6000   8000 km

MODIFIED GALL PROJECTION

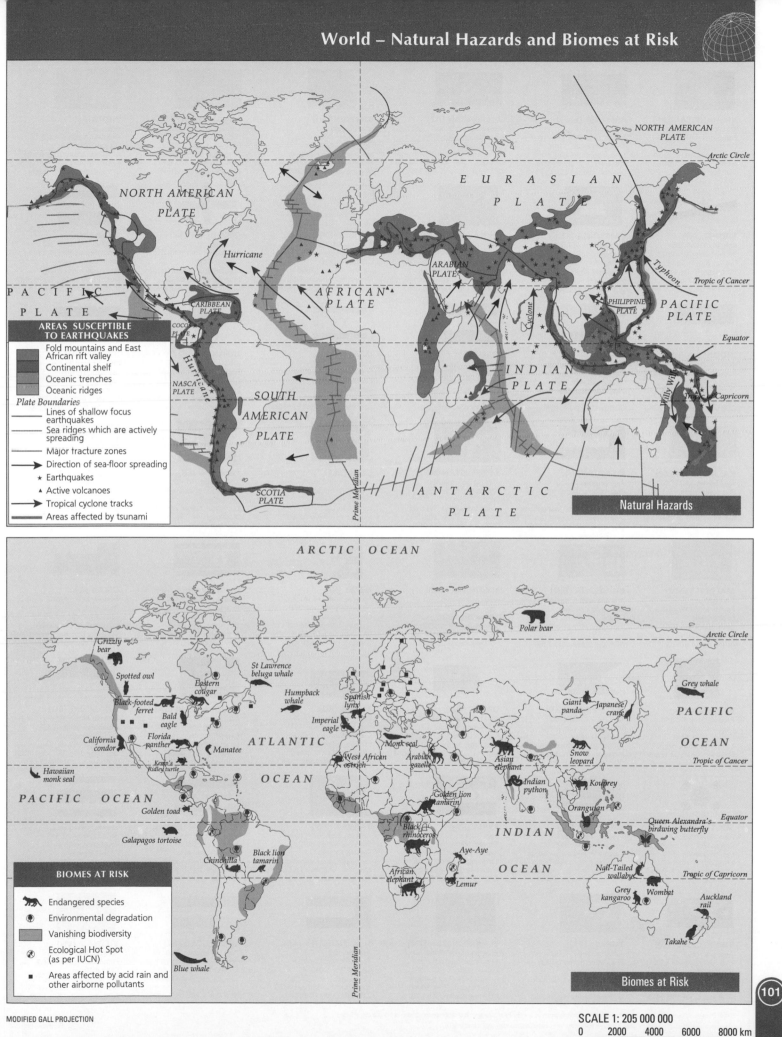

Natural Hazards

AREAS SUSCEPTIBLE TO EARTHQUAKES

- Fold mountains and East African rift valley
- Continental shelf
- Oceanic trenches
- Oceanic ridges

Plate Boundaries

- Lines of shallow focus earthquakes
- Sea ridges which are actively spreading
- Major fracture zones
- Direction of sea-floor spreading
- ★ Earthquakes
- ▲ Active volcanoes
- Tropical cyclone tracks
- Areas affected by tsunami

NORTH AMERICAN PLATE
EURASIAN PLATE
Arctic Circle
PACIFIC PLATE
ARABIAN PLATE
AFRICAN PLATE
CARIBBEAN PLATE
COCOS PLATE
Tropic of Cancer
PHILIPPINE PLATE
PACIFIC PLATE
Equator
NASCA PLATE
INDIAN PLATE
SOUTH AMERICAN PLATE
Tropic of Capricorn
ANTARCTIC PLATE
SCOTIA PLATE
Prime Meridian

Hurricane
Typhoon
Cyclone
Willy Willy

Biomes at Risk

ARCTIC OCEAN

BIOMES AT RISK

- 🐆 Endangered species
- ⊕ Environmental degradation
- Vanishing biodiversity
- ⊛ Ecological Hot Spot (as per IUCN)
- ■ Areas affected by acid rain and other airborne pollutants

Grizzly bear
Spotted owl
Black-footed ferret
Bald eagle
California condor
Florida panther
Eastern cougar
St Lawrence beluga whale
Humpback whale
Manatee
Kemp's Ridley turtle
Hawaiian monk seal
Golden toad
Galapagos tortoise
Chinchilla
Black lion tamarin
Blue whale
Polar bear
Spanish lynx
Imperial eagle
Monk seal
West African ostrich
Arabian gazelle
Golden lion tamarin
Black rhinoceros
African elephant
Aye-Aye
Lemur
Giant panda
Japanese crane
Grey whale
Snow leopard
Asian elephant
Indian python
Kouprey
Orangutan
Queen Alexandra's birdwing butterfly
Nail-Tailed wallaby
Grey kangaroo
Wombat
Auckland rail
Takahe

ATLANTIC OCEAN
PACIFIC OCEAN
PACIFIC OCEAN
INDIAN OCEAN
Arctic Circle
Tropic of Cancer
Equator
Tropic of Capricorn
Prime Meridian

MODIFIED GALL PROJECTION

SCALE 1: 205 000 000

0   2000   4000   6000   8000 km

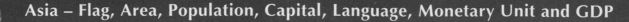

Asia – Flag, Area, Population, Capital, Language, Monetary Unit and GDP

AFGHANISTAN (AF)
Area (sq. km): 652,225
Population (million): 29.1
Capital: Kabul
Language: Dari Persian, Pushtu
Monetary Unit: Afghani (AFA)
GDP (per capita US$): 366

ARMENIA (AM)
Area (sq. km): 3.1
Population (million): 3,016
Capital: Yerevan
Language: Armenian, Yezidi
Monetary Unit: Dram (AMD)
GDP (per capita US$): 3,873

AZERBAIJAN (AZ)
Area (sq. km): 86,600
Population (million): 9.0
Capital: Baku
Language: Azerbaijani, Armenian
Monetary Unit: Az. Manat (AZM)
GDP (per capita US$): 5,315

BAHRAIN (BH)
Area (sq. km): 691
Population (million): 1.3
Capital: Manama
Language: Arabic, English
Monetary Unit: Bahraini Dinar (BHD)
GDP (per capita US$): 28,240

BANGLADESH (BD)
Area (sq. km): 143,998
Population(million): 164.4
Capital: Dhaka
Language: Bengali, English
Monetary Unit: Taka (BDT)
GDP (per capita US$): 497

BHUTAN (BT)
Area (sq. km): 38,394
Population (million): 0.7
Capital: Thimphu
Language: Dzongkha, Nepali
Monetary Unit: Ngultrum (BTN)
GDP (per capita US$): 1,869

BRUNEI (BN)
Area (sq. km): 5,765
Population (million): 0.4
Capital: Bandar Seri Begawan
Language: Malay, English
Monetary Unit: Br. Dollar (BND)
GDP (per capita US$): NA

CAMBODIA (KH)
Area (sq. km): 181,000
Population (million): 15.1
Capital: Phnom Penh
Language: Khmer, French
Monetary Unit: Riel (KHR)
GDP (per capita US$): 711

CHINA (CN)
Area (sq. km): 9,562,000
Population (million): 1,338.1
Capital: Beijing
Language: Mandarin, Wu
Monetary Unit: Yuan Renminbi (CNY)
GDP (per capita US$): 3,267

CYPRUS (CY)
Area (sq. km): 9,251
Population (million): 1.1
Capital: Nicosia
Language: Greek, Turkish
Monetary Unit: Euro (EUR)
GDP (per capita US$): 31,410

GEORGIA (GE)
Area (sq. km): 69,700
Population (million): 4.6
Capital: T'bilisi
Language: Georgian, Russian
Monetary Unit: Lari (GEL)
GDP (per capita US$): 2,970

INDIA (IN)
Area (sq. km): 3,287,263
Population (million): 1,210.2
Capital: New Delhi
Language: Hindi, English
Monetary Unit: Ind. Rupee (INR)
GDP (per capita US$): 1,017

INDONESIA (ID)
Area (sq. km): 1,919,445
Population (million): 235.5
Capital: Jakarta
Language: Indonesian
Monetary Unit: Rupiah (IDR)
GDP (per capita US$): 2,246

IRAN (IR)
Area (sq. km): 1,648,000
Population (million): 75.1
Capital: Tehran
Language:Farsi, Azeri
Monetary Unit: Iranian Rial (IRR)
GDP (per capita US$): NA

IRAQ (IQ)
Area (sq. km): 438,317
Population (million): 31.5
Capital: Baghdad
Language: Arabic, Kurdish
Monetary Unit: Iraqi Dinar (IQD)
GDP (per capita US$): NA

ISRAEL (IL)
Area (sq. km): 20,770
Population (million): 7.6
Capital: Jerusalem
Language: Hebrew, Arabic
Monetary Unit: Sheqel (ILS)
GDP (per capita US$): 27,652

JAPAN (JP)
Area (sq. km): 377,727
Population (million): 127.4
Capital: Tokyo
Language: Japanese
Monetary Unit: Yen (JPY)
GDP (per capita US$): 38,455

JORDAN (JO)
Area (sq. km): 89,206
Population (million): 6.5
Capital: Amman
Language: Arabic
Monetary Unit: Jord. Dinar (JOD)
GDP (per capita US$): 3,596

KAZAKHSTAN (KZ)
Area (sq. km): 2,717,300
Population (million): 16.3
Capital: Astana
Language: Kazakh, Russian
Monetary Unit: Tenge (KZT)
GDP (per capita US$): 8,513

KUWAIT (KW)
Area (sq. km): 17,818
Population (million): 3.1
Capital: Kuwait City
Language: Khalka (Mongolian)
Monetary Unit: Kuwaiti Dinar (KWD)
GDP (per capita US$): 54,260

KYRGYZSTAN (KG)
Area (sq. km): 198,500
Population (million): 5.3
Capital: Bishkek
Language: Kyrgyz, Russian
Monetary Unit: Ky. Som (KGS)
GDP (per capita US$): 958

LAOS (LA)
Area (sq. km): 236,800
Population (million): 6.4
Capital: Vientiane
Language: Lao
Monetary Unit: Kip (LAK)
GDP (per capita US$): 893

LEBANON (LB)
Area (sq. km):10,452
Population (million): 4.3
Capital: Beirut
Language: Arabic, Armenian
Monetary Unit: Leb. Pound (LBP)
GDP (per capita US$): 6,978

MALAYSIA (MY)
Area (sq. km): 332,965
Population (million): 28.9
Capital: Kuala Lumpur/Putrajaya
Language: Malay, English
Monetary Unit: Ringgit (MYR)
GDP (per capita US$): 8,209

     ...

MALDIVES (MV)
Area (sq. km): 298
Population (million): 0.3
Capital: Male
Language: Divehi (Maldivian)
Monetary Unit: Rufiyaa (MVR)
GDP (per capita US$): 4,135

MONGOLIA (MN)
Area (sq. km): 1,565,000
Population (million): 2.8
Capital: Ulan Bator
Language: Mongolian, Kazakh
Monetary Unit: Tugrik (MNT)
GDP (per capita US$): 1,991

MYANMAR (MM)
Area (sq. km): 676,577
Population (million): 53.4
Capital: Naypyidaw
Language: Burmese, Karen
Monetary Unit: Kyat (MMK)
GDP (per capita US$): NA

NEPAL (NP)
Area (sq. km): 147,181
Population (million): 28.0
Capital: Katmandu
Language: Nepali, Maithili
Monetary Unit: Nep. Rupee (NPR)
GDP (per capita US$): 438

NORTH KOREA (KP)
Area (sq. km): 120,538
Population (million): 22.8
Capital: Pyongyang
Language: Korean
Monetary Unit: N. K. Won (KPW)
GDP (per capita US$): NA

OMAN (OM)
Area (sq. km): 309,500
Population (million): 3.1
Capital: Muscat
Language: Arabic, Baluchi
Monetary Unit: Rial Omani (OMR)
GDP (per capita US$): NA

     ...

PAKISTAN (PK)
Area (sq. km): 803,940
Population (million): 184.8
Capital: Islamabad
Language: Urdu, Punjabi
Monetary Unit: Pak. Rupee (PKR)
GDP (per capita US$): 991

PHILIPPINES (PH)
Area (sq. km): 300,000
Population (million): 94.0
Capital: Manila
Language: Filipino, English
Monetary Unit: Ph. Peso (PHP)
GDP (per capita US$): 1,847

QATAR (QA)
Area (sq. km): 11,437
Population (million): 1.7
Capital: Doha
Language: Arabic
Monetary Unit: Qatari Riyal (QAR)
GDP (per capita US$): NA

RUSSIA (RU)
Area (sq. km): 17,075,400
Population (million): 141.9
Capital: Moscow
Language: Russian, Tatar
Monetary Unit: Rouble (RUB)
GDP (per capita US$): 11,832

SAUDI ARABIA (SA)
Area (sq. km): 2,200,000
Population (million): 29.2
Capital: Riyadh
Language: Arabic
Monetary Unit: Saudi Rial (SAR)
GDP (per capita US$): 19,022

SINGAPORE (SG)
Area (sq. km): 639
Population (million): 5.1
Capital: Singapore
Language: Chinese, English
Monetary Unit: Sin. Dollar (SGD)
GDP (per capita US$): 37,597

     ...

SOUTH KOREA (KR)
Area (sq. km): 99,274
Population (million): 48.9
Capital: Seoul
Language: Korean
Monetary Unit: S. K. Won (KRW)
GDP (per capita US$): 19,115

SRI LANKA (LK)
Area (sq. km): 65,610
Population (million): 20.7
Capital: Sri Jayawardenapura
Language: Sinhalese, Tamil
Monetary Unit: Sri L. Rupee (LKR)
GDP (per capita US$): 2,013

SYRIA (SY)
Area (sq. km): 185,180
Population (million): 22.5
Capital: Damascus
Language: Arabic, Kurdish
Monetary Unit: Syrian Pound (SYP)
GDP (per capita US$): 2,682

TAIWAN (TW)
Area (sq. km): 36,179
Population (million): 23.2
Capital: T'aipei
Language: Mandarin, Min
Monetary Unit: New Tai. Dollar (TWD)
GDP (per capita US$): NA

TAJIKISTAN (TJ)
Area (sq. km): 143,100
Population (million): 7.6
Capital: Dushanbe
Language: Tajik, Uzbek
Monetary Unit: Tajik Rouble (TJR)
GDP (per capita US$): 751

THAILAND (TH)
Area (sq. km): 513,115
Population (million): 68.1
Capital: Bangkok
Language: Thai, Lao
Monetary Unit: Baht (THB)
GDP (per capita US$): 4,043

TIMOR-LESTE (TP)
Area (sq. km): 14,874
Population (million): 1.2
Capital: Dili
Language: Portuguese, Tetun
Monetary Unit: US Dollar (USD)
GDP (per capita US$): 453

TURKEY (TR)
Area (sq. km): 779,452
Population (million): 73.6
Capital: Ankara
Language: Turkish, Kurdish
Monetary Unit: Turkish Lira (TRL)
GDP (per capita US$): 9,942

TURKMENISTAN (TM)
Area (sq. km): 488,100
Population (million): 5.2
Capital: Ashgabat
Language: Turkmen, Uzbek
Monetary Unit: Turk. Manat (TMM)
GDP (per capita US$): 3,039

U. A. EMIRATES (AE)
Area (sq. km): 77,700
Population (million): 5.4
Capital: Abu Dhabi
Language: Arabic, English
Monetary Unit: Dirham (AED)
GDP (per capita US$): NA

UZBEKISTAN (UZ)
Area (sq. km): 447,400
Population (million): 28.1
Capital: Tashkent
Language: Uzbek, Russian
Monetary Unit: Uzb. Som (UZS)
GDP (per capita US$): 1023

VIETNAM (VN)
Area (sq. km): 329,565
Population (million): 88.9
Capital: Hanoi
Language: Vietnamese, Thai
Monetary Unit: Dong (VND)
GDP (per capita US$): 1,051

Gross Domestic Product (GDP) is the total value of goods and services produced in a country and are given in US$ per person, adjusted for the local cost of living.
Country codes and currency codes are given in brackets along with country names and monetary units respectively.
Two major official languages are given for each country.

Data Source
Population - PRB 2010
GDP - HDR 2010

YEMEN (YE)
Area (sq. km): 527,968
Population (million): 23.6
Capital: San'a
Language: Arabic
Monetary Unit: Riyal (Yer)
GDP (per capita US$): 1,160

EUROPE

ALBANIA (AL)
Area (sq. km): 28,748
Population (million): 3.2
Capital: Tirana
Language: Albanian, Greek
Monetary Unit: Lek (ALL)
GDP (per capita US$): 3,911

ANDORRA (AD)
Area (sq. km): 465
Population (million): 0.1
Capital: Andorra la vella
Language: Spanish, Catalan
Monetary Unit: Euro (EUR)
GDP: NA

AUSTRIA (AT)
Area (sq. km): 83,855
Population (million): 8.4
Capital: Vienna
Language: German, Croatian
Monetary Unit: Euro (EUR)
GDP (per capita US$): 49,599

BELARUS (BY)
Area (sq. km): 207,600
Population (million): 9.5
Capital: Minsk
Language: Belarusian, Russian
Monetary Unit: Belarussian Rouble (BYR)
GDP (per capita US$): 6,230

BELGIUM (BE)
Area (sq. km): 30,520
Population (million): 10.8
Capital: Brussels
Language: Dutch , French
Monetary Unit: Euro (EUR)
GDP (per capita US$): 47,085

BOSNIA-HERZEGOVINA (BA)
Area (sq. km): 51,130
Population (million): 3.8
Capital: Sarajevo
Language: Bosnian, Serbian
Monetary Unit: Convertible Mark (BAM)
GDP (per capita US$): 4,906

BULGARIA (BG)
Area (sq. km): 110,994
Population (million): 7.5
Capital: Sofia
Language: Bulgarian, Turkish
Monetary Unit: Lev (BGL)
GDP (per capita US$): 6,546

CROATIA (HR)
Area (sq. km): 56,538
Population (million): 4.4
Capital: Zagreb
Language: Croatian, Serbian
Monetary Unit: Kuna (HRK)
         Croatian Dinar (HRD)
GDP (per capita US$): 15,637

CZECH REPUBLIC (CZ)
Area (sq. km): 78,864
Population (million): 10.5
Capital: Prague
Language: Czech, Moravian
Monetary Unit: Czech Koruna (CZK)
GDP (per capita US$): 20,673

DENMARK (DK)
Area (sq. km): 43,075
Population (million): 5.5
Capital: Copenhagen
Language: Danish
Monetary Unit: Danish Krone (DKK)
GDP (per capita US$): 62,118

ESTONIA (EE)
Area (sq. km): 45,200
Population (million): 1.3
Capital: Tallinn
Language: Estonian, Russian
Monetary Unit: Kroon (EEK)
GDP (per capita US$): 17,454

FINLAND (FI)
Area (sq. km): 338,145
Population (million): 5.4
Capital: Helsinki
Language: Finnish, Swedish
Monetary Unit: Euro (EUR)
GDP (per capita US$): 51,323

FRANCE (FR)
Area (sq. km): 543,965
Population (million): 63.0
Capital: Paris
Language: French
Monetary Unit: Euro (EUR)
GDP (per capita US$): 44,508

GERMANY (DE)
Area (sq. km): 357,022
Population (million): 81.6
Capital: Berlin
Language: German, Turkish
Monetary Unit: Euro (EUR)
GDP (per capita US$): 44,446

GREECE (GR)
Area (sq. km): 131,957
Population (million): 11.3
Capital: Athens
Language: Greek
Monetary Unit: Euro (EUR)
GDP (per capita US$): 31,670

HOLY SEE (VA)
Area (sq. km): 0.5
Population (million): NA
Capital: Vatican City
Language:
Monetary Unit: Euro (EUR)
GDP (per capita US$): NA

HUNGARY (HU)
Area (sq. km): 93,030
Population (million): 10.0
Capital: Budapest
Language: Hungarian
Monetary Unit: Forint (HUF)
GDP (per capita US$): 15,408

ICELAND (IS)
Area (sq. km): 102,820
Population (million): 0.3
Capital: Reykjavik
Language: Icelandic
Monetary Unit: Icelandic Krona (ISK)
GDP (per capita US$): 52,479

IRELAND (IE)
Area (sq. km): 70,282
Population (million): 4.5
Capital: Dublin
Language: English, Irish
Monetary Unit: Euro (EUR)
GDP (per capita US$): 60,460

ITALY (IT)
Area (sq. km): 301,245
Population (million): 60.5
Capital: Rome
Language: Italian
Monetary Unit: Euro (EUR)
GDP (per capita US$): 38,492

LATVIA (LV)
Area (sq. km): 63,700
Population (million): 2.2
Capital: Riga
Language: Latvian, Russian
Monetary Unit: Lats (LVL)
GDP (per capita US$): 14,908

LIECHTENSTEIN (LI)
Area (sq. km): 160
Population (million): 0.04
Capital: Vaduz
Language: German
Monetary Unit: Swiss franc (CHF)
GDP: NA

LITHUANIA (LT)
Area (sq. km): 65,200
Population (million): 3.3
Capital: Vilnius
Language: Lithuanian, Russian
Monetary Unit: Litas (LTL)
GDP (per capita US$): 14,098

LUXEMBOURG (LU)
Area (sq. km): 2,586
Population (million): 0.5
Capital: Luxembourg
Language: Luxembourgish, German
Monetary Unit: Euro (EUR)
GDP (per capita US$): 109,903

MACEDONIA (MK)
Area (sq. km): 25,713
Population (million): 2.1
Capital: Skopje
Language: Macedonian, Albanian
Monetary Unit: Dinar (MKD)
GDP (per capita US$): 4,664

MALTA (MT)
Area (sq. km): 316
Population (million): 0.4
Capital: Valletta
Language: Maltese, English
Monetary Unit: Euro (EUR)
GDP (per capita US$): NA

MOLDOVA (MD)
Area (sq. km): 33,700
Population (million): 4.1
Capital: Chisinau
Language: Romanian, Ukrainian
Monetary Unit: Moldavian Leu (MDL)
GDP (per capita US$): NA

MONACO (MC)
Area (sq. km): 2
Population (million): 0.04
Capital: Monaco
Language: French, Monegasque
Monetary Unit: Euro (EUR)
GDP (per capita US$): NA

NETHERLANDS (NL)
Area (sq. km): 41,526
Population (million): 16.6
Capital: Amsterdam, The Hague
Language: Dutch, Frisian
Monetary Unit: Euro (EUR)
GDP (per capita US$): 52,963

NORWAY (NO)
Area (sq. km): 323,878
Population (million): 4.9
Capital: Oslo
Language: Norwegian
Monetary Unit: Norwegian Krone, (NOK)
GDP (per capita US$): 94,759

POLAND (PL)
Area (sq. km): 312,683
Population (million): 38.2
Capital: Warsaw
Language: Polish, German
Monetary Unit: New Zloty (PLL)
GDP (per capita US$): 13,845

PORTUGAL (PT)
Area (sq. km): 88,940
Population (million): 10.7
Capital: Lisbon
Language: Portuguese
Monetary Unit: Euro (EUR)
GDP (per capita US$): 22,923

ROMANIA (RO)
Area (sq. km): 237,500
Population (million): 21.5
Capital: Bucharest
Language: Romanian, Hungarian
Monetary Unit: Romanian Leu (ROL)
GDP (per capita US$): 9,300

SAN MARINO (SM)
Area (sq. km): 61
Population (million): 0.03
Capital: San Marino
Language:Italian
Monetary Unit: Euro (EUR)
GDP (per capita US$): NA

SERBIA (RS)
Area (sq. km): 88,361
Population (million): 7.3
Capital: Belgrade
Language:Serbian, Albanian
Monetary Unit: Serbian Dinar (CSD)
GDP (per capita US$): 6,811

SLOVAKIA (SK)
Area (sq. km): 49,035
Population (million): 5.4
Capital: Bratislava
Language: Slovakian, Hungarian
Monetary Unit: Slovak Koruna (SKK)
GDP (per capita US$): 18,212

SLOVENIA (SI)
Area (sq. km): 20,251
Population (million): 2.1
Capital: Ljubljana
Language: Slovenian, Croatian
Monetary Unit: Tolar (SIT)
GDP (per capita US$): 27,019

SPAIN (ES)
Area (sq. km): 504,782
Population (million): 47.1
Capital: Madrid
Language: Spanish, Castilian
Monetary Unit: Euro (EUR)
GDP (per capita US$): 35,215

SWEDEN (SE)
Area (sq. km): 449,964
Population (million): 9.4
Capital: Stockholm
Language: Swedish
Monetary Unit: Swedish Krona (SEK)
GDP (per capita US$): 51,950

SWITZERLAND (CH)
Area (sq. km): 41,293
Population (million): 7.8
Capital: Berne
Language: German, French
Monetary Unit: Swiss Franc (CHF)
GDP (per capita US$): 64,327

UKRAINE (UA)
Area (sq. km): 603,700
Population (million): 45.9
Capital: Kiev
Language: Ukrainian, Russian
Monetary Unit: Hryvnia (UAH)
         Karbovanet (UAK)
GDP (per capita US$): 3,899

UNITED KINGDOM (GB)
Area (sq. km): 243,609
Population (million): 62.2
Capital: London
Language: English, Welsh
Monetary Unit: Pound Sterling (GBP)
GDP (per capita US$): 43,451

ALGERIA (DZ)
Area (sq. km): 2,381,741
Population (million): 36.0
Capital: Algiers
Language: Arabic, French
Monetary Unit: Alg. Dinar (DZD)
GDP (per capita US$): 4,845

ANGOLA (AO)
Area (sq. km): 1,246,700
Population (million): 19.0
Capital: Luanda
Language: Portuguese, Bantu
Monetary Unit: New Kwanza (AON)
GDP (per capita US$): 4,714

BENIN (BJ)
Area (sq. km): 112,620
Population (million): 9.8
Capital: Porto-Novo
Language: French, Fon
Monetary Unit: CFA Franc (XAF)
GDP (per capita US$): 771

BOTSWANA (BW)
Area (sq. km): 581,370
Population (million): 1.8
Capital: Gaborone
Language: Yoruba, Adja
Monetary Unit: Pula (BWP)
GDP (per capita US$): 6,982

BURKINA FASO (BF)
Area (sq. km): 274,200
Population (million): 16.2
Capital: Ouagadougou
Language: French, Moore
Monetary Unit: CFA Franc (XAF)
GDP (per capita US$): 522

BURUNDI (BI)
Area (sq. km): 27,835
Population (million): 8.5
Capital: Bujumbura
Language: Kirundi (Hutu, Tutsi)
Monetary Unit: Bur. Franc (BIF)
GDP (per capita US$): 144

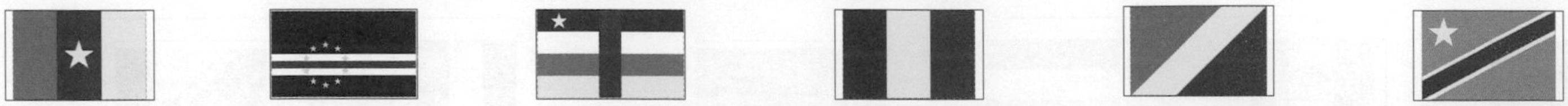

CAMEROON (CM)
Area (sq. km): 475,442
Population (million): 20.0
Capital: Yaoundé
Language: French English, Fang
Monetary Unit: CFA Franc (XAF)
GDP (per capita US$): 1,226

CAPE VERDE (CV)
Area (sq. km): 4,033
Population (million): 0.5
Capital: Praia
Language: Portuguese, Creole
Monetary Unit: C. V. Escudo (CVE)
GDP (per capita US$): 3,193

CENTRAL AFRICAN REP. (CF)
Area (sq. km): 622,436
Population (million): 4.8
Capital: Bangui
Language: French, Sangho
Monetary Unit: CFA Franc (XAF)
GDP (per capita US$): 458

CHAD (TD)
Area (sq. km):1,284,000
Population (million): 11.5
Capital: N'Djamena
Language: Arabic, French
Monetary Unit: CFA Franc (XAF)
GDP (per capita US$): 770

CONGO (CG)
Area (sq. km): 342,000
Population (million): 3.9
Capital: Brazzaville
Language: French, Kongo
Monetary Unit: CFA Franc (XAF)
GDP (per capita US$): 2,966

CONGO DEM. REP. (CD)
Area (sq. km): 2,345,410
Population (million): 67.8
Capital: Kinshasa
Language: French, Lingala
Monetary Unit: Con. Franc (CDF)
GDP (per capita US$): 182

COTE D'IVOIRE (CI)
Area (sq. km): 322,464
Population (million): 22.0
Capital: Yamoussoukro
Language: French, Creole
Monetary Unit: CFA Franc (XAF)
GDP (per capita US$): 1,137

DJIBOUTI (DJ)
Area (sq. km): 23,200
Population (million): 0.9
Capital: Djibouti
Language: Somali, Afar
Monetary Unit: Djib. Franc (DJF)
GDP (per capita US$): 1,030

EGYPT (EG)
Area (sq. km): 1,000,250
Population (million): 80.4
Capital: Cairo
Language: Arabic
Monetary Unit: Egyptian Pound (EGP)
GDP (per capita US$): 1,991

EQUATORIAL GUINEA (GQ)
Area (sq. km): 28,051
Population (million): 0.7
Capital: Malabo
Language: Spanish, French
Monetary Unit: CFA Franc (XAF)
GDP (per capita US$): 28,103

ERITREA (ER)
Area (sq. km): 117,400
Population (million): 5.2
Capital: Asmara
Language:Tigrinya, Tigre
Monetary Unit: E. Nakfa (ERN, ETB)
GDP (per capita US$): 336

ETHIOPIA (ET)
Area (sq. km): 1,133,880
Population (million): 85.0
Capital: Addis Ababa
Language: Oromo, Amharic
Monetary Unit: Eth. Birr (ETB)
GDP (per capita US$): 317

GABON (GA)
Area (sq. km): 267,667
Population (million): 1.5
Capital: Libreville
Language: French, Fang
Monetary Unit: CFA Franc (XAF)
GDP (per capita US$): 10,037

GAMBIA (GM)
Area (sq. km): 11,295
Population (million): 1.8
Capital: Banjul
Language:English, Mandinka
Monetary Unit: Dalasi (GMD)
GDP (per capita US$): 489

GHANA (GH)
Area (sq. km): 238,537
Population (million): 24.0
Capital: Accra
Language:English, Hausa
Monetary Unit: Cedi (GHC)
GDP (per capita US$): 713

GUINEA (GN)
Area (sq. km): 245,857
Population (million): 10.8
Capital: Conakry
Language: French, Fulani
Monetary Unit: G. Syli (Franc) (GNS)
GDP (per capita US$): 386

KENYA (KE)
Area (sq. km): 582,646
Population (million): 40.0
Capital: Nairobi
Language:Kiswahili, English
Monetary Unit: Ken. Shilling (KES)
GDP (per capita US$): 783

LESOTHO (LS)
Area (sq. km): 30,355
Population (million):,1.9
Capital: Maseru
Language:Sesotho, English
Monetary Unit: LSL, LSM, ZAR
GDP (per capita US$): 791

LIBERIA (LR)
Area (sq. km): 111,369
Population (million): 4.1
Capital: Monrovia
Language: English, Creole
Monetary Unit: Lib. Dollar (LRD)
GDP (per capita US$): 222

LIBYA (LY)
Area (sq. km): 1,759,540
Population (million): 6.5
Capital: Tripoli
Language:Arabic, Berber
Monetary Unit: Libyan Dinar (LYD)
GDP (per capita US$): 14,802

MADAGASCAR (MG)
Area (sq. km): 587,041
Population (million): 20.1
Capital: Antananarivo
Language: Malagasy, French
Monetary Unit: Malagasy Franc (MGF)
GDP (per capita US$): 495

MALAWI (MW)
Area (sq. km): 118,484
Population (million): 15.4
Capital: Lilongwe
Language:Chichewa, English
Monetary Unit: M. Kwacha (MWK)
GDP (per capita US$): 288

MALI (ML)
Area (sq. km): 1,240,140
Population (million): 15.2
Capital: Bamako
Language: French, Bambara
Monetary Unit: CFA Franc (XAF)
Malian Franc (MLF)
GDP (per capita US$): 688

MAURITANIA (MR)
Area (sq. km): 1,030,700
Population (million): 3.4
Capital: Nouakchott
Language:Arabic, French
Monetary Unit: Ouguiya (MRO)
GDP (per capita US$): 889

MAURITIUS (MU)
Area (sq. km): 2,040
Population (million): 1.3
Capital: Port Louis
Language: English, Creole
Monetary Unit: Mau. Rupee (MUR)
GDP (per capita US$): 7,345

MOROCCO (MA)
Area (sq. km): 446,550
Population (million): 31.9
Capital: Rabat
Language: Arabic, Berber
Monetary Unit: Mor. Dirham (MAD)
GDP (per capita US$): 2,769

MOZAMBIQUE (MZ)
Area (sq. km): 799,380
Population (million): 23.4
Capital: Maputo
Language: Portuguese, Makhuwa
Monetary Unit: Metical (MZM)
GDP (per capita US$): 440

NAMIBIA (NA)
Area (sq. km): 824,292
Population (million): 2.2
Capital: Windhoek
Language:English, Afrikaans
Monetary Unit: N. Dollar (NAD)
South African Rand (ZAR)
GDP (per capita US$): 4,149

NIGER (NE)
Area (sq. km): 1,267,000
Population (million): 15.9
Capital: Niamey
Language:French, Hausa
Monetary Unit: W. A. Frane (XOF)
CFA Franc (XAF)
GDP (per capita US$): 364

NIGERIA (NG)
Area (sq. km): 923,768
Population (million): 158.3
Capital: Abuja
Language:English, Hausa
Monetary Unit: Naira (NGN)
GDP (per capita US$): 1,370

RWANDA (RW)
Area (sq. km): 26,338
Population (million): 10.4
Capital: Kigali
Language: Kinyarwanda, French
Monetary Unit: Rw. Franc (RWF)
GDP (per capita US$): 458

SENEGAL (SN)
Area (sq. km): 196,720
Population (million): 12.5
Capital: Dakar
Language:French, Wolof
Monetary Unit: W.A. Franc (XOF)
CFA Frane (XAF)
GDP (per capita US$): 1,087

SEYCHELLES (SC)
Area (sq. km): 455
Population (million): 0.1
Capital: Victoria
Language:English, French
Monetary Unit: Sey. Rupee (SCR)
GDP (per capita US$): 9,580

SOMALIA (SO)
Area (sq. km): 637,657
Population (million): 9.4
Capital: Mogadishu
Language:Somali, Arabic
Monetary Unit: S. Shilling (SOS)
GDP: NA

SOUTH AFRICA (ZA)
Area (sq. km): 1,219,090
Population (million): 49.9
Capital: Pretoria/Cape Town
Language: Afrikaans, English
Monetary Unit: Rand (ZAR)
GDP (per capita US$): 5,678

SUDAN (SD)
Area (sq. km): 2,505,813
Population (million): 43.2
Capital: Khartoum
Language: Arabic, Dinka
Monetary Unit: S. Pound (SDG)
GDP (per capita US$): 1,353

SWAZILAND (SZ)
Area (sq. km): 17,364
Population (million): 1.2
Capital: Mbabane
Language:Swazi, English
Monetary Unit: Lilangeni (SZL)
GDP (per capita US$): 2,429

TANZANIA (TZ)
Area (sq. km): 945,087
Population (million): 45.0
Capital: Dodoma
Language:Swahili, English
Monetary Unit: Tan. Shilling (TZS)
GDP (per capita US$): 496

TUNISIA (TN)
Area (sq. km): 164,150
Population (million): 10.5
Capital: Tunis
Language:Arabic, French
Monetary Unit: Tunisian Dinar (TND)
GDP (per capita US$): 3,903

UGANDA (UG)
Area (sq. km): 241,038
Population (million): 33.8
Capital: Kampala
Language: English, Swahili
Monetary Unit: Ug. Shilling (UGS)
GDP (per capita US$): 453

ZAMBIA (ZM)
Area (sq. km): 752,614
Population (million): 13.3
Capital: Lusaka
Language: English, Bemba
Monetary Unit: Zam. Kwacha (ZMK)
GDP (per capita US$):1,134

ZIMBABWE (ZW)
Area (sq. km): 390,759
Population (million): 12.6
Capital: Harare
Language: English, Shona
Monetary Unit: Zimbabwean Dollor ZWD
GDP (per capita US$): NA

America and Oceania – Flag, Area, Population, Capital, Language, Monetary Unit and GDP

NORTH AMERICA

ANTIGUA & BARBUDA (AG)
Area (sq. km): 442
Population (million): 0.1
Capital: St John's
Language: English, Creole
Monetary Unit: East C. Dollar (Xcd)
GDP (per capita US$): 14,048

BAHAMAS (BS)
Area (sq. km): 13,939
Population (million): 0.3
Capital: Nassau
Language: English, Creole
Monetary Unit: Bah. Dollar (Bsd)
GDP (per capita US$): NA

BARBADOS (BB)
Area (sq. km): 430
Population (million): 0.3
Capital: Bridgetown
Language: English, Creole
Monetary Unit: Bar. Dollar (BBD)
GDP (per capita US$): 14,426

BELIZE (BZ)
Area (sq. km): 22,965
Population (million): 0.3
Capital: Belmopan
Language: English, Spanish
Monetary Unit: Belize Dollar (BZD)
GDP (per capita US$): 4,218

CANADA (CA)
Area (sq. km): 9,984,670
Population (million): 34.1
Capital: Ottawa
Language: English, French
Monetary Unit: Can. Dollar (CAD)
GDP (per capita US$): 45,070

COSTA RICA (CR)
Area (sq. km): 51,100
Population (million): 4.6
Capital: San José
Language: Spanish
Monetary Unit: C. R. Colón (CRC)
GDP (per capita US$): 6,564

CUBA (CU)
Area (sq. km): 110,860
Population (million): 11.2
Capital: Havana
Language: Spanish
Monetary Unit: Cuban Peso (CUP)
GDP (per capita US$): NA

DOMINICA (DM)
Area (sq. km): 750
Population (million): 0.1
Capital: Roseau
Language: English, Creole
Monetary Unit: East C. Dollar (XCD)
GDP (per capita US$): 4,883

DOMINICAN REP. (DO)
Area (sq. km): 48,442
Population (million): 9.9
Capital: Santo Domingo
Language: Spanish, Creole
Monetary Unit: Dom. Rep. Peso (DOP)
GDP (per capita US$): 4,576

EL SALVADOR (SV)
Area (sq. km): 21,041
Population (million): 6.2
Capital: San Salvador
Language: Spanish
Monetary Unit: US Dollar (USD)
GDP (per capita US$): 3,605

GREENLAND (GL)
Area (sq. km): 2,175,600
Population (million): NA
Capital: Nuuk
Language: Kalaallisut
Monetary Unit: Danish Krone (GLK)
GDP (per capita US$): NA

GRENADA (GD)
Area (sq. km): 378
Population (million): 0.1
Capital: St George's
Language: English, Creole
Monetary Unit: East C. Dollar (XCD)
GDP (per capita US$): 6,162

GUATEMALA (GT)
Area (sq. km): 108,890
Population (million): 14.4
Capital: Guatemala City
Language: Spanish
Monetary Unit: Quetzal (GTQ)
GDP (per capita US$): 2,848

HAITI (HT)
Area (sq. km): 27,750
Population (million): 9.8
Capital: Port-au-Prince
Language: French, Creole
Monetary Unit: Gourde (HTG)
GDP (per capita US$): 729

HONDURAS (HN)
Area (sq. km): 112,088
Population (million): 7.6
Capital: Tegucigalpa
Language: Spanish
Monetary Unit: Lempira (HNL)
GDP (per capita US$): 1,823

JAMAICA (JM)
Area (sq. km): 10,991
Population (million): 2.7
Capital: Kingston
Language: English, Creole
Monetary Unit: Jam. Dollar (JMD)
GDP (per capita US$): 5,438

MEXICO (MX)
Area (sq. km): 1,972,545
Population (million): 110.6
Capital: Mexico City
Language: Spanish
Monetary Unit: M. New Peso (MXN)
GDP (per capita US$): 10,232

NICARAGUA (NI)
Area (sq. km): 130,000
Population (million): 6.0
Capital: Managua
Language: Spanish
Monetary Unit: Córdoba (NIC)
GDP (per capita US$): 1,163

PANAMA (PA)
Area (sq. km): 77,082
Population (million): 3.5
Capital: Panama City
Language: Spanish, English
Monetary Unit: Balboa (PAB)
         US Dollar (USD)
GDP (per capita US$): 6,793

ST KITTS & NEVIS (KN)
Area (sq. km): 261
Population (million): 0.1
Capital: Basseterre
Language: English, Creole
Monetary Unit: East Car. Dollar (XCD)
GDP (per capita US$): 11,046

ST LUCIA (LC)
Area (sq. km): 616
Population (million): 0.2
Capital: Castries
Language: English, Creole
Monetary Unit: East Car. Dollar (XCD)
GDP (per capita US$): 5,854

ST VINCENT & GRE. (VC)
Area (sq. km): 389
Population (million): 0.1
Capital: Kingstown
Language: English, Creole
Monetary Unit: East Car. Dollar (XCD)
GDP (per capita US$): 5,480

TRINIDAD & TOBAGO (TT)
Area (sq. km): 5,130
Population (million): 1.3
Capital: Port of Spain
Language: English, Creole, Hindi
Monetary Unit: Tri. & Tob. Dollar (TTD)
GDP (per capita US$): 18,108

U. S. OF AMERICA (US)
Area (sq. km): 9,826,635
Population (million): 309.6
Capital: Washington DC
Language: English, Spanish
Monetary unit: US Dollar (USD)
GDP (per capita US$): 46,350

SOUTH AMERICA

ARGENTINA (AR)
Area (sq. km): 2,766,889
Population (million): 40.5
Capital: Buenos Aires
Language: Spanish, Italian,
Monetary Unit: Austral (ARA)
Argentinian Neuvo Peso (ARS)
GDP (per capita US$): 8,236

BOLIVIA (BO)
Area (sq. km): 1,098,581
Population (million): 10.4
Capital: La Paz/Sucre
Language: Spanish, Quechua
Monetary Unit : Boliviano (BOB)
         Bol. Peso (BOP)
GDP (per capita US$): 1,720

BRAZIL (BR)
Area (sq. km): 8,514,879
Population (million): 193.3
Capital: Brasília
Language: Portuguese
Monetary Unit: Cruzeiro Real (BRR)
GDP (per capita US$): 8,205

CHILE (CL)
Area (sq. km): 756,945
Population (million): 17.1
Capital: Santiago
Language: Spanish
Monetary Unit: Un. de Fomento (CLF)
         Chilean Peso (CLP)
GDP (per capita US$): 10,084

COLOMBIA (CO)
Area (sq. km): 1,141,748
Population (million): 45.5
Capital: Bogotá
Language: Spanish
Monetary Unit: Col. Peso (COP)
GDP (per capita US$): 5,416

ECUADOR (EC)
Area (sq. km): 272,045
Population (million): 14.2
Capital: Quito
Language: Spanish, Quechua
Monetary Unit: US Dollar (USD)
GDP (per capita US$): 4,056

GUYANA (GY)
Area (sq. km): 214,969
Population (million): 0.8
Capital: Georgetown
Language: English, Creole
Monetary Unit: Gu. Dollar (GYD)
GDP (per capita US$): 1,513

PARAGUAY (PY)
Area (sq. km): 406,752
Population (million): 6.5
Capital: Asunción
Language: Spanish, Creole
Monetary Unit: Guaraní (PYG)
GDP (per capita US$): 2,561

PERU (PE)
Area (sq. km): 1,285,216
Population (million): 29.5
Capital: Lima
Language: Spanish, Quechua
Monetary Unit: Inti (PEI) New Sol (PEN)
GDP (per capita US$): 4,477

SURINAME (SR)
Area (sq. km): 163,820
Population (million): 0.5
Capital: Paramaribo
Language: Dutch, Surinamese
Monetary Unit: S. Guilder (SRG)
GDP (per capita US$): 5,888

URUGUAY (UY)
Area (sq. km): 176,215
Population (million): 3.4
Capital: Montevideo
Language: Spanish
Monetary Unit: Ur. New Peso (UYU)
GDP (per capita US$): 9,654

VENEZUELA (VE)
Area (sq. km): 912,050
Population (million): 28.8
Capital: Caracas
Language: Spanish, Amerindian
Monetary Unit: Bolivar Fuerte (VEF)
GDP (per capita US$): 11,246

OCEANIA

AUSTRALIA (AU)
Area (sq. km): 7,692,024
Population (million): 22.4
Capital: Canberra
Language: English
Monetary Unit: Aus. Dollar (AUD)
GDP (per capita US$): 47,370

FIJI (FI)
Area (sq. km): 18,330
Population (million): 0.9
Capital: Suva
Language: English, Fijian
Monetary Unit: Fiji Dollar (FJD)
GDP (per capita US$): 4,253

KIRIBATI (KI)
Area (sq. km): 717
Population (million): 0.1
Capital: Tarawa
Language:
Gilbertese, English
Monetary Unit: Aus. Dollar (AUD)
GDP (per capita US$): 1,414

MARSHALL IS (MH)
Area (sq. km): 181
Population (million): 0.1
Capital: Majuro
Language: English, Marshallese
Monetary Unit: US Dollar (USD)
GDP (per capita US$): 2,655

MICRONESIA (FM)
Area (sq. km): 701
Population (million): 0.1
Capital: Palikir
Language: English, Chuukese
Monetary Unit: US Dollar (USD)
GDP (per capita US$): 2,334

NAURU (NR)
Area (sq. km): 21
Population (million): 0.01
Capital: Yaren
Language: Nauruan, English
Monetary Unit: Aus. Dollar (AUD)
GDP (per capita US$): NA

NEW ZEALAND (NZ)
Area (sq. km): 270,534
Population (million): 4.4
Capital: Wellington
Language: English, Maori
Monetary Unit: New Z. Dollar (NZD)
GDP (per capita US$): 30,439

PAPUA NEW GUINEA (PG)
Area (sq. km): 462,840
Population (million): 6.8
Capital: Port Moresby
Language: English, Tok Pisin
Monetary Unit: Kina (PGK)
GDP (per capita US$): 1,253

SOLOMON IS (SB)
Area (sq. km): 28,370
Population (million): 0.5
Capital: Honiara
Language: English, Creole
Monetary Unit: Sol. Is. Dollar (SBD)
GDP (per capita US$): 1,263

TONGA (TO)
Area (sq. km): 748
Population (million): 0.1
Capital: Nuku'alofa}
Language: Tongan, English
Monetary Unit: Pa'anga (TOP)
GDP (per capita US$): 2,687

TUVALU (TV)
Area (sq. km): 25
Population (million): 0.01
Capital: Funafuti
Language: Tuvaluan, English
Monetary Unit: Aus. Dollar (AUD)
GDP (per capita US$): NA

VANUATU (VU)
Area (sq. km): 12,190
Population (million): 0.2
Capital: Port Vila
Language: English, Bislama
Monetary Unit: Vatu (VUV)
GDP (per capita US$): 2,521

105

GDP per capita, 2008

Gross domestic product (GDP) in US$ per person, adjusted for the local cost of living

Highest GDP per capital	(in US $)	Lowest GDP per capita	(in US$)
Luxembourg	109,903	Burundi	144
Norway	94,759	Congo (Democratic Republic of the)	182
Switzerland	64,327	Liberia	222
Denmark	62,118	Guinea-Bissau	273
Ireland	60,460	Malawi	288
		Ethiopia	317

INDIA 1,017

Life expectancy, 2010

Average expected lifespan of babies born in 2009 (years)

Highest life expectancy		Lowest life expectancy	
Switzerland	82.2	Afghanistan	44.6
Japan	83.2	Lesotho	45.9
Iceland	82.1	Swaziland	47.0
Hong Kong, China (SAR)	82.5	Zimbabwe	47.0
Australia	81.9	Zambia	47.3

INDIA 64.4

Literacy and Schooling, 2005-2008

Percentage of people aged 15 and above who can, with understanding, both read and write a short, simple statement on their everyday life

Highest literacy levels		Lowest literacy levels	
Norway	100	Mali	26.2
Australia	100	Burkina Faso	28.7
New Zealand	100	Niger	28.7
United States	100	Chad	32.7
Ireland	100	Ethiopia	35.9
Liechtenstein	100	Sierra Leone	39.8
Netherlands	100	Benin	40.8
Canada	100	Senegal	41.9
Sweden	100	Gambia	45.3
Germany	100	Guinea-Bissau	51.0

INDIA 62.8

Health care, 2000 – 2009

Number of doctors per 10 000 people

Most doctors per 10 000 people		Fewest doctors per 10 000 people	
Cuba	64	Ethiopia	<0.5
Greece	54	Niger	<0.5
Belarus	49	Sierra Leone	<0.5
Georgia	45	Chad	<0.5
Russian Federation	43	Liberia	<0.5
		Burundi	<0.5
		Mozambique	<0.5
		Guinea-Bissau	<0.5
		Tanzania (United Republic of)	<0.5
		Gambia	<0.5

INDIA 6

Human Development Index (HDI), 2010

HDI measures the relative social and economic progress of a country. It combines life expectancy, adult literacy, average number of years of schooling and purchasing power.

Highest HDI		Lowest HDI	
Norway	0.938	Zimbabwe	0.140
Australia	0.937	Congo (Democratic Republic of the)	0.239
New Zealand	0.907	Niger	0.261
United States	0.902	Burundi	0.282
Ireland	0.895	Mozambique	0.284

INDIA 0.519

Population below income poverty line (PPP US$1.25 a day), 2000–2008

The proportion of the population with a standard of living below the national poverty line

Highest percentage of population	
Tanzania (United Republic of)	88.5
Liberia	83.7
Burundi	81.3
Rwanda	76.6
Mozambique	74.7
Malawi	73.9
Guinea	70.1
Madagascar	67.8
Niger	65.9

INDIA 41.6

Gross National Income (GNI), 2010

The decent standard of living component of a country is measured by Gross National Inclome (GNI) per capita (PPP US$).

Highest GNI		Lowest GNI	
Liechtenstein	81,011	Zimbabwe	176
Qatar	79,426	Congo (Democratic Republic of the)	291
Norway	58,810	Liberia	320
United Arab Emirates	58,006	Burundi	402
Kuwait	55,719	Guinea-Bissau	538

INDIA 3,337

Fertility rate, 2010 – 2015 (births per woman)

Average number of children born to childbearing woman

Largest families	
Niger	6.9
Afghanistan	6.3
Somalia	6.2
Timor-Leste	6.0
Uganda	5.9
Chad	5.8
Burkina Faso	5.6
Congo (Democratic Republic of the)	5.5
Guinea-Bissau	5.4

INDIA 2.5

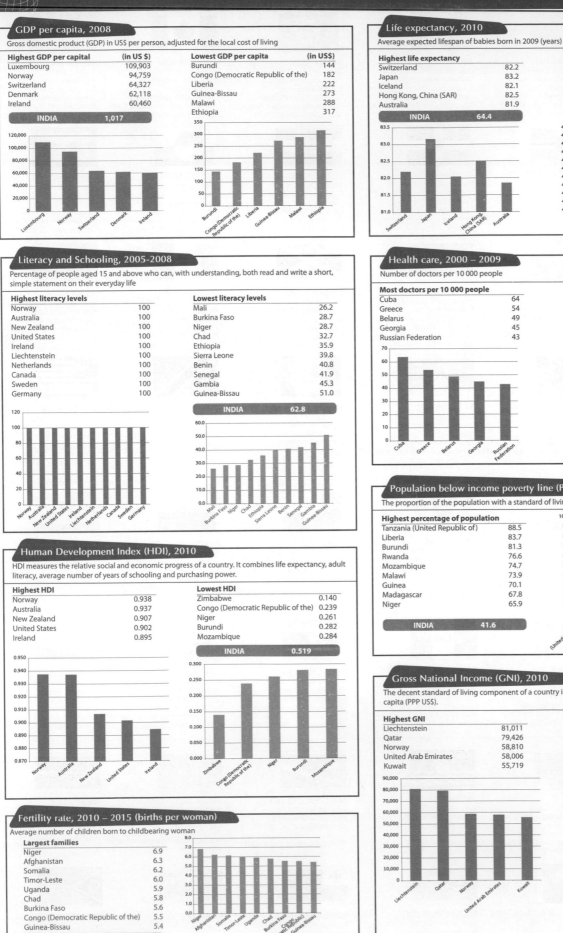
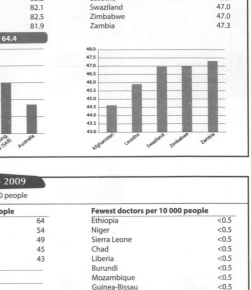

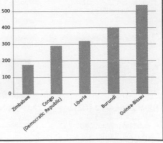
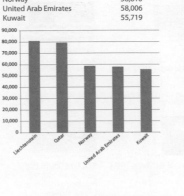

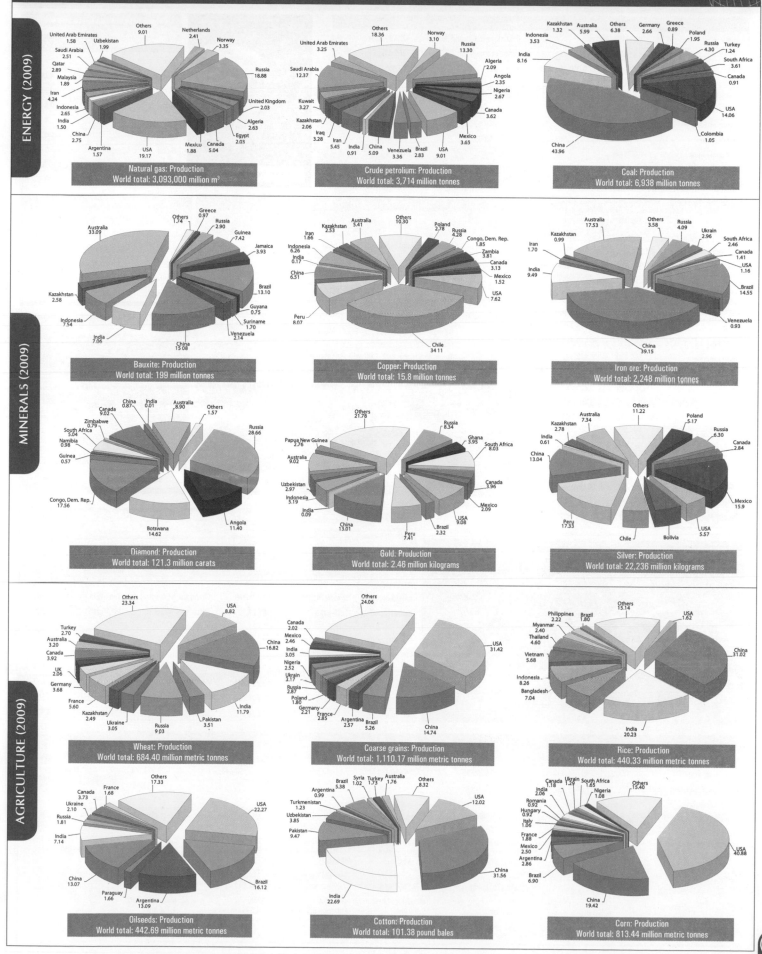

ENERGY (2009)

Natural gas: Production
World total: 3,093,000 million m³

Others 9.01
Netherlands 2.41
Norway 3.35
Russia 18.88
United Kingdom 2.03
Algeria 2.63
Egypt 2.03
Canada 5.04
Mexico 1.88
USA 19.17
Argentina 1.57
China 2.75
India 1.50
Indonesia 2.65
Iran 4.24
Malaysia 1.89
Qatar 2.89
Saudi Arabia 2.51
United Arab Emirates 1.58
Uzbekistan 1.99

Crude petroleum: Production
World total: 3,714 million tonnes

Others 18.36
Norway 3.10
Russia 13.30
Algeria 2.09
Angola 2.35
Nigeria 2.67
Canada 3.62
Mexico 3.65
USA 9.01
Brazil 2.83
Venezuela 3.36
China 5.09
India 0.91
Iran 5.45
Iraq 3.28
Kazakhstan 2.06
Kuwait 3.27
Saudi Arabia 12.37
United Arab Emirates 3.25

Coal: Production
World total: 6,938 million tonnes

Kazakhstan 1.32
Australia 5.99
Others 6.38
Germany 2.66
Greece 0.89
Poland 1.95
Russia 4.30
Turkey 1.24
South Africa 3.61
Canada 0.91
USA 14.06
Colombia 1.05
China 43.96
India 8.16
Indonesia 3.53

MINERALS (2009)

Bauxite: Production
World total: 199 million tonnes

Australia 33.09
Others 1.74
Greece 0.97
Russia 2.90
Guinea 7.42
Jamaica 3.93
Brazil 13.10
Guyana 0.75
Suriname 1.70
Venezuela 2.14
China 15.08
India 7.06
Indonesia 7.54
Kazakhstan 2.58

Copper: Production
World total: 15.8 million tonnes

Others 10.30
Poland 2.78
Russia 4.28
Congo, Dem. Rep. 1.85
Zambia 3.81
Canada 3.13
Mexico 1.52
USA 7.62
Chile 34.11
Peru 8.07
China 6.51
India 0.17
Indonesia 6.26
Iran 1.66
Kazakhstan 2.53
Australia 5.41

Iron ore: Production
World total: 2,248 million tonnes

Australia 17.53
Others 3.58
Russia 4.09
Ukrain 2.96
South Africa 2.46
Canada 1.41
USA 1.16
Brazil 14.55
Venezuela 0.93
China 39.15
India 9.49
Iran 1.70
Kazakhstan 0.99

Diamond: Production
World total: 121.3 million carats

China 0.87
India 0.01
Australia 8.90
Others 1.57
Russia 28.66
Canada 9.02
Zimbabwe 0.79
South Africa 5.04
Namibia 0.98
Guinea 0.57
Congo, Dem. Rep. 17.56
Botswana 14.62
Angola 11.40

Gold: Production
World total: 2.46 million kilograms

Others 21.78
Russia 8.34
Ghana 3.95
South Africa 8.03
Canada 3.96
Mexico 2.09
USA 9.08
Brazil 2.32
Peru 7.41
China 13.01
India 0.09
Indonesia 5.19
Uzbekistan 2.97
Australia 9.02
Papua New Guinea 2.76

Silver: Production
World total: 22,236 million kilograms

Others 11.22
Poland 5.17
Russia 6.30
Canada 2.84
Mexico 15.9
USA 5.57
Bolivia
Chile
Peru 17.33
China 13.04
India 0.61
Kazakhstan 2.78
Australia 7.34

AGRICULTURE (2009)

Wheat: Production
World total: 684.40 million metric tonnes

Others 23.34
USA 8.82
Turkey 2.70
Australia 3.20
Canada 3.92
UK 2.06
Germany 3.68
France 5.60
Kazakhstan 2.49
Ukraine 3.05
Russia 9.03
Pakistan 3.51
India 11.79
China 16.82

Coarse grains: Production
World total: 1,110.17 million metric tonnes

Others 24.06
Canada 2.02
Mexico 2.46
China 3.05
India 3.05
Nigeria 2.52
Ukraine 2.17
Russia 2.87
Poland 1.80
Germany 2.21
France
Argentina 2.57
Brazil 5.26
China 14.74
USA 31.42

Rice: Production
World total: 440.33 million metric tonnes

Others 15.14
USA 1.62
Philippines 2.22
Brazil 1.80
Myanmar 2.40
Thailand 4.60
Vietnam 5.68
Indonesia 8.26
Bangladesh 7.04
India 20.23
China 31.02

Oilseeds: Production
World total: 442.69 million metric tonnes

Others 17.33
France 1.68
Canada 3.73
Ukraine 2.10
Russia 1.81
India 7.14
China 13.07
Paraguay 1.66
Argentina 13.09
Brazil 16.12
USA 22.27

Cotton: Production
World total: 101.38 pound bales

Others 8.32
Brazil 5.38
Syria 1.02
Turkey 1.73
Australia 1.76
USA 12.02
Argentina 0.99
Turkmenistan 1.23
Uzbekistan 3.85
Pakistan 9.47
India 22.69
China 31.56

Corn: Production
World total: 813.44 million metric tonnes

Others 15.40
Canada 1.18
Ukrain 1.24
South Africa 1.65
Nigeria 1.08
India 2.06
Romania 0.92
Hungary 0.92
Italy 1.06
France 1.88
Mexico 2.50
Argentina 2.86
Brazil 6.90
China 19.42
USA 40.88

Earth-Fact File

Situation	Milky Way Galaxy	Orbital speed (around Sun)	29.79 km/sec.
Age	4.6 billion years	Period of revolution	365 days 5 hrs.
Mass	5,940,000,000,000,000,000,000 Metric tones	Axial tilt	23.45º
Equatorial circumference	40, 066 km	Average surface temperatures	13º C
Polar circumference	39,992 km	Surface area	510,100,500 sq km
Equatorial diameter	12,756 km	Land surface	148,950,800 sq km
Polar diameter	12,710 km	No. of satellites	1 (Moon)
Equatorial radius	6,376 km	Nearest star	Sun
Polar radius	6,355 km	Solar light reaches Earth in	8 min. 20 sec.
Distance from Sun	149 407 000 km	Escape velocity	11.2 km/sec.

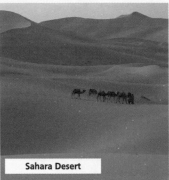

Earth from Moon

Composition of the Earth and Moon

	Earth (in per cent)	Moon (in per cent)
Iron	34.6	9.3
Oxygen	29.5	42.0
Silicon	15.2	19.6
Magnesium	12.7	18.7
Carbon	1.1	4.3
Aluminum	1.1	4.2
Nickel	2.4	0.6
Sodium	0.6	0.07
Sulphur	1.9	0.3

World, Continents and Oceans

	Area - Sq. km	Area - Miles	%
World			
The World	484,510,420	207,934,764	
Land	148,800,420	57,412,764	30.71
Water	335,710,000	150,522,000	69.29
Continents			
Asia	45,036,492	17,388,686	30.27
Africa	30,343,578	11,715,721	20.39
North America	24,680,331	9,529,129	16.59
South America	17,815,420	6,878,572	11.97
Antarctica	12,093,000	4,669,133	8.13
Europe	9,908,599	3,825,731	6.66
Australia and Oceania	8,923,000	3,405,792	6.00
World Land	**148,800,420**	**57,412,764**	**100.00**
Oceans			
Pacific Ocean	166,241,000	64,186,000	49.52
Atlantic Ocean	86,557,000	33,420,000	25.78
Indian Ocean	73,427,000	28,350,000	21.87
Arctic Ocean	9,485,000	24,566,000	2.83
World Water	**335,710,000**	**150,522,000**	**100.00**

Highest Waterfalls of the World

Name(s)	Location	Source/River	Height (in metres)
Angel	Canaima National Park, Venezuela	Upper tributary of Rio Caroni	979
Tugela	NatalNat'l Park, South Africa	Tugela	947
Utigord	Norway	Glacier stream	800
Monge	Marstein, Norway	Mongebeck	774
Gocta Cataracts	Chachapoyas, Peru	--	771
Mutarazi	Nyanga National Park, Zimbabwe	Mutarazi	762
Yosemite	Yosemite National Park, California	Yosemite Creek	739

Angel Fall

World's largest deserts

Desert	Location	Sq. km
Sahara	North Aftrica	9,065,000
Gobi	Mongolia-China	1,295,000
Kalahari	Southern Africa	582,000
Great Victoria	Australia	338,500
Great Sandy	Australia	338,500

Sahara Desert

Mount Everest

Highest Peaks and Longest Rivers in the World

Peak	Location	Height (in meters / feet)	River	Country	Length (in kilometers)
Mount Everest	Nepal/China	8,850 / 29,035	Nile	Egypt/Africa	6,695
K2	India	8,611 / 28,251	Amazon	Brazil/South America	6,516
Kangchenjunga	India/Nepal	8,586 / 28,169	Chang Jiang (Yangtze)	China/Asia	6,380
Lhotse	Nepal	8,516 / 27,939	Mississippi-Missouri	USA/North America	5,969
Makalu	Nepal	8,463 / 27,765	Ob'-Irtysh	Asia	5,568
Cho Oyu	Nepal/China	8,201 / 26,906	Yenisei-Angara	Russia/Asia	5,550
Dhaulagiri	Nepal	8,167 / 26,794	Huang He (Yellow)	China/Asia	5,464
Manaslu	Nepal	8,163 / 26,781	Congo	Africa	4,667
Nanga Parbat	India	8,126 / 26,660	Parana (Rio de la Plata)	South America	4,500
Annapurna I	Nepal	8,091 / 26,545	Mekong	Asia	4,425

Continental extremes

Continent	Asia	Europe	North America	South America	Africa	Oceania	Antarctica
Area (in sq. km)	45,036,492	9,908,599	24,680,331	17,815,420	30,343,578	8,923,000	12,093,000
Estimated Population (in thousand)	3,679,737	727,986	315,915	349,510	795,671	31,043	--
No. of Countries	48	50	23	12	54	14	--
Highest Point	Mt Everest, Nepal/China; 29,035 ft (8,850 m)	Mt Elbrus, Russia/Georgia; 18,510 ft (5,642 m)	Mt McKinley, Alaska; 20,320 ft (6,194 m)	Mt Aconcagua, Argentina; 22,834 ft (6,960 m)	Mt Kilimanjaro, Tanz.; 19,340 ft (5,895 m)	Kosciusko, Australia; 7,316 ft (2,228 m)	Vinson Massif, Ellsworth Mts; 16,066 ft (4,897 m)
Lowest Point	Dead Sea; 1341 ft below sea level (409 m bsl)	Caspian Sea Shore; 92 ft below sea level (28 m bsl)	Death Valley; 282 ft below sea level (86 m bsl)	Valdes Peninsula; 131 ft below sea level (40 m bsl)	Lake Assal; 512 ft below sea level (156 m bsl)	Lake Eyre; 52 ft below sea level (16 m bsl)	8327 ft below sea level (2,538 m bsl)
Largest Island	Borneo; 745,561 sq. km	Great Britain; 218,476 sq. km	Greenland; 2,175,600 sq. km	Tierra del Fuego; 47,000 sq. km	Madagascar; 587,040 sq. km	New Guinea; 808,510 sq. km	
Longest river	Chang Jiang (Yangtze); 6,380 km	Volga; 3,688 km	Mississippi-Missouri; 5,969 km	Amazonas (Amazon); 6,516 km	Nile; 6,695 km	Murray-Darling; 3,750 km	
Largest lake	Caspean Sea; 371,000 sq. km	Lake Ladoga; 18,390 sq. km	Lake Superior; 82,100 sq. km	Lake Titicaca; 8,340 sq. km	Lake Victoria; 68,800 sq. km	Lake Eyre; 9, 000 sq. km	--

Tanz.: Tanzania

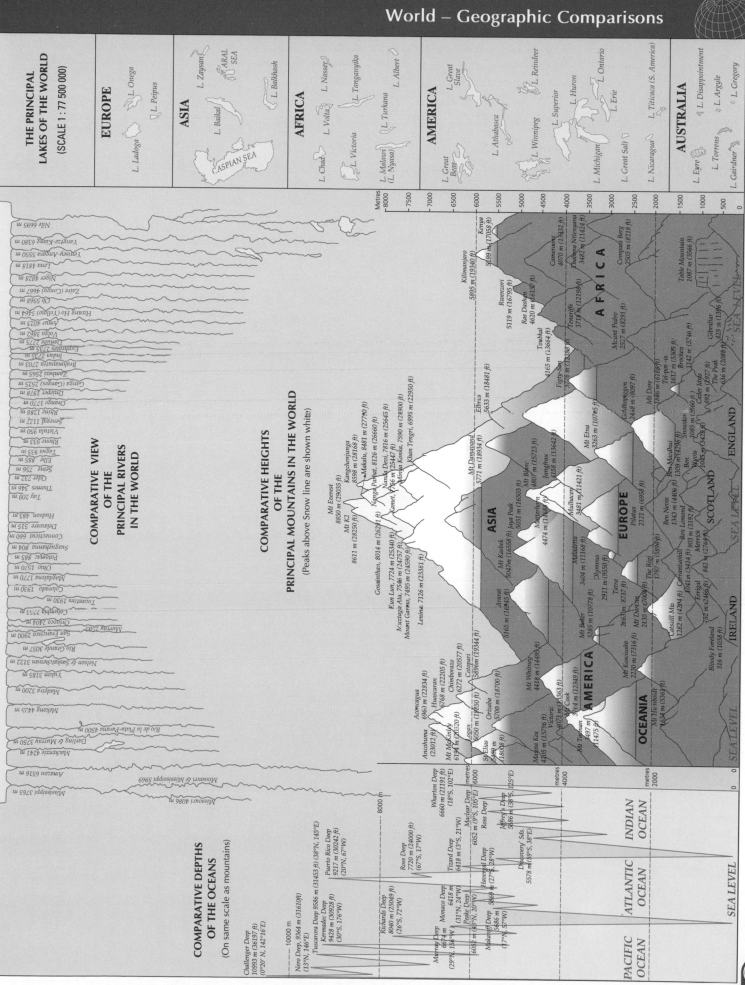

THE PRINCIPAL LAKES OF THE WORLD
(SCALE 1 : 77 500 000)

EUROPE
L. Ladoga
L. Onega
L. Peipus

ASIA
L. Zaysam
ARAL SEA
L. Balkhash
L. Baikal
CASPIAN SEA

AFRICA
L. Chad
L. Volta
L. Nasser
L. Victoria
L. Tanganyika
L. Turkana
L. Malawi (L. Nyasa)
L. Albert

AMERICA
L. Great Slave
L. Great Bear
L. Athabasca
L. Reindeer
L. Winnipeg
L. Superior
L. Huron
L. Michigan
L. Ontario
L. Erie
L. Great Salt
L. Nicaragua
L. Titicaca (S. America)

AUSTRALIA
L. Eyre
L. Disappointment
L. Torrens
L. Argyle
L. Gairdner
L. Gregory

COMPARATIVE VIEW OF THE PRINCIPAL RIVERS IN THE WORLD

Nile 6695 m
Yangtze-Kiang 6380 m
Yenisey-Angara 5550 m
Lena 4818 m
Niger 4828 m
Zaïre (Congo) 4667 m
Ob 5568 m
Huang Ho (Yellow) 5464 m
Amur 4023 m
Volga 3862 m
Danube 2775 m
Euphrates 2735 m
Indus 2735 m
Brahmaputra 2703 m
Zambezi 2565 m
Ganga (Ganges) 2525 m
Dnieper 1978 m
Orange 1770 m
Rhine 1288 m
Senegal 1127 m
Vistula 950 m
Rhone 933 m
Tagus 933 m
Elbe 885 m
Seine 756 m
Oder 732 m
Thames 346 m
Tay 209 m
Hudson 483 m
Delaware 515 m
Connecticut 660 m
Susquehanna 804 m
Potomac 885 m
Magdalena 1770 m
Ohio 1570 m
Colorado 1930 m
Tocantins 1930 m
Orinoco 2404 m
Columbia 2374 m
San Francisco 2900 m
Rio Grande 3057 m
Nelson & Saskatchewan 5122 m
Yukon 3185 m
Madeira 3200 m
Mekong 4425 m
Rio de la Plata-Paraná 4500 m
Darling & Murray 3750 m
Murray 2520 m
Mackenzie 4241 m
Amazon 6516 m
Mississippi 3765 m
Missouri & Mississippi 5969 m
Missouri 4086 m

COMPARATIVE HEIGHTS OF THE PRINCIPAL MOUNTAINS IN THE WORLD
(Peaks above Snow line are shown white)

ASIA
Mt Everest 8850 m (29035 ft)
Mt K2 8611 m (28250 ft)
Kangchenjunga 8598 m (28168 ft)
Makalu, 8481 m (27790 ft)
Nanga Parbat, 8126 m (26660 ft)
Gosainthan, 8014 m (26291 ft)
Kamet, 7766 m (25447 ft)
Namka Barwa, 7816 m (25645 ft)
Minya Konka, 7590 m (24900 ft)
Kun Lun, 7724 m (25340 ft)
Muztagia Ata, 7546 m (24757 ft)
Mount Garmo, 7495 m (24590 ft)
Khan Tengri, 6995 m (22950 ft)
Lenina 7126 m (23381 ft)

AFRICA
Kilimanjaro 5895 m (19340 ft)
Kenya 5199 m (17058 ft)
Ruwenzori 5119 m (16795 ft)
Ras Dashan 4620 m (16137 ft)
Cameroon 4070 m (13332 ft)
Thabana Ntlenyana 3482 m (11424 ft)
Compass Berg 2505 m (8218 ft)
Toubkal 4165 m (13665 ft)
Teneriffe 3718 m (12198 ft)
Mount Pedro 2527 m (8291 ft)
Table Mountain 1087 m (3566 ft)

EUROPE
Elbrus 5633 m (18481 ft)
Mt Damavand 5771 m (18934 ft)
Mt Blanc 4807 m (15723 ft)
Matterhorn 4474 m (14688 ft)
Jungfrau 4158 m (13642 ft)
Mt Etna 3263 m (10705 ft)
Mulhacen 3481 m (11421 ft)
Mt Kasbek 5047 m (16558 ft)
Jaya Peak 5031 m (16503 ft)
Olympus 2911 m (9550 ft)
Tatra 2663 m (8737 ft)
Gerlachovka 2448 m (8097 ft)
Mt Dore 1886 m (6187 ft)
Pilatus 2121 m (6958 ft)
Tel-pos-iis 1617 m (5305 ft)
Ben Nevis 1343 m (4406 ft)
Brocken 1142 m (3746 ft)
Ben Macdhui 1309 m (4296 ft)
Snowdon 1085 m (3560 ft)
Corrantuohill 1041 m (3414 ft)
Errigal 903 m (3192 ft)
Ben Lomond 903 m (3192 ft)
Merrick 842 m (2764 ft)
Cader Idris 892 m (3429 ft)
The Peak 636 m (2088 ft)
Gibraltar 425 m (1396 ft)
The Rigi 1797 m (5899 ft)
Catskill Mts 1282 m (4204 ft)
Bloody Foreland 316 m (1038 ft)

AMERICA
Aconcagua 6961 m (22834 ft)
Huascaran 6768 m (22205 ft)
Chimborazo 6272 m (20577 ft)
Cotopaxi 5896 m (19344 ft)
Orizaba 5700 m (18700 ft)
Mt McKinley 6194 m (20320 ft)
Logan 6050 m (19850 ft)
St Elias 5489 m (18008 ft)
Mt Whitney 4418 m (14495 ft)
Mauna Kea 4205 m (13796 ft)
Mt Koscuisko 2230 m (7316 ft)

OCEANIA
Victoria 4073 m (13363 ft)
Mt Cook 3764 m (12349 ft)
Mt Tarbun 2497 m (11475 ft)
Mt Hornbild 1634 m (5361 ft)
Mt Kinabalu

AFRICA
ASIA
EUROPE
ENGLAND
SCOTLAND
IRELAND
AMERICA
OCEANIA
SEA LEVEL

COMPARATIVE DEPTHS OF THE OCEANS
(On same scale as mountains)

Challenger Deep 10993 m (36197 ft) (0°20' N, 142°16'E)
Nero Deep, 9364 m (30610ft) (13°N, 146°E)
Tuscarora Deep 9586 m (31453 ft) (38°N, 145°E)
Kermadec Deep 9428 m (30928 ft) (30°S, 176°W)
Puerto Rico Deep 9217 m (30242 ft) (20°N, 67°W)
Richards Deep 8040 m (25049 ft) (26°S, 72°W)
Ross Deep 7720 m (24000 ft) (67°S, 17°W)
Wharton Deep 6660 m (21191 ft) (18°S, 102°E)
Tizard Deep 6418 m (3°S, 21°W)
Maclear Deep 6052 m (9°S, 105°E)
Ross Deep
Monaco Deep 6674 m (29°N, 16°W)
Peake Deep 6418 m (31°N, 24°W)
Murray Deep
Makaroff Deep 5860 m (45°N, 20°W)
Haverell Deep (17°S, 37°W)
Jeffrey's Deep 5686 m (38°S, 125°E)
Discovery Sds. 5578 m (59°S, 38°E)

PACIFIC OCEAN
ATLANTIC OCEAN
INDIAN OCEAN
SEA LEVEL

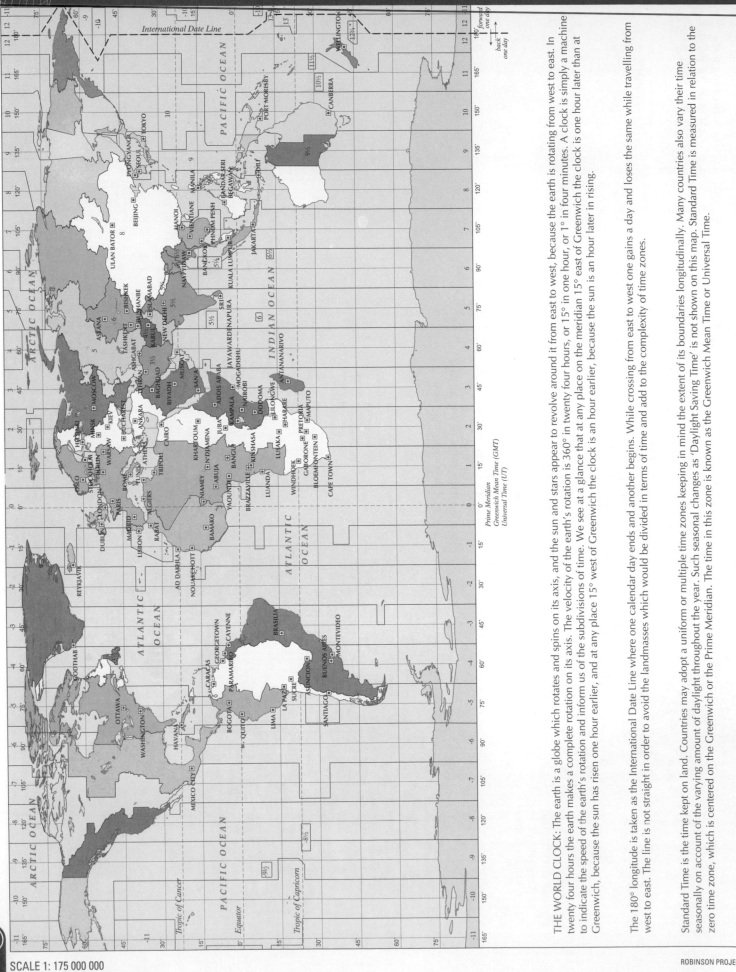

THE WORLD CLOCK: The earth is a globe which rotates and spins on its axis, and the sun and stars appear to revolve around it from west to east, because the earth is rotating from west to east. In twenty four hours the earth makes a complete rotation on its axis. The velocity of the earth's rotation is 360° in twenty four hours, or 15° in one hour, or 1° in four minutes. A clock is simply a machine to indicate the speed of the earth's rotation and inform us of the subdivisions of time. We see at a glance that at any place on the meridian 15° east of Greenwich the clock is one hour later than at Greenwich, because the sun has risen one hour earlier, and at any place 15° west of Greenwich the clock is an hour earlier, because the sun is an hour later in rising.

The 180° longitude is taken as the International Date Line where one calendar day ends and another begins. While crossing from east to west one gains a day and loses the same while travelling from west to east. The line is not straight in order to avoid the landmasses which would be divided in terms of time and add to the complexity of time zones.

Standard Time is the time kept on land. Countries may adopt a uniform or multiple time zones keeping in mind the extent of its boundaries longitudinally. Many countries also vary their time seasonally on account of the varying amount of daylight throughout the year. Such seasonal changes as 'Daylight Saving Time' is not shown on this map. Standard Time is measured in relation to the zero time zone, which is centered on the Greenwich or the Prime Meridian. The time in this zone is known as the Greenwich Mean Time or Universal Time.

SCALE 1: 175 000 000

0   1500   3000   4500   6000 km

ROBINSON PROJECTION

How to use this Index

The place names or features in this index are arranged in alphabetical order. Each entry in the index starts with the name of the place or feature, followed by the name of the country or region in which it is located. This is followed by the number of the most appropriate page on which the name appears, usually the largest scale map. Next comes the coordinate reference i.e., latitude and longitude, which gives a more exact description of the position of a name or feature. For example, the index entry for Aachen is given as follows:

Aachen Germany (67) 50.47N 6.05E

Aachen is in Germany and appears on page 67. Its latitude is 50 degrees and 47 minutes north of the equator and its longitude is 6 degrees and 05 minutes east of the prime meridian.

Names of the physical features such as rivers, lakes, mountains, etc. are followed by a description, which has been shortened to one or two or three letters, e.g. Everest mountain is written as Everest, Mt. The names of rivers have been indexed either according to their origins or according to their mouths.

Where there is more than one place with the same name, the country name is used to decide the order.

Abbreviations used in the index and maps

Arch.	Archipelago	Pt	Point
C.	Cape	R.	River
E.	East	Ra.	Range
I.	Island	Rep.	Republic
Is	Islands	Res.	Reservoir
L.	Lake	S.	South
Mt	Mount	S.E.	South east
Mts	Mountains	Str.	Strait
N.	North	Terr.	Territory
N.W.	North West	UK	United Kingdom
NSW	New South Wales	USA	United States of America
Pen.	Peninsular/Peninsula	Vol.	Volcano
Prov.	Province	W.	West

Names	Country/Region	Pg.No.	Lat.	Long.
A				
Aachen	Germany	67	50.47N	6.05E
Abadan	Iran	65	30.27N	48.25E
Abaetetuba	Brazil	83	1.45S	48.54W
Abapo	Bolivia	81	18.50S	63.27W
Abashiri	Japan	63	44.00N	144.15E
Abbottabad	Pakistan	14	34.09N	73.15E
Aberdeen	Scotland	69	57.09N	2.05W
Aberystwyth	Wales	69	52.24N	4.05W
Abha	Saudi Arabia	65	18.00N	42.34E
Abidjan	Cote d' Ivoire	73	5.26N	3.58W
Abquaiq	Saudi Arabia	65	26.00N	49.45E
Abu Dhabi	United Arab Emirates	59	24.28N	54.25E
Abu	Rajasthan	23	24.40N	72.45E
Abuja	Nigeria	73	9.06N	7.19E
Abuna	Brazil	83	9.41S	65.20W
Acapulco	Mexico	77	17.00N	100.00W
Acarau	Brazil	83	2.55S	40.05W
Accra	Ghana	73	5.31N	0.15W
Achalpur	Maharashtra	20	21.18N	77.33E
Achill, Is.	Rep. of Ireland	69	53.57N	10.00W
Aconcagua, Mt	Argentina	80	32.30S	67.30W
Ad Damman	Saudi Arabia	65	26.20N	50.05E
Adam's Bridge	Sri Lanka	21	9.05N	79.35E
Adam's Peak	Sri Lanka	21	6.49N	80.30E
Addanki	Andhra Pradesh	20	15.49N	80.01E
Addis Ababa	Ethiopia	73	9.02N	38.44E
Adelaide	South Australia	85	35.57S	136.38E
Aden	Yemen	65	12.45N	45.04E
Adilabad	Andhra Pradesh	27	19.40N	78.32E
Adirampattinam	Tamil Nadu	21	10.21N	79.25E
Adoni	Andhra Pradesh	27	15.38N	77.19E
Adriatic Sea	Italy, etc.	66	43.00N	15.00E
Aegean Sea	Greece	67	39.00N	25.00E
AFGHANISTAN	Asia	59	34.00N	65.00E
Africa, Continent	**World**	**92**		
Agartala	Tripura	13	23.30N	91.30E
Agra	Uttar Pradesh	24	27.10N	78.05E
Ahmadabad	Gujarat	12	23.03N	72.40E
Ahmadnagar	Maharashtra	27	19.05N	74.48E
Ahmadpur East	Pakistan	10	29.06N	71.18E
Ahwa	Gujarat	23	20.44N	73.42E
Aizawl	Mizoram	25	23.36N	93.00E
Ajaccio	Corsica	67	41.55N	8.40E
Ajanta Range	Maharashtra	20	20.20N	77.10E
Ajanta	Maharashtra	27	20.33N	75.48E
Ajmer	Rajasthan	23	26.27N	74.42E
Akalkot	Maharashtra	20	17.31N	76.51E
Akbarpur	Uttar Pradesh	24	26.26N	79.57E
Akita	Japan	63	39.40N	140.00E
Akola	Maharashtra	27	20.42N	77.02E
Akot	Maharashtra	20	21.06N	77.06E
Akron	Ohio, USA	79	41.07N	81.31W
Aksu	China	62	41.04N	80.05E
Al Amarah	Iraq	65	31.55N	47.15E
Alagoinhas	Brazil	83	12.09S	38.21W
Alappuzha	Kerala	28	9.30N	76.23E
Alaska	USA	79	65.00N	150.00W
Alaska, Gulf of	Alaska, USA	79	58.30N	145.00W
ALBANIA	S. Europe	67	41.00N	20.00E
Albany	W. Australia	85	35.00S	118.00E
Albany, R.	Canada	76	51.30N	83.35W
Albert, L.	Uganda, etc.	72	1.50N	31.00E
Albuquerque	New Mexico, USA	79	35.00N	106.40W
Aldershot	England	69	51.17N	0.45W
Alegrete	Brazil	83	29.45S	55.40W
Alessandria	Italy	70	44.54N	8.39E
Aleutian, Is	Bering Sea, USA	79	51.00N	180.00E
Alexandria	Egypt	73	34.12N	29.53E
ALGERIA	N.W. Africa	73	28.30N	2.00E
Algiers	Algeria	73	36.50N	3.00E
Alhillah	Iraq	65	32.30N	44.25E
Alhufuf	Saudi Arabia	65	22.25N	49.48E
Alibag	Maharashtra	27	18.39N	72.55E
Aligarh	Uttar Pradesh	24	27.30N	79.40E
Alipur Duar	W. Bengal	25	26.30N	89.35E
Alipur	W. Bengal	25	22.32N	88.24E
Alipura	Madhya Pradesh	16	25.10N	79.22E
Alirajpur	Madhya Pradesh	26	22.16N	74.24E
Aliwal	South Africa	75	30.41S	26.42E
Aljawf	Saudi Arabia	65	29.55N	39.45E
Allahabad	Uttar Pradesh	24	25.28N	81.54E
Almaty	Kazakhstan	71	43.12N	76.45E
Almora	Uttarakhand	24	29.37N	79.40E
Almubarraz	Saudi Arabia	65	25.30N	49.40E
Along	Arunachal Pradesh	25	28.08N	94.43E
Alps, Southern	New Zealand	85	44.00S	170.00E
Alps, The	Switzerland	70	46.00N	7.00E
Alqatif	Saudi Arabia	65	26.35N	50.00E
Alqunfidha	Saudi Arabia	65	19.03N	41.04E
Altai, Mts	Mongolia	62	47.00N	90.00E
Altamira	Brazil	83	3.13S	52.15W
Altyn Tagh, Mts	China	64	38.40N	90.00E
Aluva	Kerala	28	10.07N	76.24E
Alwar	Rajasthan	23	27.34N	76.38E
Amambai	Brazil	83	23.04S	55.16W
Amapa	Brazil	83	2.00N	50.50W
Amarapura	Myanmar	13	21.55N	96.04E
Amaravati	Andhra Pradesh	27	16.50N	80.15E
Amarnath Cave	J & K, India	22	34.12N	75.30E
Amazon, R.	S. America	80	3.00S	60.00W
Amb	Pakistan	14	34.20N	72.52E
Ambala	Haryana	22	30.21N	76.52E
Ambala	Haryana	22	30.21N	76.52E
Ambasamudram	Tamil Nadu	21	8.43N	77.29E
Ambassa	Tripura	25	23.51N	91.48E
Ambikapur	Chhattisgarh	26	23.10N	83.15E
Ambovombe	Madagascar	75	25.11S	46.08E
Amethi	Uttar Pradesh	24	26.08N	81.50E
Amindivi, Is	Arabian Sea	29	10.00N	73.00E
Amirante, Is	Indian Ocean	88	6.00S	53.00E
Amlekhganj	Nepal	15	27.15N	85.00E
Amman	Jordan	59	31.57N	35.56E
Ampani	Odisha	17	19.43N	82.40E
Amrawati	Maharashtra	27	20.56N	77.48E
Amreli	Gujarat	23	21.37N	71.14E
Amreli	Gurajat	23	21.36N	71.15E
Amritsar	Punjab	22	31.37N	74.55E
Amroha	Uttar Pradesh	24	28.54N	78.31E
Amsterdam	The Netherlands	67	52.22N	4.53E
Amu Darya	Turkmenistan	71	38.00N	65.00E
Amur, R.	Russia	71	50.30N	127.30E
Anadyr, Gulf of	Russia	71	65.00N	178.00W
Anaimalai Hills	Tamil Nadu	21	10.24N	76.40W
Anand	Gujarat	23	22.34N	72.56E
Anandpur	Punjab	14	31.15N	76.34E
Ananindeua	Brazil	83	1.22S	48.20W
Anantapur	Andhra Pradesh	27	14.41N	77.36E
Anantapur	Andhra Pradesh	27	14.41N	77.39E
Anantnag	Jammu & Kashmir	22	33.43N	75.17E
Anapolis	Brazil	83	16.19S	48.58W
Ancohuma, Mt	Bolivia	80	16.00S	68.50W
Ancona	Italy	70	43.36N	13.31E
Andaman & Nicobar Islands, Union Terr.	India	13	12.00N	92.40E
Andes, Mts	S. America	80	10.00S	77.00W
Andhra Pradesh, State	India	13	16.00N	80.0E
Andkhui	Afghanistan	65	36.56N	65.05E
Andorra	South Europe	67	42.31N	1.32E
Andorra-la-Vella	Andorra	67	42.31N	1.32E
Angel Falls	Venezuela	80	6.00N	63.00W
Angers	France	70	47.28N	0.33W
ANGOLA	S. Africa	73	13.00S	15.00E
Angouleme	France	70	45.39N	0.10E
Angul	Odisha	26	24.50N	85.06E
Angul	Odisha	26	20.48N	85.05E
Anini	Arunachal Pradesh	25	28.47N	95.54E
Anju	N. Korea	63	39.32N	125.32E
Ankara	Turkey	65	39.57N	32.54E
Ankleshwar	Gujarat	23	21.38N	73.02E
Annam	Vietnam	64	15.00N	108.00E
Annapurna, Mt	Nepal	15	28.35N	83.57E
Anqing	China	62	30.34N	117.81E
Anshan	China	62	41.03N	122.58E
Antalya	Turkey	65	36.52N	30.45E
Antananarivo	Madagascar	73	18.54S	47.33E
ANTIGUA & BARBUDA	West Indies	77	17.20N	61.48W
Antilles, Greater	West Indies	76	18.00N	74.00W
Antofagasta	Chile	83	23.40S	70.23W
Antsiranana	Madagascar	75	12.19S	49.17E
Antwerp	Belgium	70	51.13N	4.24E
Anupgarh	Rajasthan	23	29.07N	73.06E
Anuppur	Madhya Pradesh	26	23.05N	81.43E
Anuradhapura	Sri Lanka	61	8.22N	80.23E
Anxi	China	62	40.21N	96.10E
Anyang	China	62	36.07N	114.26E
Apennine, Mts	Italy	66	44.00N	12.00E
Apia	Samoa	87	13.50S	171.44W
Appalachian, Mts	USA	76	38.30N	80.00E
Aqaba	Jordan	65	29.31N	35.00E
Aquidauana	Brazil	83	20.27S	55.45W
Ara	Bihar	24	25.34N	84.32E
Arabia, Pen.	S.W. Asia	65	25.00N	45.00E
Arabian Sea	Indian Ocean	58	17.00N	66.00E
Aracaju	Brazil	83	10.54S	37.07W
Aracati	Brazil	83	4.32S	37.45W
Arad	Romania	70	46.11N	21.19E
Arafura Sea	Pacific Ocean	84	10.50N	132.00E
Araguania	Brazil	83	7.16S	48.18W
Araguari	Brazil	83	18.38S	48.13W
Arakan Yoma	Myanmar	10	20.00N	94.20E
Arakkonam	Tamil Nadu	28	13.05N	79.43E
Aral Sea	Kazakhstan	71	45.00N	60.00E
Arambagh	W. Bengal	25	22.53N	87.50E
Aran, I.	Rep. of Ireland	69	53.05N	9.35W
Arantangi	Tamil Nadu	21	10.10N	79.02E
Arapiraca	Brazil	83	9.45S	36.40W
Araraquara	Brazil	83	21.46S	48.08W
Araria	Bihar	24	26.11N	87.32E
Aravali Range	Rajasthan	10	25.00N	73.10E
Araxa	Brazil	83	19.37S	46.50W
Arcot	Tamil Nadu	21	12.56N	79.24E
Arctic Ocean	**World**	**92**		
Ardnamurchan, Pt	Scotland	69	56.43N	6.09W
Arequipa	Peru	81	16.28S	71.30W
ARGENTINA	South America	81	35.00S	65.00W
Arica	Chile	83	18.30S	70.20W
Aripuana	Brazil	83	7.00S	60.30W
Ariquemes	Brazil	83	9.55S	63.06W
Ariyalur	Tamil Nadu	28	11.11N	79.03E
Arkansas, R.	USA	76	38.20N	100.00W
Arkhangelsk	Russia	71	64.33N	40.33E
Arles	France	70	43.40N	4.38E
Armagh	N. Ireland	69	54.22N	6.39W
ARMENIA	Asia	59	40.00N	45.00E
Armur	Andhra Pradesh	20	18.48N	78.16E
Arni	Tamil Nadu	21	12.40N	79.19E
Arran, I.	Scotland	69	55.35N	5.15W
Artigas	Uruguay	83	30.25S	56.28W
Arunachal Pradesh, State	India	13	28.00N	95.00E
Aruppukkottai	Tamil Nadu	21	9.31N	78.08E
Arwal	Bihar	24	25.14N	84.40E
Asansol	W. Bengal	18	23.42N	87.01E
Ashgabat	Turkmenistan	59	37.45N	58.30E
Ashoknagar	Madhya Pradesh	26	24.35N	77.43E
Ashti	Maharashtra	20	21.12N	78.14E
Asia, Continent	**World**	**92**		
Asir	Saudi Arabia	65	20.00N	42.00E
Asmar	Afghanistan	14	35.03N	71.30E
Asmara	Eritrea	73	15.20N	38.56E
Assam, State	India	25	26.00N	93.00E
Assis	Brazil	83	22.37S	50.25W
Astana	Kazakhstan	59	51.10N	71.30E
Astrakhan	Russia	71	46.15N	48.04E
Asuncion	Paraguay	83	25.15S	57.40W
Aswan	Egypt	73	24.05N	32.57E
Asyut	Egypt	73	27.14N	31.07E
Atacama Desert	Chile	80	24.00S	69.20W
Athabasca, L. & R.	Canada	76	59.00N	110.00W
Athens	Greece	67	37.54N	23.52N
Athgarh	Odisha	17	20.32N	85.41E
Athlone	Rep. of Ireland	69	53.26N	7.56E
Athni	Karnataka	20	16.44N	75.06E
Atico	Peru	83	16.12S	73.38W
Atlanta	Georgia, USA	79	33.45N	84.21W
Atlantic Ocean	**World**	**92**		
Atlas, Mts	Morocco	72	32.00N	5.00W
Atmakur	Andhra Pradesh	20	14.37N	79.40E
Attock	Pakistan	14	33.53N	72.17E
Attur	Tamil Nadu	21	11.36N	78.39E
Atur	Tamil Nadu	21	10.16N	77.53E
Auckland	New Zealand	85	36.52S	174.42E
Augsburg	Germany	70	48.22N	10.53E
Augusta	Georgia, USA	79	33.29N	81.59W
Augusta	Maine, USA	79	44.20N	69.45W
Auraiya	Uttar Pradesh	24	26.26N	79.32E
Aurangabad	Bihar	24	24.45N	84.25E
Aurangabad	Maharashtra	27	19.53N	75.23E
Austin	Texas, USA	79	30.16N	97.43W
AUSTRALIA	Oceania	85	25.00S	135.00E
AUSTRIA	Europe	67	47.00N	14.00E
Avignon	France	70	43.57N	4.49E
Ayaviri	Peru	83	14.53S	70.35W
Aydin	Turkey	65	37.45N	27.40E
Ayodhya	Uttar Pradesh	24	26.48N	82.14E
Ayr	Scotland	69	55.28N	4.39W
Ayutthaya	Thailand	64	14.23N	100.35E
Azamgarh	Uttar Pradesh	24	26.03N	83.13E
AZERBAIJAN	Asia	59	40.00N	47.00E
B				
Babol	Iran	65	36.30N	52.49E
Badami	Karnataka	28	15.55N	75.45E
Badanah	S audi Arabia	65	30.58N	41.30E
Badarinath	Uttarakhand	24	30.44N	79.32E
Bad-el-Mandeb	Str. of Africa, etc.	72	13.00N	43.10E
Badgam	Jammu & Kashmir	22	34.06N	74.44E
Badnur	Madhya Pradesh	16	21.80N	77.90E
Badulla	Sri Lanka	61	6.59N	81.05E
Baffin, Bay & I.	Canada	76	73.00N	65.00W
Bagalkot	Karnataka	28	16.12N	75.45E
Bagdogra	West Bengal	18	26.42N	88.19E
Bage	Brazil	83	31.22S	54.06W
Bageshwar	Uttarakhand	24	29.50N	79.49E
Baghdad	Iraq	59	33.20N	44.27E
Baghelkhand	Madhya Pradesh	17	24.10N	82.00E
Baghmara	Meghalaya	25	25.11N	90.38E
Baghpat	Uttar Pradesh	24	28.56N	77.17E
BAHAMAS	North America	77	24.00N	75.00W
Baharampur	West Bengal	25	24.06N	88.15E
Baharampur	W. Bengal	25	24.06N	88.19E
Bahawalpur	Pakistan	14	28.24N	71.47E
Bahia Blanca	Argentina	81	38.40S	62.13W
Bahraich	Uttar Pradesh	24	27.34N	81.38E
BAHRAIN	Persian Gulf	65	26.00N	50.35E
Baikal, L.	Russia	58	54.00N	108.00E
Baikunthpur	Chhattisgarh	26	23.16N	82.33E
Bairiki	Kiribati	87	01.20N	172.59E
Baku	Azerbaijan	59	40.22N	49.50E
Balaghat	Madya Pradesh	26	21.48N	80.15E
Balaghat, Ra.	Maharashtra	10	18.37N	76.14E
Balama	Mozambique	75	13.20S	38.35E
Balaton, L.	Hungary	70	46.50N	17.40E
Balearic, Is	Spain	67	39.30N	2.00E
Baleshwar	Odisha	26	21.30N	86.54E
Bali, I.	Indonesia	64	8.20S	115.00E
Balia	Bangladesh	18	25.09N	89.18E
Balikesir	Turkey	65	39.35N	27.58E
Balkan, Mts	Bulgaria	66	42.45N	24.20E
Balkhash	Kazakhstan	71	46.50N	74.50E
Balkhash, L.	Kazakhstan	58	46.30N	75.00E
Balkonda	Andhra Pradesh	20	19.05N	78.20E
Ballarat	Australia	85	37.35S	143.55E
Ballarshah	Maharastra	27	19.55N	79.23E
Ballary	Karanataka	28	15.09N	76.55E
Ballia	Uttar Pradesh	24	25.44N	84.11E
Balrampur	Uttar Pradesh	24	27.25N	82.15E
Baltic Sea	N. Europe	67	56.00N	16.00E
Baltimore	Maryland, USA	79	39.18N	76.37W
Baltistan	Jammu & Kashmir	14	35.30N	76.00E
Baluchistan	Pakistan	14	28.00N	65.00E
Balurghat	W. Bengal	25	25.14N	88.47E
Bamako	Mali	73	12.34N	7.55W
Bamberg	Germany	70	49.54N	10.53E
Banas, R.	Rajsthan	19	26.13N	76.13E
Banda Atjeh	Sumatra	64	5.30N	95.00E
Banda	Uttar Pradesh	24	25.20N	80.22E

Names	Country/Region	Pg.No.	Lat.	Long.
Banda, Is and Sea	Indonesia	64	5.00S	128.00E
Bandar Abbas	Iran	65	27.12N	56.15E
Bandar Seri Begawan	Brunei	64	4.56N	114.58E
Bandar-e-Pahiavi	Iran	65	37.30N	49.30E
Bandipore	Jammu & Kashmir	22	34.25N	74.39E
Bandjarmasin	Borneo	64	3.20S	114.35E
Bandra	Maharastra	27	19.03N	72.52E
Banff	Scotland	69	57.31N	2.32W
Banganapalle	Andhra Pradesh	27	15.19N	78.17E
Bangkok	Thailand	64	13.42N	100.30E
BANGLADESH	South Asia	59	24.00N	90.00E
Bangui	Central African Re	73	4.23N	18.37E
Bangweulu, L.	Zimbabwe	72	12.00S	30.00E
Banjul	Gambia	73	13.28N	16.40W
Banka	Bihar	24	24.53N	86.55E
Banki	Odisha	17	20.21N	85.33E
Bankipore	Bihar	17	25.40N	85.12E
Banks, I.	Canada	76	73.30N	120.00W
Bankura	W. Bengal	25	23.14N	87.07E
Bannu	Pakistan	14	33.00N	70.39E
Bansi	Uttar Pradesh	17	27.10N	82.56E
Banswara	Rajasthan	23	23.30N	74.24E
Bantval	Karnataka	21	12.53N	75.05E
Bara Banki	Uttar Pradesh	24	26.53N	81.12E
Baragarh	Odisha	26	21.20N	83.37E
Baraj	Uttar Pradesh	17	26.16N	83.46E
Baramba	Odisha	17	20.25N	85.23E
Baramula	Jammu & Kashmir	22	34.10N	74.30E
Baran	Rajasthan	23	25.05N	76.33E
Barannda	Madhya Pradesh	17	25.03N	80.40E
Barasat	West Bengal	25	22.43N	88.29E
Barbacena	Brazil	83	21.13S	43.47W
BARBADOS	West Indies	77	10.10N	59.30W
Barcelona	Spain	67	41.22N	2.10E
Barcelos	Brazil	83	00.59S	62.58W
Barddhaman	W. Bengal	25	23.16N	87.54E
Bardi	Madhya Pradesh	17	24.30N	82.26 E
Bareilly	Uttar Pradesh	24	28.22N	79.27E
Barents Sea	Arctic Ocean	89	73.00N	42.00E
Bargarh	Odisha	26	21.20N	83.37E
Baripada	Odisha	26	21.56N	86.46E
Barisal	Bangladesh	18	22.43N	90.24E
Barmer	Rajasthan	23	25.45N	71.25E
Barnala	Punjab	14	30.25N	75.35E
Barnaul	Russia	71	53.23N	83.40E
Barnstaple	England	69	51.05N	4.15W
Barpeta	Assam	25	26.19N	91.00E
Barrackpur	W. Bengal	18	22.46N	88.24E
Barranquilla	Colombia	81	10.50N	74.48
Barreiras	Brazil	83	12.09S	44.58W
Barrow	England	69	54.07N	3.15W
Barrow, Pt	Alaska, USA	79	71.22N	156.30W
Barshi	Maharashtra	27	18.13N	75.44E
Barwani	Madhya Pradesh	26	22.03N	74.57E
Basavana Bagevadi	Karnataka	28	16.32N	76.03E
Basra	Iraq	65	30.28N	47.51E
Bass , Str.	Australia	85	39.20S	145.00E
Bassein	Myanmar	13	16.54N	94.50E
Basseterre	St Kitts & Nevis	77	17.18N	62.44W
Basti	Uttar Pradesh	24	26.48N	82.46E
Batala	Punjab	14	31.49N	75.14E
Batan, Is	Philippines	64	20.25N	121.59E
Bath	England	69	51.24N	2.20W
Bathinda	Punjab	22	30.11N	75.00E
Bathurst	N.S.W., Australia	85	33.30S	149.35E
Batticaloa	Sri Lanka	65	7.43N	81.44E
Battle Harbour	Labrador, Canada	77	52.19N	55.57W
Batumi	Georgia	65	41.41N	41.38E
Baudh	Odisha	26	20.50N	84.19E
Baurul	Brazi	83	22.20S	49.05W
Bay of Bengal	South Asia	58	16.00N	88.00E
Bayonne	France	70	43.29N	1.28W
Bayreuth	Germany	70	49.57N	11.34E
Beachy Head	England	69	50.44N	0.15E
Bear Great, L.	Canada	76	66.00N	120.00W
Beaufort Sea	Canada	76	72.00N	140.0W
Beaumont	Texas, USA	79	30.05N	94.08W
Beawar	Rajasthan	23	26.06N	74.21E
Begusarai	Bihar	24	25.26N	86.13E
Beijing	China	62	39.55N	116.24E
Beira	Mozambique	75	19.50S	34.52E
Beirut	Lebanon	65	33.50N	35.25E
Bela	Pakistan	14	26.20N	66.20E
Bela	Uttar Pradesh	24	25.56N	82.02E
BELARUS	Europe	67	53.00N	30.00E
Beldanga	W. Bengal	18	23.58N	88.20E
Belem (Para)	Brazil	83	1.27S	48.27W
Belem	Brazil	83	1.20S	48.30W
Belfast	N. Ireland	69	54.35N	5.56W
Belfort	France	70	47.38N	6.52E
Belgaum	Karnataka	28	15.52N	74.34E
BELGIUM	W. Europe	67	51.00N	5.00E
Belgrade	Serbia	67	44.50N	20.30E
Belitung, I.	Indonesia	64	2.30S	108.10E
BELIZE	Central America	77	17.29N	88.14W
Bellary	Karnataka	28	15.09N	76.56E
Belle Ile	France	70	47.20N	3.10W
Bellinghausen Sea	Antarctica	89	66.00S	81.00W
Belmopan	Belize	77	17.14N	88.46W
Belo Horizonte	Brazil	83	19.55S	43.56W
Ben Nevis	Scotland	69	56.48N	5.00W
Bendigo Victoria	Australia	85	36.46S	144.17E

Names	Country/Region	Pg.No.	Lat.	Long.
Bengaluru	Karnataka	28	12.58N	77.38E
Benghazi	Libya	73	32.10N	20.10E
Benguela	Angola	73	12.37S	13.25E
BENIN	West Africa	73	8.00N	2.00E
Benjamin Constant	Brazil	83	4.23S	69.58W
Benxi	China	62	41.16N	123.45E
Berber	Sudan	73	18.01N	34.04E
Berbera	Somali Rep	73	10.27N	45.01E
Bergamo	Italy	70	45.42N	9.41E
Bering , Str.	Asia-N. America	58	65.00N	169.00W
Bering Sea	East Asia	58	58.00N	179.00E
Berlin	Germany	67	52.32N	13.25E
Bermuda	Atlantic Ocean	88	32.19N	64.50W
Bern	Switzerland	67	46.55N	7.30E
Berwick on Tweed	England	69	55.48N	2.00W
Besancon	France	70	47.14N	6.02E
Betroka	Madagascar	75	23.16S	46.05E
Bettiah	Bihar	24	26.48N	84.33E
Betul	Madhya Pradesh	26	21.88N	77.98E
Beypore	Kerala	21	11.10N	75.50E
Beziers	France	70	43.21N	3.14E
Bhabua	Bihar	24	25.01N	83.43E
Bhadohi	Uttar Pradesh	17	25.24N	82.38E
Bhadra	Rajasthan	19	29.15N	75.30E
Bhadrachalam	Andhra Pradesh	27	17.40N	80.56E
Bhadrak	Odisha	26	21.03N	86.33E
Bhadravati	Karnataka	28	13.52N	75.40E
Bhadreswar	W. Bengal	25	22.49N	88.20E
Bhagalpur	Bihar	24	25.15N	87.02E
Bhalki	Karnataka	20	18.04N	77.10E
Bhamo	Myanmar	13	24.16N	97.17E
Bhandara	Maharashtra	27	21.09N	79.42E
Bharatpur	Rajasthan	23	27.15N	77.30E
Bharuch	Gujarat	23	21.41N	73.01E
Bhatgaon	Nepal	15	27.39N	85.22E
Bhatpara	W. Bengal	18	22.54N	88.25E
Bhavnagar	Gujarat	23	21.46N	72.11E
Bhawanipatna	Odisha	26	19.58N	83.12E
Bhilwara	Rajasthan	23	25.21N	74.40E
Bhind	Madhya Pradesh	26	26.36N	78.46E
Bhinmal	Rajasthan	23	25.00N	72.19E
Bhiwani	Haryana	22	28.46N	76.18E
Bhopal	Madhya Pradesh	12	23.16N	77.36E
Bhubaneshwar	Odisha	13	20.15N	85.52E
Bhuj	Gujarat	23	23.15N	69.49E
Bhusawal	Maharashtra	27	21.02N	75.47E
BHUTAN	Asia	59	27.30N	90.00E
Biagoveshchensk	Russia	71	50.20N	127.39E
Bialystok	Poland	67	53.06N	23.18E
Biaora	Madhya Pradesh	26	23.55N	76.57E
Bibao	Spain	70	43.16N	2.56W
Bid	Maharashtra	27	19.00N	75.50E
Bidar	Karnataka	28	17.57N	77.39E
Bihar Sharif	Bihar	24	25.10N	85.36E
Bihar, State	India	24	25.37N	85.32E
Bijapur	Karnataka	28	16.49N	75.43E
Bijapur	Chhattisgarh	26	18.50N	80.50E
Bijawar	Madhya Pradesh	17	24.38N	79.32E
Bijna	Madhya Pradesh	17	25.27N	79.05E
Bijnor	Uttar Pradesh	24	29.23N	79.11 E
Bikaner	Rajasthan	23	28.01E	73.22E
Bilaspur	Himachal Pradesh	22	31.19N	76.50E
Bilaspur	Chhattisgarh	26	22.05N	82.13E
Bingerville	Cote D Ivoire	73	5.18N	3.53W
Birjand	Iran	65	32.57N	59.10E
Birkenhead	England	69	53.24N	3.02W
Birmingham	Alabama, USA	79	33.30N	86.49W
Birmingham	England	69	52.30N	1.55W
Biscay, Bay of	France, etc	70	45.00N	2.30W
Bishkek	Kyrgystan	71	42.59N	74.00E
Bishnupur	W. Bengal	25	23.05N	87.23E
Bismarck	N. Dakota, USA	79	46.49N	100.49W
Bissau	Guinea Bissau	73	11.53N	15.38W
Black Sea	S.E. Europe	66	43.00N	33.00E
Blackpool	England	69	53.50N	3.02W
Blanco, C.	W. Africa	73	21.00N	16.59W
Blantyre	Malawi	73	15.47S	35.02E
Bloemfontein	South Africa	75	29.07S	26.14E
Blue, Mts	N.S.W., Australia	85	34.00S	150.00E
Blumenau	Brazil	83	27.00S	49.00W
Boa Vista	Brazil	83	02.48N	60.30W
Bobbili	Andhra Pradesh	20	18.34N	83.25E
Bodh Gaya	Bihar	24	24.41N	85.02E
Bodinayakkanur	Tamil Nadu	21	10.01N	77.24E
Bogota	Colombia	81	4.43N	74.12W
Bogra	Bangladesh	18	24.51N	89.26E
Boise	Idaho, USA	79	43.36N	116.15W
Bokaro	Jharkhand	24	23.46N	85.58E
Bolangir	Odisha	26	20.41N	83.32E
BOLIVIA	South America	81	15.00S	65.00W
Bologna	Italy	70	44.30N	11.21E
Bolzano	Italy	70	46.31N	11.22E
Bom Jesus da Lapa	Brazil	83	13.14S	43.23W
Bomdila .	Arunachal Pradesh	25	27.20N	92.22E
Bongaigaon	Assam	25	26.26N	90.31E
Bonifacio, Str. of	Corsica-Sardinia	66	41.23N	9.08E
Bonn	Germany	70	40.44N	9.04E
Boothia, Gulf of and Pen.	Canada	76	71.00N	90.00W
Bordeaux	France	70	44.50N	0.34W
Borneo, I.	Indonesia	64	1.00N	115.00E
BOSNIA-HERZEGOVINA	S. Europe	67	44.00N	17.00E
Bosporus, Str.	Black Sea	66	41.10N	29.00E

Names	Country/Region	Pg.No.	Lat.	Long.
Boston	USA	79	42.22N	71.02W
Bothnia, Gulf of	Baltic Sea	66	63.00N	20.00E
BOTSWANA	Africa	73	23.00S	22.00E
Boudh	Odisha	26	20.49N	84.24E
Bourges	France	70	47.05N	2.23E
Bournemouth	England	69	50.44N	1.50W
Boyne, R.	Rep. of Ireland	69	53.44N	6.15W
Bradford	England	69	53.46N	1.40W
Braganca	Brazil	83	1.02S	46.46W
Brahmanbaria	Bangladesh	18	23.58N	91.09E
Brahmaputra, R.	Assam	18	26.45N	93.30E
Brahmpur	Odisha	26	19.18N	84.51E
Brasileia	Brazil	83	10.59S	68.45W
Brasilia	Brazil	83	16.13S	44.29W
Bratislava	Slovakia	70	48.09N	17.07E
BRAZIL	South America	81	10.00S	55.00W
Brazilian Highlands	Brazil	83	18.00S	46.30W
Brazzaville	Congo	73	4.15S	15.20E
Bremen	Germany	70	53.05N	8.50E
Brescia	Italy	70	45.33N	10.15E
Brest	Poland	70	52.05N	23.42E
Bridgetown	Barbados	77	13.05N	59.30W
Brighton	England	69	50.50N	0.10W
Brisbane	Queensland, Aust.	85	27.30S	153.00E
Bristol	England	69	51.27N	2.35W
British Isles	N.W. Europe	69	55.00N	2.00W
British Isles	United Kingdom	69	53.00N	2.00W
Brno	Czech Republic	70	49.12N	16.37E
Broken Hill	N.S.W., Australia	84	30.58S	141.27E
Brownsville	Texas, USA	79	25.56N	97.25W
BRUNEI	S.E. Asia	59	4.55N	114.57E
Brussels	Belgium	70	50.52N	4.22E
Buchan Ness	Scotland	69	57.28N	1.46W
Bucharest	Romania	67	44.25N	26.07E
Budapest	Hungary	67	47.29N	19.03E
Budaun	Uttar Pradesh	24	28.02N	79.10E
Budejovice	Czech Republic	70	48.58N	14.28E
Buea	Cameroon	73	4.09N	9.06E
Buenaventura	Colombia	81	3.55N	77.11W
Buenos Aires	Argentina	81	34.35S	58.20W
Buffalo	New York, USA	79	42.53N	78.50W
Buir Nur	Mongolia	62	47.50N	117.35E
Bujumbura	Burundi	73	3.24S	29.22E
Bukhara	Uzbekistan	65	39.52N	64.30E
Bulandshahr	Uttar Pradesh	24	28.24N	77.54E
Bulawayo	Zimbabwe	75	20.10S	28.43E
Buldhana	Maharashtra	27	20.32N	76.14E
BULGARIA	S.E. Europe	70	42.10N	24.00E
Bundelkhand	Madhya Pradesh	17	24.40N	80.00E
Bundi	Rajasthan	23	25.27N	75.41E
Burgin	China	65	48.00N	86.70E
Burhanpur	Madhya Pradesh	16	21.17N	76.16E
BURKINA FASO	E. Africa	73	12.00N	2.00W
Bursa	Turkey	65	40.10N	29.01E
Buru, I.	Moluccas	64	3.20S	126.30E
BURUNDI	Africa	73	3.00S	30.00E
Busan	South Korea	63	35.07N	129.02E
Butte (But)	Montana, USA	79	46.00N	112.33W
Buxar	Bihar	24	25.34N	84.01E
Bydgoszcz	Poland	70	53.03N	18.00E

C

Names	Country/Region	Pg.No.	Lat.	Long.
Cabinda	Angola	73	5.00S	12.30E
Cabo	Brazil	83	8.14S	34.58W
Caceres	Spain	70	39.29N	6.23W
Cachoeira do Sul	Brazil	83	30.03S	52.52W
Cachoeira	Brazil	83	12.35S	39.59W
Cadiz	Spain	67	36.32N	6.17W
Caen	France	70	49.11N	0.22W
Caernarvon	Wales	69	53.08N	4.15W
Cagliari	Sardinia, Italy	67	39.15N	9.05E
Cairns	Queensland, Aust.	85	16.54S	145.44E
Cairo	Egypt	73	30.02N	31.15E
Calais	France	70	50.55N	1.50E
Calama	Chile	83	22.30S	68.55W
Calgary	Canada	77	51.02N	114.20W
Cali	Colombia	81	3.25N	76.35W
California	USA	79	40.00N	120.00W
California, Gulf of	Mexico	76	27.00N	111.00W
Callao	Peru	81	12.00S	77.00W
Calvinia	South Africa	75	31.25S	19.47E
Camacupa	Angola	73	12.03S	17.50E
Camaguey	Cuba	77	21.20N	78.00W
CAMBODIA	S.E. Asia	59	12.00S	105.00E
Cambrai	France	70	50.11N	3.14E
Cambrian, Mts	Wales	69	52.00N	3.50W
Cambridge	England	69	52.12N	0.10E
CAMEROON	West Africa	73	5.30N	13.00E
Cameroun, Mt	Cameroon	72	4.11N	9.09E
Cameta	Brazil	83	2.13S	49.30W
Camocim	Brazil	83	2.55S	40.50W
Campina Grande	Brazil	83	7.15S	35.50W
Campo Grande	Brazil	83	20.25S	54.40W
Campo Mourao	Brazil	83	24.01S	52.24W
Campos	Brazil	83	21.20S	41.20W
Canacona	Goa	20	14.50N	74.08E
CANADA	North America	77	60.00N	100.00W
Canadian, R.	USA	79	35.20N	100.00W
Canary, Is	Atlantic Ocean	88	28.00N	15.30W
Canberra	Australia	85	35.17S	149.18E
Cangamba	Angola	75	13.41S	19.51E
Cannes	France	70	43.33N	6.59E
Canoas	Brazil	83	28.55S	51.10W
Canterbury Bight	New Zealand	85	44.10S	172.00E

Names	Country/Region	Pg.No.	Lat.	Long.
Cape Lopez	Gabon	73	0.50S	8.30E
Cape Province	S. Africa	73	32.00S	24.00E
Cape Town	South Africa	75	33.56S	18.28E
CAPE VERDE	West Africa	73	17.00N	25.00W
Car Nicobar	Andaman & Nicobar Is	29	9.12N	92.48E
Carajas	Brazil	83	6.02S	50.10W
Caraoas	Venezuela	81	10.31N	67.05W
Caratinga	Brazil	83	19.50S	42.06W
Carcassonne	France	70	43.13N	2.21E
Cardamom Hills	Kerala	21	9.27N	76.52E
Cardiff	Wales	69	51.30N	3.10W
Cardigan, Bay	Wales	69	52.05N	4.39W
Cariacica	Brazil	83	20.15S	40.23W
Caribbean Sea	West Indies	76	15.00N	73.00W
Carlisle	England	69	54.54N	3.00W
Carolina	Brazil	83	7.21S	47.22W
Carpathian, Mts	S.E. Europe	66	49.00N	22.30E
Carpentaria, G. of	Queensland, Aust.	84	15.00S	139.00E
Carson City	Nevada, USA	79	39.08N	119.45W
Cartagena	Spain	67	37.39N	0.55W
Cartagena	Columbia	81	10.22N	75.32W
Casablanca	Morocco	73	33.39N	7.35W
Cascade, Ra.	N. America	76	47.00N	121.30W
Cascavel	Brazil	83	4.10S	38.15W
Caspian Sea	Europe-Asia	71	42.00N	52.00E
Cassel (Kassel)	Germany	70	51.20N	9.30E
Castries	St Lucia	77	14.01N	60.59W
Caucaia	Brazil	83	3.44S	38.45W
Caucasus, Mts	Georgia	58	43.00N	44.00E
Cavan	Rep. of Ireland	69	54.00N	7.30W
Caxias do Sul	Brazil	83	29.14S	51.10W
Caxias	Brazil	83	4.53S	43.20W
Cayenne	Fr. Guiana	81	4.58N	52.18W
Cayman's, Is	West Indies	76	19.40N	80.30W
Celebes, I.	Indonesia	64	2.00S	120.00E
CENTRAL AFRICAN REPUBLIC	Africa	73	5.00N	20.00E
Ceuta	North Africa	73	35.53N	5.20W
CHAD	Africa	73	15.00N	17.15E
Chad, L.	Africa	73	13.20N	14.00E
Chagos, Arch.	Indian Ocean	58	6.00S	72.00E
Chaibasa	Jharkhand	24	22.33N	85.51E
Chakdarra	Pakistan	14	34.40N	72.06E
Chakwal	Pakistan	14	32.56N	72.53E
Chalgali	Chhattisgarh	17	23.18N	83.42E
Chalisgaon	Maharashtra	27	20.33N	75.10E
Chalons-sur-Saone	France	70	46.47N	4.52E
Chamarajanagar	Karnataka	28	11.55N	76.56E
Chamba	Himachal Pradesh	22	32.29N	76.10E
Chambal, R.	Madhya Pradesh	26	26.40N	76.20E
Chambery	France	70	45.34N	5.56E
Champa	Chhattisgarh	26	22.02N	82.43E
Champawat	Uttarakhand	24	29.21N	80.07E
Champhai	Mizoram	25	23.29N	93.17E
Chamrajnagar	Karnataka	28	11.56N	77.00E
Chanaral	Chile	83	26.23S	70.40W
Chandauli	Uttar Pradesh	24	25.15N	83.16E
Chandausi	Uttar Pradesh	17	28.27N	78.49E
Chandel	Manipur	25	24.17N	93.56E
Chanderi	Madhya Pradesh	16	24.42N	78.11E
Chandigarh, Union Terr.	India	12	30.42N	76.54E
Chandrakona	W. Bengal	18	22.44N	87.33E
Chandrapur	Maharashtra	27	19.57N	79.21E
Chanduria	W. Bengal	18	22.56N	88.55E
Changara	Mozambique	75	16.50S	33.17E
Changchun	China	62	43.54N	125.20E
Changhua	Taiwan	62	24.02N	120.30E
Changlang .	Arunachal Pradesh	25	27.04N	95.39E
Changsha	China	62	28.09N	112.45E
Channapatna	Karnataka	21	12.38N	77.13E
Channel, Is	English Channel	69	49.30N	2.30W
Charkhari	Uttar Pradesh	17	25.26N	79.45E
Charkhi Dadri	Punjab	14	28.37N	76.19E
Charleston	S. Carolina, USA	79	32.50N	79.58W
Charleston	W. Virginia, USA	79	38.23N	81.40W
Charsadda	Pakistan	14	34.08N	71.46E
Chartres	France	70	48.27N	1.30E
Chatra	Jharkhand	24	24.12N	84.56E
Cheduba, I.	Myanmar	10	18.40N	93.30E
Cheju Do (Quelpart), I.	S. Korea	63	33.29N	126.34E
Chelyuskin, C.	Russia	71	77.52N	104.30E
Chemnitz	Germany	70	50.50N	12.55E
Chenab, R.	India	22	32.00N	77.14E
Chengalpattu	Tamil Nadu	21	12.42N	80.01E
Chengde	China	62	40.59N	117.55E
Chengdu	China	62	30.40N	104.12E
Chennai	Tamil Nadu	28	13.04N	80.17E
Cherbourg	France	70	49.40N	1.40W
Chernivih	Ukraine	67	51.29N	31.19E
Chernivtsi(Cernauti)	Ukraine	70	48.18N	25.56E
Cherrapunji	Meghalaya	25	25.17N	91.47E
Chesapeake	Virginia, USA	79	38.00N	76.12W
Cheyenne	Wyoming, USA	79	41.09N	104.19W
Chhapra	Bihar	24	25.47N	84.47E
Chhatarpur	Madhya Pradesh	26	24.54N	79.38E
Chhatrapur	Odisha	26	19.21N	85.03E
Chhattisgarh, State	India	26	21.00N	81.00E
Chhindwara	Madhya Pradesh	26	22.03N	78.59E
Chiang Mai	Thailand	64	18.50N	98.53E
Chicago	Illinois, USA	79	42.00N	87.40E
Chidambaram	Tamil Nadu	28	11.24N	79.44E
Chik Ballapur	Karnataka	28	13.29N	77.42E

Names	Country/Region	Pg.No.	Lat.	Long.
Chikmagalur	Karnataka	28	13.18N	75.49E
Chiknayakanhalli	Karnataka	21	13.25N	76.40E
CHILE	South America	81	30.00S	71.00W
Chilika, L.	Odisha	26	9.50N	85.30E
Chiloe, I.	Chile	80	42.52S	74.00W
Chimbay	Uzbekistan	65	43.00N	59.43E
Chimborazo, Vol.	Equador	80	1.30S	79.11W
CHINA	S.E. Asia	64	33.00N	105.00E
Chinde	Mozambique	75	18.35S	36.28E
Chindwin, R.	Myanmar	11	22.30N	95.00E
Chingola	Zambia	75	12.31S	27.53E
Chinhoyi	Zimbabwe	75	17.21S	30.11E
Chiniot	Pakistan	14	31.44N	73.01E
Chinju	S. Korea	63	35.12N	128.02E
Chipata	Zambia	75	13.40S	32.42E
Chiromo	Malawi	75	16.33S	35.10E
Chisinau	Maldova	67	47.00N	28.55E
Chisinau	Moldova	71	47.02N	28.52E
Chita	Russia	71	53.10N	113.40E
Chitembo	Angola	73	13.32S	16.46E
Chitradurga	Karnataka	28	14.14N	76.26E
Chitrakootdham	Uttar Pradesh	24	25.15N	80.41E
Chitral	Pakistan	14	35.48N	71.52E
Chittagong	Bangladesh	18	22.21N	91.53E
Chittaranjan	W. Bengal	25	23.50N	87.00E
Chittaurgarh	Rajasthan	23	24.54N	74.42E
Chittoor	Andhra Pradesh	27	13.13N	79.08E
Chittur	Kerala	21	10.42N	76.47E
Chongjin	N. Korea	63	41.51N	129.58E
Chongju	S. Korea	63	35.50N	127.04E
Chongqing	China	62	29.32N	106.50E
Choybalsun	Mongolia	62	48.03N	114.28E
Christchurch	New Zealand	85	43.30S	172.40E
Chukchi Sea	Arctic Ocean	89	68.00N	175.00W
Chunar	Uttar Pradesh	17	25.08N	82.56E
Chunchura	W. Bengal	25	22.53N	88.27E
Chur	Switzerland	70	46.52N	9.22E
Churachandpur	Manipur	25	24.18N	93.39E
Churchill	Canada	77	58.44N	94.15W
Churu	Rajasthan	23	28.19N	75.01E
Cincinnatl	Ohio, USA	79	39.07N	84.30W
Circars, Northern	Andhra Pradesh	20	17.00N	82.20E
Ciudad Bolivar	Venezuela	81	8.08N	63.57W
Ciudad del Este	Paraguay	83	25.32S	54.34W
Clermont Ferrand	France	70	45.46N	3.06N
Cleveland	Ohio, USA	79	41.28N	81.40W
Cluj-Napoca	Romania	67	46.46N	23.35E
Clyde, Firth of	Scotland	69	54.40N	4.30W
Coast, Ra.	N. America	76	40.00N	123.00W
Cobh	Rep. of Ireland	69	51.55N	8.19W
Cobija	Bolivia	81	11.01S	68.45W
Cochabamba	Bolivia	80	17.26S	66.10W
Cochrane	Ontario, Canada	79	49.00N	81.00W
Cocos-Keeling, Is	Indian Ocean	88	12.12S	96.54E
Codajas	Brazil	83	3.55S	62.00W
Codo	Brazil	83	4.28S	43.51W
Coimbatore	Tamil Nadu	28	11.00N	77.00E
Colgong	Bihar	17	25.16N	87.17E
Cologne	Germany	70	50.56N	6.57E
COLOMBIA	South America	81	5.00N	75.00W
Colombo	Sri Lanka	59	6.56N	79.56E
Colon	Panama	77	9.21N	79.56W
Colorado, R.	Argentina	80	38.00S	65.00W
Colorado, R.	USA	79	37.30N	109.43W
Columbia	S. Carolina, USA	79	34.0N	81.00W
Columbia, R.	USA	79	48.25N	118.12W
Columbus	Georgia, USA	79	32.30N	84.56W
Columbus	Ohio, USA	79	39.57N	83.02W
Comilla	Bangladesh	18	23.25N	91.13E
Como	Italy	70	45.48N	9.05E
Comorin, C.	Tamil Nadu	28	8.04N	77.36E
COMOROS	Africa/Indian Oean	73	11.55S	44.30E
Conakry	Guinea	73	9.29N	13.42W
Concepcion	Chile	81	36.50S	73.10W
Concord	New Hampshire, USA	79	43.15N	71.34W
Conepclon	Paraguay	81	23.22S	57.26W
CONGO	W. Africa	73	1.00S	16.00E
CONGO, DEMOCRATIC REPUBLIC	Africa	73	5.00S	15.00E
Constanta	Romania	67	44.12N	28.38E
Cook , Str.	New Zealand	85	41.00S	171.30E
Cook, Is	Pacific Ocean	87	20.00S	160.00W
Coolgardie	W. Australia	85	30.57S	121.10E
Copenhagen	Denmark	67	55.40N	12.30E
Copiapo	Chile	83	27.18S	70.24W
Coral Sea	Australia	84	15.00S	150.00E
Cordoba	Argentina	81	31.22S	64.15W
Cork	Rep. of Ireland	69	51.54N	8.29W
Coromandel Coast	Tamil Nadu	10	12.00N	80.30E
Corsica, I.	France	66	42.00N	9.00E
Corumba	Brazil	83	19.00S	57.30W
COSTA RICA	Central America	77	10.00N	85.00W
COTE D' IVOIRE	Africa	72	06.51N	5.18W
Cotswold Hills	England	69	51.40N	2.20W
Coventry	England	69	52.24N	1.30W
Covington	Kentucky, USA	79	39.05N	84.30W
Cox's Bazar	Bangladesh	18	21.27N	92.01E
Coxim	Brazil	83	18.30S	54.55W
Crete, Is	Greece	66	35.10N	25.00E
Crewe	England	69	53.07N	2.27W
Crimea	Ukraine	67	45.30N	35.00E
CROATIA	S. Europe	70	45.00N	16.00E
Crownest Pass	Canada	76	49.40N	114.40W
Croydon	England	69	51.22N	0.06W
CUBA	West Indies	73	22.00N	80.00W
Cuddalore	Tamil Nadu	28	11.43N	79.49E
Cuddapah	Andhra Pradesh	27	14.30N	78.42E
Cuddapah	Andhra Pradesh	27	14.28N	78.52E
Cuiaba	Brazil	83	15.30S	56.00W
Curitiba	Brazil	83	25.26S	49.20W
Cuttack	Odisha	26	20.28N	85.54E
Cuxhaven	Germany	70	53.53N	8.42E
Cuzco	Peru	83	13.32S	72.05W
CYPRUS	Mediterranean	59	35.00N	33.00E
CZECH REPUBLIC	Central Europe	67	49.00N	16.00E

D

Names	Country/Region	Pg.No.	Lat.	Long.
Dabhoi	Gujarat	23	22.11N	73.25E
Dadra & Nagar Haveli, Union Terr.	India	12	20.10N	72.90E
Dahej	Gujarat	23	21.42N	72.38E
Dahod	Gujarat	23	22.46N	74.18E
Dakar	Senegal	73	14.34N	17.29W
Dakshin Gangotri	Antarctica	89	70.00S	12.00E
Dalandzadgad	Mongolia	62	43.37N	104.17E
Dalap-Uliga-Darrit	Marshall Is	87	7.07N	171.22E
Dalian	China	62	38.51N	121.37E
Dallas	Texas, USA	79	34.45N	96.48W
Dalmau	Uttar Pradesh	17	26.07N	81.05E
Dalmianagar	Bihar	24	24.53N	84.09E
Daltenganj	Jharkhand	24	24.02N	84.04E
Daly Waters	N. Terr., Australia	84	16.19S	133.28E
Daman & Diu, Union Terr.	Western India	12	20.25N	72.50E
Daman, Union Terr.	Western India	12	20.25N	72.53E
Damascus	Syria	59	33.30N	36.14E
Damavand, Mt	Iran	65	36.00N	52.00E
Damietta	Egypt	65	31.24N	31.48E
Damodar, R.	W. Bengal	25	23.17N	87.35E
Damoh	Madhya Pradesh	26	23.50N	79.29E
Danapur	Bihar	17	25.38N	85.05E
Dandot	Pakistan	14	32.41N	72.59E
Dantewara	Chhattisgarh	26	18.52N	81.26E
Danube, R.	Europe	66	44.00N	25.00E
Danzig (Gdansk)	Poland	70	54.20N	18.45E
Daporijo	Arunachal Pradesh	25	27.59N	94.18E
Dar es Salaam	Tanzania	73	6.50S	39.17E
Darbhanga	Bihar	24	26.10N	85.57E
Dargai	Pakistan	14	34.30N	71.53E
Darjiling	West Bengal	25	27.03N	88.18E
Darling, R.	Australia	84	33.00S	142.30E
Darlington	England	69	54.32N	1.33W
Darmstadt	Germany	70	49.52N	8.39E
Darrang	Assam	17	26.45N	92.40E
Dartmoor	England	69	50.40N	4.00W
Darwin	N. Terr., Australia	84	12.30S	131.00E
Daska	Pakistan	14	32.17N	74.24E
Datia	Madhya Pradesh	26	25.39N	78.27E
Daulatabad	Maharashtra	27	19.57N	75.15E
Daund	Maharashtra	27	18.32N	74.40E
Dausa	Rajasthan	23	26.50N	76.21E
Davangere	Karnataka	28	14.31N	75.58E
Davis, Str.	Canada-Greenland	76	67.00N	58.00W
Dawson	Canada	77	64.05N	139.20W
De Aar	South Africa	75	30.40S	24.00E
Dead Sea	Israel/Jordan	66	31.30N	35.00E
Debagarh	Odisha	26	21.32N	84.44E
Deccan	S. India	10	18.00N	77.00E
Dee, R.	Scotland	69	57.05N	2.15W
Dehra Dun	Uttarakhand	12	30.19N	78.04E
Delaram	Afghanistan	12	32.10N	65.30E
Delft, I.	Sri Lanka	21	9.30N	79.40E
Delgado, C.	Mozambique	72	10.45S	40.40E
Delhi, Union Territory	India	12	28.38N	77.12E
Denizli	Turkey	65	37.42N	29.02E
DENMARK	N.W. Europe	67	56.30N	8.00E
Denver	Colorado, USA	79	39.45N	105.00W
Deogarh	Jharkhand	24	24.29N	86.42E
Deogarh	Odisha	26	21.32N	84.46E
Deoghar	Jharkhand	24	24.29N	84.42E
Deoli	Maharashtra	20	20.39N	78.32E
Deoria	Uttar Pradesh	24	26.23N	83.42E
Dera Ghazi Khan	Pakistan	14	30.04N	70.49E
Dera	Syria	65	32.36N	36.07E
Derby	England	69	52.58N	1.25W
Des Moines	USA	79	41.35N	93.37W
Detroit	Michigan, USA	79	42.21N	83.03W
Devakottai	Tamil Nadu	21	9.57N	78.53E
Devarkonda	Andhra Pradesh	20	16.42N	78.58E
Devli	Rajasthan	23	25.46N	75.25E
Dewangiri	Bhutan	18	26.51N	91.27E
Dewas	Madhya Pradesh	26	22.58N	76.06E
Dezful	Iran	65	32.24N	48.32E
Dezhnev, C.	Russia	71	66.10N	169.03W
Dhaka	Bangladesh	59	23.43N	90.26E
Dhamra	Odisha	17	20.48N	86.56E
Dhamtari	Chhattisgarh	26	20.42N	81.34E
Dhanbad	Jharkhand	24	23.47N	86.30E
Dhandhuka	Gujarat	19	22.21N	72.02E
Dhankuta	Nepal	15	26.55N	87.20E
Dhanushkodi	Tamil Nadu	21	09.13N	79.24E
Dhar	Madhya Pradesh	26	22.35N	75.20E
Dharapuram	Tamil Nadu	21	10.45N	77.34E
Dharmapuri	Tamil Nadu	28	12.08N	78.13E
Dharmavaram	Andhra Pradesh	27	14.25N	77.00E
Dharmshala	Himachal Pradesh	22	32.16N	76.23E
Dharwad	Karnataka	28	15.27N	75.05E
Dhaulagiri	Nepal	11	29.11N	83.00E
Dhaulpur	Rajasthan	23	26.42N	77.53E
Dhebar, L.	Rajasthan	19	24.30N	74.00E
Dhemaji	Assam	25	27.32N	94.43E
Dhenkanal	Odisha	26	20.40N	85.38E
Dholera	Gujarat	19	22.15N	72.15E
Dholka	Gujarat	19	22.44N	72.29E
Dhrangadhra	Gujarat	23	22.59N	71.31E
Dhubri	Assam	25	26.02N	90.02E
Dhule	Maharashtra	27	20.58N	74.47E
Diamantina	Brazil	83	18.17S	43.40W
Diamond Harbour	W. Bengal	25	22.11N	88.14E
Dibrugarh	Assam	25	27.27N	94.55E
Didwana	Rajasthan	23	27.17N	74.25E
Dieppe	France	70	49.58N	1.00E
Dig	Rajasthan	19	27.28N	77.20E
Digboi	Assam	25	27.33N	95.40E
Dijon	France	70	47.20N	5.03E
Dili	East Timor	59	08.34S	125.34E
Dimapur	Nagaland	25	25.51N	93.48E
Dinajpur	Bangladesh	18	25.37N	88.40E
Dinaric Alps	Croatia	66	44.00N	17.00E
Dindigul	Tamil Nadu	28	10.22N	78.00E
Dindori	Madhya Pradesh	26	22.57N	81.41E
Dingwall	Scotland	69	57.36N	4.26E
Diphu	Assam	25	25.49N	93.26E
Disa	Gujarat	23	24.14N	72.13E
Dispur	Assam	25	26.09N	91.50E
Diu, Union Terr.	Western India	12	20.42N	71.01E
Divinopolis	Brazil	83	20.08S	44.55W
Djibouti	E. Africa	73	11.34N	43.01E
Dneiper, R.	Ukraine-Belarus	66	50.00N	32.00E
Dnepropetrovsk	Ukraine	67	48.28N	35.02E
Dniester, R.	Ukraine	66	46.00N	29.50E
Doda	Jammu & Kashmir	22	33.08N	75.37E
Dodabetta, Mt	Tamil Nadu	10	11.25N	76.46E
Dod-Ballapur	Karnataka	21	13.14N	77.23E
Dodoma	Tanzania	73	06.10S	35.44E
Doha	Qatar	59	25.15N	51.36E
Dohad	Gujarat	23	22.52N	74.15E
Dolomites, Mts	Italy	70	46.15N	12.00E
DOMINICA	West Indies	77	15.20N	61.20W
DOMINICAN REP.	West Indies	77	19.00N	70.00W
Don, R.	Scotland	69	57.11N	2.05W
Don, R.	Russia	71	50.10N	40.00E
Donegal	Rep. of Ireland	69	54.39N	8.06W
Donegal, Bay	Rep. of Ireland	69	52.08N	10.16W
Donetsk (Stalino)	Ukraine	67	48.00N	37.38E
Dongargarh	Chhattisgarh	12	21.12N	80.50E
Dongola	Sudan	73	19.10N	30.26E
Doranda	Jharkhand	17	23.22N	85.22E
Dortmund	Germany	70	51.31N	7.27E
Douglas	Isle of Man., UK	69	54.12N	4.25W
Dourados	Brazil	83	22.09S	54.52W
Dover	England	69	51.08N	1.15E
Dover, Str. of	England/France	69	51.00N	1.30E
Drakensberg	Southern Africa	72	28.30S	29.00E
Dras	Jammu & Kashmir	14	34.22N	75.50E
Drazinda	Pakistan	14	31.47N	70.05E
Dresden	Germany	70	51.03N	13.45E
Drogheda	Rep. of Ireland	69	52.44N	6.23W
Duala (Douala)	Cameroon	73	4.05N	9.40E
Dublin	Ireland	67	53.21N	6.16W
Dublin	Rep. of Ireland	69	53.21N	6.16W
Duisburg	Germany	70	51.26N	6.45E
Duki	Pakistan	14	30.10N	68.35E
Duluth	Minnesota, USA	79	46.49N	92.09W
Dumfries	Scotland	69	55.05N	3.37W
Dumka	Jharkhand	24	24.15N	87.16E
Dun Laoghaire	Rep. of Ireland	69	53.17N	6.09W
Duncansby Head	Scotland	69	58.4	3.00W
Dundalk	Rep. of Ireland	69	54.00N	6.25W
Dundee	Scotland	69	56.29N	3.00W
Dunedin	New Zealand	85	45.40S	170.30E
Dungarpur	Rajasthan	23	23.50N	73.50E
Dunnet Head	Scotland	69	58.38N	3.22W
Durban	South Africa	75	29.53S	31.00E
Durg	Chhattisgarh	26	21.12N	81.18E
Durgapur	Bangladesh	18	25.00N	90.50E
Durgapur	W. Bengal	25	23.30N	87.20E
Dushanbe	Tajikistan	71	38.50N	69.20E
Dusseldorf	Germany	70	51.13N	6.47E
Dwarka	Gujarat	23	22.14N	69.01E

E

Names	Country/Region	Pg.No.	Lat.	Long.
East London	South Africa	75	33.00S	27.54E
East Sea	Asia	59	39.00N	137.00E
East Siberian Sea	Russia	71	73.00N	160.00E
ECUADOR	South America	81	2.00S	78.00E
Edinburgh	Scotland	69	55.56N	3.12W
Edmonton	Canada	77	55.35N	113.30W
EGYPT	N. Africa	73	25.00N	30.00E
El Alamein	Egypt	73	30.50N	28.57E
El Faiyum	Egypt	65	29.19N	30.50E
El Giza	Egypt	73	31.01N	31.13E
El Obeid	Sudan	73	13.16N	29.48E
El Paso	Texas USA	79	31.49N	106.31W
EL SALVADOR	Central America	77	13.50N	89.00W
Elarish	Egypt	65	31.08N	33.50E
Elba, I.	Italy	70	42.45N	10.10E
Elbe, R.	Germany	66	53.50N	9.00E
Elbert, Mt	USA	79	39.05N	106.27W
Elbrus, Mt	Russia	71	42.23N	42.27E
Elburz, Mts	Iran	65	36.10N	52.00E
Elgin	Scotland	69	57.40N	3.20W
Ellenabad	Haryana	14	29.26N	74.54E
Ellesmere, I.	Canada	76	79.30N	80.00W
Ellora	Maharashtra	27	20.02N	75.13E
Eluru	Andhra Pradesh	27	16.43N	81.09E
Empangeni	South Africa	75	28.45S	31.55E
England	U.K.	67	53.00N	1.00W
English Channel	England/France	69	50.00N	2.00W
Ennore	Tamil Nadu	21	13.14N	80.22E
Entebbe	Uganda	73	0.02N	32.30E
EQUATORIAL GUINEA	Africa	72	03.45N	08.47E
Eregli	Turkey	65	41.15N	31.30E
Erfurt	Germany	70	50.58N	11.02E
Erie, L.	Canada-USA	79	42.00N	81.00W
Erimo, C.	Japan	63	41.50N	143.15E
ERITREA	Africa	73	15.20N	38.55E
Ernakulam	Kerala	28	10.00N	76.15E
Erode	Tamil Nadu	28	11.20N	77.46E
Erramala, Ra.	Andhra Pradesh	20	15.20N	78.00E
Erz Gebirge	Germany	70	50.40N	13.30E
Erzurbum	Turkey	65	39.55N	41.10E
Eskisehir	Turkey	65	39.50N	30.35E
Essen	Germany	70	51.28N	7.01E
Estancia	Brazil	83	11.15S	37.28W
ESTONIA	Europe	67	58.20N	27.00E
Etah	Uttar Pradesh	24	27.35N	78.40E
Etawah	Uttar Pradesh	24	26.47N	79.02E
ETHIOPIA	N. E. Africa	73	10.00N	40.00E
Ethiopian Highlands	E. Africa	73	10.00N	37.00E
Etna, Mt	Sicily	66	37.45N	15.00E
Euphrates, R.	Iraq	65	33.30N	43.10E
Europe, Continent	**World**	**92**		
Everest, Mt	Nepal-China	15	28.05N	86.58E
Exeter	England	69	50.42N	3.30W
Eyre, L.	S. Australia	84	28.30S	137.20E
Eyre, Pen.	S. Australia	84	34.00S	137.00E

F

Names	Country/Region	Pg.No.	Lat.	Long.
Fairbanks	Alaska, USA	79	64.59N	148.10W
Faisalabad	Pakistan	14	31.30N	73.05E
Faizabad	Uttar Pradesh	24	26.47N	82.12E
Fale	Tokelau	87	9.22 S	171.14 W
Falkland, Is	S. Atlantic Ocean	81	52.00S	59.00W
False Point	Odisha	17	20.20N	86.46E
Farafangana	Madagascar	75	22.48S	47.48E
Farah	Afghanistan	61	32.30N	62.10E
Farewell, C.	Greenland	77	59.47N	43.40W
Faridabad	Haryana	22	28.25N	77.22E
Faridkot	Punjab	22	30.40N	74.57E
Faroe, Is	Denmark	67	62.00N	7.00W
Fatehabad	Haryana	22	29.31N	75.30E
Fatehgarh	Uttar Pradesh	24	27.23N	79.40E
Fatehgarh Sahib	Punjab	22	30.41N	76.28E
Fatehjang	Pakistan	14	33.34N	72.38E
Fatehpur	Rajasthan	23	28.00N	75.02E
Fatehpur	Uttar Pradesh	24	25.55N	80.52E
Fazilka	Punjab	22	30.25N	74.04E
Fderik	Mauritania	73	22.40N	12.45W
Ferrara	Italy	70	44.51N	11.28E
Fez	Morocco	73	34.08N	5.06W
Fianarantsoa	Madagascar	75	21.27S	47.07E
Fife Ness	Scotland	69	56.16N	2.35W
FIJI	Pacific Ocean/Oceania	87	16.00N	180.00E
FINLAND	N. Europe	67	62.00N	25.00E
Firozabad	Uttar Pradesh	24	27.09N	78.24E
Firozepur	Punjab	22	30.55N	74.40E
Fishguard	Wales	69	51.59N	4.59W
Fiume (Reijeka)	Croatia	70	45.20N	14.25E
Flamborough Head	England	69	54.07N	0.05W
Flores, I.	Indonesia	64	8.30S	121.00E
Floriano	Brazil	83	6.46S	42.59W
Florianopolis	Brazil	83	27.37S	48.27W
Florida	USA	79	27.00N	82.00W
Folkestone	England	69	51.04N	1.10E
Fongafale	Tuvalu	87	8.31S	179.13E
Forfar	Scotland	69	56.40N	2.50W
Formosa	Brazil	83	15.30S	47.22W
Fort Munro	Pakistan	14	29.55N	70.03E
Fort Smith	Canada	77	60.05N	112.00W
Fort Smith	Arkansas USA	79	35.25N	94.25W
Fort William	Scotland	69	56.48N	5.05W
Fort Worth	Taxas, USA	79	32.43N	97.20W
Fort Yukon	Alaska, USA	79	66.20N	145.00W
Fortaleza	Brazil	83	3.50S	38.28W
Fort-de-France	Martinique	87	14.36N	61.02W
Forth, Firth of	Scotland	69	56.03N	3.00W
Fouta Djallon	W. Africa	72	11.20N	12.10W
Foxe Basin	Canada	77	68.00N	78.00W
Foz do Iguacu	Argentina	81	25.33S	54.31W
Franca	Brazil	83	20.33S	47.27W
FRANCE	W. Europe	67	48.00N	2.00E
Franceville	Gabon	73	1.40S	13.31E
Francistown	Bostwana	75	21.11S	27.32E
Frankfort	Kentucky, USA	79	33.12N	85.44W
Frankfurt-am-Main	Germany	70	50.06N	8.40E
Frankfurt-an-der-Oder	Germany	70	52.22N	14.33W
Fraserburgh	Scotland	69	57.42N	2.00E
Fredericton	Canada	77	45.55N	66.32W
Freetown	Sierra Leone	73	8.30N	13.10W
Freiburg	Germany	70	48.00N	7.52E
Fremantle	W. Australia	85	32.05S	115.40E
French Guiana	South America	81	4.00N	53.00W
French Polynesia	Pacific Ocean	87	20.00S	145.00W
Frisian, Is	Germany/Netherlands	70	53.40N	7.00E

Names	Country/Region	Pg.No.	Lat.	Long.
Fuji San, Mt	Japan	63	35.20N	138.20E
Fukui	Japan	63	35.25N	135.09E
Fukuoka	Japan	63	33.30N	131.00E
Fundy, Bay of	Nova Scotia, Canada	76	45.00N	66.00W
Fushun	China	62	42.00N	123.59E
Fuzhou	China	62	26.07N	119.21E

G

Names	Country/Region	Pg.No.	Lat.	Long.
Gabes, Gulf of	Tunisia	73	34.00N	10.20E
GABON	Africa	73	1.00S	12.00E
Gaborone	Bostwana	73	24.45S	25.55E
Gadag	Karnataka	28	15.25N	75.42E
Gadchiroli	Maharashtra	27	20.11N	80.03E
Gadwel	Andhra Pradesh	27	16.13N	77.48E
Galapagos, I.	Ecuador	80	1.00S	90.00W
Galati	Romania	67	45.28N	28.04E
Galle	Sri Lanka	61	6.01N	80.14E
Galveston	Taxas, USA	79	29.19N	94.50W
Galway (Gaillimh)	Rep. of Ireland	69	53.16N	9.05W
GAMBIA	W. Africa	73	13.25N	16.00W
Ganawati	Karnataka	20	15.30N	76.36E
Gandak, R.	Bihar	24	26.30N	84.30E
Ganderbal	Jammu & Kashmir	22	34.14N	74.47E
Gandhinagar	Gujarat	12	23.10N	72.41E
Ganga (Ganges), R.	India	11	21.30N	89.40E
Ganganagar	Rajasthan	23	29.49N	73.50E
Gangotri	Uttarakhand	24	30.54N	78.54E
Gangtok	Sikkim	25	27.20N	88.40E
Ganjam	Odisha	26	19.22N	85.06E
Gar	China	62	31.45N	80.21E
Garanhuns	Brazil	83	8.53S	36.28W
Garhwa	Jharkhand	24	24.10N	83.52E
Garo Hills (Tura)	Meghalaya	11	25.30N	90.30E
Garonne, R.	France	70	44.34N	0.10E
Garrauli	Madhya Pradesh	17	25.05N	79.24E
Gartha	Madhya Pradesh	16	24.25N	78.03E
Gauriganj	Uttar Pradesh	24	26.13N	81.41E
Gaurihar	Madhya Pradesh	17	25.16N	80.12E
Gautemala City	Guatemala	77	14.38N	90.33W
Gavle	Sweden	67	60.40N	17.00E
Gawilgarh	Maharashtra	20	21.22N	77.25E
Gaya	Bihar	24	24.48N	85.00E
Gdynia	Poland	70	54.34N	18.35E
Geelong	Victoria, Australia	85	38.10S	144. 21E
Geneva	Switzerland	70	46.13N	6.07E
Genoa	Italy	70	44.24N	8.57E
Georgetown	Guyana	81	6.50N	58.12W
GEORGIA	Asia	59	41.40N	45.00E
Gereshk	Afghanistan	12	31.50N	64.38E
GERMANY	Europe	66	52.0N	12.00E
Gerona	Spain	70	41.59N	2.49E
Ghadames	Libya	73	30.10N	9.30E
Ghaghara, R.	Uttar Pradesh	17	27.30N	81.20E
GHANA	W. Africa	73	6.00N	1.00W
Ghanzi	Bostwana	75	21.42S	21.39E
Ghatampur	Uttar Pradesh	17	26.08N	80.13E
Ghats, Eastern	S. India	10	16.00N	80.00E
Ghats, Western	S. India	11	16.00N	74.00E
Ghaziabad	Uttar Pradesh	24	28.40N	77.28E
Ghazipur	Uttar Pradesh	24	25.34N	83.35E
Ghazni	Afghanistan	14	33.34N	68.17E
Ghent	Belgium	70	51.03N	3.45E
Ghotaru	Rajasthan	23	27.22N	70.02E
Gibraltar	Spain	67	36.08N	5.19W
Gifu	Japan	63	35.30N	135.45E
Gilgit	India	22	35.55N	74.22E
Gir	Gujarat	16	21.00N	71.00E
Giridih	Jharkhand	24	24.10N	86.21E
Girvan	Scotland	69	55.15N	4.50W
Gisborne	New Zealand	85	38.40S	178.03E
Glasgow	Scotland	69	55.52N	4.15W
Gloucester	England	69	51.52N	2.15W
Goa, State	India	12	14.20N	74.00E
Goalpara	Assam	25	26.11N	90.41E
Gobabis	Namibia	75	22.30S	18.58E
Gobi, The	Mongolia	62	44.00N	108.00E
Gobindpur	Jharkhand	17	23.51N	86.34E
Godavari, R.	Andhra Pradesh	20	16.35N	82.15E
Godda	Jharkhand	24	24.50N	87.13E
Godhra	Gujarat	23	22.45N	73.40E
Godthaab	Greenland	77	64.10N	51.32W
Godwin Austen (K2), Mt	Jammu & Kashmir	10	35.30N	76.32E
Gogri	Bihar	17	25.28N	86.38E
Goiania	Brazil	83	16.43S	49.18W
Goias	Brazil	83	15.57S	50.07W
Gokak	Karnataka	28	16.11N	74.52E
Golaghat	Assam	25	26.30N	94.00E
Golconda	Andhra Pradesh	20	17.23N	78.27E
Gomati, R.	Uttar Pradesh	17	27.15N	80.38E
Gonda	Uttar Pradesh	24	27.28N	82.01E
Gondal	Gujarat	23	21.55N	70.52E
Gondar	Ethiopia	73	12.35N	37.28E
Gondia	Maharashtra	27	21.28N	80.29E
Good Hope, Cape of	S. Africa	73	34.12S	18.23E
Gooty	Andhra Pradesh	27	15.07N	77.41E
Gopalganj	Bihar	24	26.28N	84.26E
Gopalpur	Odisha	26	19.16N	84.57E
Gopeshwar	Uttarakhand	24	30.23N	79.24E
Gorakhpur	Uttar Pradesh	24	26.45N	83.24E
Gorlitz	Germany	70	51.09N	14.59E
Gorontalo	Celebes	64	0.32N	123.13E
Goteborg	Sweden	67	57.42N	12.00E
Gotland I.	Sweden	67	57.30N	18.30E
Gottingen	Germany	70	51.30N	10.00E
Goulburn	N.S.W., Australia	85	34.50S	149.45E
Grahamstown	South Africa	75	33.19S	26.32E
Grampians	Scotland	69	56.52N	4.00W
Gran Chaco, El	S. America	80	23.30S	60.00W
Grande Rio	Mexico, etc.	76	26.10N	98.30W
Graz	Austria	70	47.04N	15.26E
Great Barrier Reef	Queensland, Aust.	84	18.00S	148.00E
Great Indian Desert	Rajasthan	10	27.00N	71.00E
Great Salt, L.	USA	79	41.15N	112.30W
GREECE	S. E. Europe	67	38.00N	23.00E
Green Bay	Wisconsin, USA	79	44.30N	88.00W
GREENLAND	N. America	77	72.15N	40.00W
Greenock	Scotland	69	55.57N	4.45W
GRENADA	West Indies	77	12.10N	61.40W
Grenadines	West Indies	77	13.00N	61.10W
Grenoble	France	70	45.11N	5.43E
Grimsby	Great England	69	53.34N	0.04E
Groningen	Netherlands	70	53.13N	6.34E
Grootfontein	Namibia	75	19.32S	18.05E
Grossglockner	Austria	70	47.06N	12.35E
Groznyy	Russia	67	43.20N	45.45E
Guadalajara	Mexico	77	20.40N	103.20W
Guadalquivir, R.	Spain	66	36.45N	6.18W
Guadalupe, I.	Mexico	76	28.40N	118.12W
Guadeloupe, I.	West Indies	77	16.10N	61.45W
Guajara Mirim	Brazil	83	10.50S	65.20W
Guangzhou (Canton)	China	62	23.11N	113.14E
GUATEMALA	Central America	77	14.38N	90.22W
Guayaquil	Ecuador	81	2.15S	79.52W
Gudiyatam	Tamil Nadu	21	12.57N	78.55E
Gudur	Andhra Pradesh	27	14.09N	79.54E
Guernsey	Channel Is	70	49.30N	2.35W
Guiana Highlands	S. America	80	5.00N	60.00W
GUINEA	W. Africa	73	11.00N	12.00W
Guinea, Gulf of	W. Africa	72	3.00N	2.00E
GUINEA-BISSAU	W. Africa	73	12.00N	15.00W
Guiyang	China	62	26.33N	106.39E
Gujar Khan	Pakistan	14	33.16N	73.20E
Gujarat, State	W. India	12	23.00N	72.00E
Gujranwala	Pakistan	14	32.10N	74.14E
Gulbarga	Karnataka	28	17.20N	76.50E
Gulmarg	Jammu & Kashmir	22	34.15N	74.25E
Gumla	Jharkhand	24	23.03N	84.33E
Guna	Madhya Pradesh	26	24.40N	77.20E
Guntakal	Andhra Pradesh	27	15.11N	77.25E
Guntur	Andhra Pradesh	27	16.18N	80.29E
Gurdaspur	Punjab	22	32.03N	75.27E
Gurgaon	Haryana	22	28.37N	77.04E
Guryev	Kazakhstan	71	47.15N	51.52E
Guthrie	Oklahoma USA	79	35.55N	97.30W
Guwahati	Assam	25	26.12N	91.42E
GUYANA	South America	81	5.00N	60.00W
Guyenne	France	70	42.15N	1.00E
Gwallior	Madhya Pradesh	26	26.15N	78.10E
Gweru	Zimbabwe	75	19.27S	29.49E
Gyalshing	Sikkim	25	27.18N	88.16E
Gyor	Hungary	70	47.41N	17.38E

H

Names	Country/Region	Pg.No.	Lat.	Long.
Haarlem	Netherlands	70	52.24N	4.40E
Haeju	N. Korea	63	38.12N	125.41E
Haflong	Assam	25	25.08N	93.03E
Haifa	Israel	65	32.49N	36.00E
Hailakandi	Assam	25	24.39N	92.35E
Hainan, I.	China	62	19.00N	110.0E
HAITI	West Indies	77	19.00N	72.00W
Hajipur	Bihar	24	25.41N	85.14E
Hakodate	Japan	63	41.46N	140.44E
Halifax	Nova Scotia, Canada	77	44.38N	63.35W
Halle	Germany	70	51.28N	11.58E
Halmahera, I.	Moluccas	64	1.00N	128.00E
Hamadan	Iran	65	34.49N	48.27E
Hamah	Syria	65	35.05N	36.40E
Hamamatsu	Japan	63	34.45N	137.45E
Hamburg	Germany	70	53.35N	10.00E
Hami	China	62	42.54N	93.28E
Hamilton Inlet	Labrador, Canada	76	54.00N	59.00W
Hamilton	Ontario, Canada	79	43.16N	79.48W
Hamirpur	Himachal Pradesh	22	31.38N	76.35E
Hamirpur	Uttar Pradesh	24	25.58N	80.12E
Hammerfest	Norway	67	70.40N	23.30E
Hampi (Vijaynagar)	Karnataka	28	15.20N	76.30E
Hanamkonda	Andhra Pradesh	27	18.03N	79.32E
Hangayn Nuruu, Mt	Mongolia	62	48.00N	99.00E
Hangzhou	China	62	30.16N	120.08E
Hangzhou Wan	China	62	30.30N	121.03E
Hanoi	Vietnam	59	21.02N	105.52E
Hanover	Germany	70	52.23N	9.00E
Hansi	Haryana	14	29.06N	76.00E
Hanumangarh	Rajasthan	23	29.35N	74.21E
Haora	W. Bengal	25	22.35N	88.23E
Harappa	Pakistan	14	30.35N	72.58E
Harare	Zimbabwe	73	17.50S	31.03E
Harbin	China	62	45.40N	126.37E
Harda	Madhya Pradesh	26	22.20N	77.06E
Hardoi	Uttar Pradesh	24	27.23N	80.10E
Haridwar	Uttarakhand	24	29.58N	78.13E
Harihar	Karnataka	20	14.31N	75.52E
Haripur	Pakistan	14	34.00N	72.58E
Harnahalli	Karnataka	21	13.15N	76.12E
Harnai	Pakistan	14	30.08N	68.00E
Harpanahalli	Karnataka	28	14.47N	75.58E
Harrisburg	Penn., USA	79	40.18N	76.52E
Harrogate	England	69	54.00N	1.30W
Harwich	England	69	51.56N	1.15E
Haryana, State	India	12	30.30N	74.60E
Hassan	Karnataka	28	13.01N	76.10E
Hassan Abdal	Pakistan	14	33.48N	72.45E
Hathras	Uttar Pradesh	24	27.36N	78.06E
Hauraki, Gulf	New Zealand	84	36.25S	175.05E
Havana	Cuba	77	23.08N	82.22W
Haveri	Karnataka	28	14.45N	75.26E
Hawai	Arunachal Pradesh	25	27.04N	93.22E
Hawaiian, Is	Pacific Ocean	87	20.00N	155.00W
Hawick	Scotland	69	55.27N	2.47W
Hawke, Bay	New Zealand	85	39.30S	176.30E
Hazaribag	Jharkhand	24	23.59N	85.25E
Hazro	Pakistan	14	33.55N	72.32E
Hearst	Canada	79	49.40N	83.40W
Hebrides, Is	Scotland	69	57.40N	7.00W
Hefei	China	62	31.51N	117.19E
Hegang	China	62	47.13N	130.13E
Heibronn	Germany	70	19.08N	9.13E
Heidelberg	Germany	70	49.24N	8.42E
Helder	Netherlands	70	52.58N	4.45E
Helena	Montana, USA	79	46.35N	112.01W
Heligoland, I.	Germany	70	54.11N	7.55E
Helmand, R.	Afghanistan	10	32.00N	61.00E
Helsinki	Finland	67	60.09N	24.57E
Hengyang	China	62	26.52N	112.33E
Herat	Afghanistan	61	34.22N	62.08E
Hijaz	Saudi Arabia	65	25.00N	39.00E
Himachal Pradesh, State	N. India	12	32.29N	76.10E
Himalayan, Ra.	N. India	10	28.00N	88.00E
Himatnagar	Gujarat	23	23.42N	73.02E
Hindol	Odisha	17	20.36N	85.14E
Hindu Kush, Mts	Afghanistan	10	36.10N	71.30E
Hinganghat	Maharashtra	27	20.34N	78.53E
Hinggan Ling	China	62	47.00N	120.00E
Hingoli	Maharashtra	27	19.43N	77.11E
Hirakud Dam and Res.	Odisha	17	21.30N	84.00E
Hiriyur	Karnataka	20	13.57N	76.40E
Hiroshima	Japan	63	34.30N	132.30E
Hisar	Haryana	22	29.10N	75.46E
Hispaniola	West Indies	77	19.00N	72.00W
Ho Chi Minh City	Vietnam	64	10.49N	106.00E
Hobart	Tasmania	85	42.53S	147.00E
Hoggar Plateau	Sahara	72	23.30N	6.00E
Hokkaido, I.	Japan	63	43.00N	140.00E
Hole Narsipur	Karnataka	21	12.47N	76.17E
HOLI SEE	S. Europe	67	41.55N	12.27E
Holo, Is	Philippines	64	5.00N	121.30E
Holyhead	Wales	69	53.20N	4.42W
Homer	Alaska, USA	79	59.40N	151.35W
Homnabad	Karnataka	28	17.43N	77.12E
Homs	Syria	65	34.40N	36.45E
Honavar	Karnataka	21	14.17N	74.29E
HONDURAS	Central America	77	14.40N	86.30W
Hong Kong	China	62	22.12N	114.12E
Honiara	Solomon Is	87	9.26S	159.57E
Honnali	Karnataka	28	14.15N	75.41W
Honolulu	Hawaiian Is	87	22.00N	156.00E
Honshu, I.	Japan	63	37.00N	139.00E
Horn, C.	S. America	80	55.58S	67.16W
Hosapete	Karnataka	28	15.16N	76.26E
Hosdurga	Karnataka	28	13.48N	76.20E
Hoshangabad	Madhya Pradesh	26	22.46N	77.45E
Hoshiarpur	Punjab	22	31.32N	75.57E
Hosur	Tamil Nadu	28	12.44N	77.52E
Hotan	China	62	37.07N	80.02E
Houston	Texas, USA	79	29.49N	95.20W
Hovd (Jirgalanta)	Mongolia	62	48.00N	91.40E
Hovsgol Nuur	Mongolia	62	51.00N	100.30E
Hradec Kraiove	Czech Republic	70	50.13N	15.49E
Hrodna	Belarus	67	53.41N	23.49E
Hsenwi	Myanmar	13	23.18N	98.00E
Hsinchu	Taiwan	62	24.55N	121.00E
Hualien	Taiwan	62	24.00N	121.30E
Huamba (Nova Lisboa)	Angola	73	13.20S	15.30E
Huambo	Angola	73	12.44S	15.47E
Huancayo	Peru	83	12.05S	75.12W
Huang He	China	62	37.40N	118.40E
Huanuco	Peru	83	09.55S	76.15W
Huascaren, Mt	Peru	80	9.08S	77.63W
Hubballi	Karnataka	28	15.20N	75.12E
Hudson, Bay	Canada	76	60.00N	88.00W
Hudson, Str.	Canada	76	62.00N	70.00W
Hue	Vietnam	64	16.27N	107.33E
Hugli, R.	W. Bengal	18	22.00N	88.00E
Hull	England	69	53.45N	0.20E
Humaita	Brazil	83	07.30S	63.01W
Humber, R.	England	69	54.35N	0.00E
HUNGARY	S.E. Europe	67	47.00N	19.00E
Hunsur	Karanataka	21	12.18N	76.19E
Hurghada	Egypt	73	27.15N	33.50E
Huron, L.	Canada-USA	76	44.30N	82.00W
Hwange	Zimbabwe	75	18.22S	26.29E
Hyderabad	Andhra Pradesh	13	17.22N	78.28E
Hyderabad	Pakistan	14	25.25N	68.38E
Hyderabad	Andhra Pradesh	27	17.20N	78.30E

I

Names	Country/Region	Pg.No.	Lat.	Long.
Iasi	Romania	67	47.12N	27.35E
Ibadan	Nigeria	73	7.23N	3.56E
Ibotirama	Brazil	83	12.13S	43.12W
Ica	Peru	83	14.00S	75.48W
Icana	Brazil	83	00.21N	67.19W
ICELAND	N.W. Europe	67	65.00N	17.00W
Ichak	Jharkhand	17	24.05E	85.25E
Ichchapuram	Andhra Pradesh	27	19.07N	84.44E
Ifni	N.W. Africa	73	29.10N	10.20W
Igatpuri	Maharashtra	20	19.40N	73.35E
Iguape	Brazil	83	24.37S	47.30W
Iguatu	Brazil	83	6.22S	39.17W
Ihosy	Madagascar	75	22.23S	46.09E
Ilebo	Congo Dem. Rep.	73	5.00S	21.10E
Ilheus	Brazil	83	14.49S	39.02W
Imperatriz	Brazil	83	5.32S	47.28W
Imphal	Manipur	13	24.44N	93.58E
INDIA	South Asia	59	20.00N	78.00E
Indian Ocean	**World**	**92**		
Indianapolis	Indian, USA	79	39.45N	86.16W
INDONESIA	S.E. Asia	64	5.00S	115.00E
Indore	Madhya Pradesh	26	22.44N	75.50E
Indravati, R.	Chhattisgarh	17	19.03N	81.00E
Indus, R.	Jammu & Kashmir	22	33.30N	78.00E
Ingraj Bazar	W. Bengal	25	25.00N	88.11E
Inhambane	Mozambique	75	23.51S	35.29E
Innsbruck	Austria	70	47.16N	11.23E
Inuvik	Canada	77	68.25N	135.05W
Invercargill	New Zealand	85	46.30S	168.30E
Inverness	Scotland	69	57.30N	4.15W
Ionian, Is	Greece	66	38.00N	20.00E
Ipatinga	Brazil	83	19.32S	32.30W
Ipswich	England	69	52.06N	1.10E
Ipu	Brazil	83	4.32S	40.44W
Iquique	Chile	83	20.19S	70.05W
Iquitos	Peru	81	3.45S	73.10W
IRAN	S.W. Asia	59	33.00N	55.00E
IRAQ	S.W. Asia	59	32.00N	45.00E
IRELAND	W. Europe	67	53.00N	8.00W
Irkutsk	Russia	71	52.36N	104.10E
Irrawaddy, R.	Myanmar	11	20.40N	95.00E
Irtysh, R.	Russia	71	53.36N	75.30E
Isa Khel	Pakistan	14	32.41N	71.19E
Isfahan	Iran	65	32.37N	51.38E
Ishinomaki	Japan	63	38.32N	141.20E
Islamabad	Pakistan	59	33.44N	73.10E
Isle of Man	Irish Sea	69	54.05N	4.37W
ISRAEL	W. Asia	59	32.30N	35.30E
Issyk Kul	Kyrgystan	71	42.30N	77.00E
Istanbul (Constantinople)	Turkey	65	41.00N	29.00E
Itabaiana	Brazil	83	10.42S	37.37W
Itabuna	Brazil	83	14.28S	39.19W
Itaituba	Brazil	83	4.15S	55.56W
Itajai	Brazil	83	26.50S	48.39W
ITALY	S. Europe	67	42.00N	12.00E
Itanagar	Arunachal Pradesh	13	27.08N	93.40E
Itapipoca	Brazil	83	3.29S	39.35W
Itaqui	Brazil	83	29.10S	56.30W
Itarsi	Madhya Pradesh	26	22.30N	77.55E
Iturup, I.	Russia	71	45.00N	148.00E
Izmir (Smyma)	Turkey	65	38.24N	27.06E

J

Names	Country/Region	Pg.No.	Lat.	Long.
Jabalpur	Madhya Pradesh	26	23.10N	79.59E
Jaboatao	Brazil	83	8.05S	35.00W
Jackson	Mississipi, USA	79	32.17N	90.08W
Jacksonville	Florida, USA	79	30.21N	81.40W
Jacobabad	Pakistan	14	28.17N	68.29E
Jacobina	Brazil	83	11.13S	40.30W
Jaffna	Sri Lanka	61	9.45N	80.02E
Jagannathganj	Bangladesh	18	24.39N	89.50E
Jagatsinghapur	Odisha	26	20.13N	86.18E
Jagdalpur	Chhattisgarh	26	19.05N	82.04E
Jaggayyapeta	Andhra Pradesh	20	16.52N	80.09E
Jaghbub	Libya	73	29.55N	24.00E
Jagtiyal	Andhrya Pradesh	27	18.48N	79.09E
Jahanabad	Bihar	24	25.13N	85.05E
Jahazpur	Rajasthan	23	25.38N	75.19E
Jaipur	Rajasthan	12	26.55N	75.52E
Jakarta	Indonesia	64	6.12S	106.50E
Jalalabad	Afghanistan	14	34.24N	70.26E
Jalalpur Pirwala	Pakistan	14	29.30N	71.16E
Jalandhar	Punjab	22	31.18N	75.40E
Jalaun	Uttar Pradesh	17	26.08N	79.23E
Jalgaon	Maharashtra	27	21.05N	75.40E
Jalna	Maharashtra	27	19.51N	75.56E
Jalor	Rajasthan	23	25.22N	72.58E
Jalpaiguri	W. Bengal	25	26.32N	88. 46E
JAMAICA	West Indies	77	18.00N	77.00W
Jamalpur	Bihar	17	25.19N	86.32E
Jamalpur	Bangladesh	18	24.56N	90.00E
Jamkhandi	Karnataka	20	16.30N	75.20E
Jamkhed	Maharashtra	27	18.43N	75.24E
Jammalamadugu	Andhra Pradesh	20	14.12S	78.25E
Jammu	Jammu & Kashmir	22	32.43N	74.54E
Jammu & Kashmir, State	India	12	32.44N	74.54E
Jamnagar	Gujarat	23	22.27N	70.07E
Jampur	Pakistan	14	29.39N	70.38E
Jamshedpur	Jharkhand	24	22.50N	86.10E
Jamtara	Jharkhand	24	23.57N	86.36E
Jamui	Bihar	24	24.55N	86.13E
Jamuna, R.	Bangladesh	18	24.25N	89.50E

Names	Country/Region	Pg.No.	Lat.	Long.
Janakpur	Chhattisgarh	17	23.43E	81.50E
Jandiala	Punjab	14	31.51N	75.37E
Jangipur	W. Bengal	18	24.28N	88.05E
Jani Khel	Pakistan	14	32.48N	70.27E
Janjgir	Chhattisgarh	26	22.02N	82.35E
Janjira	Maharashtra	20	18.18N	73.00E
JAPAN	E. Asia	59	40.00N	135.00E
Japvo, Mt	Nagaland	18	25.32N	94.10E
Jaru	Brazil	83	10.24S	62.45W
Jasdan	Gujarat	23	22.04N	71.01E
Jashpurnagar	Chhattisgarh	26	22.53N	84.12E
Jaso	Madhya Pradesh	17	24.30N	80.32E
Jath	Maharashtra	27	17.03N	75.15E
Jaunpur	Uttar Pradesh	24	25.46N	82.44E
Java, I.	Indonesia	64	7.30S	110.00E
Javadi Hills	Tamil Nadu	21	12.40N	78.40E
Jawalamukhi	Himachal Pradesh	14	31.53N	76.22E
Jawhar	Maharashtra	20	19.52N	73.21E
Jaynagar	Bihar	24	26.35N	86.09E
Jaypur	Odisha	26	18.52N	82.38E
Jefferson City	Missouri, USA	79	38.35N	92.11W
Jequie	Brazil	83	13.52S	40.06W
Jersey	Channel Is	70	49.15N	2.00W
Jerusalem	Israel	59	31.46N	35.14E
Jessore	Bangladesh	18	23.10N	89.10E
Jhabua	Madhya Pradesh	26	22.45N	74.38E
Jhajjar	Haryana	22	28.36N	76.39E
Jhal	Pakistan	14	28.18N	67.30E
Jhalawar	Rajasthan	23	24.35N	76.11E
Jhang	Pakistan	14	31.16N	72.22E
Jhansi	Uttar Pradesh	24	25.27N	78.37E
Jharia	Jharkhand	24	23.50N	86.33E
Jharkhand, State	India	13	24.02N	86.00E
Jharsuguda	Odisha	26	21.54N	84.05E
Jhunjhunun	Rajasthan	23	28.05N	75.29E
Jiamusi	China	62	46.47N	130.15E
Jiddah	Saudi Arabia	65	21.32N	39.10E
Jigni	Uttar Pradesh	17	25.44N	79.25E
Jihlava	Czech Republic	70	49.24N	15.35E
Jilin	China	62	43.53N	126.33E
Jinan	China	62	36.38N	117.01E
Jind	Haryana	22	29.19N	76.23E
Jinzhou	China	62	41.10N	121.02E
Joao Pessoa	Brazil	83	7.06S	34.53W
Jobat	Madhya Pradesh	16	22.29N	74.37E
Jodhpur	Rajasthan	23	26.18N	73.04E
Jog Falls	Karnataka	20	14.18N	74.55E
Jogindernagar	Himachal Pradesh	14	31.50N	76.45E
Johannesburg	South Africa	75	26.10S	28.02E
Joinville	Brazil	83	26.20S	48.55W
Jolarpettai	Tamil Nadu	21	12.34N	78.37E
JORDAN	W. Asia	59	32.00N	35.00E
Jorhat	Assam	25	26.46N	94.16E
Jowai	Meghalaya	25	25.18N	92.09E
Juan Fernandez, Is	Chile	81	33.36S	78.55W
Juazeiro do Norte	Brazil	83	7.10S	39.18W
Juba	Sudan	73	4.56N	32.20E
Juiz de Fora	Brazil	83	21.47S	43.23W
Juliaca	Peru	83	15.29S	70.09W
Jumla	Nepal	15	29.17N	82.13E
Junagadh	Gujarat	23	21.31N	70.36E
Junagarh	Odisha	26	19.52N	82.59E
Jundiai	Brazil	83	23.10S	46.54W
Juneau	Alaska, USA	79	58.21N	134.20W
Junnar	Maharashtra	20	19.12N	73.50E

K

Names	Country/Region	Pg.No.	Lat.	Long.
Kabul	Afghanistan	14	34.30N	69.18E
Kabul, R.	Afghanistan	14	34.32N	69.20E
Kabwe	Zambia	75	14.29S	28.25E
Kachchh, Gt. Rann of	Gujarat	19	24.00N	70.00E
Kachchh, Gulf of	Gujarat	19	22.35N	69.40E
Kachchh, Little Rann of	Gujarat	19	23.26N	71.20E
Kadiri	Andhra Pradesh	20	14.07N	78.14E
Kadoma	Zimbabwe	75	18.21S	29.55E
Kaduna	Nigeria	73	10.30N	7.28E
Kaesong	N. Korea	63	38.01N	126.46E
Kafue	Zambia	75	15.44S	28.10E
Kagoshima	Japan	63	31.36N	130.33E
Kailashahar	Tripura	25	24.22N	92.06E
Kaintira	Odisha	17	20.45N	84.37E
Kaithal	Haryana	22	29.48N	76.26E
Kajalgaon	Assam	25	26.31N	90.31E
Kakinada	Andhra Pradesh	27	16.57N	82.15E
Kalabagh	Pakistan	14	32.58N	71.36E
Kalaburgi	Karanataka	28	17.19N	76.54E
Kalahandi	Odisha	26	20.05N	83.12E
Kalahari Desert	S. Africa	72	23.00S	22.00E
Kalam	Pakistan	14	35.27N	72.30E
Kalemie	Congo Dem. Rep.	73	7.00S	29.12E
Kalgoorlie	W. Australia	85	30.50S	121.20E
Kalingapatnam	Andhra Pradesh	21	18.20N	84.10E
Kaliningrad	Russia	71	54.42N	20.30E
Kalol	Gujarat	23	23.15N	72.33E
Kalomo	Zambia	75	17.02S	26.29E
Kalpetta	Kerala	28	11.37N	76.04E
Kaluga	Russia	67	54.30N	36.16E
Kalutara	Sri Lanka	61	6.34N	79.54E
Kalyan	Maharashtra	27	19.14N	73.10E
Kalyani	Karnataka	20	17.53N	76.59E
Kamachatka, Pen.	Russia	71	57.00N	158.00E
Kamalia	Pakistan	14	30.44N	72.42E
Kamareddi	Andhra Pradesh	27	18.18N	78.22E

Names	Country/Region	Pg.No.	Lat.	Long.
Kambham	Andhra Pradesh	27	15.34N	79.19E
Kamet, Mt	Uttarakhand	10	30.56N	79.36E
Kampala	Uganda	73	0.19N	32.35E
Kampli	Andhra Pradesh	20	15.25N	76.39E
Kamptee	Maharashtra	20	21.14N	79.15E
Kanazawa	Japan	63	36.30N	136.38E
Kancheepuram	Tamil Nadu	28	12.50N	79.45E
Kandahar	Afghanistan	61	31.37N	65.30E
Kandla	Gujarat	23	23.00N	70.10E
Kandukur	Andhra Pradesh	20	15.12N	79.57E
Kandy	Sri Lanka	21	7.18N	80.40E
Kangaroo, I.	S. Australia	84	35.50S	137.20E
Kangchenjunga	India	18	27.42N	88.11E
Kangra	Himachal Pradesh	22	32.05E	76.18E
Kanigiri	Andhra Pradesh	27	15.23N	79.32E
Kanker	Chhattisgarh	26	20.16N	81.32E
Kankesanturai	Sri Lanka	61	9.51N	80.05 E
Kannauj	Uttar Pradesh	24	27.03N	79.58 E
Kannur	Kerala	28	11.52N	75.25E
Kano	Nigeria	73	12.00N	8.30E
Kanpur	Uttar Pradesh	24	26.28N	80.24E
Kansas City	Kansas USA	79	39.05N	94.35W
Kanye	Botswana	75	24.59S	25.10E
Kapurthala	Punjab	22	31.23N	75.25E
Kara Sea	Arctic Ocean	89	75.00N	70.00E
Karabala	Iraq	65	32.35N	44.07E
Karachi	Pakistan	14	24.51N	67.04E
Karad	Maharashtra	27	17.15N	74.12E
Karaganda	Kazakhstan	71	49.50N	73.00E
Karaikal	Puducherry	28	10.55N	79.52E
Karakoram, Ra.	India	10	36.10N	75.00E
Karanja	Maharashtra	20	20.29N	77.32E
Karanjia	Odisha	17	21.43N	87.07E
Karasburg	Namibia	75	28.00S	18.43E
Karativo, I.	Sri Lanka	21	8.22N	79.52E
Karauli	Rajasthan	23	26.30N	77.04E
Kargil	Jammu & Kashmir	22	34.30N	76.13E
Kariba Dam	Zambia/Zimbabwe	73	16.51S	28.50E
Karibib	Namibia	75	21.59S	15.51E
Karimganj	Assam	25	24.40N	92.30E
Karimnagar	Andhra Pradesh	27	18.28N	79.06E
Karkala	Karnataka	21	13.12N	75.00E
Karlsruhe	Germany	70	49.01N	8.23E
Karnal	Haryana	22	29.42N	77.02E
Karnataka, State	India	12	15.00N	75.00E
Karshi	Uzbekistan	65	38.48N	65.48E
Karur	Tamil Nadu	28	10.58N	78.07E
Karwar	Karnataka	28	14.48N	74.11E
Kasaragod	Kerala	28	12.30N	75.00E
Kasauli	Himachal Pradesh	14	30.53N	77.01E
Kasempa	Zambia	75	13.28S	25.48E
Kasganj	Uttar Pradesh	24	27.49N	78.39E
Kashi	China	62	39.20N	74.04E
Kassel	Germany	70	51.19N	9.28E
Kasur	Pakistan	14	31.07N	74.31E
Kataba	Zambia	75	16.02S	25.03E
Katangi	Madhya Pradesh	26	21.47N	79.51E
Kathiawar, Pen.	Gujarat	10	22.00N	71.00E
Kathiraveli	Sri Lanka	61	8.13N	81.23E
Kathua	Jammu & Kashmir	22	32.17N	75.36E
Katihar	Bihar	24	25.30N	87.40E
Katmandu	Nepal	59	27.42N	85.12E
Katni	Madhya Pradesh	26	23.50N	80.26E
Katowice	Poland	70	50.16N	19.03E
Katoya	W. Bengal	18	23.39N	88.11E
Kaushambi	Uttar Pradesh	24	25.33N	81.33E
Kavali	Andhra Pradesh	27	14.55N	80.03E
Kavaratti	Lakshadweep	12	10.33N	72.39E
Kaveri, R.	Tamil Nadu, etc.	21	11.20N	77.50E
Kawardha	Chhattisgarh	26	22.00N	81.17E
Kayalpatnam	Tamil Nadu	21	8.34N	78.10E
Kayseri	Turkey	65	38.42N	35.25E
KAZAKHSTAN	Asia	59	48.00N	70.00E
Kazan	Russia	71	55.48N	49.10E
Kecskemet	Hungary	70	46.55N	19.35E
Keetmanshoop	Namibia	75	26.36S	18.08E
Keewatin	N.W. Terr., Canada	77	63.00N	94.00E
Kekirawa	Sri Lanka	21	8.02N	80.36E
Kekri	Rajasthan	23	25.56N	75.20E
Kellam	Kerala	28	8.53N	76.36E
Kendal	England	69	54.20N	2.45W
Kendrapara	Odisha	26	20.30N	86.28E
Kendujhar	Odisha	26	21.38N	85.37E
KENYA	East Africa	73	1.00N	38.00E
Kenya, Mt	E. Africa	72	0.10S	37.18E
Kerala, State	S. India	12	10.00N	76.25E
Kerguelen, I.	Indian Ocean	88	48.30S	69.40E
Kerki	Turkemenistan	65	37.50N	65.12E
Kermadec, Is	S. Pacific Ocean	87	30.03S	178.40W
Kerman	Iran	65	30.20N	57.10E
Key West	Florida, USA	79	24.40N	81.48W
Khabarovsk	Russia	71	48.40N	135.05E
Khagaria	Bihar	24	25.29N	86.31E
Khairagarh	Chhattisgarh	17	21.26N	81.02E
Khairpur	Pakistan	14	27.28N	68.44E
Khalilabad	Uttar Pradesh	24	26.46N	83.06E
Khambhat	Gujarat	23	22.19N	72.38E
Khambhat, Gulf of	Gujarat	19	21.00N	72.30E
Khammam	Andhra Pradesh	27	17.15N	80.11E
Khandpara	Odisha	17	20.16N	85.13E
Khandwa	Madhya Pradesh	26	21.50N	76.23E
Khaniadhana	Madhya Pradesh	16	25.01N	78.07E
Khanka, L.	Russia	71	45.00N	132.30E
Khanpur	Pakistan	14	28.30N	70.40E

Names	Country/Region	Pg.No.	Lat.	Long.
Khapa	Maharashtra	20	21.25N	79.02E
Kharagpur	W. Bengal	25	22.30N	87.20E
Khargone	Madhya Pradesh	26	21.48N	75.41E
Kharkiv	Ukraine	67	48.58N	36.11E
Kharsawan	Jharkhand	17	22.48N	85.52E
Khartoum	Sudan	73	15.35N	32.35E
Khasi and Jaintia Hills	Meghalaya	18	25.30N	91.30E
Khed	Maharashtra	20	18.51N	73.56E
Kheda	Gujarat	23	22.45N	72.45E
Khedbrahma	Gujarat	23	24.03N	73.04E
Kheri	Uttar Pradesh	24	27.54N	80.48E
Kherson	Ukraine	67	46.38N	32.36E
Khilok	Russia	71	51.30N	110.45E
Khiva	Uzbekistan	65	41.30N	60.18E
Khonsa	Arunachal Pradesh	25	26.57N	95.33E
Khordha	Odisha	26	20.11N	85.40E
Khorramshahr	Iran	65	30.30N	48.30E
Khulna	Bangladesh	18	22.49N	89.37E
Khunti	Jharkhand	24	23.01N	85.16E
Khurai	Madhya Pradesh	16	24.03N	78.23E
Khurja	Uttar Pradesh	17	28.15N	77.50E
Khurrambad	Iran	65	33.30N	48.25E
Khushab	Pakistan	14	32.18N	72.24E
Khyber Pass	Pakistan	10	34.06N	71.05E
Kidare	Rep. of Ireland	69	53.09N	6.54W
Kiev	Ukraine	67	50.28N	30.11E
Kigali	Rwanda	73	1.59S	30.05E
Kigoma	Tanzania	73	4.52S	29.36S
Kilabira	Odisha	17	21.49N	84.15E
Kilakarai	Tamil Nadu	21	9.14N	78.50E
Kilchu	N. Korea	63	41.00N	129.20E
Kilimanjaro, Mt	E. Africa	72	3.40S	37.00E
Kilkenny	Rep. of Ireland	69	52.39N	7.15W
Kilmarnock	Scotland	69	55.36N	4.30W
Kimberley	South Africa	75	28.45S	24.46E
Kingston	Jamaica	77	17.59N	76.50W
Kingston	Ontario, Canada	79	44.16N	76.30W
Kingstown	St Vincent&Grenadines	77	13.10N	61.14W
Kinshasa	Congo Dem. Rep.	73	4.20S	15.18E
Kiphire	Nagaland	25	25.54N	94.47E
KIRIBATI	Pacific Ocean	87	5.00S	180.00E
Kirkcaldy	Scotland	69	56.05N	3.10W
Kirkcudbright	Scotland	69	54.51N	4.03W
Kirkuk	Iraq	65	35.30N	44.21E
Kirkwall	Scotland	69	59.09N	3.00W
Kirov	Russia	67	58.35N	49.40E
Kisangani	Congo Dem. Rep.	73	0.30N	25.10W
Kishanganj	Bihar	24	26.08N	98.57E
Kishangarh	Rajasthan	19	27.53N	70.37E
Kishorganj	Bangladesh	18	24.26N	90.49E
Kishtwar	Jammu & Kashmir	22	33.19N	75.48E
Kismayu	Somali Rep.	73	0.03S	49.30E
Kitakyushu	Japan	63	33.50N	130.50E
Kitwe	Zambia	75	0.08S	30.30E
Kizil Irmak	Turkey	65	41.20N	35.40E
Klagenfurt	Austria	70	46.38N	14.18E
Klondike Goldfields	Canada	79	64.00N	139.20W
Kobdo	Mongolia	62	48.02N	91.39E
Kobe	Japan	63	34.41N	135.12E
Koch Bihar	W. Bengal	25	26.20N	89.29E
Kochi	Kerala	28	9.55N	76.14E
Kochi	Japan	63	33.30N	133.35E
Kodaikkanal	Tamil Nadu	28	10.13N	77.32E
Kodarma	Jharkhand	24	24.27N	85.36E
Kodiak, I.	Alaska, USA	79	57.30N	153.00W
Kodikkarai	Tamil Nadu	28	10.18N	79.52E
Kohat	Pakistan	14	33.36N	71.29E
Kohima	Nagaland	13	25.40N	94.07E
Kohima	Negaland	25	25.40N	94.08E
Kokrajhar	Assam	25	26.24N	90.16E
Kolar	Karnataka	28	13.09N	78.11E
Kolasib	Mizoram	25	24.10N	92.42E
Kolhapur	Maharashtra	27	16.42N	74.14E
Kolkata	West Bengal	13	22.34N	88.24E
Kollam	Kerala	28	08.53N	76.36E
Kollegal	Karnataka	21	12.09N	77.09E
Kolleru, L.	Andhra Pradesh	20	16.40N	81.10E
Kollur	Karnataka	28	13.53N	74.53E
Koluapur	Maharashtra	27	16.42N	74.16E
Komsomolsk	Russia	71	50.30N	137.00E
Konarka	Odisha	26	19.53N	86.08E
Kondalwadi	Maharashtra	20	18.15N	77.43E
Kondapalli	Andhra Pradesh	20	16.38N	80.36E
Kongwa	Tanzania	73	6.20S	36.30E
Konosha	Russia	67	60.58N	40.08E
Konya	Turkey	65	37.52N	32.28E
Koppal	Karnataka	28	15.21N	76.09E
Koraput	Odisha	26	18.49N	82.48E
Koratla	Andhra Pradesh	20	18.43N	78.41E
Korba	Chhattisgarh	26	22.21N	82.42E
Korea	South Asia	63	36.00N	128.00E
Korea, Str.	Korea-Japan	63	34.00N	129.30E
Koror	Palau	59	07.21N	134.28E
Korsakov	Russia	71	46.30N	142.42E
Korwai	Madhya Pradesh	16	24.07N	78.05E
Kosi, R.	Bihar	17	26.00N	87.06E
Kostroma	Russia	67	57.45N	40.58E
Kot Kapura	Punjab	14	30.34N	74.52E
Kota	Rajasthan	23	25.10N	75.52E
Kota Kinabulu	Sabah	64	5.55N	116.12E
Kotapad	Odisha	17	19.04N	82.24E
Kothi	Madhya Pradesh	17	24.45N	80.40E
Kottagudem	Andhra Pradesh	20	17.30N	80.40E
Kottayam	Kerala	28	9.36N	76.34E

Names	Country/Region	Pg.No.	Lat.	Long.
Kottbus	Germany	70	51.46N	14.20E
Kotturu	Karnataka	20	14.49N	76.16E
Koyna, R.	Maharashtra	20	17.30N	73.45E
Kozhikode	Kerala	28	11.15N	75.49E
Kragujevac	Serbia	70	44.01N	20.56E
Krakow	Poland	67	50.50N	19.50E
Krasnodar	Russia	67	45.03N	38.53E
Krasnovodsk	Turkmenistan	71	40.01N	52.52E
Krasnoyarsk	Russia	71	56.08N	93.00E
Krishnagiri	Tamil Nadu	28	12.32N	78.16E
Krishnanagar	W. Bengal	25	23.24N	88.33E
Krishnarajasagara, Res.	Karnataka	21	12.20N	76.32E
Krisnha, R.	Andhra Pradesh	20	15.55N	81.10E
Kristiansand	Norway	67	58.08N	7.59E
Krugersdorp	South Africa	75	26.06S	27.46E
Kuala Lumpur	Malaysia	59	3.11N	101.40E
Kuching	Sarawak	64	1.30N	110.20E
Kudremukh, Peak	Karnataka	21	13.10N	75.15E
Kuito	Angola	73	12.25S	16.56E
Kukawa	Nigeria	73	12.55N	13.30E
Kukshi	Madhya Pradesh	16	22.13N	74.48E
Kulachi	Pakistan	14	31.56N	70.30E
Kulgam	Jammu & Kashmir	22	33.39N	75.01E
Kullu	Himachal Pradesh	22	31.57N	77.06E
Kumamoto	Japan	63	32.50N	130.40E
Kumbakonam	Tamil Nadu	28	10.58N	79.25E
Kumta	Karnataka	28	14.26N	74.27E
Kunashir	Russia	71	44.00N	146.00E
Kundapura	Karnataka	28	13.50N	74.40E
Kunlun, Mts	China, etc.	62	36.00N	85.00E
Kunming	China	62	25.02N	102.42E
Kunsan	S. Korea	63	35.59N	126.45E
Kupwara	Jammu & Kashmir	22	34.31N	74.20E
Kuril, Is	Russia	71	46.0N	160.00E
Kurnool	Andhra Pradesh	27	15.50N	78.05E
Kursk	Russia	67	51.42N	36.11E
Kurukshetra	Haryana	22	29.57N	76.52E
Kurunegala	Sri Lanka	21	7.31N	80.22E
Kushiro	Japan	63	43.00N	144.30E
Kushka	Turkmenistan	71	35.12N	62.30E
Kushtia	Bangladesh	18	23.55N	89.10E
Kusma	Nepal	15	28.16N	83.40E
Kutaisi	Georgia	65	42.19N	42.40E
Kutru	Chhattisgarh	17	19.03N	80.53E
Kuvango	Angola	73	14.27S	16.20E
KUWAIT	Asia	59	28.59N	47.52E
Kuwait City	Kuwait	59	29.12N	47.59E
Kuybyshev, Res.	Rusia	67	55.00N	50.00E
Kwekwe	Zimbabwe	75	18.55S	29.49E
Kyakhta	Russia	71	50.04N	106.20E
Kyelang	Himachal Pradesh	22	32.33N	77.05E
Kyle of Lochalsh	Scotland	69	7.16N	5.43W
Kyoto	Japan	63	35.01N	135.34E
KYRGYZSTAN	Asia	59	42.00N	75.00E
Kyushu, I.	Japan	63	32.30N	131.00E
Kyzyl	Russia	71	51.50N	94.30E
Kyzyl-Orda	Kazakhstan	71	44.50N	65.33E

L

Names	Country/Region	Pg.No.	Lat.	Long.
La Coruna	Spain	67	43.21 N	8.24 W
La Guaira	Venezuela	81	10.35N	67.02E
La Paz / Sucre	Bolivia	81	16.31S	67.68W
La Plata	Argentina	80	34.53S	58.00W
La Rochelle	France	70	46.10N	1.09W
Laayoune	Western Sahara	73	27.09 N	13.12 W
Labrador, Coast of	Canada	76	54.00 N	64.00 W
Labrea	Brazil	83	7.20S	64.46W
Ladakh, Ra.	Jammu & Kashmir	10	32.00N	80.00E
Ladysmith	South Africa	75	28.34S	29.47E
Ladysmith	Canada	77	48.57N	123.50W
Laghman	Afghanistan	14	34.30N	70.00E
Lagoas	Nigeria	73	6.27N	3.28E
Lagos	Nigeria	73	6.25N	3.27E
Lahara	Odisha	17	21.26N	85.14E
Lahore	Pakistan	14	31.37N	74.26E
Lajes	Brazil	83	27.48S	50.20W
Lakhimpur	Uttar Pradesh	24	27.57N	80.49E
Lakhimpur	Assam	25	27.32N	94.01E
Lakhisarai	Bihar	24	25.09N	86.07E
Lakhnadon	Madhya Pradesh	26	22.36N	79.39E
Lakhpat	Gujarat	23	23.49N	68.48E
Lakki	Pakistan	14	32.37N	70.57E
Lakshadweep, Union Territory	India	12	10.00N	73.00E
Lala Musa	Pakistan	14	32.40N	74.01E
Lalbagh	W. Bengal	18	24.13N	88.19E
Lalitpur	Uttar Pradesh	24	24.22N	78.28E
Lalsot	Rajashtan	23	26.34N	76.23E
Lamphelpat	Manipur	25	24.49N	93.54E
Land's End	England	69	50.04N	5.45W
Landshut	Germany	70	48.27N	12.10E
Lansing	Michigan, USA	79	42.44N	84.33W
Lanzhou	China	62	36.02N	103.50E
LAOS	S.E. Asia	59	19.00N	104.00E
Lapland	N. Europe	66	67.00N	25.00E
Laptev Sea	Arctic Ocean	71	76.00N	125.00E
Lar	Iran	65	27.40N	54.15E
Laredo	Texas, USA	79	27.30N	99.30W
Larentian Uplands	Canada	76	50.00N	75.00W
Larissa	Greece	67	39.36N	22.25E
Larkana	Pakistan	14	27.33N	68.15E
Larne	N. Ireland	69	54.51N	5.49W
Lashkar	Madhya Pradesh	16	26.10N	78.10E

Names	Country/Region	Pg.No.	Lat.	Long.
Latakia	Syria	65	35.30N	35.45E
Latehar	Jharkhand	24	23.46N	84.35E
Latur	Maharashtra	27	18.24N	76.36E
LATVIA	Europe	67	57.00N	24.00E
Launceston	Tasmania	85	41.25S	147.10E
Lausanne	Switzerland	70	46.31N	6.38E
Laval	France	70	48.04N	0.46W
Lawngtlai	Mizoram	25	22.31N	92.57E
Laying-Yangte	Arunachal Pradesh	25	27.54N	93.21E
Leadville	Colorado, USA	79	39.17N	106.23W
LEBANON	W. Asia	59	33.00N	35.00E
Leeds	England	69	53.48N	1.30W
Lefkosia (Nicosia)	Cyprus	59	35.10N	33.22E
Leh (Ladakh)	Jammu & Kashmir	22	34.09N	77.36E
Leiah	Pakistan	14	30.58N	70.58E
Leicester	England	69	52.38N	1.05W
Leipzig	Germany	70	51.20N	12.23E
Leith	Scotland	69	55.58N	3.10W
Lemans	France	70	48.01N	0.12E
Lena, R.	Russia	71	70.00N	126.00E
Lerwick	Scotland	69	60.10N	1.00W
LESOTHO	S. Africa	73	30.00S	28.00E
Lethbridge	Canada	79	49.43N	112.50W
Levis	Canada	79	46.48N	71.09W
Lewis, I.	Scotland	69	58.10N	6.40W
Leyte, I.	Philippines	64	11.25N	124.36E
Lhasa	Tibet, China	59	29.40N	91.05E
Liaqatabad	Pakistan	14	32.17N	71.24E
LIBERIA	W. Africa	73	6.00N	9.00W
Libreville	Gabon	73	0.26N	9.25E
LIBYA	N. Africa	73	25.00N	15.00E
Libyan, Desert	N. Africa	72	25.00N	26.00E
Lichinga	Mozambique	75	13.19S	35.13E
LIECHTENSTIEN	Centtral Europe	67	47.10N	9.50E
Liege	Belgium	70	50.38N	6.34E
Ligurian, Sea	Italy	70	53.30N	9.00E
Lille	France	70	50.40N	3.00E
Lilongwe	Malawi	73	13.58S	33.49E
Lima	Peru	81	12.02S	77.02W
Limbdi	Gujarat	23	22.34N	71.53E
Limerick	Rep. of Ireland	69	52.40N	8.37W
Limoges	France	70	45.50N	1.16E
Limpopo, R.	S. Africa	72	23.20S	30.00E
Lincoln	England	69	53.12N	0.30W
Lincoln	USA	79	40.50N	96.42W
Lingsugur	Karnataka	28	16.07N	76.34E
Lini	China	62	35.02N	118.10E
Linsia	China	62	35.50N	103.00E
Linz	Austria	70	48.18N	14.18E
Lions, G. of	France	70	43.10N	4.00E
Lisbon	Portugal	67	38.44N	9.09W
LITHUANIA	Europe	67	54.40N	25.30E
Little Rock	Arkansas, USA	79	34.41N	92.15W
Liverpool	England	69	53.24N	2.58W
Livingstone	Zambia	73	17.55S	25.48E
Livingstone	USA	79	45.40N	110.33W
Livingstonia	Malawi	73	10.35S	34.05E
Lizard, Pt	England	69	49.56N	5.15W
Ljubljana	Solvenia	70	46.03N	14.31E
Llano Estacado	USA	79	34.00N	100.03W
Lleida	Spain	70	41.38N	0.38E
Lobatse	Botswana	75	25.11S	25.40E
Lobito	Angola	73	12.20S	13.34E
Lodoga, L.	Russia	67	60.00N	32.00E
Lodz	Poland	70	51.46N	19.26E
Lofoten, Is	Norway	66	68.00N	12.50E
Lohardaga	Jharkhand	24	23.26N	84.42E
Loharu	Haryana	14	28.16N	75.45E
Loire, R.	France	70	47.17N	2.10W
Loktak, L.	Manipur	18	24.30N	93.55E
Lombok, I.	Indonesia	64	8.30S	116.20E
Lome	Togo	73	6.09N	1.13E
Lonavala	Maharashtra	27	18.44N	73.28E
Londa	Karnataka	20	15.60N	74.50E
London	United Kingdom	67	51.30N	0.05W
London	Canada	79	42.58N	81.15W
London	Ontario, Canada	79	43.00N	91.15W
Londonderry	N. Ireland	69	55.00N	7.20W
Londrina	Brazil	83	23.18S	51.13W
Long Beach	California, USA	79	33.46N	118.12W
Long, I.	USA	79	40.45N	73.00W
Longleng	Nagaland	25	26.31N	94.56E
Loralai	Pakistan	14	30.24N	68.36E
Lord Howe, I.	Pacific Ocean	84	31.46S	159.08E
Lorient	France	70	47.45N	3.21W
Los Angeles	California, USA	79	34.03N	118.17W
Louis Trichardt	South Africa	75	23.01S	29.43E
Louisiade, Arch.	New Guinea	84	11.30S	152.00E
Louisville	Kentucky, USA	79	38.16N	85.47W
Luanda	Angola	73	8.50S	13.14E
Luang Prabang	Laos	64	19.55N	102.05E
Luanshya	Zambia	75	13.09S	28.24E
Lubango	Angola	75	14.55S	13.30E
Lubeck	Germany	70	53.50N	10.40E
Lublin	Poland	70	51.15N	22.34E
Lubumbashi	Congo Dem. Rep.	73	11.40S	27.28E
Lucerne	Switzerland	70	47.03N	8.18E
Lucknow	Uttar Pradesh	13	26.55N	80.59E
Lucusse	Angola	75	12.33S	20.51E
Luderitz	Namibia	75	26.38S	15.10E
Luderitz .	S.W. Africa	73	27.00S	16.00E
Ludhiana	Punjab	22	30.55N	75.54E
Luena	Angola	75	11.47S	19.52E
Lulea	Sweden	67	65.35N	22.10E

Names	Country/Region	Pg.No.	Lat.	Long.
Lunavada	Gujarat	23	23.08N	73.37E
Lundy, I.	England	69	51.12N	4.40W
Luneburg	Germany	70	53.16N	10.26E
Lunglei	Mizoram	25	22.56N	92.49E
Luni, R.	Rajasthan	19	26.01N	73.02E
Lusaka	Zambia	73	18.26S	28.20E
Luton	England	69	51.53N	0.25W
LUXEMBOURG	W. Europe	67	49.38N	6.10E
Luziania	Brazil	83	16.16S	47.57W
Luzon, I.	Philippines	64	16.00N	121.00E
Lviv	Ukraine	70	49.50N	24.00E
Lyme, Bay	England	69	50.43N	2.56W
Lyons	France	67	45.25N	4.50E

M

Names	Country/Region	Pg.No.	Lat.	Long.
Ma'an	Jordan	65	30.11N	35.43E
Mabalane	Mozambique	75	23.51S	32.38E
Macapa	Brazil	83	0.04N	51.04W
Macau	China	62	22.15N	113.33E
MACEDONIA	S. Europe	67	42.00N	21.32E
Maceio	Brazil	83	1.32S	27.16E
Macgillicuddy's Reeks	Rep. of Ireland	69	52.10N	9.45W
Machilipatnam	Andhra Pradesh	27	16.09N	81.12E
Macias Nguema	W. Africa	73	3.30N	8.40E
Mackenzie, R.	Canada	76	67. 26N	131.00W
Macon	France	70	46.18N	4.50E
Macon	Georgia, USA	79	32.50N	83.37W
MADAGASCAR	Indian Ocean	73	20.00S	46.00E
Madakasira	Andhra Pradesh	20	13.57N	77.19E
Madaripur	Bangladesh	18	23.14N	90.15E
Maderia, Is	Atlantic Ocean	88	32.50N	17.00W
Maderia, R.	S. America	80	5.30S	61.20W
Madhepura	Bihar	24	25.57N	86.51E
Madhubani	Bihar	24	26.21N	86.07E
Madhupur	Jharkhand	24	24.18N	86.37E
Madhya Pradesh, State	India	26	23.30N	80.00E
Madicine Hat	Canada	77	50.00N	110.45W
Madikeri	Karnataka	28	12.26N	75.47E
Madison	Wisconsin, USA	79	43.05N	89.25W
Madre, Sierra	Mexico	76	25.00N	105.00W
Madrid	Spain	67	40.24N	3.42W
Madurai	Tamil Nadu	28	9.58N	78.10E
Madurantakam	Tamil Nadu	21	12.30N	79.56E
Magdeburg	Germany	70	53.08N	11.38E
Magellan	Strait of Chile	81	52.30S	69.00W
Magnitogorsk	Russia	71	53.30N	59.00E
Mahabaleshwar	Maharashtra	27	17.58N	73.43E
Mahabubnagar	Andhra Pradesh	27	16.42N	77.58E
Mahadeo Hills	Madhya Pradesh	11	22.24 N	78.00E
Mahajanga	Madagascar	75	15.40S	46.20E
Mahanadi, R.	Odisha	17	20.19N	86.45E
Maharajganj	Uttar Pradesh	24	27.11N	83.37E
Maharashtra, State	India	27	20.00N	76.00E
Mahasamund	Chhattisgarh	26	21.11N	82.10E
Mahe	Puducherry	28	11.41N	75.30E
Mahendragarh	Chhattisgarh	17	23.21N	82.21E
Mahesana	Gujarat	23	23.42N	72.37E
Maheshwar	Madhya Pradesh	26	22.11N	75.37E
Mahi, R.	Gujarat	23	22.20N	73.05E
Mahoba	Uttar Pradesh	24	25.17N	79.54E
Mahrajganj	Uttar Pradesh	24	27.08N	83.34E
Mahuva	Gujarat	23	21.10N	71.45E
Maihar	Madhya Pradesh	17	24.16N	80.49E
Maijdi	Bangladesh	18	22.48N	91.09E
Maimana	Afghanistan	65	35.55N	64.48E
Mainpuri	Uttar Pradesh	24	27.14N	79.03E
Majitha	Punjab	14	31.46N	75.01E
Majorca (Mallorca)	Balearic Is	66	39.30N	3.00E
Makasar (Makassar)	Celebes	64	5.05 S	119.30E
Makhach-Kala	Russia	71	42.52N	47.50E
Malabo	Equatorial Guinea	73	3.45N	8.48E
Malacca and Strait	Malaysia	64	2.10N	102.14E
Malaga	Spain	67	36.43N	4.25W
Malappuram	Kerala	28	11.03N	76.03E
Malatya	Turkey	65	38.20N	38.20E
MALAWI	East Africa	73	13.00S	34.00E
Malawi L.	East Africa	72	12.00 S	34.30E
MALAYSIA	S. E. Asia	59	5.00N	105.00E
Maldah	West Bengal	18	25.03N	88.09E
MALDIVES	Indian Ocean	59	5.30N	73.00E
MALDOVA	Europe	67	47.00N	28.55E
Male	Maldives	59	4.00N	73.28E
Malegaon	Maharashtra	20	20.30N	74.40E
Malema	Mozambique	75	14.57S	37.25E
Maler Kitla	Punjab	14	30.31N	75.59E
MALI	W. Africa	73	15.00N	5.00W
Malkangiri	Odisha	26	18.22N	81.56E
Malkapur	Maharashtra	20	20.53N	76.17E
Malmesbury	South Africa	75	33.28S	18.43E
Malmo	Sweden	67	55.40N	13.00E
MALTA	Mediterranean	67	36.00N	14.30E
Malvan	Maharashtra	27	16.03N	73.30E
Malwa Plateau	Madhya Pradesh	10	24.00N	76.00E
Mamallapuram	Tamil Nadu	28	12.37N	80.14E
Mamit	Mizoram	25	23.52N	92.32E
Manama	Bahrain	59	26.12N	50.35E
Manaus	Brazil	83	3.10 S	60.00W
Manchester	England	69	53.28N	2.12W
Manchouli	China	62	49.46N	117.24E
Mandalay	Myanmar	13	21.59N	96.08E
Mandi	Himachal Pradesh	22	31.39N	76.58E
Mandla	Madhya Pradesh	26	22.35N	80.23E

Names	Country/Region	Pg.No.	Lat.	Long.
Mandsaur	Madhya Pradesh	26	24.03N	75.10E
Mandvi	Gujarat	23	22.51N	68.32E
Mandya	Karnataka	28	12.33N	76.53E
Mangalagiri	Andhra Pradesh	20	16.26N	80.36E
Mangaldai	Assam	25	26.27N	92.05E
Mangalore	Karnataka	28	12.52N	74.53E
Mangan	Sikkim	25	27.30N	88.32E
Mangaon	Maharashtra	20	18.15N	73.20E
Mangyai	China	62	38.06N	91.37E
Manica	Mozambique	75	18.56S	32.52E
Manila	Philippines	64	14.30N	121.30E
Manipur, State	India	13	24.44N	93.58W
Manisa	Turkey	65	38.38N	27.30E
Manitoba, Prov.	Canada	77	52.00N	97.00W
Mankheri	Jharkhand	17	23.40N	84.33E
Manmad	Maharashtra	20	20.15N	74.29E
Mannar	Sri Lanka	61	8.59N	79.55E
Mannar, Gulf of.	India-Sri Lanka	11	8.50N	79.50E
Mannargudi	Tamil Nadu	21	10.40N	79.29E
Mansa	Punjab	22	29.58N	75.24E
Mansa	Zambia	75	11.10S	28.52E
Mansar	Maharashtra	20	21.24N	79.19E
Manugua	Nicaragua	81	12.10N	86.51W
Manvi	Karnataka	20	15.57N	76.58E
Manwat	Maharashtra	20	19.18N	76.30E
Manzai	Pakistan	14	32.12N	70.15E
Maputo	Mozambique	75	25.58S	32.35E
Mar Del Plata	Argentina	81	37.59 S	57.30W
Maraba	Brazil	83	5.23S	49.10W
Maracaibo	Venezuela	81	10.37N	71.41W
Mardan	Pakistan	14	34.10N	72.03E
Margao	Goa	27	15.15N	73.59E
Mariental	Namibia	75	24.36S	17.59E
Maringa	Brazil	83	23.26S	52.02W
Markham, Mt	Antarctica	89	83.00S	164.00E
Marmara, Sea of	Turkey	65	40.40N	27.35E
Marmugao	Goa	27	15.25N	73.43E
Marrakech	Morocco	73	31.38N	7.59W
Marseilles	France	67	43.20N	3.30E
MARSHALL IS	Pacific Ocean	87	13.00N	170.00E
Martaban	Myanmar	13	16.30N	97.40E
Martaban, Gulf of	Myanmar	11	16.00N	97.00E
Martigny	Switzerland	70	46.07N	7.05E
Martinique	West Indies	77	14.40N	61.00W
Mary	Turkmenistan	71	37.32N	61.58E
Maryborough	Queensland, Aust.	85	25.35 S	152.43E
Maseru	Lesotho	75	29.19S	27.29E
Mashhad	Iran	65	36.16N	59.36E
Massawa	Ethiopia	73	15.36N	39.28E
Mastuj	Pakistan	14	36.16N	72.36E
Masvingo	Zimbabwe	75	20.50S	30.50E
Matadi	Congo Dem, Rep.	73	5.42 S	13.31E
Matale	Sri Lanka	61	7.28N	80.37E
Matanzas	Cuba	77	23.01N	81.39W
Matara	Sri Lanka	61	5.57N	80.33E
Matheran	Maharashtra	27	18.59N	73.18E
Mathura	Uttar Pradesh	24	27.28N	77.41E
Mato Grosso	Brazil	83	15.00S	60.00W
Mattancheri	Kerala	21	9.57N	76.17E
Mau	Madhya Pradesh	17	22.15N	80.13E
Mauganj	Madhya Pradesh	17	24.40N	81.56E
Maunath Bhanjan	Uttar Pradesh	24	25.57N	83.36E
MAURITANIA	West Africa	73	19.00N	13.00W
MAURITIUS	Indian Ocean/Africa	73	20.00S	57.00E
Mawlaik	Myanmar	18	23.36N	94.26E
Mawlamyaing	Myanmar	13	16.30N	97.38E
Mayiladutural	Tamil Nadu	21	11.06N	79.42E
Mayo	Canada	79	63.38N	135.57W
Mayotte	Indian Ocean	73	12.50S	45.10E
Mazabuka	Zambia	75	15.50S	27.47E
Mazalgaon	Maharashtra	20	19.08N	76.13E
Mazar-i-sharif	Afghanistan	65	36.45N	67.09E
Mazatlan	Mexico	77	23.15N	106.30W
Mbabane	Swaziland	75	26.20S	31.08E
Mecca	Saudi Arabia	65	21.25N	39.54E
Medak	Andhra Pradesh	27	18.01N	78.15E
Medan	Sumatra	64	3.40N	78.38E
Medellin	Colombia	81	6.15N	75.45W
Medina	Saudi Arabia	65	24.33N	39.53E
Medinipur	W. Bengal	25	22.25N	87.21E
Mediterranean Sea	S. Europe, etc.	70	37.00N	15.00E
Meerut	Uttar Pradesh	24	29.01N	77.45E
Meghalaya, State	India	13	25.30N	91.00E
Meherpur	Bangladesh	18	23.47N	88.40E
Mekong, R.	S.E. Asia	64	15.00N	106.00E
Melbourne	Victoria Australia	85	37.50 S	144.59E
Melilla	North Africa	73	35.21N	2.57W
Melo	Ururuay	81	32.22S	54.10W
Melville, I.	Canada	76	75.30N	113.00W
Memphis	Tennessee USA	79	35.08N	90.01W
Mendocino, C.	USA	79	40.26N	124.23W
Mendoza	Argentina	81	32.50 S	68.52W
Menongue	Angola	75	14.36S	17.48E
Mentawei, Is	Sumatra	64	2.00 S	99.00E
Mergui, Arch.	Myanmar	11	12.32N	98.07E
Merida	Mexico	79	20.54N	89.40W
Merida	Venezuela	81	8.20N	71.08W
Merta	Rajasthan	23	26.39N	74.06E
Merthyr Tydfil	Wales	69	51.46N	3.20W
Messanjore	Jharkhand	17	24.05N	87.21E
Messina	Italy	67	38.13N	15.13E
Messina	South Africa	75	22.23S	30.00E
Mettupalaiyam	Tamil Nadu	21	11.18N	76.59E
Mettur Dam	Tamil Nadu	21	11.52N	77.50E

Names	Country/Region	Pg.No.	Lat.	Long.
Metz	France	70	49.05N	6.12E
MEXICO	N. America	77	19.26N	99.01W
Mexico City	Mexico	77	19.26N	99.08W
Mexico, Gulf of	Mexico	76	26.00N	92.00W
Miami	Florida USA	79	25.46N	80.12W
Miani	Pakistan	14	32.32N	73.08E
Mianwali	Pakistan	14	32.35N	71.33E
Michigan, L.	USA	76	44.00N	87.00W
MICRONESIA, FED. STATES OF	Oceania	85	6.55N	158.11E
Middelburg	South Africa	75	31.28S	25.01E
Middlesbrough	England	69	54.34N	1.15W
Milan	Italy	70	45.27N	9.10E
Milwaukee	Wisconsin, USA	79	43.03N	87.55W
Mindanao, I.	Philippines	64	8.00N	125.00E
Mindoro, I.	Philippines	64	13.00N	121.00E
Mingin	Myanmar	18	22.51N	94.34E
Minicoy, I.	India	12	8.10N	73.00E
Minneapolis	Minnesota, USA	79	44.59N	93.17W
Minorca	Balearic Is	66	40.00N	4.00E
Minsk	Belarus	67	53.55N	27.35E
Minyuwa	Myanmar	18	22.00N	94.06E
Miraj	Maharashtra	27	16.49N	74.43E
Miram Shah	Pakistan	14	33.00N	70.04E
Mirpur	Jammu & Kashmir	22	33.12N	73.51E
Mirzapur	Uttar Pradesh	24	25.10N	82.37E
Mississippi, R.	USA	79	34.00N	91.00W
Missouri, R.	USA	79	48.00N	107.00W
Mitchell, Mt	USA	79	35.44N	82.15W
Mito	Japan	63	36.20N	140.30E
Miyako	Japan	63	39.40N	141.75E
Miyazaki	Japan	63	32.00N	131.30E
Mizoram, State	India	13	23.30N	92.52E
Mobile	Alabama, USA	79	30.41N	88.03W
Mocambique	Mozambique	75	15.03S	40.45E
Mocuba	Mozambique	75	16.52S	36.57E
Modena	Italy	70	44.38N	10.55E
Moga	Punjab	22	30.49N	75.14E
Mogadishu	Somali Rep.	73	2.05N	45.25E
Mohali	Punjab	14	30.78N	76.69E
Mokameh	Bihar	24	25.24N	85.55E
Mokokchung	Nagaland	25	26.18N	94.30E
Mokpo	S. Korea	63	35.50N	126.30E
Moldova	Europe	66	47.40N	28.00E
Molepolole	Botswana	75	24.25S	25.30E
Mollendo	Peru	83	17.00S	72.00W
Moluccas, Is	Indonesia	64	2.00S	128.00E
Mombasa	Kenya	73	4.00S	39.40E
Mominabad	Maharashtra	20	18.44N	76.23E
Mon	Nagaland	25	26.40N	95.01E
MONACO	Europe	67	43.43N	07.25E
Monaco	Riviera, France	70	43.44N	7.24E
Monaco	Monaco, Europe	71	43.43N	7.25E
Monaragala	Sri Lanka	61	6.52N	81.22E
MONGOLIA	Asia	59	46.00N	105.00E
Mongu	Zambia	75	15.13S	23.09E
Monrovia	Liberia	73	6.18N	10.45W
Mons	Belgium	70	50.27N	3.57E
Mont Blanc	France	70	45.49N	6.52E
Montauban	France	70	44.02N	1.22E
MONTENEGRO	Europe	67	43.01N	19.05E
Montepelier	Vermont, USA	79	44.16N	72.35W
Monteral	Canada	77	45.31N	73.34W
Montero	Bolivia	81	17.20S	63.15W
Monterrey	Mexico	79	25.42N	100.14W
Montes Claros	Brazil	83	16.45S	43.52W
Montevideo	Uruguay	81	34.55S	56.11W
Montgomery	Alabama, USA	79	32.21N	85.20W
Montpellier	France	70	43.36N	3.53E
Montreal	Scotland	69	56.44N	2.28W
Montserrat	West Indies	77	16.40N	62.10W
Moradabad	Uttar Pradesh	24	28.51N	78.49E
Morar	Madhya Pradesh	16	26.13N	78.14E
Moratuwa	Sri Lanka	61	6.53N	79.56E
Moray Firth	Scotland	69	57.45N	3.45W
Morbi	Gujarat	23	22.49N	70.54E
Morea	Greece	66	37.20N	22.00E
Morecambe, Bay	England	69	54.00N	3.00W
Morena	Madhya Pradesh	26	26.23N	78.04E
Morigaon	Assam	25	26.14N	92.23E
Morioka	Japan	63	39.45N	141.08E
MOROCCO	N.W. Africa	73	32.00N	5.00W
Morondava	Madagascar	75	20.19S	44.17E
Moroni	Comoros Is	73	11.39S	43.14E
Moscow	Russian Federation	67	55.45N	37.37E
Mossamedes	Angola	73	15.07S	12.15E
Mossel Bay	South Africa	73	34.11S	22.09E
Mostar	Bosnia-Herzegovina	70	43.02N	17.49E
Mosul	Iraq	65	36.20N	43.05E
Motihari	Bihar	24	26.37N	84.57E
Mourne Mts	N. Ireland	69	54.10N	6.05W
MOZAMBIQUE	S. E. Africa	73	15.02 S	40.48E
Mozambique Channel	S. E. Africa	73	15.00 S	42.00E
Mucia	Spain	67	37.59N	1.07W
Muddedihal	Karnataka	20	16.20N	76.10E
Mudhol	Andhra Pradesh	20	19.00N	77.52E
Mudhol	Karnataka	28	16.20N	75.20E
Mufulira	Zambia	75	12.30S	28.12E
Mugal Sarai	Uttar Pradesh	17	25.17N	83.11E
Muhammadgarh	Madhya Pradesh	16	23.39N	78.13E
Mukher	Maharashtra	20	18.42N	77.24E
Muktinath	Nepal	15	28.54N	83.49E
Muktsar	Punjab	22	30.30N	74.43E

Names	Country/Region	Pg.No.	Lat.	Long.
Mul	Maharashtra	20	20.04N	79.43E
Mulbagal	Karnataka	21	13.11N	78.14E
Mulhouse	France	70	47.45N	7.20E
Mull, I.	Scotland	69	56.20N	6.00W
Mullaittivu	Sri Lanka	61	9.16N	80.48E
Mulshi, L.	Maharashtra	20	18.50N	73.50E
Mumbai	Maharashtra	27	18.55N	72.54E
Mundra	Gujarat	23	22.49N	69.52E
Munger	Bihar	24	25.23N	86.30E
Munich	Germany	67	48.08N	11.35E
Murmansk	Russia	67	68.50N	33.10E
Muroran	Japan	63	42.25N	141.00E
Murray, R.	Australia	84	35.25 S	139.30E
Murree	Pakistan	14	33.55N	73.27E
Murrumbidgee, R.	Australia	84	35.35 S	149.07E
Murshidabad	W. Bengal	25	24.11N	88.19E
Murud	Maharashtra	27	18.18N	72.59E
Murwara	Madhya Pradesh	26	23.51N	80.02E
Murzug	Libya	73	25.52N	14.10E
Musa Khel Bazar	Pakistan	14	30.53N	69.54E
Muscat	Oman	59	23.37N	58.36E
Muscogee	USA	79	35.50N	95.25W
Mushalpur	Assam	25	26.40N	91.22E
Mussoorie	Uttarakhand	24	30.27N	78.06E
Mutarara	Mozambique	75	17.30S	32.40E
Mutare	Zimbabwe	75	18.58S	32.40E
Muzaffarabad	Jammu & Kashmir	22	34.24N	73.22E
Muzaffargarh	Pakistan	14	30.05N	71.14E
Muzaffarnagar	Uttar Pradesh	24	29.28N	77.44E
Muzaffarpur	Bihar	24	26.07N	85.27E
Mwanza	Tanzania	73	2.35S	32.56E
MYANMAR	S. Asia	59	20.20N	96.00E
Myitkyina	Myanmar	13	25.24N	97.26E
Myittha, R.	Myanmar	18	23.12N	94.18E
Mymensingh	Bangladesh	18	24.45N	90.27E
Mysore	Karnataka	28	12.18N	76.42E
Mzuzu	Malawi	75	11.31S	34.00E

N

Names	Country/Region	Pg.No.	Lat.	Long.
N. Ireland	UK, British Isles	69	53.00N	2.00W
N'Djamena	Chad	73	12.10N	14.59E
Naharangapur	Odisha	20	10.17N	82.37E
Nabha	Punjab	14	30.25N	76.09E
Nacala	Mozambique	75	14.34S	40.40E
Nachana	Rajasthan	19	27.29N	71.45E
Nadiad	Gujarat	23	22.41N	72.55E
Naga Hills	Nagaland	18	26.00N	94.20E
Nagaland, State	India	13	26.00N	94.20E
Nagaon	Assam	25	26.21N	92.45E
Nagappattinam	Tamil Nadu	28	10.46N	79.51E
Nagar Karnul	Andhra Pradesh	20	16.30N	78.19E
Nagarcoil	Tamil Nadu	28	8.10N	77.26E
Nagarjunasagar Dam	Andhra Pradesh	20	16.50N	79.20E
Nagasaki	Japan	63	32.47N	129.52E
Nagaur	Rajasthan	23	27.11N	73.40E
Nagercoil	Tamil Nadu	28	8.11N	77.29E
Nagina	Uttar Pradesh	24	29.27N	78.29E
Nagod (Unchahra)	Madhya Pradesh	17	24.33N	80.37E
Nagoya	Japan	63	35.07N	136.56E
Nagpur	Maharashtra	27	21.09N	79.09E
Nagrota	Himachal Pradesh	14	32.07N	76.23E
Nahan	Himachal Pradesh	22	30.33N	77.17E
Naini Tal	Uttarakhand	24	29.23N	79.30E
Nairn	Scotland	69	57.36N	3.53W
Nairobi	Kenya	73	1.18S	36.52E
Najin	N. Korea	63	42.12N	130.15E
Nalbari	Assam	25	26.25N	91.29E
Naldrug	Maharashtra	20	17.49N	76.20E
Nalgonda	Andhra Pradesh	27	17.03N	79.02E
Nallamalai, Ra.	Andhra Pradesh	20	15.00N	78.38E
Namakkal	Tamil Nadu	28	11.13N	78.13E
Namchi	Sikkim	25	27.07N	88.23E
Namib Desert	S. W. Africa	72	22.30W	15.00E
Namibe	Angola	75	15.10S	12.09E
NAMIBIA	S. W. Africa	73	23.00S	15.00E
Nampula	Mozambique	75	15.09S	39.14E
Namur	Belgium	70	50.28N	4.53E
Nanchang	China	62	28.34N	115.48E
Nancy	France	70	48.40N	6.15E
Nanda Devi, Mt	Uttarakhand	24	30.23N	80.01E
Nanded	Maharashtra	27	19.09N	77.27E
Nandigama	Andhra Pradesh	20	16.46N	80.20E
Nandikotkur	Andhra Pradesh	20	15.52N	78.18E
Nandod	Gujarat	19	21.54N	73.34E
Nandurbar	Maharashtra	27	21.23N	74.19E
Nandyal	Andhra Pradesh	27	15.29N	78.32E
Nanga Parbat, Mt	Jammu & Kashmir	14	35.14N	74.35E
Nanguneri	Tamil Nadu	21	8.29N	77.44E
Nanjangud	Karnataka	28	12.07N	76.44E
Nanjing	China	62	32.04N	118.50E
Nanning	China	62	22.49N	108.24E
Nantes	France	70	47.13N	1.32W
Naoshera	Jammu & Kashmir	14	33.13N	74.17E
Napier	New Zealand	85	39.29S	176.55E
Naples	Italy	67	40.51N	14.26E
Naraina	Rajasthan	19	26.50N	74.11E
Narasapur	Andhra Pradesh	20	16.26N	81.45E
Narasaraopet	Andhra Pradesh	20	16.14N	80.06E
Narayanganj	Bangladesh	18	23.37N	90.32E
Narayanpet	Andhra Pradesh	20	16.46N	77.27E
Narayanpur	Chhattisgarh	26	19.43N	81.14E
Narbonne	France	70	43.11N	3.01E
Narmada, R.	India	16	21.48N	74.00E
Narnaul	Haryana	22	28.02N	76.14E
Narsinghgarh	Madhya Pradesh	26	23.44N	77.08E
Narsinghpur	Odisha	17	20.28N	85.07E
Narsinghpur	Madhya Pradesh	26	22.56N	79.12E
Narsipatnam	Andhra Pradesh	20	17.40N	82.39E
Narvik	Norway	67	68.25N	17.30E
Nashik	Maharashtra	27	20.02N	73.50E
Nashville	Tennessee, USA	79	36.11N	86.50W
Nasirabad	Pakistan	14	28.24N	68.28E
Nasirabad	Rajasthan	19	26.18N	74.40E
Nassau	Bahamas	77	25.04N	77.20W
Nasser, L.	Egypt	72	23.00N	32.30E
Natal	S. Africa	73	29.00 S	30.30E
Natuna, Is	Indonesia	64	4.00N	108.00E
Naugarh	Uttar Pradesh	24	27.18N	83.06E
NAURU	Pacific Ocean	87	1.00S	166.00E
Navadwip	W. Bengal	18	23.24N	88.23E
Navsari	Gujarat	23	21.07N	73.40E
Nawabganj	Uttar Pradesh	17	26.56N	82.12E
Nawabshah	Pakistan	14	26.08N	68.28E
Nawada	Bihar	24	24.53N	85.35E
Nawanshahr	Punjab	22	31.06N	76.09E
Nayagarh	Odisha	26	20.08N	85.08E
Naypyidaw	Myanmar	59	19.45N	96.06E
Nazca	Peru	83	14.53S	74.54W
Nazwa	Oman	65	22.56N	57.31E
Ndola	Zambia	75	13.00S	28.39E
Neagh, L.	N. Ireland	69	54.36N	6.25W
Neemuch	Madhya Pradesh	26	24.26N	74.57E
Negombo	Sri Lanka	21	7.12N	79.50E
Negro, R.	S. America	80	40.00S	64.00W
Negros, I.	Philippines	64	10.00N	122.55E
Neijiang	China	62	29.35N	105.10E
Nejd	Saudi Arabia	65	25.40N	47.00E
Nellore	Andhra Pradesh	27	14.27N	80.02E
Nelma	Russia	71	47.30N	139.00E
Nelson	Canada	79	49.29N	117.20W
Nelson	New Zealand	85	41.15S	173.20E
Nelson, R.	Canada	76	55.20N	96.52W
Nemawar	Madhya Pradesh	16	22.30N	77.00E
Nemuro	Japan	63	43.20N	145.35E
NEPAL	Asia	59	28.00N	85.00E
Nepalganj	Nepal	15	27.59N	81.40E
NETHERLANDS	W. Europe	67	53.00N	5.00E
Netrakona	Bangladesh	18	24.53N	90.47E
Nevada	Sierra, USA	76	40.00N	120.00W
Nevers	France	70	47.00N	3.09E
New Brunswick	Canada	77	46.50N	66.30W
New Caledonia I.	Pacific Ocean	84	21.30S	166.00E
New Delhi	India	12	28.37N	77.12E
New Guinea	Pacific Ocean	87	5.00S	142.00E
New Haven	Connecticut, USA	79	41.20N	72.54W
New Orleans	Louisiana, USA	79	30.00N	90.01W
New Plymouth	New Zealand	85	39.05S	174.05E
New Port News	USA	79	37.02N	76.54W
New Siberian Is	Russia	71	74.20N	148.00E
New South Wales, State	Australia	85	32.00 S	146.00E
New Tehri	Uttarakhand	24	30.23N	78.29E
New Westminster	Canada	79	49.13N	122.52W
New York	USA	79	40.43N	74.01W
NEW ZEALAND	Oceania	85	40.00S	175.00E
Newcastle	England	69	54.58N	1.35W
Newcastle	N.S.W., Aust.	85	33.00S	151.40E
Newfoundland	Canada	77	49.00N	57.00W
Newhaven	England	69	50.46N	0.05E
Neyveli	Tamil Nadu	28	11.31N	79.29E
Nguru	Nigeria	73	12.30N	10.00E
Nha-Trang	Vietnam	64	12.16N	109.10E
Niagara Falls	Canada-USA	76	43.07N	79.02W
Niamey	Niger	73	13.27N	2.06E
Nias, I.	Sumatra	64	1.00N	97.30E
NICARAGUA	Central America	77	12.00N	86.00W
Nicaragua, L.	Central America	76	12.00N	85.30W
Nice	France	70	43.41N	7.18E
Nicosia	Cyprus	59	35.10N	33.22E
NIGER	West Africa	73	18.00N	10.00E
Niger, R.	West Africa	72	15.00N	2.03E
NIGERIA	W. Africa	73	10.00N	8.00E
Nighasan	Uttar Pradesh	17	28.14N	80.55E
Nijgata	Japan	63	37.58N	139.04E
Nikolayevsk	Russia	71	53.18N	140.44E
Nilagiri	Odisha	17	21.27N	86.49E
Nile, R.	N. E. Africa	72	28.00N	32.00E
Nilgiri Hills	Kerala-Karnataka-Tamil Nadu	10	11.28N	76.47E
Nimas	France	70	43.50N	4.22E
Nimbahera	Rajasthan	23	24.37N	74.45E
Ningbo	China	62	29.50N	121.30E
Nipigon, L.	Ontario, Canada	79	49.50N	88.30W
Nirmal	Andhra Pradesh	27	19.06N	78.25E
Niteroi	Brazil	83	22.54S	43.06W
Nizamabad	Andhra Pradesh	27	18.40N	78.10E
Nizampatnam	Andhra Pradesh	20	15.54N	80.43E
Nizhniy Novgorod	Russia	71	56.15N	43.38E
Nohar	Rajasthan	19	29.11N	74.49E
Noida	Uttar Pradesh	24	28.33N	77.37E
Nome	Alaska, USA	79	64.45N	165.25W
Nongpoh	Meghalaya	25	25.53N	91.55E
Nongstoin	Meghalaya	25	25.28N	91.17E
Norfolk	Virginia, USA	79	36.51N	76.18W
Norfolk, I.	Pacific Ocean	84	29.00S	170.00E
Norrkoping	Sweden	67	58.35N	16.15E
North America, Continent	**World**	**92**		
North Channel	Scotland-Ireland	69	55.10N	6.00W
NORTH KOREA	North Asia	59	40.00N	126.00E
North Lakhimpur	Assam	25	27.10N	94.07E
North Sea	N. W. Europe	66	55.00N	2.30E
North, C.	Norway	66	71.12N	25.45E
Northampton	England	69	52.41N	0.55W
Northern Ireland	Great Britain	69	55.00N	7.00W
Northern Marianas	Pacific Ocean	87	17.00N	145.00E
Northern Territory	Australia	85	15.00N	135.00E
Northwest Territories	Canada	77	65.00N	100.00W
NORWAY	N. W. Europe	67	62.00N	10.00E
Norwich	England	69	52.40N	1.15E
Nottingham	England	69	59.57N	1.10E
Nouakchott	Mauritania	73	18.06N	15.58W
Nova Scotia	Canada	77	45.00N	64.00W
Novaya Zemlya	Russia	71	73.00N	55.00E
Novi Sad	Serbia	70	45.16N	19.50E
Novosibirsk	Russia	71	55.20N	83.42E
Nowshera	Pakistan	14	34.00N	72.00E
Nuapara	Odisha	26	20.46N	82.35E
Nubian Desert	Sudan	72	21.00N	34.00E
Nuh	Haryana	22	28.07N	77.01E
Nuku'alofa	Tonga	87	21.80S	175.12W
Nukus	Uzbekistan	65	42.30N	59.40E
Nurnberg (Nuremberg)	Germany	70	49.27N	11.05E
Nuuk	Greenland	77	64.10N	51.44W
Nuwara Eliya	Sri Lanka	21	6.59N	80.47E
Nyainqentangiha, Ra.	China	62	30.30N	95.00E

O

Names	Country/Region	Pg.No.	Lat.	Long.
Oakland	California, USA	79	37.40N	122.19W
Oaxaca	Mexico	79	17.02N	96.40W
Ob, R.	Russia	71	68.00N	74.00E
Oban	Scotland	69	56.26N	5.28W
Obbia .	Somali Rep.	73	5.20N	48.30E
Obluch'ye	Russia	71	49.10N	130.50E
Oceania, Continent	**World**	**92**		
Odessa	Ukraine	67	46.27N	30.48E
Odisha, State	India	13	21.10N	85.00E
Offenbach	Germany	70	50.06N	8.45E
Oghi	Pakistan	14	34.32N	73.02E
Ohio, R.	USA	76	37.20N	88.00W
Okara	Pakistan	14	30.50N	73.30E
Okhotsk	Russia	71	59.30N	143.20E
Okhotsk, Sea of	Russia	71	55.00N	145.00E
Okinawa	Japan	63	26.40N	128.00E
Oklahoma City	Oklahoma, USA	79	35.29N	97.31W
Oldenburg	Germany	70	53.09N	8.13E
Olinda	Brazil	83	8.00S	34.51E
Olympia	Washington, USA	79	47.00N	122.58W
Omagh	N. Ireland	69	54.36N	7.19W
Omaha	Nebraska, USA	79	41.16N	95.58E
OMAN	Asia	59	23.00N	58.00E
Oman, Gulf of	Iran/Arabia	65	23.30N	57.00E
Omdurman	Sudan	73	15.36N	32.47E
Omsk	Russia	71	55.00N	73.38E
Onega, L.	Russia	71	61.30N	35.00E
Ongole	Andhra Pradesh	27	15.30N	80.06E
Ontario, L.	Canada-USA	79	43.40N	78.00W
Oppeln (Opole)	Poland	70	50.41N	17.55E
Orai	Uttar Pradesh	24	25.59N	79.30E
Oran	Algeria	73	35.45N	0.39W
Orange, R.	S. Africa	72	29.40S	16.22E
Oras	Maharashtra	27	16.04N	73.31E
Orchha	Madhya Pradesh	16	25.21N	78.38E
Orel	Russia	67	52.56N	36.05E
Orenburg	Russia	71	54.46N	55.07E
Orhon Gol	Mongolia	62	49.30N	106.00E
Orinoco, R.	Venezuela	80	6.00N	67.30W
Orizaba	Mexico	79	18.49N	97.04W
Orkney, Is	Scotland	69	59.00N	3.00W
Orleans	France	70	47.54N	1.54E
Orsk	Russia	71	51.15N	58.34E
Osaka	Japan	63	34.39N	135.27E
Osend	Belgium	70	51.13N	2.57E
Oslo	Norway	67	59.54N	10.45E
Osmanabad	Maharashtra	27	18.09N	76.05E
Osnabruck	Germany	70	52.17N	8.03E
Ottawa	Canada	79	45.27N	75.42W
Ouagodougou	Burkina Faso	73	12.25N	1.30W
Oudtshoorn	South Africa	75	33.35S	22.12E
Oulu	Finland	67	65.03N	25.35E
Ouse, R.	England	69	52.40N	0.21E
Oxford	England	69	51.46N	1.15W

P

Names	Country/Region	Pg.No.	Lat.	Long.
Pabna	Bangladesh	18	24.01N	89.18E
Pachmarhi	Madhya Pradesh	26	22.30N	78.22E
Pachora	Maharashtra	27	20.38N	75.29E
PACIFIC OCEAN	**World**	**92**		
Padang	Sumatra	64	0.55S	100.20E
Padmanabhapuram	Tamil Nadu	21	9.06N	76.50E
Padra	Gujarat	19	22.15N	73.07E
Padrauna	Uttar Pradesh	24	26.52N	84.01E
Padua (Padova)	Italy	70	45.23N	11.54E
Paharpur	Pakistan	14	32.07N	71.02E
Painavu	Kerala	28	9.46N	77.01E
Paisley	Scotland	69	55.51N	4.24W
Paithan	Maharashtra	27	19.29N	75.26E
Pakala	Andhra Pradesh	21	13.30N	79.00E
Pakaur	Jharkhand	24	24.38N	87.54E
PAKISTAN	S. Asia	59	30.00N	70.00E
Pakpattan	Pakistan	14	30.21N	73.26E
Pakur	Jharkhand	24	24.38N	87.51E
Palakkad	Kerala	28	10.46N	76.42E
Palakollu	Andhra Pradesh	20	16.31N	81.46E
Palamu	Jharkhand	24	23.52N	84.17E
Palani	Tamil Nadu	28	10.27N	77.33E
Palanpur	Gujarat	23	24.12N	72.28E
PALAU	Asia	59	07.21N	119.00E
Palawan, I.	Philippiness	64	10.00N	134.20E
Palayankottai	Tamil Nadu	28	8.43N	77.46E
Palembang	Sumatra	64	3.00S	104.39E
Palermo	Italy	67	38.07N	13.23E
Palestine	Asia	59	32.30N	35.30E
Pali	Rajasthan	23	25.46N	73.25E
Palikir	Micronesia, Fed. States of	87	06.55N	158.11E
Palitana	Gujarat	23	21.31N	71.53E
Palk, Str.	India-Sri Lanka	11	10.00N	80.00E
Palkonda	Andhra Pradesh	20	18.36N	83.48E
Palkonda, Ra.	Andhra Pradesh	20	13.50N	79.20E
Palkot	Jharkhand	17	22.52N	84.41E
Palladam	Tamil Nadu	21	10.59N	77.20E
Palmyras, Pt	Odisha	17	20.45N	87.02E
Palni Hills	Tamil Nadu	21	10.20N	77.10E
Palwal	Haryana	22	28.24N	76.35E
Pamirs	Tajikistan	71	38.00N	73.00E
Pampas	S. America	80	30.00S	60.00W
Pamplona	Spain	70	42.50N	1.38W
Panaji	Goa	12	15.30N	73.55E
PANAMA	Central America	77	9.00N	79.35W
Panama City	Panama	77	8.59N	79.31W
Panay, I.	Philippines	64	11.10N	122.30E
Panchkula	Haryana	22	30.42N	76.53E
Pandaria	Chhattisgarh	17	22.15N	81.27E
Pandharpur	Maharashtra	27	17.41N	75.23E
Panikoili	Odisha	26	20.48N	86.24E
Panipat	Haryana	22	29.23N	77.10E
Panna	Madhya Pradesh	26	24.44N	80.14E
Panruti	Tamil Nadu	21	11.47N	79.35E
Papeete	Fr. Polynesia	87	17.32S	149.34W
PAPUA NEW GUINEA	Oceania	85	8.00S	145.00E
Parachinar	Pakistan	14	33.55N	70.00E
Paradwip	Odisha	26	20.30N	86.55E
PARAGUAY	South America	81	25.16S	57.40W
Paraguay and R.	South America	81	23.00S	58.00W
Paralakhemundi	Odisha	26	18.47N	84.08E
Paramakkudi	Tamil Nadu	21	9.31N	78.39E
Paramaribo	Suriname	81	5.42N	55.11W
Parana, R.	S. America	80	30.00S	60.00W
Parangipettai	Tamil Nadu	21	11.30N	79.48E
Parasnath, Mt	Bihar	17	24.00N	86.11E
Parbhani	Maharashtra	27	19.08N	76.50E
Parenda	Maharashtra	20	18.16N	75.30E
Paricatuba	Brazil	83	18.00S	49.00W
Paris	France	67	48.50N	2.20E
Parlakot	Chhattisgarh	17	19.45N	80.48E
Parli	Maharashtra	20	18.53N	76.36E
Parma	Italy	70	44.48N	10.21E
Parnaiba	Brazil	83	2.58S	41.46W
Paro	Bhutan	18	27.24N	89.14E
Paron	Madhya Pradesh	16	24.57N	76.50E
Partabgarh	Rajasthan	23	24.02N	74.40E
Partabpur	Chhattisgarh	17	19.59N	80.50E
Parvatipuram	Andhra Pradesh	20	18.47N	83.28E
Pashat	Afghanistan	14	34.42N	71.05E
Pasighat	Arunachal Pradesh	25	28.00N	95.22E
Pasrur	Pakistan	14	32.16N	74.43E
Passau	Germany	70	48.34N	13.27E
Passo Fundo	Brazil	83	28.16S	52.20W
Patagonia	Argentina	80	43.00S	70.00W
Patan	Nepal	15	27.38N	85.13E
Patan	Rajasthan	19	27.49N	76.01E
Patan	Gujarat	23	23.52N	72.10E
Patancheru	Andhra Pradesh	20	17.36N	78.20E
Pataudi	Haryana	16	28.18N	76.48E
Pathanamthitta	Kerala	28	9.18N	76.51E
Pathankot	Punjab	22	32.17N	75.42E
Pathari	Madhya Pradesh	16	23.56N	78.15E
Pathri	Maharashtra	20	19.20N	76.30E
Patiala	Punjab	22	30.20N	76.25E
Patkai Bum	N. E. India	11	27.00N	95.30E
Patna	Bihar	13	25.37N	85.13E
Patos	Brazil	83	6.55S	37.15W
Patrai	Greece	67	38.14N	21.48E
Pattikonda	Andhra Pradesh	20	15.24N	77.04E
Pattukkottai	Tamil Nadu	28	10.26N	79.22E
Patuakhali	Bangladesh	18	22.20N	90.22W
Pau	France	70	43.18N	0.22W
Pauni	Maharashtra	20	20.48N	79.40E
Pauri	Uttarakhand	24	30.10N	78.48E
Paysandu	Uruguay	81	32.19S	58.08W
Peace , R.	Canada	76	56.15N	117.18W
Peak, The	England	69	53.24N	1.50W
Pecs	Hungary	70	46.04N	18.13E
Peddapuram	Andhra Pradesh	20	17.05N	82.11E
Pegu	Myanmar	13	17.20N	96.29E
Pegu Yoma (Pago)	Myanmar	11	20.00N	96.00E
Pehowa	Haryana	14	29.57N	76.37E
Peipus, L.	Estonia-Russia	66	58.30N	27.30E
Pembroke	Wales	69	51.40N	4.55W
Penganga, R.	Maharashtra	20	20.00N	77.00E
Pennine Chain	England	69	54.00N	2.00W
Pensacola	Florida, USA	79	30.30N	87.10W

Names	Country/Region	Pg.No.	Lat.	Long.
Saskatchewan, R.	Canada	76	53.25N	104.00W
Saskatoon	Canada	77	52.09N	106.40W
Satara	Maharashtra	27	17.42N	74.02E
Satluj, R.	Punjab	14	31.00N	75.00E
Satna	Madhya Pradesh	26	24.34N	80.55E
Satpura, Ra.	Madhya Pradesh	16	21.40N	75.00E
Sattenapalle	Andhra Pradesh	20	16.24N	80.11E
Sattur	Tamil Nadu	21	9.21N	77.58E
Satyamangalam	Tamil Nadu	21	11.30N	77.17E
SAUDI ARABIA	W. Asia	59	25.00N	40.00E
Savannah	Georgia, USA	79	32.06N	81.05W
Savantvadi	Maharashtra	20	15.54N	73.52E
Savanur	Karnataka	20	14.58N	75.19E
Sawai Madhopur	Rajasthan	23	25.58N	76.30E
Saynshand	Mongolia	62	44.50N	110.20E
Scarborough	England	69	54.17N	0.24W
Scilly, Is	England	69	50.00N	6.00W
Scotland	Great Britain	69	56.00N	4.00W
Scutari (Uskudar)	Turkey	65	49.01N	29.02E
Seattle	Washington, USA	79	47.36N	122.21W
Secunderabad	Andhra Pradesh	27	17.27N	78.33E
Sehore	Madhya Pradesh	26	23.12N	77.00E
Seine, R.	France	70	49.30N	1.00E
Semipalatinsk	Kazakhstan	71	50.28N	80.13E
Senapati	Manipur	25	25.15N	94.07E
SENEGAL	West Africa	73	14.00N	15.00W
Senegal, R.	West Africa	72	16.10N	16.25W
Sengottai	Tamil Nadu	21	8.59N	77.18E
Senhor do Bonfim	Brazil	83	10.28S	40.11W
Seoni	Madhya Pradesh	26	22.06N	79.35E
Seoul	South Korea	59	37.31N	127.06E
Seppa	Arunachal Pradesh	25	27.20N	92.56E
Serampore	W. Bengal	18	22.45N	88.23E
SERBIA	Europe	67	43.30N	20.00E
Serchhip	Mizoram	25	23.18N	92.53E
Serenje	Zambia	75	13.12S	30.15E
Serowe	Botswana	75	22.24S	26.42E
Serra	Brazil	83	20.06S	40.16W
Seshachalam Hills	Andhra Pradesh	20	14.10N	78.30E
Sevastopol	Ukraine	67	44.37N	33.35E
Severn, R.	England-Wales	69	51.40N	2.40W
Seville (Sevilla)	Spain	67	37.25N	5.58W
SEYCHELLES	Indian Ocean/Africa	73	4.00S	55.00E
Shahabad	Uttar Pradesh	17	27.30N	80.05E
Shahabad	Rajasthan	19	25.10N	77.20E
Shahabad	Andhra Pradesh	20	17.10N	78.11E
Shahdol	Madhya Pradesh	26	23.00N	81.30E
Shahjahanpur	Uttar Pradesh	24	27.54N	79.57E
Shahpura	Madhya Pradesh	17	23.10N	80.45E
Shajapur	Madhya Pradesh	26	23.26N	76.18E
Shanghai	China	62	31.15N	121.29E
Shannon, R.	Rep. of Ireland	69	53.50N	8.00W
Sharjah	UAE	65	25.20N	55.24E
Sheffield	England	69	53.22N	1.30W
Shegaon	Maharastra	20	20.48N	76.46E
Shekhpura	Bihar	24	25.07N	85.53E
Shenyang (Mukden)	China	62	41.48N	123.25E
Sheohar	Bihar	24	26.31N	85.18E
Sheopur	Madya Pradesh	26	25.39N	76.41E
Shetland, Is	Scotland	69	60.30N	1.00W
Shevaroy Hills	Tamil Nadu	21	12.00N	78.30E
Shijiazhuang	China	62	38.00N	114.30E
[illegible]ikoku, I.	Japan	63	33.40N	133.30E
[illegible]uri	W. Bengal	25	26.42N	88.25E
[illegible]	Russia	71	52.00N	115.52E
[illegible]	Meghalaya	25	25.34N	91.56E
[illegible]	Himachal Pradesh	12	31.06N	77.13E
[illegible]	Karnataka	28	14.00N	75.17E
[illegible]	Japan	63	33.40N	131.00E
[illegible]	Afghanistan	65	33.18N	62.15E
[illegible]	Pakistan	14	31.45N	69.49E
[illegible]	Iran	65	29.38N	52.31E
[illegible]	Iran	65	13.56N	75.38E
[illegible]	Madhya Pradesh	26	25.40N	77.44E
Shkoder (Scutari)	Albania	70	42.03N	19.31E
Shravasti	Uttar Pradesh	24	27.24N	82.07E
Shrewsbury	England	69	52.44N	2.45W
Shrigonda	Maharashtra	20	18.41N	74.44E
Shrirangapattana	Karnataka	28	12.26N	76.43E
Shupiyan	Jammu & Kashmir	22	33.43N	74.50E
Sialkot	Pakistan	14	32.31N	74.36E
Sibi	Pakistan	14	29.30N	67.55E
Sicily, I.	Italy	66	37.35N	14.10E
Sidhauli	Uttar Pradesh	17	27.18N	80.50E
Sidhi	Madhya Pradesh	26	24.25N	81.54E
Sidhout	Andhra Pradesh	20	14.28N	79.01E
Sidi-Bel-Abbes	Algeria	73	35.13N	0.01W
Sidipett	Andhra Pradesh	20	18.07N	78.50E
Sidra, Gulf of	Libya	73	31.30N	18.30E
SIERRA LEONE	W. Africa	73	9.00N	12.00W
Sihora	Madhya Pradesh	17	23.29N	80.09E
Sikandra	Uttar Pradesh	16	27.13N	77.58E
Sikar	Rajasthan	23	27.36N	75.15E
Sikkim, State	India	13	27.30N	88.30E
Sil Garhi	Nepal	15	29.12N	81.06E
Silchar (Cachar)	Assam	25	24.47N	92.48E
Silvassa	Dadra & Nagar Haveli	12	20.13N	73.03E
Simdega	Jharkhand	24	22.35N	84.32E
Sindgi	Karnataka	20	16.58N	76.13E
Sindhnur	Karnataka	20	15.45N	76.43E
Sindkheda	Maharashtra	20	21.18N	74.50E
SINGAPORE	S. E. Asia	59	1.17N	103.51E
Singareni Collieries	Andhra Pradesh	20	17.27N	80.20E
Singrauli	Madhya Pradesh	17	24.78N	82.83E

Names	Country/Region	Pg.No.	Lat.	Long.
Sinop	Turkey	65	42.01N	35.11E
Sinuiju N.	Korea	63	39.59N	124.30E
Sioux City	Iowa, USA	79	42.32N	96.25W
Sioux Falls	S. Dakota, USA	79	43.35N	96.40W
Sirajganj	Bangladesh	18	24.27N	89.47E
Sirohi	Rajasthan	23	24.53N	72.54E
Sironcha	Maharastra	20	18.51N	80.01E
Sironj	Madhya Pradesh	16	24.06N	77.44E
Sirpur	Andhra Pradesh	20	19.32N	79.45E
Sirsa	Haryana	22	29.32N	75.07E
Sirsi	Karnataka	20	14.36N	74.54E
Sirur	Maharashtra	20	18.50N	74.23E
Sitamarhi	Bihar	24	26.35N	85.32E
Sitapur	Uttar Pradesh	24	27.32N	80.43E
Sitka	Alaska, USA	79	57.04N	135.10W
Sitpur	Pakistan	14	29.11N	70.51E
Sittwe	Myanmar	13	20.09N	92.57E
Siuri	West Bengal	25	23.54N	87.34E
Sivaganga	Tamil Nadu	28	9.51N	79.32E
Sivas	Turkey	65	39.43N	36.58E
Sivasagar	Assam	25	26.59N	94.41E
Sivasamudram, I.	Karnataka	21	12.16N	77.13E
Siwalik, Ra.	India	10	30.00N	77.30E
Siwan	Bihar	24	26.12N	84.13E
Siwana	Rajasthan	23	25.36N	72.27E
Skagway	Alaska, USA	79	59.30N	135.20W
Skegness	England	69	53.09N	0.21E
Skopje	Macedonia	67	41.59N	21.27E
Skye, I. of	Scotland	69	57.20N	6.20W
Slave, Great L.	Canada	76	62.00N	114.00W
Sligo	Rep. of Ireland	69	54.16N	8.30W
SLOVAKIA	Europe	67	49.00N	20.00E
SLOVENIA	S. Europe	67	46.00N	15.00E
Slvudyanka	Russia	71	51.40N	103.30E
Smolensk	Russia	67	54.45N	32.01E
Smyrna (Izmir)	Turkey	65	38.24N	27.06E
Snowdon, Mt	Wales	69	53.04N	4.10W
Sobral	Brazil	83	3.45S	40.20W
Sobraon	Punjab	14	31.07N	74.54E
Socotra, I.	Indian Ocean	88	12.30N	50.00E
Sofala	Mozambique	75	20.00S	34.00E
Sofia	Bulgaria	67	42.40 N	23.20E
Sogamoso	Colombia	83	5.43N	72.60W
Sohagpur	Madhya Pradesh	16	22.42N	78.17E
Sohan, R.	Pakistan	14	32.10N	72.05E
Sohawal	Madhya Pradesh	17	24.35N	80.50E
Sohela	Odisha	17	21.18N	83.26E
Sokoto	Nigeria	73	13.02N	5.16E
Solan	Himachal Pradesh	22	30.55N	77.09E
Solapur	Maharastra	27	17.40N	75.56E
SOLOMON IS	Pacific Ocean	87	8.00S	158.00E
Solway Firth	England-Scotland	69	54.52N	2.30W
SOMALIA	E. Africa	73	5.00N	45.00E
Somnath (Patan)	Gujarat	23	21.04N	70.26E
Sonakhan	Chhattisgarh	17	21.36N	82.36E
Sonepur	Odisha	26	20.51N	83.59E
Sonhat	Chhattisgarh	17	23.29N	82.30E
Sonipat	Haryana	22	28.59N	77.04E
Sonpur	Bihar	24	25.42E	85.13E
Sopron	Hungary	70	47.41N	16.36E
Sopur	Jammu & Kashmir	14	34.19N	74.30E
Soron	Uttar Pradesh	16	27.52N	78.48E
Sosnowiec	Poland	70	50.07N	19.30E
SOUTH AFRICA	Africa	73	25.00S	25.00E
South America, Continent	**World**	**92**		
South Georgia, I.	Antarctica	89	54.15S	38.00W
SOUTH KOREA	Asia	59	36.00N	127.00E
South Orkney, Is	Antarctica	89	60.30S	45.00W
South Shetland, Is	Antarctica	89	63.00N	62.00W
South Snieids	England	69	55.00N	1.27W
SOUTH SUDAN	E. Africa	73	07.00N	30.00E
Southern Ocean	**World**	**92**		
Soutnampton	England	69	50.54N	1.24W
SPAIN	S.W. Europe	67	40.00N	5.00W
Spencer, Gulf	S. Australia	84	34.00S	137.00E
Spey, R.	Scotland	69	57.38N	3.07W
Spezia	Italy	70	44.06N	9.50E
Spokane	Washington, USA	79	47.39N	117.26W
Springbok	South Africa	75	29.44S	17.56E
Springfield	Louisiana, USA	79	39.58N	89.40W
Sri Jayawardenapura	Sri Lanka	59	6.54N	75.54E
SRI LANKA	S. Asia	59	8.00N	81.00E
Sriharikota, I.	Andhra Pradesh	21	13.45N	80.20E
Srikakulam	Andhra Pradesh	27	18.18N	83.54E
Srikakulam	Andhra Pradesh	27	18.17N	83.57E
Srikalahasti	Andhra Pradesh	27	13.45N	79.44E
Srinagar	Jammu & Kashmir	22	34.06N	74.51E
Srirangam	Tamil Nadu	28	10.52N	78.44E
Srivilliputtur	Tamil Nadu	28	9.31N	77.40E
Srungavarapukota	Andhra Pradesh	20	18.06N	83.11E
St Brieuc	France	70	48.31N	2.46W
St Charles, C.	Labrador, Canada	76	52.11N	55.38W
St Etienne	France	70	45.25N	4.25E
St Gallen	Switzerland	70	47.10N	2.15E
St George's Channel	Wales-Ireland	69	52.00N	6.00W
St George's	Grenada	77	12.05N	61.48W
St Helena	Atlantic Ocean	88	15.58S	5.42W
St John	Canada	77	45.14N	66.04W
St Johns	Newfoundland, Canada	77	47.33N	52.40W
St John's	Antigua & Barbuda	81	17.06N	61.51E
St Kilda, I.	Scotland	69	57.49N	8.34W
ST KITTS & NEVIS	West Indies	77	17.20N	62.40W
St Lawrence, Gulf of	Canada	76	48.30N	62.00W

Names	Country/Region	Pg.No.	Lat.	Long.
St Lawrence, R.	Canada	76	47.00N	70.00W
St Louis	Senegal	73	16.01N	16.30W
ST LUCIA	West Indies	77	14.00N	60.50W
St Luis	Missouri, USA	79	38.39N	90.13W
St Malo	France	70	48.39N	2.01W
St Nazaire	France	70	47.17N	2.12W
St Paul	Minnesota, USA	79	44.59N	93.08W
St Petersburg (Leningrad)	Russia	67	59.57N	30.20E
ST VINCENT & GRENADINES	West Indies	77	13.00N	61.10W
St Andrews	Scotland	69	56.21N	2.48W
Stanley Falls	Congo Dem. Rep.	72	0.00N	25.20E
Stavanger	Norway	67	58.58N	5.46E
Stavropol	Russia	67	45.02N	41.58E
Stettin (Szczecin)	Poland	70	53.25N	14.34E
Stewart I.	New Zealand	85	47.00S	168.00E
Stirling	Scotland	69	56.09N	3.54W
Stockholm	Sweden	67	59.20N	18.00E
Stoke-upon-Trent	England	69	53.00N	2.10W
Stonehaven	Scotland	69	56.58N	2.15W
Stornoway	Scotland	69	58.14N	6.23W
Stralsund	Germany	70	54.18N	13.06E
Stranraer	Scotland	69	54.54N	5.00W
Strasbourg	France	70	48.35N	7.50E
Stromboli	Italy	70	38.47N	15.03E
Stuttgart	Germany	67	48.47N	9.11E
Suakin	Sudan	73	19.08N	37.17E
Subarnapur	Odisha	26	20.51N	83.54E
Subarnarekha, R.	Jharkhand	17	22.10N	87.00E
Subotica	Serbia	70	46.05N	19.40E
Sucre	Bolivia	81	19.02S	65.17W
SUDAN	E. Africa	73	11.00N	30.00E
Sudbury	Ontario, Canada	79	46.30N	80.56W
Suez	Egypt	73	30.00N	32.30E
Sujangarh	Rajasthan	19	27.42N	74.31E
Sujanpur	Punjab	14	31.50N	76.33E
Sukhumi	Georgia	65	43.00N	41.00E
Sukkur	Pakistan	15	27.42N	68.55E
Sula Is	Indondesia	64	1.50S	125.00E
Sulaiman, Ra.	Pakistan	10	30.00N	70.00E
Sulaimaniya	Iraq	66	35.35N	45.20E
Sultanpur	Punjab	14	31.58N	77.07E
Sultanpur	Uttar Pradesh	24	26.16N	82.07E
Sulu Sea	Indonesia	64	8.00N	120.00E
Sumatra, I.	Indonesia	64	0.00N	100.00E
Sumba, I.	Indonesia	64	9.30S	119.40E
Sumbawa	Indonesia	64	8.26S	117.30E
Sunamganj	Bangladesh	18	25.04N	91.26E
Sunda, Is	Indonesia	59	9.00S	110.00E
Sundarbans	India -Bangladesh	11	22.00N	89.00E
Sundargarh	Odisha	26	22.06N	84.00E
Sunderland	England	69	54.56N	1.25W
Sunkam	Chhattisgarh	17	18.22N	81.46E
Supaul	Bihar	24	25.55N	86.25E
Superior, L.	Canada-USA	79	47.30N	88.00W
Surabaya	Java	64	7.18S	112.46E
Surada	Odisha	17	19.45N	84.29E
Surapur	Karnataka	20	16.31N	76.48E
Surat	Gujarat	23	21.10N	72.50E
Surat	Gujarat	23	21.12N	72.52E
Suratgarh	Rajasthan	23	29.19N	73.57E
Surendranagar	Gujarat	23	22.43N	71.43E
Surgana	Maharashtra	20	20.33N	73.20E
Suriapet	Andhra Pradesh	20	17.10N	79.19E
SURINAME	S. America	81	5.00N	55.00W
Suva	Fiji	87	18.07S	178.28E
Suzhou	China	62	31.18N	120.40E
Svalbard (Spitsbergen)	Norway	66	78.0N	17.00E
Sverdlovsk	Russia	71	56.50N	60.39E
Svobodny	Russia	71	51.20N	128.00E
Swabi	Pakistan	14	34.07N	72.33E
Swansea	Wales	69	51.38N	3.55W
SWAZILAND	S. E. Africa	73	26.23S	31.30E
SWEDEN	N. Europe	67	62.00N	15.00E
Swellendam	South Africa	75	34.02S	20.27E
SWITZERLAND	Europe	67	47.00N	8.00E
Sydney	Australia	85	33.52S	151.12E
Sylhet	Bangladesh	18	24.53N	91.55E
Syrdarya, R.	Central Asia	71	45.00N	63.00E
SYRIA	S.W. Asia	59	35.00N	37.00E
Szeged	Hungary	70	46.15N	20.11E

T

Names	Country/Region	Pg.No.	Lat.	Long.
Tabora	Tanzania	73	5.00S	32.50E
Tabriz	Iran	65	38.02N	46.20E
Tabuk	Saudi Arabia	65	28.30N	36.25E
Tacheng	China	62	46.50N	83.01E
Tacna	Peru	83	18.00S	70.15W
Tacoma	Washington DC, USA	79	47.15N	122.30W
Tadatri	Andhra Pradesh	20	14.56N	78.02E
Taganrog	Russia	67	47.12N	38.57E
Tagus, R.	Spain-Portugal	66	39.00N	7.00W
Taimir, Penn.	Russia	71	76.00N	103.00E
Tainan	Taiwan	62	23.00N	120.11E
Taipei	Taiwan	62	25.02N	121.30E
Taitung	Taiwan	62	22.43N	121.04E
TAIWAN	E. Asia	59	24.00N	121.00E
Taiyuan	China	62	37.52N	112.28E
TAJIKISTAN	Asia	59	35.30N	70.00E
Takht-i-Sulaiman, Mt	Pakistan	10	31.30N	70.02E
Takla Makan	China	62	39.40N	85.00E
Takoradi	Ghana	73	4.55N	1.45W

Names	Country/Region	Pg.No.	Lat.	Long.
Talagang	Pakistan	14	32.56N	72.28E
Talaimannar	Sri Lanka	21	9.10N	79.40E
Talcher	Odisha	26	20.57N	85.16E
Talguppa	Karnataka	20	14.10N	74.52E
Tallahassee	Florida, USA	79	30.26N	84.18W
Tallinn	Estonia	67	59.24N	24.45E
Taloda	Maharashtra	20	21.34N	74.19E
Tamatave	Madagascar	75	18.00S	49.00E
Tamenglong	Manipur	25	24.53N	93.30E
Tamil Nadu, State	India	13	11.00N	78.00E
Tamluk	W. Bengal	25	22.18N	87.58E
Tampa	Florida, USA	79	27.59N	82.29W
Tampico	Mexico	79	22.16N	97.50W
Tamsag Bulag	Mongolia	62	47.15N	117.05E
Tana, L.	Ethiopia	72	12.00N	37.15E
Tanakpur	Uttarakhand	24	29.10N	80.18E
Tanda	Punjab	14	31.40N	75.41E
Tanda	Uttar Pradesh	17	26.33N	82.42E
Tandur	Andhra Pradesh	20	171.17N	77.30E
Tangail	Bangladesh	18	24.14N	89.56E
Tanganyika, L.	Cent. Africa	72	7.00S	30.00E
Tangier	Morocco	73	35.49N	5.52W
Tangshan	China	63	39.34N	118.13E
Tanimbar, Is	Indonesia	64	8.00S	131.00E
Tank	Pakistan	14	32.14N	70.25E
Tantpur	Rajasthan	19	26.51N	77.32E
Tanuku	Andhra Pradesh	20	16.45N	81.44E
TANZANIA	E. Africa	73	4.00S	34.00E
Taolanaro	Madagascar	75	25.02S	46.58E
Tapajos, R.	S. America	80	4.30S	56.10W
Tapi, R.	Gujarat	19	21.20N	74.30E
Tarangambadi	Tamil Nadu	21	11.01N	79.54E
Tarapoto	Peru	83	6.31S	76.23W
Tarapur	Maharashtra	20	19.52N	72.42E
Tarawa	Kiribati	87	01.28N	173.02E
Tarija	Bolivia	81	21.33S	65.02W
Tarikere	Karnataka	20	13.42N	75.51E
Tarn Taran Sahib	Punjab	22	31.27N	74.55E
Tashkent	Uzbekistan	59	41.30N	69.20E
Tashkurghan	Afghanistan	65	36.44N	67.41E
Tasmania, I.	Australia	84	42.00S	146.30E
Taunton	England	69	51.02N	3.05W
Taupo, L.	New Zealand	85	38.45S	176.00E
Tavoy, Pt	Myanmar	11	14.07N	98.18E
Tawang	Arunachal Pradesh	25	27.35N	91.59E
Taxila	Pakistan	14	33.40N	72.50E
Tay, R. and firth	Scotland	69	56.27N	3.30W
Tayma	Saudi Arabia	65	27.39N	38.28E
Tbilisi	Georgia	59	41.42N	44.46E
Tefe	Brazil	83	3.24S	64.45W
Tegucigalpa	Honduras	77	14.05N	87.12W
Tehran	Iran	59	35.41N	51.25E
Tehri	Uttarakhand	24	30.20N	78.53E
Tehuantepec	Mexico	76	16.00N	95.00W
Tekari	Bihar	17	24.57N	84.53E
Tenali	Andhra Pradesh	20	16.15N	80.35E
Tenasserim	Myanmar	13	12.06N	99.03E
Teni	Tamil Nadu	28	9.55N	77.23E
Tenkasi	Tamil Nadu	28	8.58N	77.21E
Tennessee, R.	USA	76	35.10N	86.00W
Teofilo Otoni	Brazil	83	17.52S	41.31W
Teplice	Czech Republic	70	50.38N	13.49E
Terai Swamp	India-Nepal	11	29.00N	80.00E
Teroina	Brazil	83	5.09S	42.46W
Termez	Uzbekistan	65	37.14N	67.15E
Tete	Mozambique	75	16.10S	33.35E
Tetyukhe Pristan	Russia	71	44.45N	135.40E
Tezpur	Assam	25	26.36N	92.49E
Tezu	Arunachal Pradesh	25	27.55N	96.11E
Tha Kurgaon	Bangladesh	18	26.02N	88.34E
THAILAND	S. E. Asia	59	12.00N	102.00E
Thakurgaon	Bangladesh	18	26.02N	88.34E
Thal	Pakistan	14	33.24N	70.36E
Thalasseri	Kerala	28	11.45N	75.32E
Thames, R.	England	69	51.30N	0.30E
Thandway	Myanmar	13	18.28N	94.27E
Thane	Maharashtra	27	19.12N	73.03E
Thanesar	Haryana	14	29.58N	76.56E
Thanjavur	Tamil Nadu	28	10.47N	79.10E
Thard	Gujarat	15	24.23N	71.37E
The Hague	The Netherlands	67	52.06N	4.20E
Theni	Tamil Nadu	28	10.04N	77.45E
Thessaloniki	Greece	67	40.38N	22.59E
Thimphu	Bhutan	59	27.32N	89.53E
Thiruvananthapuram	Kerala	12	8.29N	76.59E
Thiruvarur	Tamil Nadu	28	10.46N	79.37E
Thoothukkudi	Tamil Nadu	28	08.48N	78.08E
Thoubal	Manipur	25	24.38N	93.58E
Thrissur	Kerala	28	10.30N	76.15E
Thunder, B.	USA	79	45.00N	83.20E
Thursday, I.	Queensland, Aust.	84	10.40 S	142.20E
Thurso	Scotland	69	58.37N	3.33W
Thurston, I.	Antarctica	80	73.00 S	100.00W
Tianjin	China	62	39.04N	117.15E
Tibesti, Mts	Niger-Chad, Africa	72	21.00N	15.00E
Tibet	China	62	30.00N	88.00E
Tieling	China	62	42.25N	123.51E
Tien Shan, Mts	China	62	43.00N	85.00E
Tierra del Fuego	S. America	81	54.00 S	69.00W
Tigiria	Odisha	17	20.28N	84.34E
Tigris, R.	Iraq	65	35.20N	43.31E
Tikamgarh	Madhya Pradesh	26	24.45N	78.53E
Tilaiya	Bihar	17	24.20N	85.31E
Tilpara	W. Bengal	18	23.58N	87.32E